# W R I T I N G

# Analytically

*SECOND EDITION*

**David Rosenwasser**     **Jill Stephen**
*Muhlenberg College*

**HARCOURT COLLEGE PUBLISHERS**

Fort Worth   Philadelphia   San Diego   New York   Orlando   Austin   San Antonio
Toronto   Montreal   London   Sydney   Tokyo

| | |
|---:|:---|
| PUBLISHER | *Earl McPeek* |
| ACQUISITIONS EDITOR | *Julie McBurney* |
| MARKET STRATEGIST | *John Meyers* |
| DEVELOPMENTAL EDITOR | *Michell Phifer* |
| PROJECT EDITOR | *Kathryn M. Stewart* |
| ART DIRECTOR | *Sue Hart* |
| PRODUCTION MANAGER | *Angela Williams Urquhart* |

ISBN: 0-15-508070-9
Library of Congress Catalog Card Number: 98-89701

*Address for Domestic Orders*
Harcourt, Inc., 6277 Sea Harbor Drive, Orlando, FL 32887-6777
800-782-4479

*Address for International Orders*
International Customer Service
Harcourt, Inc., 6277 Sea Harbor Drive, Orlando, FL 32887-6777
407-345-3800
(fax) 407-345-4060
(e-mail) hbintl@harcourtbrace.com

*Address for Editorial Correspondence*
Harcourt College Publishers, 301 Commerce Street, Suite 3700, Fort Worth, TX 76102

*Web Site Address*
http://www.harcourtcollege.com

Harcourt College Publishers will provide complimentary supplements or supplement packages to those adopters qualified under our adoption policy. Please contact your sales representative to learn how you qualify. If as an adopter or potential user you receive supplements you do not need, please return them to your sales representative or send them to: Attn: Returns Department, Troy Warehouse, 465 South Lincoln Drive, Troy, MO 63379.

Printed in the United States of America

9 0 1 2 3 4 5 6 7 8    039    9 8 7 6 5 4 3

# About the Authors

David Rosenwasser and Jill Stephen are Associate Professors of English at Muhlenberg College in Allentown, Pennsylvania, where they have codirected a Writing Across the Curriculum (WAC) program since 1987. They began teaching writing to college students in the early 1970s—David at the University of Virginia and then at the College of William and Mary, and Jill at New York University and then at Hunter College (CUNY). *Writing Analytically* has grown out of their undergraduate teaching, their direction of the college writing center, and, more directly, the seminars on writing and writing instruction that they have offered to faculty across the curriculum at Muhlenberg.

# PREFACE

Both our own students and the faculty we have taught in Writing Across the Curriculum seminars have repeatedly told us that they need *models* for thinking analytically—that when a professor writes "develop" in the margin of a draft and when a student reads that advice, neither is sure what to do next. In trying to respond to our faculty's requests, we discovered that writing texts rarely give more than a slim chapter to analysis and that many slight academic writing in general. Our faculty needed models and guidelines that would help them teach students to do the kind of writing expected of them in their academic courses: not issue-based argument or personal reflection, but analysis, with its sustained inquiry into the meaning of data.

*Writing Analytically* is about how to have and develop ideas in an academic setting and beyond. It is deeply committed to the concept of *writing to learn*—the idea that writing can facilitate and enrich students' understanding of their academic courses, or of anything else that they care to think more clearly about. The book is suitable for composition courses as a central text and for writing-intensive courses across the curriculum as a supplementary text. It would also work well in more advanced expository writing courses, first-year seminars, and as a guide for writing center tutors and teaching assistants. The book is really for anyone who wishes to learn how to use writing as a tool of thought.

*Writing Analytically* offers alternatives to oversimplified thinking of the like/dislike, agree/disagree variety. It argues that an idea is not the same thing as an opinion and demonstrates how to respect the complexity of subjects where there is no single right answer It values understanding over judgment, promoting a model of analysis in which writers examine evidence in depth rather than leaping too quickly to generalizations.

The book also addresses the anti-analytical bias that many people harbor. It demonstrates that analysis is not destructive (ripping things apart) but instead fosters an exploratory attitude towards experience that searches out questions before rushing to answers.

The book's methodology is indebted primarily to the process-oriented approach to writing and to the critical thinking movement. From process, it takes the openness to exploration, the emphasis on invention, and the dedication to drafting and redrafting. From critical thinking, it takes the concern with logical rigor and close analysis. In combining these two approaches, we have attempted to avoid certain problems that sometimes accompany each as it is commonly taught. The book situates attention to critical thinking *within* the writing process rather than relegating it to product-oriented exercises on identifying logical errors. it also brings the process model to bear more fully on academic writing, given that process-oriented approaches have tended to underestimate analysis and academic writing in general.

We believe that in order to be substantive and explicit about thinking, writing texts have to find ways of letting students eavesdrop on someone thinking—not just in the abstract, but about some subject (a painting, media representation of political unrest in China, ways of defining the Renaissance, or whatever). Throughout the text we offer extended revision-oriented analyses of student writing on these and other subjects from across the curriculum. Our aims in these step-by-step accounts are to involve students in the inner dialogue that produces analytical writing, while also generating templates they can follow and apply.

The book has more to say about what students shouldn't do than is usually the case in writing texts. While we are sensitive to the dangers of negativism, we have found that students have a hard time developing new skills until they've come to understand what is counterproductive about features of their current practice. We believe in the motivational and other practical values of talking overtly with students about where their writing typically goes wrong. So, for example, we discuss at some length the shortcomings of five-paragraph form (a slot-filler organizational scheme most students have learned, which we demonstrate to be a barrier to careful thinking and writing); we offer a chapter on kinds of weak thesis statements, with explanations of why they are weak and practical advice on how to fix them; and we critique common definitions of the thesis for saying too little on the necessity of making the thesis *evolve* in response to the analysis of evidence.

The book does acknowledge that various academic disciplines differ in their expectations of student writing. And so, interspersed throughout the text are boxes labelled *Voices from Across the Curriculum*. These were written for the book by professors in various disciplines who offer their disciplinary perspective on such matters as reasoning back to premises and determining what counts as evidence. These Voices are especially prominent in the chapter entitled "Matters of Form," which explains the rationale for disciplinary formats and offers advice on how to use these to arrive at ideas rather than just to arrange them in the final product. As we believe these Voices demonstrate, the area of faculty consensus about the ingredients of effective writing is larger and more significant than the areas of disciplinary difference.

*Writing Analytically* is prescriptive, but it does not impose a system that students and professors must follow in every particular. It scrupulously attempts to avoid patronizing students, instead addressing them as thinking adults. Our hope is to provide a basis for conversation—between faculty and students, between students and students, and especially, between writers and their own writing.

## How to Use This Book

*Writing Analytically* is designed to accompany writing-intensive courses in a wide variety of subject areas without requiring that the course be built around it. The book is also designed to be used as the central text in first-year writing courses or seminars wherein the instructor provides his or her own readings and specific paper topics. An assumption of the book is that most professors will want to supply their own subject matter for students to write about. The book does, however, contain writing-oriented exercises throughout that can be adapted to a wide range of course contents and types of assignments.

These exercises, called Applications, can be used to generate in-class writing and discussion as well as more polished drafts of varying lengths, including a research paper. We have tried to arrange the chapters and the applications so that they move from lesser to more complex writing and thinking skills. Chapter 1, for example, provides a series of concrete writing strategies for discovering the meaning of details in any subject; the examples in this chapter are largely visual, since these are easily discussed in class. Chapters 2 and 3 add on to this initial scheme with various short analytical exercises designed to give practice in specific thinking and writing skills. The book deliberately waits until Chapter 4 to elicit the kind of complex thesis statements that might govern a longer paper. This approach reflects our conviction that students might spend as much as the first third of a writing-intensive course doing short, exploratory analyses and practicing highly specific skills. This is not to say that many of the Applications in the first three chapters couldn't be expanded to generate longer papers if an instructor so desired.

Attention to organization (Chapter 5) and to topics (Chapter 6)—the traditional expository modes—are deliberately located after the thesis chapters, at the point at which most students would be ready to think in more detail about matters of form. The book does not, however, make a simple distinction between process and product, between the prewriting phase and the drafting phases. And so, for example, Chapters 5 and 6 demonstrate that organizational schemes are also useful for generating ideas.

These chapters are followed by one on conversing with secondary sources (Chapter 7), which comes late in the book because it treats one of the most complex of writing skills that students need to learn. A two-chapter mini-handbook on editing and an appendix on documentation styles end *Writing Analytically*.

Although the chapters of the book build on one another if read sequentially, they are also designed to stand independently, so that they can be used in any order. An instructor might, for example, have students consult the topics chapter (Chapter 6) periodically as they go about locating and narrowing an angle on a writing project. Each time that students prepare to submit a final draft, they can consult Chapters 8 and 9 on editing for correctness and style. If students working on a research paper worry that they are summarizing the experts too much and contributing too little of their own analysis, Chapter 7 on using secondary sources will help. And so forth.

## What's New in This Edition

We have done some re-ordering to make the book's conceptual progression more logical and have added exercises and more short models of good student writing to make the book easier to use both in the classroom and out. We have thoroughly revised for greater clarity and directness; briefer, more economical lists of writing strategies have in many cases replaced lengthier analysis of examples. See, for example, the new list of Strategies in Chapter 1—the five analytical moves.

**1.** Re-ordering of chapters

- The chapter on evidence now appears *before* rather than after the thesis chapters in order to give students practice with strategies for analyzing evidence in depth before they move to thesis formulation.
- Chapters on form (disciplinary formats and essay organization) and topics now appear *after* rather than before the thesis chapters; the chapter on form brings together two chapters from the first edition, on formats and on introductions and conclusions.
- The order of the last two chapters has been reversed, so that editing for correctness precedes editing for style.
- The discussion of logical fallacies has been integrated into relevant chapters rather than being separated into a glossary-style appendix.

**2.** Key Word lists and Applications in each chapter

- The book intersperses throughout each chapter short exercises (called Applications) that offer a compressed review of chapter concepts coupled with suggestions for writing; the applications are designed to work with a wide range of subjects to elicit in-class writing as well as more extended drafts.
- A list of Key Words now precedes the Guidelines at the end of each chapter; terms appear in the order of presentation within the chapter.

**3.** More models of good student writing from across the curriculum

- Additions include writing in history, biology, cultural studies, film, philosophy and more.

**4.** New contributors added to Voices from Across the Curriculum

- Professors of dance, history, psychology, and biology have written new Voices boxes on a range of subjects.

**5.** New additions to chapters

- The chapter on evidence now includes sections on kinds of evidence and what counts as evidence across the curriculum.
- The chapter on secondary sources now includes a section on using and evaluating electronic sources, written by a reference librarian.

- The chapter on form now includes a section on the psychology of form containing advice on locating concessions and refutations, organizing comparisons and contrasts, climactic order, thesis shape, and the shaping force of transitions.

## Chapter Outline

Chapter 1, **Writing and Thinking Analytically**, defines analysis and discusses how it resembles and differs from other forms of writing, such as summary, personal response, and argument. The chapter addresses sources of uneasiness about analytical thinking, and offers a set of strategies (the five moves)—with examples from student writing—for analyzing virtually anything. The five moves are especially useful for prewriting (the evidence and idea-gathering stage) and for group brainstorming sessions.

Chapter 2, **Analyzing Evidence**, promotes a model of analysis in which students examine a restricted pool of evidence in great detail. The chapter stresses the importance of reasoning from observations to implications to conclusions and of constantly testing and refining theories of what the evidence means rather than leaping prematurely to broad generalizations. It also includes discussions of kinds of evidence and what counts as evidence.

Chapter 3, **Recognizing and Fixing Weak Thesis Statements**, isolates the basic types of weak theses, explains why they inhibit effective analysis, and shows how to rewrite them—especially those that rely on personal likes and dislikes and overly categorical thinking.

Chapter 4, **Making the Thesis Evolve**, shows how to arrive at a thesis and make it evolve in response to evidence, rather than repeating the same general idea in more or less the same language throughout the paper. The chapter begins with an argument against the ubiquitous five-paragraph form and ends by offering a substitute organizational scheme that is more flexible and thus more conducive to careful thinking.

Chapter 5, **Matters of Form**, explains the rationale for disciplinary formats and offers advice on how to use these as tools for thinking rather than just as ways of organizing final drafts. A section entitled "The Psychology of Form" discusses the rhetorical features of forms and formats, addressing such matters as climactic order and the shapes of different kinds of thesis statements. A closing section demonstrates basic strategies for constructing introductions and conclusions, and targets some of the most common problems.

Chapter 6, **Making Your Response to Topics More Analytical**, treats topic construction as part of the writing process rather than a prelude to it. It offers students ways of making the expository kinds of writing, such as summary, comparison and contrast, personal response (the "reaction" piece) and definition more analytical.

Chapter 7, **Using Secondary Sources**, puts the emphasis in research-writing on *using* sources rather than just plugging in unanalyzed quotations and summaries as "answers." The chapter includes advice on making the most productive use of library resources, with an emphasis on the reference room. There is also a section on using and evaluating electronic sources.

Chapter 8, **Editing for Correctness**, offers a brief guide to grammar and usage. It illustrates nine kinds of basic writing errors that are most likely to interfere with meaning and gives tips for recognizing and fixing them. The chapter also contains a glossary of grammatical terms. Taken together, the last two chapters cover most of the problems that students routinely encounter in producing a final draft.

Chapter 9, **Editing for Style**, concentrates on the choices of words and sentence structures available to writers as they edit drafts for greater clarity and effect. It discusses such matters as the pros and cons of using the active versus the passive voice, the role of jargon, and the effect of word order on emphasis.

An **Appendix** at the end of the book explains and illustrates MLA (Modern Language Association)and APA (American Psychological Association) documentation styles. The appendix also includes guidelines on citing electronic sources.

## Acknowledgments

Our thanks go first to the faculty of Muhlenberg College, without whom this textbook would never have been conceived. The insights they shared with us in the summer seminars on writing across the curriculum and the questions they raised have changed the way we think about writing.

We are especially grateful to the eleven Muhlenberg colleagues who contributed to the *Voices from Across the Curriculum* sections: Kelly Cannon, Karen Dearborn, Jack Gambino, James Marshall, Robert Milligan, Richard Niesenbaum, Frederick Norling, Ellen Poteet, Laura Snodgrass, Alan Tjeltveit, and Bruce Wightman. Nor could we have written the book without the colleagues, friends, and students who have generously contributed samples of their writing—in particular, Anna Adams, Jane Elliot, and Dennis Slade.

Further thanks are due to Thomas Cartelli, a prince among department heads; to Carol Proctor, who was always there when we needed her; to the many colleagues at Muhlenberg who have given us feedback after using the book, most notably Grant Scott, Jim Bloom, Linda Miller, and Barri Gold; and to Dean Curtis Dretsch and his predecessors, Richard Hatch and Nelvin Vos, for their support.

We would also like to thank the many collegues who reviewed the book; we are grateful for their insight: Joan Livingston-Weber, Western Illinois University; Paul Johnson, Winona State University; Susanmarie Harrington, Indiana University-Purdue University, Indianapolis; David Blakesley, Southern Illinois University; Carmen Werder, Western Washington University; Michael Lueker, University of Missouri, Columbia; Liane Bryson, San Diego State University; Christine Farris, Indiana University, Bloomington; Vicki Stewart, Western Michigan University; and finally special thanks to Paul Heilker at Virginia Polytechnic Institute and State University, to Mary Sauer at Indiana University-Purdue University, and (again) to Christine Farris at Indiana University for arranging workshops on our book and to all of the workshops' attendees for their useful advice.

The book continues to be indebted to Karl Yambert, former developmental editor at Harcourt, for his critical acuity, generosity, and wit.

Sincere appreciation goes to our Harcourt Brace staff: Julie McBurney, Acquisitions Editor; Michell Phifer, Developmental Editor; John Meyers, Marketing Strategist; Kathryn Stewart, Project Editor; Sue Hart, Art Director; and Angela Urquhart, Production Manager.

Finally, special thanks to our families—Mark, Lesley and Sarah; Deborah and Elizabeth—for their continued support.

# Contents in Brief

# CONTENTS

CHAPTER 2

ANALYZING EVIDENCE    31

## CHAPTER 6
## MAKING YOUR RESPONSE TO TOPICS
## MORE ANALYTICAL    187

CHAPTER 7

**USING SECONDARY SOURCES**    219

## CHAPTER 8
## EDITING FOR CORRECTNESS   265

APPENDIX
## DOCUMENTATION STYLES    339

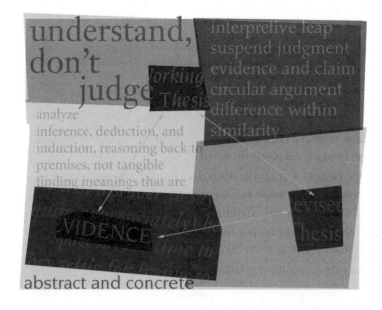

## CHAPTER 1

# WRITING AND THINKING ANALYTICALLY

The aim of this book is to help you become both a better writer and a better thinker, because these two skills go hand in hand. Good ideas rarely spring to life of their own accord. In fact, most writers will tell you that, more often than not, they are unsure of what they will write until they start writing. The common observation, "I know what I want to say; I'm just having trouble getting it down on paper," is a half-truth at best. This is because, even when you are certain about what you plan to write, putting words on paper almost always alters your ideas and leads you to discover thoughts you didn't know you had.

Having good ideas, then, is less a matter of luck than of practice, of learning how to make best use of the writing process. Sudden flashes of inspiration do, of course, occur; sometimes our best ideas seem to come unbidden. But those who write regularly know that inspirational moments can, in fact, be courted and that inspiration is actually a rather small part of what is required in order to think well in writing. The rest of this book will offer you ways of courting and then realizing the full potential of your ideas.

We'll begin by defining and explaining the importance of the kind of thinking—analysis—that the book addresses. We'll then offer five basic "moves"—five reliable ways of proceeding—for courting ideas analytically. The chapter will also address some of the fears people typically express about analysis and will differentiate analytical writing from the other forms you may often be called upon to do: argument, summary, and personal expression.

## What Is Analysis and How Does It Work?

To analyze something is to ask what that something *means*. It is to ask *how* something does what it does or *why* it is as it is. Analysis is the kind of thinking you'll most often be asked to do in your work life and in school; it is not the rarefied and exclusive province of scholars and intellectuals. It is, in fact, one of the most common of our mental activities.

If, for example, you find yourself being followed by a large dog, your first response, other than breaking into a cold sweat, will be to analyze the situation. What does being followed by a large dog mean for me, here, now? Does it mean the dog is vicious and about to attack? Does it mean the dog is curious and wants to play? Similarly, if you are losing a game of tennis or you've just left a job interview or you are looking at a painting of a woman with three noses, you will begin to analyze. How can I play differently to increase my chances of winning? Am I likely to get the job, and why (or why not)? Why did the artist give the woman three noses?

As these examples suggest, most people already analyze all the time, but they often don't realize that this is what they're doing. A first step, then, toward becoming a better analytical thinker and writer is to *become more aware of your own thinking processes, building on skills that you already possess, and eliminating habits that get in the way.* Toward this end, here are five moves to practice consciously, five activities people engage in when they analyze.

### Move 1: Suspend Judgment

This first move, suspending judgment, is a singularly difficult thing for most people to do. As the psychologist Carl Rogers and others have argued, our habitual tendency is to evaluate. Walking out of a movie, for example, most people will immediately voice their approval or disapproval, usually in either/or terms: I liked it *or* didn't like it; it was right/wrong, good/bad, interesting/boring. The other people in the conversation will then offer their own evaluation plus their judgment of the others' judgments: I think that it was a good movie and that you are wrong to think it was bad. And so on.

There are several problems with this kind of reflex move to evaluation. Such comments, because they are so general, really don't say much of significance about the subject. The fact that you liked or didn't like a movie probably says more about you—your tastes, interests, biases, and experiences—than it does about the movie. And, although you might go on to substantiate your judgment, saying that you thought the leading man was miscast or the dialogue too long-winded, these further comments tend to be motivated more by your desire to defend your position than by your desire to understand what the film was trying to accomplish. When people leap to judgment, they usually land in the mental pathways they've grown accustomed to traveling, guided by family or friends or popular opinion. Moving through these pathways can become so automatic that thinking stops. If you can break the evaluation reflex and press yourself to analyze before judging a subject, you will often be surprised at how much your initial responses change.

As a general rule, you should seek to understand the subject you are analyzing before moving to a judgment about it. Try to *figure out what your subject means before deciding how you feel about it.*

## Move 2: Define Significant Parts and How They're Related

Whether you are analyzing an awkward social situation, an economic problem, a painting, a substance in a chemistry lab, or your chances of succeeding in a job interview, the process of analysis is the same:

- Divide the subject into its defining parts, its main elements or ingredients.
- Consider how these parts are related, both to each other and to the subject as a whole.

In the case of the large dog, you might notice that he's dragging a leash, has a ball in his mouth, and is wearing a bright red scarf. Having broken your larger subject into these defining parts, you would try to see the connection among them and determine what they mean, what they allow you to decide about the nature of the dog: apparently somebody's lost pet, playful, probably not hostile, unlikely to bite me.

Analysis of the painting of the woman with three noses, a subject more like the kind you might be asked to write about in a college course, would proceed in the same way. Your result—ideas about the nature of the painting—would be determined, as with the dog, not only by your noticing its various parts, but also by your familiarity with the subject. If you knew little about art history, scrutiny of the painting's parts would not tell you, for instance, that it is an example of the movement known as Cubism. Even without this context, however, you would still be able to draw some analytical conclusions—ideas about the meaning and nature of the subject. You might conclude, for example, that the artist is interested in perspective or in the way we see, as opposed to realistic depictions of the world.

One common denominator of all effective analytical writing is that it pays close attention to detail. We analyze because our global responses, to a play, for example, or to a speech or a social problem, are too general. If you comment on an entire football game, you'll find yourself saying things like "great game," which is a generic response, something you could say about almost anything. This "one-size-fits-all" kind of comment doesn't tell us very much except that you probably liked the game. In order to say more, you would necessarily become more analytical—shifting your attention to the significance of some important aspect of the game, such as "they won because the offensive line was giving the quarterback all day to find his receivers" or "they lost because they couldn't defend against the safety blitz."

This move from generalization to analysis, from the larger subject to its key components, is characteristic of good thinking. To understand a subject, we need to get past our first, generic, evaluative response in order to discover what the subject is "made of," the particulars that contribute most strongly to the character of the whole.

If all that analysis did, however, was to take subjects apart, leaving them broken and scattered, the activity would not be worth very much. The student who presents a draft of a paper to his or her professor with the words, "Go ahead, rip it apart," reveals a disabling misconception about analysis—that, like dissecting a frog in a biology lab, analysis takes the life out of its subjects. Clearly, analysis means more than breaking a subject into its parts. When you analyze a subject you ask not just "what is it made of?" but also *"how do these parts help me to understand the meaning of the subject as a whole?"* A good analysis seeks to locate the life of its subject, the ideas that energize it.

## Move 3: Make the Implicit Explicit

A definition of analytical writing to which this book will return repeatedly is that it makes explicit (overtly stated) what is implicit (suggested but not overtly stated) in both your subject and your own thinking. This process of converting suggestions into direct statements is essential to analysis, but it is also the feature of analysis least understood by inexperienced writers. They fear that, like the emperor's new clothes, implications aren't really "there," but are instead the phantasms of an overactive imagination. "Reading between the lines" is the common and telling phrase that expresses this anxiety. We will have more to say against the charge that analysis makes something out of nothing—the spaces between the lines—rather than out of what is there in black and white.

But for now, let's look at a hypothetical example of this process of drawing out implications, pausing first to offer a couple of definitions. The process of drawing out implications is also known as *making inferences. Inference* and *implication* are related but not synonymous terms, and the difference is a useful one to know. The term *implication* is used to describe something suggested by the material itself; implications reside in the matter you are studying. The term *inference* is used to describe your thinking process. In short, *you infer what the subject implies.*

Now, let's move on to the example, which will suggest not only how the process of making the implicit explicit works, but also how often we do it in our everyday lives.

Imagine that you are driving down the highway and find yourself analyzing a billboard advertisement for a brand of beer. Such an analysis might begin with your noticing what the billboard photo contains, its various "parts"—six young, athletic, and scantily clad men and women drinking beer while pushing kayaks into a fast-running river. At this point, you have produced not an analysis but a summary—a description of what the photo contains. If, however, you go on to consider what the particulars of the photo *imply,* your summary would become analytical.

You might infer, for example, that the photo implies that beer is the beverage of fashionable, healthy, active people, not just of older men with large stomachs dozing in armchairs in front of the television. Thus, the advertisement's meaning goes beyond its explicit contents; your analysis would lead you to *convert to direct statement meanings that are suggested but not overtly stated,* such as the advertisement's goal of attacking a common, negative stereotype about its product (that only lazy, overweight men drink beer). The naming and renaming of parts that you undertake when analyzing should carry you from the actual details to the meanings they imply. By making the implicit explicit (inferring what the ad implies) you can better understand the nature of your subject.

## Move 4: Look for Patterns

We have been defining analysis as the understanding of parts in relation to each other and to a whole, as well as the understanding of the whole in terms

---

**APPLICATION:**

**MAKING INFERENCES**

Locate any magazine ad that you find interesting. Ask yourself, *"What is this a picture of?"* Use our hypothetical beer ad as a model for rendering the implicit explicit. Don't settle for just one or even three answers. *Keep answering the question in different ways,* letting your answers grow in length as they identify and begin to interpret the significance of telling details. Attend to your choice of language, because your word choice as you summarize details will begin to suggest to you the ad's range of implication.

If you find yourself getting stuck, rephrase the question as "What is this ad *really about,* and *why* did the advertiser choose this particular image or set of images?" Your repeated answering of the first question should eventually lead you to answer the second question. As we will emphasize throughout the book, your best ideas will come when you allow yourself to repeatedly move over the same ground, casting and recasting the language you use to state what seems to you to be going on. So, be sure to keep answering the question, even if you are fairly satisfied with what you come up with in your first couple of tries. And, as we will also emphasize throughout, try to *write about what you see,* the details of the picture, rather than generalizing about the picture. Eventually you will arrive at some generalizations, but generalizing too soon—moving too quickly from your data to a higher level of abstraction—starves the writing process of what it needs to generate good ideas.

of the relationships among its parts. But how do you know which parts to attend to? What makes some details in the material you are studying more worthy of your attention than others? Here are three principles for selecting significant parts of the whole:

1. *Look for a pattern of repetition or resemblance.* In virtually all subjects, repetition is a sign of emphasis. In a symphony, for example, certain patterns of notes repeat throughout, announcing themselves as major themes. In a legal document, such as a warranty, a reader will quickly become aware of words that are part of a particular idea or pattern of thinking: for instance, disclaimers of accountability.

The repetition may not be exact: in Shakespeare's play *King Lear,* for example, references to seeing and eyes call attention to themselves through repetition. So a reader of the play would do well to look for various occurrences of words and other details that might be part of this pattern. Let's say you notice that references to seeing and eyes almost always occur along with another strand—a pattern of similar kinds of language—having to do with the concept of proof. How might noticing this pattern lead to an idea? You might make a start toward an idea by inferring from the pattern that the play is very concerned with ways of knowing (proving) things—with seeing as opposed to other ways of knowing, such as faith or intuition.

2. *Look for organizing contrasts.* Sometimes patterns of repetition that you begin to notice in a particular subject matter will be significant because they are part of a contrast—a basic opposition—around which the subject matter is structured. Some examples of organizing contrasts that we encounter frequently are nature/civilization, city/country, public/private, organic/inorganic, voluntary/involuntary. One advantage of detecting repetition is that it will lead you to discover organizing contrasts, which are key in helping you to locate central issues and concerns in the material you are studying. (For more on working with organizing contrasts, see "Strategies for Using Binaries Analytically" in Chapter 3.)

3. *Look for anomalies—things that seem unusual, seem not to fit.* An anomaly (*a = not, nom = name*) is literally something that cannot be named, what the dictionary defines as deviation from the normal order. Along with looking for pattern, it is also fruitful to attend to anomalous details—those that seem not to fit the pattern. Anomalies help us to revise our stereotypical assumptions. A recent TV commercial, for example, chose to advertise the Philadelphia Phillies baseball team by featuring its star, Scott Rolen, reading a novel by Dostoyevsky in the dugout during a game. In this case, the anomaly, a baseball player who reads serious literature, is being used to subvert (question, unsettle) the stereotypical assumption that sports and intellectualism don't belong together.

Just as people tend to leap to evaluative judgments, they also tend to avoid information that challenges (by not conforming to) opinions they already hold. In the desire to make things fit and keep explanations simple, people often screen out anything that would ruffle the pattern they've begun to see. The result is that they ignore the evidence that might lead them to a better theory. (For more on this process of using anomalous evidence to evolve an essay's main idea, see Chapter 4, "Making the Thesis Evolve.") Anomalies are important because noticing them often leads to new and better ideas. Most advances in scientific thought, for example, have arisen when a scientist observes some phenomenon that does not fit with a prevailing theory.

## Move 5: Keep Reformulating Questions and Explanations

Analysis, like all forms of writing, requires a lot of experimenting. Because the purpose of analytical writing is to figure something out, you shouldn't expect to know at the outset exactly where you are going, how all of your subject's parts fit together, and to what end. The key is to be patient and to know that there are procedures—in this case, questions—you can rely on to take you from uncertainty to understanding.

The following three groups of questions (organized according to the analytical moves they're derived from) are typical of what goes on in an analytical writer's head as he or she attempts to understand a subject. These questions will work with almost anything that you want to think about. As you will see,

---

**APPLICATION:**

### Looking for Patterns

Select a magazine ad that includes a significant amount of language, and then (1) identify words that repeat or that are similar to each other, (2) group the resulting categories of words into organizing contrasts, and (3) search for anomalies—significant words that appear not to fit within these patterns of similarity and difference. You may also wish to perform these three operations in relation to the visual aspect of the ad and to consider the relation between the words and the picture. The primary emphasis, though, should rest on the words.

This exercise can produce unusually fruitful results with almost any kind of material. If you are reading this book in connection with your work life or a more advanced course, try the method on something you are reading. This method offers a very useful way of starting to understand and characterize the mental habits of particular authors, experts in your field, and so forth. You can work with as little as a few paragraphs or as much as an entire article or chapter or book. By focusing on repetition, contrast, and anomalies, you press yourself to get closer to your data—to become more aware of what the subject is made of, rather than generalizing broadly about it.

the questions are geared toward helping you locate and try on explanations for the meaning of various patterns of details.

> Which details seem significant? Why?
>
> What is the significance of a particular detail? What does it mean?
>
> What else might it mean?
>
> (Moves: Define Significant Parts; Make the Implicit Explicit)
>
> How do the details fit together? What do they have in common?
>
> What does this *pattern* of details mean?
>
> What else might this same pattern of details mean? How else could it be explained?
>
> (Moves: Look for Patterns of Resemblance and of Contrast)
>
> What details *don't* seem to fit? How might they be connected with other details to form a different pattern?
>
> What does this new pattern mean? How might it cause me to read the meaning of individual details differently?
>
> (Moves: Look for Anomalies and Keep Asking Questions)

The process of posing and answering such questions—the analytical process—is one of trial and error. Learning to write well is largely a matter of learning how to frame questions. One of the main things you acquire in the study of an academic discipline is knowledge of the kinds of questions that the discipline typically asks. For example, an economics professor and a sociology professor might observe the same phenomenon, such as a sharp decline in health benefits for the elderly, and analyze its causes and significance in different ways. The economist might consider how such benefits are financed and how changes in government policy and the country's population patterns might explain the declining supply of funds for the elderly. The sociologist might ask about attitudes toward the elderly and about the social structures that the elderly rely on for support.

Whatever questions you ask, the answers you propose will often produce more questions. Like signposts on a trail, details (data) that initially seem to point in one direction may, on closer examination, lead you someplace else. Dealing with these realities of analytical writing requires patience, but it will also make you a more confident thinker, because you'll come to know that your *uncertainty is a normal and necessary part of writing.*

### Analysis at Work: An Example

Examine the following excerpt from a draft of a paper about Ovid's *Metamorphoses,* a collection of short mythological tales dating from ancient Rome. We have included annotations in boldface to suggest how a writer's ideas evolve as she looks for pattern, contrast, and anomaly, constantly remaining open to reformulation.

The draft actually begins with two loosely connected observations: that males dominate females and that many characters in the stories lose the ability to speak and thus become submissive and dominated. In the excerpt, the writer begins to connect these two observations and speculate about what this connection means.

There are many other examples in Ovid's *Metamorphoses* that show the dominance of man over woman through speech control. In the Daphne and Apollo story, Daphne becomes a tree to escape Apollo, but her ability to speak is destroyed. Likewise, in the Syrinx and Pan story, Syrinx becomes a marsh reed, also a life form that cannot talk, although Pan can make it talk by playing it. *[The writer establishes a pattern of similar detail.]* Pygmalion and Galatea is a story in which the male creates his rendition of the perfect female. The female does not speak once; she is completely silent. Also, Galatea is referred to as "she" and never given a real name. This lack of a name renders her identity more silent. *[Here the writer begins to link the contrasts of speech/silence with the absence/presence of identity.]*

Ocyrhoe is a female character who could tell the future but who was transformed into a mare so that she could not speak. One may explain this transformation by saying it was an attempt by the gods to keep the future unknown. *[Notice how the writer's thinking expands as she sustains her investigation of the overall pattern of men silencing women: here she tests her theory by adding another variable—prophecy.]* However, there is a male character, Tiresias, who is also a seer of the future and is allowed to speak of his foreknowledge, thereby becoming a famous figure. (Interestingly, Tiresias during his lifetime has experienced being both a male and a female.) *[Notice how the Ocyrhoe example has spawned a contrast based on gender in the Tiresias example. The pairing of the two examples demonstrates that the ability to tell the future is not the sole cause of silencing, because male characters who can do it are not silenced— though the writer pauses to note that Tiresias is not entirely male.]* Finally, in the story of Mercury and Herse, Herse's sister, Aglauros, tries to prevent Mercury from marrying Herse. Mercury turns her into a statue; the male directly silences the female's speech.

The woman silences the man in only two stories studied. *[Here the writer searches out an anomaly—women silencing men—that grows in the rest of the paragraph into an organizing contrast.]* In the first, "The Death of Orpheus," the women make use of "clamorous shouting, Phrygian flutes with curving

horns, tambourines, the beating of breasts, and Bacchic howlings"
(246) to drown out the male's songs, dominating his speech in
terms of volume. In this way, the quality of power within speech
is demonstrated: "for the first time, his words had no effect,
and he failed to move them [the women] in any way by his voice"
(247). Next the women kill him, thereby rendering him silent.
However, the male soon regains his temporarily destroyed power
of expression: "the lyre uttered a plaintive melody and the life-
less tongue made a piteous murmur" (247). Even after death Orpheus is able to communicate. The women were not able to destroy
his power completely, yet they were able to severely reduce his
power of speech and expression. *[The writer learns, among other things, that men are
harder to silence; Orpheus's lyre continues to sing after his death.]*

The second story in which a woman silences a man is the story
of Actaeon, in which the male sees Diana naked, and she trans-
forms him into a stag so that he cannot speak of it: "he tried to
say 'Alas!' but no words came" (79). This loss of speech leads to
Actaeon's inability to inform his own hunting team of his true
identity; his loss of speech leads ultimately to his death. *[This
example reinforces the pattern that the writer had begun to notice in the Orpheus example.]*

In some ways these two paragraphs of draft exemplify a writer in the
process of discovering a workable idea. They begin with a list of similar examples, briefly noted. As the examples accumulate, the writer begins to make
connections and formulate trial explanations. We have not included enough
of this excerpt to get to the tentative thesis the draft is working toward, although that thesis is already beginning to emerge. What we want to emphasize here is the writer's willingness to accumulate data and to locate it in various patterns of similarity and contrast.

## Using Prewriting to Find Workable Questions

As we said at the beginning of the chapter, few writers can arrive at their best
ideas before they begin to write. If you expect to have all the answers before
you start, you are more likely to settle for relatively superficial ideas. And, when
you try to conduct all of your thinking in your head, you may arrive at an idea
but not be able to explain how you got there.

Writing, unlike trying to carry all of our thinking in our heads, allows us to
follow our mental trails and to experiment with alternate routes without losing
track of where we've been. This is important because the process of having ideas

rarely moves steadily forward, traveling in an uninterrupted line from point to point like a connect-the-dots picture. Instead, thinking and writing are *recursive* activities, which means that we move forward by looking backward, by repeatedly going over the same ground, looking for wrong turns, uncovering signposts we may have missed, and reinterpreting signposts passed earlier because of what we discovered later. To figure out where we're going, we often need to revisit where we've been. Without writing, in all but the most carefully trained memories, the way back keeps vanishing, sometimes leaving us stranded.

The tentative and exploratory nature of good analytical thinking makes it especially important that you incorporate some kind of prewriting into your writing process. If you move directly from your thinking about your subject to writing a draft, without an intermediary stage of prewriting, you will almost inevitably produce an overly general analysis. The pressures of time tempt most of us to move to a conclusion about a subject before we've spent enough time examining it. We fail to dwell with the data long enough to begin to see the questions it invites us to ask. *A good paper is essentially the answer to a good question,* an explanation of some feature or features of your subject that need explaining. If you don't take the time to look for questions, you might end up writing a tidy but relatively pointless paper.

The solution to this problem of short-circuiting the writing process with premature and thus usually superficial conclusions is to *slow down.* Spend some time simply recording what you observe about your subject without worrying about where these observations might lead. By opening up your thinking in this way, you will discover more data to think with, more possible starting points from which to develop an idea. And you will be less likely to get trapped into seeing only those features of your subject that support the first conclusion you come to. When you shift from prewriting to writing a first draft, you may not—and most likely will not—have all the answers, but you will waste significantly less time chasing ill-focused and inadequately considered ideas than might otherwise have been the case.

Some guiding principles to take from this discussion are:

1. Prewrite before you draft.
2. Use prewriting to frame questions.
3. Retain the openness to ideas of your prewriting in your actual draft.

For further discussion of various prewriting techniques, see the section in Chapter 6 entitled "Making Your Response to Topics More Analytical." In particular, try the Application entitled "Passage-Based Focused Freewriting."

## A Note on the Relationship between Prewriting and the Final Draft

How much of the kind of writing we have been talking about here—the kind in which you use writing to search out meaningful patterns in your data— should end up in the final draft? Where is the line between what is called "prewriting" and "writing," that is, between writing to stimulate your own thinking and writing to make others understand your thinking? Our answer is that novice writers hinder their own development by seeing prewriting and writing as more distinct stages in the writing process than they actually are (or should be). Typically, an inexperienced writer's final draft offers a thinly developed list of his or her conclusions, from which all of the thinking about the evidence has been excised. In many cases, the evidence itself has also been excised, presumably because the writer mistakenly believes it is no longer necessary, since he or she has "finished" thinking about it.

Although there clearly is a difference between writing for an audience and writing only for ourselves, the best writing respects the connection between the two: it makes its ideas clear and accessible to the reader by retaining (in revised form) the thought processes that made those ideas clear and accessible to the writer. Here is a good phrase for keeping in mind what early and late stage drafts should have in common: *share your thought processes with the readers.* If readers can't see how you got to the position you are offering them, there is little reason for them to accept it, however smooth the sentence style, grammar, paragraphing, and organization may be.

For a quick overview of what the book offers on organizing the final draft, see "An 'All-Purpose' Organizational Scheme" at the end of Chapter 4.

The ordering principles you will find in the book have three aims: (1) to bring into the final draft the open and exploratory stance that is the best characteristic of prewriting, (2) to make the final draft flexible enough in its shape to accommodate a complex (multi-sided) act of thinking, and (3) to render the paper's organizing framework clear and visible enough to escort readers congenially through the writer's sequence of thought.

## Common Charges against Analysis

Once you accept the challenge of thinking and writing analytically—the careful, recursive, and nonjudgmental observation of your subject and of your own thoughts—you can expect to encounter another obstacle. Although analysis is an activity we call on constantly in our everyday lives, many people are deeply suspicious of it. "Why can't you just enjoy the movie rather than picking it apart?" they'll ask. Or, "Oh, you're just making that up!" You may even be accused of being an unfeeling person if you adopt an analytical stance, because it is typical of the anti-intellectual position to insist that feeling and thinking are separate and essentially incompatible activities. Some people fear that trusting our intellects will make us less feeling and less sensitive. With this fear goes the opposite one—that trusting our feelings will necessarily render us incapable of thinking. Both of these fears about analysis have long histories.

Though he was among the most astutely analytical of thinkers, the nineteenth-century English Romantic poet, William Wordsworth, wrote that "we murder to dissect," giving voice to the still-common anxiety that analysis takes the life out of things. This anxiety—so common in Romanticism as to be virtually a defining characteristic of that intellectual and artistic movement—arose in reaction against an equally extreme position from the eighteenth century (the so-called Age of Reason or Enlightenment), known for its indictment of emotion as the enemy of rationality. In response to the eighteenth century's elevation of reason over all other human faculties, the nineteenth century sought to correct the imbalance by elevating the faculties of feeling and imagination. Few thinkers of either century really adhered to these positions in such extreme forms, but suffice it to say that analysts of human beings seem always to have been perplexed about how our various capacities fit together into a functional whole. One aim of this book will be to demonstrate that taking refuge in either side of the opposition between thinking and feeling is not only counterproductive but also unnecessary.

## Charge 1: "Analysis Kills Enjoyment"

Why should enjoyment and understanding be incompatible? To begin to raise doubts about this charge, one need only listen to the conversation of football fans after a game. If analysis is interfering with their enjoyment, they apparently haven't noticed.

At the root of the "analysis kills enjoyment" complaint is the idea that analysis is critical—in the sense of disapproving and negative. From this point of view, the basic activity of analysis (asking questions), along with its deliberate delaying of evaluation, seems skeptical, uncommitted, and uncaring. But raising questions and working out the possible meanings of significant details are not necessarily negative, nor do they require a complete absence of feeling. In fact, analytical thinkers tend to be more dedicated than most people to understanding and thus to being sensitive to rather than attacking a subject. Understanding is not the enemy of enjoyment, at least not for people who enjoy thinking. In any case, the global "I like it/I don't like it" move is less common to people who have learned to think analytically, because they are more likely to make careful distinctions—deciding to like some features of a subject (for well-explained reasons) while disliking others.

## Charge 2: "Analysis Finds Meanings That Are Not There"

What about the charge that analysis "reads into" a subject things that aren't there ("reading between the lines")? What does the charge mean, and why do people make it? The phrase "reading between the lines" implies reading not the words on the page but the white space between the sentences. So, presumably, the charge means that the person producing the analysis is basing it on nothing—on white space; in other words, it's all in his or her imagination. For readers who make Charge 2, "not there" doesn't really mean nonexistent, though that's what they say. Rather, it means not overt, not tangible, and suggests as their unstated assumption that all communication is or *should be* a matter of direct statement. Proponents of this view of analysis are, in effect, committing themselves to the position that everything in life means what it says and says what it means, that meanings are always obvious and understood the same by everyone and thus don't require interpretation.

This view—that all communication is a matter of direct statement—is easily opened to question. You need think only of what people's body positions "say" in addition to (sometimes in opposition to) the words they speak in order to see the error in assuming that all things can be communicated directly.

It is, in fact, an inherent property of language that it always means more than and thus other than it says. How often have you heard a person respond to a challenging personal question with "I don't know," when what he or she really means is "I don't want to talk about it"? And doesn't the "how you doin'?" that we toss at others as we pass them in the hallway really mean "I acknowledge that you and I are acquaintances"—because in most cases we have neither the time nor the inclination to find out how they are really doing?

As these examples demonstrate, people are remarkably adept at sending and receiving complex and subtle signals. Though we may not pause to take notice, we are continually processing what goes on around us for the indirect or suggested meanings it contains. If you observe yourself for a day, you'll find yourself interpreting even the most direct-seeming statements. There's an old cartoon about the anxiety bred by the continual demands of interpretation: a person saying "Good morning" causes the one addressed to respond, "What did she mean by that?"

The truth to which this cartoon points is that a statement can have various meanings, depending on various circumstances and how it is said. *The relationship between words and meaning is always complex.* As Marshall McLuhan, one of the fathers of modern communication theory, noted, communication always involves determining not just what is being said, but also what kind of message a message is. Depending on tone and context, "Good morning" can mean a number of things.

Why does so much communication take place indirectly? When we want to understand a complex subject like love or death, we sometimes need to arrive at that understanding indirectly—by comparison with more tangible and accessible subjects like the weather, the seasons, or baseball, or chess. This is because sometimes it is possible to communicate complex ideas or feelings or situations only through comparison with something that is more immediate and more concrete. It is also the case that human beings seem inclined to think by *association* and by *analogy* (likeness). At the root of indirect communication lies *metaphor*—a mode of expression in which one thing stands for (represents) something else that remains unnamed.

Metaphor is not confined to the arts; it is a pervasive feature of communication. Many linguists argue that all language is metaphor, that we are always talking about things in terms of other things. This is the case not only when we say, "My love is like a red, red rose," but also when we say, "That movie was a piece of trash" or "I could kill you for that." The leap to language is itself metaphorical: The word *c-a-t* is not the same thing as the four-legged feline that purrs.

You can easily test some of these assertions yourself as you go through an ordinary day. What, for example, does your choice of wearing a baseball cap to a staff meeting or a class—rather than no hat or a straw hat or a beret—"say"? Note, by the way, that a communicative gesture such as the wearing of a cap need not be premeditated and entirely conscious in order to communicate something to those who see it. The cap is still "there" and available to be "read" by others as a sign of certain attitudes and a culturally defined sense of identity—with or without your intention. Things communicate meaning to others whether we wish them to or not, which is to say that the meanings of most things are socially determined.

Berets and baseball caps, for example, carry different associations because they come from different social contexts. Baseball caps convey a set of attitudes associated with the piece of American culture they come from. They suggest, for example, popular rather than high culture, casual rather than formal, young—perhaps defiantly so, especially if worn backward—rather than old, and so forth. The social contexts that make gestures, like our choice of headgear carry particular meanings that are always shifting, but some such context is always present.

Because meaning is, to a significant extent, socially determined, we can't entirely control what our clothing, our manners, our language, and even our way of walking communicate to others. This is one of the reasons that analysis makes some people suspicious and uneasy. They don't want to acknowledge that they are sending messages in spite of themselves, messages they haven't deliberately and overtly chosen.

It helps to remember that *interpretive leaps*—conclusions arrived at through analysis—about what some gesture or word choice or clothing combination or scene in a film *means* follow certain established rules of evidence. One such rule is that the conclusions of a good analysis do not rest on details taken out of context; you should instead test and support claims about the details' significance by locating them in a pattern of similar detail (see the previous section on the five analytical moves). In other words, analytical thinkers are not really free to say whatever they think, as those who are made uneasy by analysis sometimes fear.

We should acknowledge, with respect to the "reading between the lines" charge, that analysis sometimes does draw out the implications of things that are not there, because they have been deliberately omitted. Usually we recognize such omissions because we have been led to expect something that we are not given, making its absence conspicuous.

An analysis of the Nancy Drew mysteries, for example, might attach significance to the absence of a mother in the books, particularly in light of the fact that biological mothers, as opposed to wicked stepmothers, are pretty rare in many kinds of stories involving female protagonists, such as fairy tales ("Hansel and Gretel," "Cinderella," and "Snow White"). Taking note of mothers as a potentially significant omission could lead to a series of analytical questions, such as: how might this common denominator of certain kinds of children's stories

APPLICATION:

## BRINGING OUT IMPLICATIONS

Try one or more of the following exercises as means of bringing out what is "there" but not overt.

1. Look at a piece of a language to determine various ways in which it communicates indirectly. You might, for example, look at a short poem and discuss with others what the language communicates directly (through overt statement) and what it "says" indirectly. Because metaphor and other forms of suggestion/implication are not confined to deliberately artistic uses of language, you can do this exercise with virtually any written language: the rules sections of a college catalogue or other bureaucratic document are often useful targets. Consider, for example, what is communicated by the following title of a radio program about trends in the world of prime-time sports: "Only a Game."

2. Record a dream. Then determine what the dream "says" overtly and what is "there" metaphorically, that is, by suggestion. What might it mean, for example, if you have a dream in which your boyfriend or girlfriend locks you in a closet and turns into your father or mother? How would the meaning of the dream differ if he or she was inside or outside the closet?

3. The following experiment will demonstrate how much even everyday conversation depends on our ability to read what is suggested indirectly. Try writing down as much detail as you can remember about a recent, relatively brief conversation. First, write a word-for-word restatement of the conversation to the extent that you can. Include description of body language, location, and so forth. Then write an account, a summary, of the same conversation to include what you think was said that the word-for-word restatement would not reveal overtly. Make a list of things that you think were communicated indirectly and how.

be explained? What features of the stories' social, psychological, historical, economic, and other possible contexts might offer an explanation? As this example suggests, things are often left out for a reason, and a good analysis should therefore be alert to potentially meaningful omissions.

## Charge 3: "Some Subjects Weren't Meant to Be Analyzed"

The preceding examples, Nancy Drew mysteries and cigarette ads, raise the argument that it is foolish to analyze subjects that were meant only to entertain (like science-fiction movies) or to serve some practical need (like shopping

## APPLICATION:

## READING WHAT'S MISSING

Here's another example of a case in which a writer might want to pursue the implications of something being left out. Consider what you might make of a cigarette advertisement that pictures a line of laughing young men and women in unisex attire holding one of their number across their outstretched arms, but that does not include cigarettes or any sign of smoking. What might the omission of smoking in the picture mean, since its sponsor no doubt wishes to encourage the activity? What does this omission imply about the nature of the advertisement's message and its means of influencing viewers?

Try doing the same exercise with a political speech or a piece of public relations writing or coverage of the same situation in two different newspapers or magazines (in which case you would consider what one periodical left out—and why—that the other included). In what other kinds of communication might attention to what has been left out be especially revealing?

malls or blue jeans). Should analytical thinkers steer clear of subjects that supposedly weren't meant to be analyzed, like bowling and Barbie dolls and late-night television? This is a more complex question, because it runs into people's prejudices about so-called high-brow and low-brow activities. If asked to name high-brow subjects, most of us would come up with the same kind of list—Mozart's string quartets, for example, or foreign movies with subtitles. To the extent that analytical thinking is labeled a high-brow activity, highbrows are meant to stick to their own turf, being told, in effect: "Take your Mozart but leave my romance novels and fast-food favorites alone!"

The question of intention—what was and what wasn't "meant" to be analyzed—is, at least in part, an extension of the high-brow/low-brow divide. Barbie dolls, for example, and Saturday morning cartoon shows are made for children. But the fact that the makers of Barbie were trying to make money by entertaining children rather than trying to create a cultural artifact doesn't rule out analysis of Barbie's characteristics (built-in earrings, high-heeled feet), marketing, and appeal as cultural phenomena. Similarly, the makers of tough-guy movies may not have intended to produce propaganda on the value of rugged individualism and may even have produced completely different statements of their intentions. What the makers of a particular product or idea intend, however, is only a part of what their work communicates; *intention does not finally control the implications that a work possesses.* In sum, the attempt to cordon off certain subjects as too low-brow for analysis is, ironically, the elitist (in-group and exclusionary) position. Analysis knows no brow. Take any subject about which we want to understand more, and analysis will help.

APPLICATION:

## A SAMPLE PAPER TO ANALYZE

The following excerpt from a student paper is an example of a *close reading*—
a kind of analysis this book will teach you to do. A close reading *explicates:*
that is, it unfolds an interpretation by making explicit selected features of
your subject that otherwise might not be readily recognized or understood.
A close reading moves beyond the obvious, but it *does not leap to some hidden
meaning* that is unconnected to the evidence. Rather, it stays close to and
follows logically from the evidence: the meaning is implicit in the details,
waiting to be brought out by the writer who is careful enough to look closely
and questioningly.

The essay excerpt exemplifies the five moves that we have discussed so
far: suspending judgment, defining parts and how they are related, making
the implicit explicit, looking for patterns, and asking questions. It also will
allow some further discussion of the charges against analysis, especially
Charge 2, that analysis finds meanings that are not there. You may also want
to try applying the questions on page 8, since these are specifically designed
to help you look for and interpret pattern.

As you read the excerpt, look for the five moves and for evidence that the
meaning the writer is finding is "there," implied (suggested, though not explicitly named).

- Which elements of the paper seem to be factual reporting, that is, description rather than interpretation of details in the photograph the
  student is analyzing?
- Locate those places in the paper where the student writer arrives at
  conclusions about what the details of the photograph mean.
- Where has the writer made the move from implicit to explicit? What
  other conclusions might you draw from the same data?

After you've worked your way through the excerpt, on which we will do
some commenting, you will find another piece of the same essay on which
you can experiment with some of the same analytical procedures.

### EIKOH HOSOE AND THE POLITICS OF GENDER:
### AN ANALYSIS

Eikoh Hosoe is considered by some to be Japan's greatest
living photographer. Few of Hosoe's works are titled, and the majority of them are simply numbered. The print that I felt was the
strongest of the "Man and Woman" series was unnamed, and its number was not listed and was unknown to the curators. It depicts

the intricacies of male-female relationships, focusing primarily on the inherent sexual and power conflicts between the two.

In a twelve-by-twenty black and white print, we are shown a semiprofile of two figures, the left-most female and the right-most male. Upon inspection, the form of the naked male is transfigured from human to serpentine; the sinusoidal curvature of the back and the prominent abdominal muscles take on a definite reptilian quality. His left arm (facing us) is struck down facing the ground, while his right arm writhes toward the female. His arm is powerfully cocked as if to present his index finger to her mouth, which is a scant few inches away. The waist and legs are obscured in shadow, leaving only a sculpted torso and bare feet illuminated. The identity of the male is purposely vague, features obscured in shadow, and all that is shown is the head thrust forward and the prominent jawline. This is the male: tempting, cloying, and suggesting his sexuality to the female. *[Notice that the writer's choice of descriptive words has already begun to move toward interpretation: serpentine, sinusoidal, reptilian, writhes.]*

In the erotic presentation of a finger, the traditional male-female relationship has been defined: male as superior, possessing strength and control over a dominated, subservient female, a form who, by holding her hands behind her back and having her feet crossed, telegraphs an air of innocence, ignorance, and susceptibility to being controlled. She wears just a simple shirt, barely covering her young body. The noticeable protuberances of belly and breast are universal symbols of fertility, of reproductive ground ripe for conquering and colonizing. Completing the image is her head (Japanese features present), craning to accept and swallow or kiss the offered finger. *[Here the writer continues to locate significant parts of the photo and relate them to each other and to the whole. The paragraph begins with attention to a detail that the writer has selected as especially significant.]*

But what exactly does this photograph say about the role of gender in male-female relationships? Surely this is not a synthesis of equals, yet paradoxically the female is given identity, a face, whereas the male is not. Does this arrangement attempt to reshift or rebalance the power by allowing the female a presence, or does it instead drive the rift between the genders further: the male is safe in his anonymity, whereas we can see and pity the woman? *[Notice that in the first two sentences the writer has suspended judgment and is asking questions. This approach leads him to discover an anomaly that he then attempts to work out—that although the male is the dominant figure in the photo, the female is the one who has a recognizable face.]*

This series of photos was done during a period of social and cultural upheaval in a Japan that was rebuilding after World War II. That Hosoe dares to draw attention to the gender inequality inherent in his society is bold, and historically this series caused an eruption of controversy in response. And yet we are given no final solution, no answers, because the conflict, like every interpersonal relationship, is as enigmatic as the dark and large-grained print itself. *[In this paragraph the writer begins to broaden the range of his interpretation by thinking about the photo's implications in historical context—the tensions and cultural self-scrutiny of Japan in the wake of its defeat in World War II.]*

Notice that the descriptive writing in this piece of analysis is full and accurate enough to allow you to visualize the photograph as though it were in front of you. The writer's care in describing his subject and in choosing the language for that description is good not only for helping the writer to arrive at conclusions for ideas suggested by the photograph (making the implicit explicit), but also for allowing us to participate in the writer's thinking, because he has shared his data with us.

Now let's turn to another piece of the same essay. Record, at the end of each paragraph, what the paragraph does, what moves it makes, as we did with the first excerpt. Then formulate answers to the following questions:

If you were going to strengthen this analysis, how would you tighten the relationship between the details and the claims?

How, for example, might the writer make better use of the fact that the figure is perched on a fence?

How might more be done with the information we are given about the legend of the Kamaitachi?

The series entitled "Kamaitachi" is a journal of Hosoe's desolate childhood and wartime evacuation in the Tokyo countryside. He returns years later to the areas where he grew up, a stranger to his native land, perhaps likening himself to the legendary Kamaitachi, an invisible sickle-toothed weasel, intertwined with the soil and its unrealized fertility. "Kamaitachi #8" (1956), a platinum palladium print, stands alone to best capture Hosoe's alienation from and troubled expectation of the future of Japan.

The image is that of a tall fence of stark horizontal and vertical rough wood lashed together, looming above the barren rice fields. Straddling the fence, half-crouched and half-clinging, is a solitary male figure, gazing in profile to the horizon. Oblivious to the sky of dark and churning thunderclouds above, the figure instead focuses his attentions and concentrations elsewhere.

It is exactly this *elsewhere* that makes the image successful, because in studying the man we are to turn our attentions toward his and away from the photograph itself. He hangs curiously between heaven and earth, suspended on a makeshift man-made structure, in a purgatorial limbo awaiting the future. He waits with anticipation—perhaps dread?—for a time that has not yet come; he is directed away from the present, and it is this sensitivity to time that sets this print apart from the others in the series. One could argue that in effect this man, clothed in common garb, has become Japan itself, indicative of the postwar uncertainty of a country once dominant and now destroyed. What will the future (dark storm clouds) hold for this newly humbled nation?

## Distinguishing Analysis from Expressive Writing, Summary, and Argument

How does analysis resemble and differ from other kinds of thinking and writing? A common way of answering this question is to think of communication as having three possible centers of emphasis—the writer, the subject, and the audience.

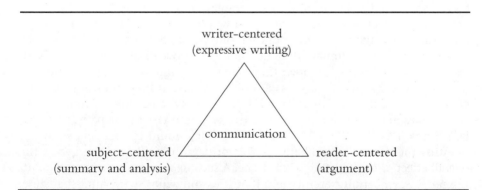

**FIGURE 1.1**

Diagram of Communication Triangle.

Communication, of course, involves all three of these centers, but some kinds of writing concentrate more on one point of the triangle than on the others. Autobiographical writing, such as diaries or memoirs or stories about personal experience, centers on the writer and his or her desire for self-expression and self-understanding. Argument, in which the writer either advocates or challenges a policy or attitude, centers on readers; its goal is to bring about a change in their actions and beliefs. Analytical writing and summary are more concerned with arriving at an understanding of a subject than they are with either achieving self-expression or changing readers' views.

Just as the three points of the triangle inevitably overlap, so, too, do the four kinds of writing we have mentioned (an argument usually involves some summarizing, for example). More to the point, summary, expressive writing, and argument all make use of analysis. How analysis figures in each of these other kinds of writing, and how it differs from them, we will now consider.

## Analysis and Summary

One of the most common kinds of writing you'll be asked to do in college, other than analysis, is summary. Summary differs from analysis, because the aim of summary is to recount, in effect, to reproduce someone else's ideas. But summary and analysis are also clearly related and usually operate together. Summary is important to analysis, because you can't analyze a subject without laying out its significant parts for your reader. Similarly, analysis is important to summary, because summarizing is more than just copying someone else's words. To write an accurate summary you have to ask analytical questions, such as:

- Which of the ideas in the reading are most significant? Why?
- How do these ideas fit together? What do the key passages in the reading mean?

Like an analysis, an effective summary doesn't assume that the subject matter can speak for itself: the writer needs to play an active role. A good summary provides perspective on the subject as a whole by explaining, as an analysis does, the meaning and function of each of that subject's parts. Moreover, like an analysis, a good summary does not aim to approve or disapprove of its subject: the goal, in both kinds of writing, is to understand rather than to evaluate.

So, summary, like analysis, is a tool of understanding and not just a mechanical task. But a summary stops short of analysis because summary typically makes much smaller interpretive leaps. A summary of the painting popularly known as *Whistler's Mother,* for example, would tell readers what the painting includes, which details are the most prominent, and even what the overall effect of the painting seems to be. A summary might say that the painting possesses a certain serenity and that it is somewhat spare, almost austere. This kind of language still falls into the category of *focused description,* which is what a summary is.

**FIGURE 1.2**

*Arrangement in Black and Grey: The Artist's Mother* by James Abbott McNeill Whistler, 1871. How would an analysis of this painting differ from a summary of it?

An analysis would include more of the writer's interpretive thinking. It might tell us, for instance, that the painter's choice to portray his subject in profile contributes to our sense of her separateness from us and of her nonconfrontational passivity. We look at her, but she does not look back at us. Her black dress and the fitted lace cap that obscures her hair are not only emblems of her self-effacement, shrouds disguising her identity like her expressionless face, but also the tools of her self-containment and thus of her power to remain aloof from prying eyes. What is the attraction of this painting (this being one of the questions that an analysis might ask)? What might draw a viewer to the sight of this austere, drably attired woman, sitting alone in the center of a mostly blank space? Perhaps it is the very starkness of the painting, and the mystery of self-sufficiency at its center, that attracts us. (See Figure 1.3.)

FIGURE 1.3

---

Summary and Analysis of *Whistler's* Mother.

---

| Data | Method of Analysis | Interpretive Leaps |
|---|---|---|
| subject in profile, not looking at us —→ | make implicit explicit —→ (speculate about what the detail might suggest) | figure strikes us as separate, nonconfrontational, passive |
| folded hands, fitted lace —→ cap, contained hair, expressionless face | locate pattern of same or —→ similar detail; make what is implicit in the pattern of details explicit | figure strikes us as self-contained, powerful in her separateness and self-enclosure—self-sufficient? |
| patterned curtain and—→ picture versus still figure and blank wall; slightly frilled lace cuffs and ties on cap versus plain black dress | locate organizing —→ contrast; make what is implicit in the contrast explicit | austerity and containment of the figure made more pronounced by slight contrast with busier, more lively, and more ornate elements and with little picture showing world outside |
| slightly slouched body —→ position and presence of support for feet | anomalies; make what is —→ implicit in the anomalies explicit | these details destabilize the serenity of the figure, adding some tension to the picture in the form of slightly uneasy posture and figure's need for support: she looks too long, drooped in on her own spine |

Observations of the sort just offered go beyond describing what the painting contains and enter into the writer's ideas about what its details imply, what the painting invites us to make of it and by what means. Notice in our analysis of the painting how intertwined the description (summary) is with the analysis. Laying out the data is key to any kind of analysis not simply because it keeps the analysis accurate but also because, crucially, it is *in the act of carefully describing a subject that analytical writers often have their best ideas.*

You may not agree with the terms by which we have summarized the painting, and thus you may not agree with such conclusions as "the mystery of self-sufficiency." Nor is it necessary that you agree, because there is no single, right answer to what the painting means. The absence of a single right answer does not, however, mean that anything goes.

A reader's willingness to accept an analytical conclusion is powerfully connected to his or her ability to see its *plausibility*—that is, how it follows from both the supporting details that the writer has selected and the language used in characterizing those details. The writer who can offer a plausible (likely, not obviously untrue) description of a subject's key features is likely to arrive at conclusions about possible meanings that others would share. This is often the best you can hope for with analytical conclusions—not that others will say, "Yes, that is obviously right," but rather, "Yes, I can see where it might be possible and reasonable to think as you do."

Here are two general rules to be drawn from this discussion of analysis and summary:

1. Describe with care. The words you choose to summarize your data will contain the germs of your ideas about what the subject means.
2. In moving from summary to analysis, scrutinize the language you have chosen, asking, "Why did I choose this word?" and "What ideas are implicit in the language I have used?"

## Analysis and Expressive Writing

In expressive writing, your primary subject is yourself, with other subjects serving as a means of evoking greater self-understanding. In analytical writing, your reasoning may derive from personal experience, but it is your reasoning and not you or your experiences that matter. Analysis asks not just the expressive question, "What do I think?," but also "How good is my thinking? How well does it fit the subject I am trying to explain?"

We don't mean to suggest that expressive writing cannot be analytical or that analytical writing cannot be expressive. Expressive (writer-centered) writing is

---

### APPLICATION:

### ANALYZING A PICTURE

Locate any portrait, preferably a good reproduction from an art book or magazine, one that shows detail clearly. Then do a version of what we've done with Whistler in the preceding columns.

Your goal is to produce an analysis of the portrait with the steps we included in analyzing *Whistler's Mother.* First, summarize the portrait, describing accurately its significant details. Do not go beyond a recounting of what the portrait includes; avoid interpreting what these details suggest.

Then use the various methods offered in this chapter to analyze the data. What repetitions (patterns of same or similar detail) do you see? What organizing contrasts suggest themselves? In light of these patterns of similarity and difference, what anomalies do you then begin to detect? Move from the data to interpretive conclusions.

This process will produce a set of interpretive leaps, which you may then try to assemble into a more coherent claim of some sort—about what the portrait "says."

analytical in its attempts to define and explain a writer's feelings, reactions, and experiences. And analysis is a form of self-expression, because it inevitably reflects the ways a writer's experiences have taught him or her to think about the world.

Although observations like those offered in the preceding "Interpretive Leaps" column go beyond simple description, they don't move from the painting into autobiography. They stay with the task of explaining the painting, rather than moving to private associations that the painting might prompt, such as effusions about old age, or rocking chairs, or the character and situation of the writer's own mother. Such associations could well be valuable unto themselves as a means of prompting a searching piece of expressive writing. They might also help a writer to interpret some feature of the painting that he or she was working to understand. But the writer would not be free to use pieces of his or her personal history as conclusions about what the painting communicates, unless these conclusions could also be reasonably inferred from the painting itself.

Let's say, for example, that a writer believed that the woman is mourning the death of a son or is patiently waiting to die and that he or she cited as substantiation the black dress, the woman's somber expression, and the relative darkness of the painting. This selection of details might be sufficient to support some kind of interpretation concerning death, but the leap to a dead son is not warranted by the data.

In formulating an interpretation involving death, however, the writer should not substitute appeals to personal experience for reasoning from particulars in the painting. Because darkness and dark clothing need not operate as symbols of death, and because the woman's expression is not unquestionably grief-stricken (she looks expressionless to us), a writer would need more evidence to jump to a narrative about the feelings and situation of the mother. If, for example, part of a coffin were showing from behind the curtain, or if there were an hourglass somewhere in the painting, a reader might more plausibly conclude that mourning and mortality are governing contexts.

A few rules are worth highlighting here:

1. The range of associations for explaining a given detail or word must be governed by context.
2. It's fine to use your personal reactions as a way into exploring what a subject means, but take care not to make an interpretive leap stretch farther than the actual details will support.
3. Because the tendency to transfer meanings from your own life onto a subject can lead you to ignore the details of the subject itself, you need always to be asking yourself: "What other explanations might plausibly account for this same pattern of detail?"

## Analysis and Argument

Analysis and argument proceed in the same way. They offer evidence, make claims about it, and supply reasons that explain and justify the claims. In other words, in both analysis and argument you respond to the questions "What have you got to go on?" (supply evidence) and "How did you get there?" (supply the principles and reasons that caused you to conclude what you did about the evidence).

Although analysis and argument proceed in essentially the same way, they differ in the kinds of questions they try to answer. Argument, at its most dispassionate, asks, "What can be said with truth about *x* or *y?*" In common practice, though, the kinds of questions that argument more often answers are more committed, directive, and *should*-centered, such as "Which is better, *x* or *y?*," "How can we best achieve *x* or *y?*," and "Why should we stop doing *x* or *y?*"

Analysis, by contrast, asks, "What does *x* or *y* mean?" In analysis the evidence (your data) is something you wish to understand, and the claims are assertions about what that evidence means. The claim that an analysis makes is usually a tentative answer to a *what, how,* or *why* question; it seeks to explain why people watch professional wrestling, or what the rising number of sexual harassment cases might mean, or how certain features of government healthcare policy are designed to allay the fears of the middle class.

The claim that an argument makes is often an answer to a *should* question: for example, readers should or shouldn't vote for bans on smoking in public buildings, or they should or shouldn't believe that gays can function effectively in the military. The writer of an analysis is more concerned with discovering how each of these complex subjects might be defined and explained than with convincing readers to approve or disapprove of them.

### Analysis vs. Debate-Style Argument

A factor that sometimes separates argument and analysis is the closer association of argument with the desire to persuade. When the aim of argument is *persuasion*—to get the audience to accept the writer's position on a given subject—argument is likely to differ significantly from analysis. For one thing, a writer concerned with persuading others may feel the need to go into the writing process with considerable certainty about the position he or she advocates. The writer of an analysis, on the other hand, usually begins and remains for an extended period in a position of uncertainty.

Analytical writers are frequently more concerned with persuading themselves, with discovering what they believe about a subject, than they are with persuading others. The writer of an analysis is thus more likely to begin with the details of a subject he or she wishes to better understand, than with a position he or she wishes to defend.

Many of you may have been introduced to writing arguments through the debate model—arguing pro or con on (for or against) a given position, with the aim of defeating an imagined opponent and convincing your audience of the rightness of your position. The agree/disagree mode of writing and thinking that you often see in editorials, hear on radio or television, and even practice sometimes in school may incline you to focus all of your energy on the bottom line—aggressively advancing a claim for or against some view—without first engaging in the exploratory interpretation of evidence that is so necessary to arriving at thoughtful arguments. But as the *American College Dictionary* says, "to argue implies reasoning or trying to understand; it does not necessarily imply opposition." It is this more exploratory, tentative, and dispassionate mode of argument that this book encourages you to practice.

Adhering to the more restrictive, debate-style definition of *argument* can create a number of problems for careful analytical writers:

1. By requiring writers to be oppositional, it inclines them to discount or dismiss problems in the side or position they have chosen; they cling to the same static position rather than testing it as a way of allowing it to evolve.
2. It inclines writers toward either/or thinking rather than encouraging them to formulate more qualified (carefully limited, acknowledging exceptions, etc.) positions that integrate apparently opposing viewpoints.
3. It overvalues convincing someone else at the expense of developing understanding.

As should now be clear, the aims of analysis and argument can sometimes be in conflict. Nevertheless, it's important to remember that, in practice, analysis and argument are inevitably linked. Even the most tentative and cautiously evolving analysis is ultimately an argument; it asks readers to accept a particular interpretation of a set of data.

Similarly, even the most passionately committed argument is an analysis. If you approach an argument with the primary goals of convincing others that you are right and defeating your opponents, you may neglect the more important goal of arriving at a fair and accurate assessment of your subject. In fact, you will be able to argue much more effectively from evidence if you first take the time to really consider what that evidence means and, thereby, to find valid positions to argue about it.

## Producing Good Thinking: Some Necessary Habits of Mind

As we have suggested throughout this chapter, there is no formula—no single set of procedures—that will automatically improve your thinking. There are, however, some habits of mind, some basic ways of approaching ideas and information that are necessary to the production of good thinking. The most important of these is the willingness to ask questions—especially about one's own assumptions—and to repeatedly reconsider conclusions. All of the following recommendations are in the service of this essential disposition, and so we include them here, even though some have not yet been explicitly addressed, as an introduction to the ideas and attitudes that the book will recommend.

1. *Suspend judgment.* Take the time to be sure you understand before you judge. Make understanding a higher priority than judging.

**2.** *Avoid oversimplification.* Qualify (limit and refine) your generalizations. Seek evidence that conflicts with your claims and use it to evolve more accurate claims. (See Chapter 4, "Making the Thesis Evolve.")

**3.** *Examine assumptions.* Reason back to and question the (often unstated) assumptions that underlie your claims. (See Chapter 3, "Recognizing and Fixing Weak Thesis Statements.")

**4.** *Don't treat opinions as facts.* Distinguish between evidence (data) and claims (ideas and judgments about the data). You have no doubt heard people say, when challenged about an opinion stated as though it were an obvious fact, that they are entitled to their opinions. It is true that not all of our convictions can be supported with reasons and evidence. In academic and other forms of analytical writing, however, you must substantiate your opinions or acknowledge them as unsubstantiatable.

**5.** *Support claims with evidence.* Try not to assume that the meaning and the truth of your claims are self-evident. Share your thought process with your readers. Let them see how you arrived at your claims and why you think the evidence means what you say it does.

**6.** *Question either/or statements.* Dividing possible views on a subject into two opposing sides often forces a choice between black and white when some shade of gray is fairer and more accurate. Before deciding which side of an issue you think is right, consider whether the issue has been adequately and appropriately defined.

**7.** *Choose and define your terms carefully.* Much of what goes wrong in reasoning is the product of sloppy (vague, inaccurate) and/or deliberately misleading terminology. Try thinking of your words as doorways and your arguments as the corridors these doorways lead to. See, for instance, our example in Chapter 9, "Editing for Style," of what happens when a writer chooses the word *ambivalent* rather than *ambiguous* to describe a presidential policy. The time you invest in locating and defining your doorways is time you won't waste getting stuck in or having to retrace your steps back down unproductive corridors.

## Key Words

This is the first of our lists of key words, which will appear at the end of each chapter; the words are listed in the order in which they are defined in the text. The lists are intended to help you review the chapters' chief concepts. Ideally, you should be able to define each of these words after you have read the chapter.

| | |
|---|---|
| substantiate | data |
| implicit, implication | recursive |
| explicit | metaphor |
| overt | close reading |
| inference | explication |
| opposition | interpretive leap |
| anomaly | plausibility |
| subvert | claim |

## Guidelines for Writing Analytically

1. Slow down. Take the time to record what you notice without worrying about where your observations might lead.
2. Avoid deciding what your subject means before you analyze it, and remember that analysis often operates in areas where there is no one right answer.
3. As you analyze a subject, ask not just, "What are its defining parts?" but also, "How do these parts help me to understand the meaning of the subject as a whole?"
4. Look for patterns of repetition and organizing contrasts in the data, as well as anomalies, and ask yourself questions about what these mean.
5. Make the implicit explicit: convert the suggested meanings of particular details into overt statements.
6. When you describe and summarize, attend carefully to the language you choose, because the words themselves will usually contain the germs of ideas.
7. Take special care in connecting evidence with claims, answering the question "How did I get there?" Inexperienced writers are prone to neglect or underplay this crucial move.
8. If you avoid the extreme oppositional thinking associated with debate-style argument, you are more likely, in the long run, to make your argument truly persuasive.

## CHAPTER 2

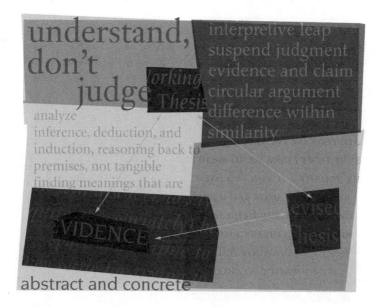

# ANALYZING EVIDENCE

## Linking Evidence and Claims

This chapter is about evidence—what it is, what it is meant to do, and how you can recognize when you are using it well. The chapter's overall argument is that you should use evidence to test, refine, and develop your ideas, rather than just to prove that they are correct. The chapter begins by analyzing two common problems: claims without evidence *(unsubstantiated claims)* and evidence without claims *(pointless evidence)*. It then moves to a discussion of strategies for analyzing evidence in depth.

By way of definition, a *claim* is what you want to prove. It is a point that you make about the meaning of your subject. The primary claim in a paper is the *thesis*—a term we use synonymously with *claim* and to which Chapters 3 and 4 will be devoted. *Evidence* refers to the information that is used to corroborate (support) a claim, though we use the term more broadly to refer to the pool of primary material (data) being analyzed.

There are many kinds of evidence; and whether or not something qualifies as acceptable evidence, as well as what it is evidence of, is often debatable. The types and amounts of evidence necessary for persuading readers and building authority also vary from one discipline to another, as does the manner in which the evidence is presented. Whereas some disciplines—the natural sciences, for

EVIDENCE <---> CLAIMS

the crucial site

**FIGURE 2.1**

example—require you to present your evidence first and then interpret it, others (the humanities and some social sciences) require you to interpret your evidence as it is presented. At the end of the chapter we will offer some examples of types of evidence typically used in different disciplines. But what we wish to stress is that it is possible to talk about methods of using evidence that apply across the curriculum. In all disciplines—and virtually any writing situation—it is important to support claims with evidence, to make your evidence lead to claims, and especially to be explicit about *how you've arrived at the connection between your evidence and your claims.*

The first step in learning to explain the connection between your evidence and your claims is to remember that *evidence rarely, if ever, can be left to speak for itself.* When you leave evidence to speak for itself, you are assuming that it can be interpreted in only one way and that others will necessarily think as you do.

Writers who think that evidence speaks for itself generally do very little with it. Sometimes they will present it without making any overt claims, stating, for example, "There was no alcohol at the party," and expecting the reader to understand this statement as a sign of approval or disapproval. Alternatively, they may simply place the evidence next to a claim. Such writers will say, for example, "The party was terrible: there was no alcohol" or "The party was great: there was no alcohol." Merely juxtaposing the evidence to the claim (just putting them next to each other) leaves out the thinking that connects them, thereby implying that the logic of the connection is obvious. But even for readers prone to agree with you, just pointing to the evidence, assuming it will speak for itself, is not enough.

## Unsubstantiated Claims

**Problem:** making claims that lack supporting evidence

**Solution:** learn to recognize and support unsubstantiated assertions

Unsubstantiated claims occur when you concentrate only on conclusions, omitting the evidence that led to them. At the opposite extreme, pointless evidence results when you offer a mass of detail attached to an overly general claim. To solve both of these problems, remember two rules. Whenever you make a claim:

1. Offer your readers the evidence that led you to it.
2. Explain how the evidence led you to that conclusion.

The word *unsubstantiated* means "without substance." An unsubstantiated claim is not necessarily false; it just offers none of the concrete "stuff" upon which the claim is based. There are two compelling reasons to avoid unsubstantiated claims:

> Making such a claim assumes that readers will believe you just because you say this or that.

> Unsubstantiated claims deprive you of details. Without details, you're left with nothing concrete to think about.

If you lack some actual "stuff" to analyze, you can easily get stuck in a set of abstractions, which tends to overstate your position, inhibit your thinking, and leave your readers wondering exactly what you mean. The farther away your language gets from the concrete references to physical detail—things that you can see, hear, count, taste, smell, and touch—the more abstract it becomes. An aircraft carrier anchored outside a foreign harbor is concrete; the phrase "intervening in the name of democracy" is abstract. (See "Concrete and Abstract Diction" in Chapter 9, "Editing for Style.")

You can see the problem of unsubstantiated assertions not only in papers but also in everyday conversation. It occurs when people get into the habit of leaping to conclusions—forming impressions so quickly and automatically that they have difficulty even recalling what it was that triggered a particular response. Ask such people why they thought a party was boring or a new acquaintance pretentious, and they will rephrase the generalization rather than offer the evidence that led to it: the party was boring because nobody did anything; the person is pretentious because he puts on airs.

Rephrasing your generalizations rather than offering evidence tends to starve your thinking; it also has the effect of shutting out readers. If, for example, you defend your judgment that a person is pretentious by saying that he puts on airs, you have ruled on the matter and dismissed it. (You have also committed a logic error known as a *circular argument;* because "pretentious" and "puts on airs" mean virtually the same thing, using one in support of the other is arguing in a circle.) If, by contrast, you include the *grounds* upon which your judgment is based—that he uses big words or always wears a bow tie— you have given readers a glimpse of your criteria. Readers are far more likely to accept your views if you give them the chance to think *with* you about the evidence. The alternative—offering groundless assertions—is to expect them to take your word for it.

There is, of course, an element of risk in providing the details that have informed your judgment. You leave yourself open to attack if, for example, your readers wear bow ties or speak in polysyllables. But this is an essential risk to take, because otherwise you leave your readers wondering why you think as you do, or worse, unlikely to credit your point of view. Moreover, in laying out

**APPLICATION:**

## DISTINGUISHING EVIDENCE FROM CLAIMS

Take an excerpt from your own writing, at least two paragraphs in length—perhaps from a paper you have already written or a draft you are working on—and at the end of every sentence, label it as either evidence (E) or claim (C). For a sentence that appears to offer both, determine which parts of the sentence are evidence and which are claim, and then decide which one, *E* or *C*, predominates. What is the ratio of evidence to claim, especially in particularly effective or weak paragraphs?

A useful variant: after you have marked your own paper or draft excerpt, exchange an unmarked copy with another member of the class, and mark each other's work with *C*s and *E*s. Then confer about each other's markings, and in cases where you have marked the same sentence differently, figure out why: what is it about the sentence that caused the disagreement?

As an alternative or a preface to the preceding exercise, mark the following paragraph with *C*'s and *E*'s. We have numbered the sentences for easier isolation and discussion. A few of them—1 and 7, for example—are arguably quite tricky to decide about: which part of the sentence is a claim, and which part is evidence? Keep in mind that you are making your decisions on the basis of the writer's *use* of the sentences, not simply on their content: is a secondary source's *judgment* that is imported into an essay as *support* for the writer's point of view ultimately *C* or *E*, for example?

[1] Though many current historians would argue that Andrew Jackson's treatment of the Native Americans was contrary to the ideals and precepts

*(continued)*

your evidence, you will be more likely to anticipate your readers' possible disagreement. This will make you more inclined to think openly and carefully about your judgments.

In order to check your drafts for unsubstantiated assertions, you first have to know how to recognize them. One of the most fundamental skills for a writer to possess is the ability to *distinguish* evidence from claims. It is sometimes difficult to separate facts from judgments, data from interpretations of data. Writers who aren't practiced in this skill can believe that they are offering evidence when they are actually offering only unsubstantiated claims. In your own reading and writing, pause once in a while to label the sentences of a paragraph as either evidence (E) or claims (C). What happens if we try to categorize the sentences of the following paragraph in this way?

The owners are ruining baseball in America. Although they claim that they are losing money, they are really just being greedy. A few years ago, they even fired the commissioner, Fay Vincent, because he took the players'

*(continued)*

of the American Revolution, one must consider the legal and moral context of both Jackson and the time period in which he lived. [2] Jackson, both as a general and as a president, had no real love for the Native American populations in the southern and western United States. [3] As a military general he had defended the borders of the United States many times against Indian attacks and negotiated treaties with some of the tribes during the term of President Monroe. [4] However, Jackson was also the archetype for the general American view on Native Americans. [5] He describes the Indians as barbarians and cruel savages in a letter to a fellow politician (Hollitz 172) and tried to convince President Monroe, during his negotiations with the Creek Indians, that Native Americans "are the subjects of the United States, inhabiting its territory and acknowledging its sovereignty" (Hollitz 174). [6] He subsequently argued that it was "absurd for the sovereign to negotiate with the subjects" (Hollitz 174). [7] Jackson and many of his contemporaries also saw the Indians as only a hindrance to America's exploitation of southern and western farmland and thought that they should be removed to facilitate American expansion. [8] This is clearly seen in a letter Jackson wrote to his wife in which he describes removing the natives of Alabama in terms of the fertile lands and wealth, as well as a secure southern border, that the removal will bring the United States (Hollitz 173). [9] They were subjects of American sovereignty. [10] In this sense, Jackson's policy of Indian removal was in line with the best wishes of the people that the ideals of the American Revolution were set aside for, the American citizens who wished for more fertile lands and safe borders. [11] Jackson was indeed providing for the citizens whom he believed the Declaration of Independence encompassed.

side. Baseball is a sport, not a business, and it is a sad fact that it is being threatened by greedy businessmen.

The first and last sentences of the paragraph are claims. They draw conclusions about as-yet-unstated evidence that the writer will need to provide. The middle two sentences are harder to classify. If particular owners have stated publicly that they are losing money, the existence of those statements is a fact. But the writer moves from evidence to claim when he suggests that the owners are lying about their financial situation and are doing so because of their greed. Both of these assertions are unsubstantiated claims. Unless the writer proceeds to ground them in evidence—relevant facts—they amount to little more than name-calling. Similarly, it is a fact that Commissioner Fay Vincent was fired, but the assertion that he was fired "because he took the players' side" is another unsubstantiated claim. The writer needs to offer evidence in support of this claim, along with his reasons for believing that the evidence means what he says it does.

Without evidence and the reasoning you've done about it, your writing asks readers to accept your opinions as though they were facts. The central claim of the baseball paragraph—that greedy businessmen are ruining baseball—is an example of an opinion treated as though it were factual information. Although many readers might be inclined to accept some version of the claim as true, they should not be asked to accept the writer's opinion as a self-evident truth.

The word *evident* comes from a Latin verb meaning "to see." To say that the truth of a statement is "self-evident" means that it does not need proving because its truth should be plainly seen by all. The problem is that very few ideas—no matter how much you may believe in them—readily attest to their own truth. And precisely because what people have taken to be common knowledge ("women can't do math," for example, or "men don't talk about their feelings") so often turns out to be wrong, you should take care to avoid unsubstantiated claims.

Be stingy about treating your claims and evidence as factual. The more concrete information you gather, the less likely you will be to accept your opinions, partial information, or misinformation as fact. The writer of the baseball paragraph, for example, offers as fact that the owners claim they are losing money. If he were to search harder, however, he would find that his statement of the owners' claim is not entirely accurate. The owners have not unanimously claimed that they are losing money; they have acknowledged that the problem has to do with poorer "small-market" teams competing against richer "large-market" teams. This more complicated version of the facts might at first be discouraging to the writer, because it reveals his original thesis ("greed") to be oversimplified. But then, as we have been saying, the function of evidence is not just to corroborate your claims; it should also help you to *test* and *refine* your ideas and to *define* your key terms more precisely.

Most writers make at least some unsubstantiated claims as they draft. To remedy this problem:

1. Identify all claims, distinguishing them from evidence.
2. Locate evidence that could substantiate and test unsubstantiated claims.
3. Allow your analysis of this evidence to develop your claims, rather than simply confirming your original formulation.

Following these three steps will help you write more thoughtfully. You will also find yourself having much more to say.

## Pointless Evidence

Problem: presenting a mass of evidence without explaining how it relates to the claims

Solution: make details speak; explain how evidence confirms or qualifies the claim

Your thinking emerges in the way that you follow through on the implications of the evidence you have selected. You need to interpret it for your readers. It is not enough to insert evidence after your claim, expecting readers to draw the same conclusion about its meaning that you have. You cannot assume that the facts can speak for themselves. You need to make the details speak.

The following example illustrates what happens when a writer leaves the evidence to speak for itself:

> Baseball is a sport, not a business, and it is a sad fact that it is being threatened by greedy businessmen. For example, Eli Jacobs, the previous owner of the Baltimore Orioles, recently sold the team to Peter Angelos for $100 million more than he had spent ten years earlier when he purchased it. Also, a new generation of baseball parks has been built—for the Orioles in Baltimore, for the White Sox in Chicago, for the Rangers in Arlington, for the Indians in Cleveland. These parks are enormously expensive and include elaborate scoreboards and luxury boxes. The average baseball players, meanwhile, now earn over a million dollars a year, and they all have agents to represent them. Barry Bonds, the left fielder for the San Francisco Giants, is paid over $7 million a season. Sure, he has won the coveted Most Valuable Player award (MVP) in his league three times, but is any ballplayer worth that much money?

Unlike the previous example, which is virtually all claims, this paragraph is all evidence, except for the opening claim and the closing question. The paragraph presents what we might call an "evidence sandwich": it encloses a series of facts between two claims. (The opening statement blames "greedy businessmen," presumably owners, and the closing statement appears to indict greedy, or at least overpaid, players.) Readers are left with two problems. First, the mismatch between the opening and concluding claims leaves it not altogether clear what the writer is saying that the evidence suggests. And second, he has not told readers why they should believe that the evidence means what he says it does. Instead, he leaves it to speak for itself.

If you look again at the example, you'll see that each sentence after the opening claim offers facts but does not overtly interpret those facts by connecting them to the claims. The closest connection between claims and evidence is between the fact that Barry Bonds earns over $7 million per year and the writer's implicit claim (phrased as a question) that no player is worth that much. Otherwise, the items of evidence do not bear directly on the claims made.

If readers are to accept the writer's implicit claims—that the spending is too much and that it is ruining baseball—he will have to show *how* and *why* the evidence supports these conclusions. The rule that applies here is that *evidence can almost always be interpreted in more than one way.*

You might, for instance, formulate at least three conclusions from the evidence offered in the baseball paragraph. You might decide that the writer believes baseball will be ruined by going broke or that he is saying its spirit will be ruined by becoming too commercial. Worst of all, you might disagree with his claim and conclude that baseball is not really being ruined, since the evidence could be read as signs of health rather than decay. The profitable resale of the Orioles, the expensive new ballparks (which, the writer neglects to mention, have drawn record crowds), and the skyrocketing salaries all could testify to the growing popularity rather than the decline of the sport.

How can you ensure that your readers will at least understand your interpretation of the data? Begin by constantly reminding yourself that the thought connections that have occurred to you will not automatically occur to others. This doesn't mean that you should assume your readers are stupid, but rather that you shouldn't expect them to read your mind and to do for themselves the thinking that you should be doing for them.

You can make the details speak if you take the time to stop and look at them, asking questions about what they imply. The two steps to follow are:

1. State explicitly what you take the details to mean.
2. State exactly how the evidence supports or qualifies your claims.

The writer of the baseball paragraph leaves both some of his claims and virtually all of his reasoning about the evidence implicit. What, for example, bothers him about the special luxury seating areas? What does this piece of information imply? Perhaps it demonstrates that economic interests are taking baseball away from its traditional fans, because the new seating areas cost far more than the average person can afford to pay. This interpretation of the evidence could be used to support the writer's governing claim, but he would need to spell out the connection. He might say, for example, that baseball's time-honored role as the all-American sport—democratic and grassroots—is being displaced by the tendency of baseball as a business to orient its efforts around attracting higher box office receipts and wealthier fans.

The writer could then make more explicit what his whole paragraph implies: that baseball's image as a popular pastime in which all Americans can participate is being tarnished by players and owners alike, whose primary concern appears to be making money. In making his evidence speak, the writer would also refine his claim by being much clearer about which aspect of baseball he thinks is being ruined. He could clarify in his revision, for instance, that the "greedy businessmen" to whom he refers include both owners and players.

The result of carefully pondering the implications of your evidence will almost always be a "smaller" idea than the one you may have set out to prove. This is *what "qualifying" a generalization means: you shrink and restrict its scope.* Sometimes it is hard to give up on the large, general assertions that were your first response to your subject. But your sacrifices in scope are exchanged for greater accuracy and validity. The sweeping claims you lose ("Greedy businessmen are ruining baseball") give way to less resounding but also more informed, more incisive, and less judgmental ideas ("Market pressures may not bring the end of baseball, but they are certainly changing the image and nature of the game").

**APPLICATION:**

## IN OTHER WORDS

It is a generally sound analytical practice to paraphrase—restate *in other words*—what a source has said. Doing so will help you to ensure that your readers will understand your interpretation of the data, but more importantly, it will also allow you to assimilate the material and begin to have ideas about it. Particularly with materials that are difficult to comprehend, paraphrasing is an essential guard against leaping to an unfounded conclusion.

Now consider the following excerpt from a philosophy paper in which the writer first quotes his source and then paraphrases it. As you will see, the paraphrase is pretty good—it accomplishes a lot in a few words—but it could be better. That is, it could more accurately reflect the thinking in the quotation, and it could more explicitly link the quoted evidence with the interpretation contained in the paraphrase.

Study the quotation and the paraphrase, and then rewrite the paraphrase. Don't worry if your revised paraphrase is longer than the original: you want to be concise, but your primary concern is accuracy. You may find it useful to discuss with others why you changed the paraphrase in the ways that you did. By way of context, the paper discusses an article entitled "The Ethics of Belief" by W. K. Clifford.

> Every time we let ourselves believe for unworthy reasons, we weaken our powers of self-control, of doubting, of judicially and fairly weighing evidence. We all suffer severely enough from the maintenance and support of false beliefs and the fatally wrong actions which they lead to, and the evil born when one such belief is entertained is great and wide. But a greater and wider evil arises when the credulous [prone to believe] character is maintained and supported, when a habit of believing for unworthy reasons is fostered and made permanent. . . . The danger to society is not merely that it should believe wrong things, though that is great enough, but that it should become credulous, and lose the habit of testing things and inquiring into them, for then it must sink back into savagery. (142)

What Clifford is saying is that people who have some beliefs based on insufficient evidence come to believe anything on insufficient evidence. Having a single belief not based on fact and inference causes a person to lose reason entirely; according to the article, this will eventually cause the destruction of our society.

As a further application of "In Other Words" in a peer editing context, circle a paragraph out of your own work, preferably a current draft, in which you are having significant trouble saying what you mean. Exchange the draft with another person, and write paraphrases of each other's paragraphs. Then, after conferring with your partner, rewrite your original paragraph, or possibly rewrite both paragraphs collaboratively.

## Evidence and Argument: Toulmin versus Aristotle

At this point in our discussion, it will be helpful to digress slightly in order to talk about the *systematic* examination of evidence as it is described in the field of logic. Logic as a discipline has offered us various, sometimes conflicting *rules of argument*—procedures for locating and using evidence in the service of a claim and for determining when that use of evidence can be judged valid. It is useful for writers to be aware of these rules because they can help you to understand more about how thinking operates.

Philosophers have long quested for forms that might lend to human argument some greater clarity and certainty, more like what is possible with formulas in math. As our discussion of one particular debate within the discipline of philosophy will demonstrate, however, the examination of evidence is necessarily an untidy process.

Probably the most common way of talking about logical argumentation goes back to the Greek philosopher Aristotle. At the heart of the Aristotelian model is the *syllogism,* which consists of three parts:

1. Major premise: a general proposition presumed to be true
2. Minor premise: a subordinate proposition also presumed to be true
3. Conclusion: a claim that follows logically from the two premises, if the argument has been properly framed.

A frequently cited example of a syllogism is:

All men are mortal (major premise).

Socrates is a man (minor premise).

Therefore, Socrates is mortal (conclusion).

A premise is a proposition (assumption) upon which an argument is based and from which a conclusion is drawn. In the syllogism, if both of the premises are true and have been stated in the proper form (both containing a shared term), then theoretically the conclusion must also be true. In the example, if it is true that all men are mortal, and if it is true that Socrates is a man, then it must follow that Socrates is mortal.

The British philosopher Steven Toulmin offered a competing model of argument in his influential book, *The Uses of Argument* (1958). The Toulmin model can be seen as motivated by a desire to describe the structure of argument in a way that comes closer to what actually happens in practice when we try to take a position. The Toulmin model consists of:

1. Data: the evidence appealed to in support of a claim; data respond to the question "What have you got to go on?"
2. Warrant: a general principle or reason used to connect the data with the claim; the warrant responds to the question "How did you get there?" (from the data to the claim)
3. Claim: a conclusion about the data

Toulmin's model was motivated by his belief that the philosophical tradition of formal logic, with its many rules for describing and evaluating the conduct of arguments, conflicts with the practice and idiom (ways of phrasing) of arguers. To radically simplify Toulmin's case, it is that the syllogism does not adequately account for what really happens when thinkers try to frame and defend various claims.

Toulmin notes that the rules governing the phrasing of syllogistic arguments are very strict, as they must be if the form of an argument alone is to disclose its validity. The Socrates syllogism earns its validity on the basis of its form. But for Toulmin, the strictness of the rules necessary for guaranteeing formal validity leaves out the greater amount of uncertainty that is a part of reasoning about most questions, issues, and problems. A syllogism is designed to reveal its soundness through the careful framing and arrangement of its terms:

All men are mortal. (All $x$'s are $y$.)

Socrates is a man. (Socrates is an $x$.)

Therefore, Socrates is mortal. (Socrates is $y$.)

But at what price, asks Toulmin, do we simplify our phrasing of complex situations in the world in order to gain this appearance of truth? In how many situations, he asks, can we say that "all $x$'s are $y$"?

Toulmin observes, using his own argument structure as a case in point, that as soon as an argument begins to add information in support of its premises, the complexity and inevitable tentativeness of the argument become apparent, rather than its evident truth.

Here is one of Toulmin's examples of what must happen to the form of an argument when a person begins to add this supporting information, which he calls *backing:*

**data:**     Harry was born in Bermuda.
**warrant:**  The relevant statutes provide that people born in the colonies of British parents are entitled to British citizenship;
**claim:**    So, presumably, Harry is a British citizen.

The backing for the warrant would inevitably involve mentioning "the relevant statutes"—acts of Parliament, statistical reports, and so forth—to prove its accuracy. The addition of such information, says Toulmin, would "prevent us from writing the argument so that its validity shall be manifest from its formal properties alone" (123).

In other words, formal logic has evaluated an argument on the basis of a tightly structured form (such as the syllogism) that makes the argument's validity visible (manifest). But as soon as the form of the argument is made to include the greater amount of information that supports its accuracy and truth, it is no longer possible to evaluate the argument solely on the basis of its adherence to the required form. On this basis, Toulmin questions the tradition of guaranteeing the soundness of arguments solely on rules of form.

The advantage of understanding Toulmin's response to Aristotle is that it provides an *antidote to the notion that there is a ready-made system for connecting evidence with claims that guarantees that an argument will always be right.* To use an analogy, if the Aristotelian syllogism appears to offer us the promise of never mistaking the forest for the trees, Toulmin's revision of that model is to never let us forget that the forest is in fact made up of trees.

As a writer, you will naturally want some guidelines and workable methods for selecting evidence and linking it to claims, and this book will do what it can to provide them. But what you can't expect to find is a set of predetermined slots into which you can drop any evidence and find the truth. Rather, as Toulmin allows us to see, analyses and arguments cannot be separated from the complex set of details and circumstances that are part of life as we live it. For you as a writer this means that good arguments and thus *good analyses attend carefully to particulars.*

## Analyzing Evidence in Depth

A common assumption about evidence is that it is "the stuff that proves I'm right." Although this way of thinking about evidence is not wrong, it is usually limited. *Corroboration (proving the validity of a claim) is one of the functions of evidence, but not the only one.*

It helps to remember that the word *prove* comes from a Latin verb meaning "to test." The noun form of prove, *proof,* has two meanings: (1) the *evidence* sufficient to establish a thing as true or believable and (2) the *act of testing* for truth or believability. When you operate on the first definition of *proof* alone, you are far more likely to seek out evidence that supports only your point of view, ignoring or dismissing other evidence that could lead to a different and possibly better idea. You might also assume that you can't begin writing until you have arrived at an idea you're convinced is right, because only then could you decide which evidence to include. Both of these practices close down your thinking instead of leading you to a more open process of formulating and testing ideas.

The more carefully you examine something, the more you will discover to say about it. But many writers (quite appropriately) believe that they don't have the space or the time to examine all of the pertinent data in depth, so they settle (perhaps inappropriately) for trying to cover everything a little. It is generally the case that such writers never develop their analysis past a superficial level. The next section of this chapter offers a basic model for *striking a compromise between coverage and depth* that promotes writing analytically.

### 10 on 1 vs. 1 on 10

> **Problem:** insufficiently analyzed evidence about which the writer repeatedly makes the same general claim

**Solution:** it is generally better to make ten points on a single representative issue or example (10 on 1) than to make the same basic point about ten related issues or examples (1 on 10).

The best way to enable yourself to say more about evidence is to narrow your focus. A paper built from detailed analysis of your most telling example is far more likely to take you to a good idea than is a paper that keeps saying the same thing about a large number of examples.

Making ten points about your most telling example (10 on 1) is a fruitful alternative to repeatedly pointing to a similarity among ten related examples (1 on 10). Certainly you need to examine more than one example in order to make a fair and accurate argument, but the problem with the method we are calling "1 on 10" is that it tries to cover too much ground and often ends by noticing little more than some general similarity that might be the starting point but should not be the final outcome of a paper. The number *10,* we should add, is arbitrarily chosen. You could make four or five or seven points. The important idea we intend 10 on 1 to communicate is that you should *draw out as much meaning as possible from your best examples.*

We recognize that the 10 on 1 formula can lead to a possible confusion. How can you get to a thesis by saying ten things about a representative example? Wouldn't you then have a paper that supported ten claims? The answer is that *you use 10 on 1 to:*

- Locate the range of possible meanings your evidence suggests
- Slow down the rush to generalization and thus help to ensure that when you leap to a claim, that claim will be more specific, and better able to account for your evidence
- Make you less inclined to cling to your first claim inflexibly, opening the way for you to discover a way of representing more fully the complexity of your subject

Here is a brief example: say that you were writing an essay on the role of disease in *The X-Files*. You locate a number of examples that all point to the same conclusion: now that the Cold War is over, the threat to America's security lies *within*. Once most writers decide that all the evidence points to the same conclusion, they tend to stop really looking at the evidence. If you were to use all of your examples to repeatedly corroborate the same point, the repetition would deter you from exploring the evidence in more depth. Writing would then become not a matter of finding things out or developing an idea, but simply of dropping each example into place next to an unchanging conclusion. *Rather than catalogue* all of the instances of festering innards in *The X-Files,* you would do better to *scrutinize the most revealing instance and then locate it in a pattern of other like instances.* By drawing out its implications, you would more likely discover the questions and understand the cultural issues that surround disease in *The X-Files*—or any subject.

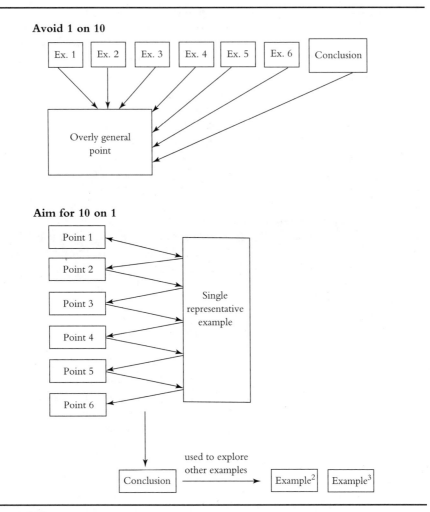

**FIGURE 2.2**

The horizontal pattern, 1 on 10 (in which *10* stands arbitrarily for any number of examples), repeatedly makes the same point about every example; its analysis of evidence is superficial. The vertical pattern, 10 on 1 (in which *10* stands arbitrarily for any number of points), successively develops a series of points about a single, representative example; its analysis of evidence is in-depth.

Here is a case in point—two paragraphs of analysis of a single episode from *The X-Files* in which the writer:

- Scrutinizes what she takes to be especially revealing details
- Argues for seeing the details as part of a coherent pattern of like detail
- Offers a theory about what the pattern signifies by drawing out its implications

**EXCERPT FROM** "Seeking the Truth and Stumbling onto the Spiritual
in *The X-Files*"

More strikingly, however, *The X-Files* has presented the abduction experience as marked by a specific, transgressive, and
unsupportable connection between women. This connection has been
staged over several episodes through the association between
Scully and the women of the Mutual UFO Network (MUFON). Although
Scully meets these women as if for the first time, they themselves recognize her as having been part of their own abduction
experiences: like Scully, all have had metal implants removed
from their necks. Although Scully initially reacts to their
recognition of her with denial and a palpable attempt at dis-
identification, she eventually espouses the connection in "Memento Mori," the episode in which her cancer was diagnosed; in
that episode, she learns that in the eleven months that have
passed since she met them, all but one of the eleven women have
died. Scully joins the remaining woman, Penny Northern, and begins treatment by the same doctor that has been treating Penny.
Through the course of the episode, Scully and Penny develop an
intense connection concretized in a scene in which Scully awak-
ens from a dream regarding her abduction to find Penny holding
her hand. While her eyes remain closed, Scully remembers that
"someone was doing something bad to me" but that Penny was there
to help her. Penny affirms that she was with Scully "during the
tests" and that she "held and comforted" Scully. As soon as Penny
validates Scully's experience in this fashion, however, Scully
opens her eyes and retreats from her own statements, rebuffing
Penny with the statement that she is "not ready to hear this now"
(*TXF*, "Memento Mori").

  Through the play between Scully's identification and dis-
identification with her fellow abductees, *The X-Files* suggests a
simultaneous need to locate abduction within a connection between
women and to keep that connection tightly controlled, both by
Scully herself and by the overarching narrative of *The X-Files* in
general. Not only does Scully acknowledge her connection with
Penny only within the realm of dreams rather than waking life, but

also the connection with Penny proves both ephemeral and short-lived; she dies by the end of the episode, leaving Scully the sole woman of the eleven she met at the MUFON meeting to survive her cancer. Furthermore, the episode itself evinces a retreat from the connection created between the two women: although a voice-over vocalizes most of "Memento Mori" through Scully, the final few scenes clearly situate the viewer with Mulder and outside of the connection between the two women. The camera follows Mulder into the hospital and with him looks through a door at Scully and Penny as they stare into each others' eyes; with Mulder, the viewer waits in the hallway until Scully emerges with the news that Penny is dead. In its suggestion that the knowledge arising from abduction creates a specific connection between women that must always be fleeting, *The X-Files* both assigns that knowledge to a space between women and marks that space as insupportable.

Although these two paragraphs are part of a much longer analysis, in this section of the paper, the writer gives a considerable amount of attention to selected features of a single episode. The claim the analysis is meant to support appears in the first sentence of the second paragraph. Most of the sentences in the two paragraphs are devoted not to generalization or to repetition of a single point, but rather to close scrutiny of relevant detail that serves to develop the writer's thinking about repeated plot elements involving the abduction of women by aliens and the women's connection with each other afterward.

In a short paper (three to five pages), you might devote as much as ninety percent of your writing to illustrating what one example reveals about the larger subject. Even in a paper that uses several examples, however, as much as fifty percent might still be devoted to analysis of and generalization from a single case. The remaining half of the paper would *make connections with other examples, testing and applying the ideas you arrived at from your single case.* In-depth analysis of your best example thus creates a center from which you can move in two directions:

Toward generalizations about the larger subject

Toward other examples, using your primary example as a tool of exploration

Faced, for example, with writing a paper about the role slavery played in causing the Civil War, an inexperienced writer might offer a broad survey with a few paragraphs on abolitionism, a few paragraphs on various congressional attempts to legislate the slavery issue, and a few paragraphs on economic rivalries between the industrial North and the agrarian South. You could cover the same body of information in far more depth, however, by focusing almost entirely on the Missouri Compromise as a representative instance. Your analysis of this legislative battle would necessarily include discussion of the abolitionists' role and the economic interests of both parties, but it would do so within a tightly focused framework. Your assumption would be that if readers can see the collision of interests that led to this compromise and its failure, they will obtain a deeper understanding of the slavery issue than a survey could provide.

This same model, applicable across a wide variety of writing situations, can be reduced to a series of steps:

1. Narrow your focus.
2. Select a representative example.
3. Provide in-depth analysis (10 on 1).
4. Test your results in similar cases.

An analysis of the representation of females on television, for example, would fare better if you focused on one show—say, *Buffy, the Vampire Slayer*— narrowed the focus to teenage girls, and tested your results against other shows with teenage heroines, such as *Sabrina, the Teenage Witch* and *My So-Called Life*. Similarly, a study of the national debt might focus on Social Security, working through specific evidence to arrive at generalizations to be tested and refined in the context of, say, health care or military spending. In sum, a close look at virtually anything will reveal its complexity, and you can bring that complex understanding to other examples for further testing and refining.

It is, of course, important to let your readers know that you are using the one primary example in this generalizable way. Note how the writer of the following discussion of the people's revolt in China in 1989 sets up his analysis. He first explains how his chosen example—a single photograph (Figure 2.3) from the media coverage of the event—illuminates his larger subject. The image is of a Chinese man in a white shirt who temporarily halted a line of tanks on their way to quell a demonstration in Tienanmen Square in Beijing.

The tank image provided a miniature, simplified version of a larger, more complex revolution. The conflict between man and tank embodied the same tension found in the conflict between student demonstrators and the Peoples' Army. The man in the white shirt, like the students, displayed courage, defiance, and rebellious individuality in the face of power. Initially, the peaceful revolution succeeded: the state allowed the students to protest; likewise, the tank spared the man's life. Empowered, the students' demands for democracy grew louder. Likewise, the man boldly jumped onto the tank and addressed the soldiers. The state's formerly unshakable dominance appeared weak next to the strength of the individual. However, the state asserted its

**FIGURE 2.3**
Tienanmen Square, Beijing, 1989.

power: the Peoples' Army marched into the square, and the tanks roared past the man into Beijing.

The image appeals to American ideology. The man in the white shirt personifies the strength of the American individual. His rugged courage draws on contemporary heroes such as Rambo. His defiant gestures resemble the demonstrations of Martin Luther King Jr. and his followers. American history predisposes us to identify strongly with the Chinese demonstrators: we have rebelled against the establishment, we have fought for freedom and democracy, and we have defended the rights of the individual. For example, the *New York Times* reported that President Bush watched the tank incident on television and said, "I'm convinced that the forces of democracy are going to overcome these unfortunate events in Tienanmen Square." Bush represents the popular American perspective of the Chinese rebellion; we support the student demonstrators.

This analysis is a striking example of 10 on 1. In the first paragraph, the writer constructs a detailed analogy between the particular image and the larger subject of which it was a part. The analogy allows the writer not just to describe but also to interpret the event. In the second paragraph, he develops his focus on the image as an image, a photographic representation tailor-made to appeal to American viewing audiences. Rather than generalizing about why Americans might find the image appealing, he establishes a number of explicit connections (10 on 1) between the details of the image and typical American heroes. By drawing out the implications of particular details, he manages to say more about the significance of the American response to the demonstrations in China than a broader survey of those events would have allowed.

The rule of thumb here is to:

- Say more about less, rather than less about more.
- Allow a carefully analyzed part of your subject to provide perspective on the whole.

### APPLICATION:

### DOING 10 ON 1

Take a piece of evidence—a representative example—from something you are studying and do 10 on 1. That is, make at least ten observations, notice ten things, about the same piece of evidence. Try not to move quickly to general ideas *about* the evidence. Instead, close read the evidence, beginning perhaps with some version of the "in other words . . ." Application earlier in the chapter. The key to doing 10 on 1 successfully is to slow down the rush to conclusions so that you can allow yourself to notice more about the evidence. The more observations you assemble about your data *before* settling on your main idea about it, the better that idea is likely to be.

To formulate your ten observations, keep in mind the strategies mentioned thus far in the book for scrutinizing evidence. These include: make details speak ("what this suggests is . . ."); make the implicit explicit; note significant repetition of the same or similar things, look for patterns of detail (which should indicate pervasive concerns); note organizing contrasts; and look for anomalies—things that call attention to themselves as somehow unusual, not easy to categorize. Individuals or small groups might do this exercise separately and then meet to compare notes.

Remember that a single paragraph from something you are reading can be enough to practice on, especially since you are working on learning to say more about less rather than less about more. Pictures and poems or the front page of a newspaper, because they present a lot of detail in a relatively small space, are good to work with if you have nothing else at hand. Or you can do 10 on 1 with the room you are sitting in. Let yourself make ten observations about the room, about things that you have perhaps not paid much attention to before, and then see what ideas these observations suggest to you.

## APPLICATION:

# "ABOUTNESS"—ANOTHER VERSION OF 10 ON 1

Another way to scrutinize material with 10 on 1 is to try answering the same question about the material ten times, making sure that you work from and with some concrete detail in your subject matter in each of your answers. A good beginning phrase for this purpose is "What this is really about is . . ." At the *end* of the process (not before, or else you will close down your examination of the evidence prematurely) you should be able to answer not just the question "What does this say?" but also "What are we to make of it, and in what context?"

As with the previous 10 on 1 Application, you might work with something you are already studying, or you might choose song lyrics, some local example of social behavior, a poem, a picture, a corporate report—anything you find interesting and want to understand better.

Use freewriting to do this Application. The method is to keep finishing the same starting phrase—"What this is really about is . . ." Let your freewriting take your thinking where it will, but follow one rule: don't wander away from the data into generalization for too long. Virtually every sentence of your writing should refer to some aspect of the evidence. If you find you have drifted too far away from the concrete into abstraction, simply break off and start again, using some particular in the evidence.

Here is a relatively simple example of what it means to ask what something is "about." On the one hand, a magazine advertisement for Virginia Slims cigarettes is obviously *about* the advantages of smoking that particular brand. The advertiser's most immediate and obvious concern is that people might choose some other brand. The advertiser is also concerned with a problem—that most people now know that smoking isn't good for you and that it is less socially acceptable than it used to be.

Looking at such an ad, however, will reveal that it is also "about" other things, which are related more subtly to the advertiser's immediate purpose. Virginia Slims are marketed mainly to women. Such ads generally feature photos of women from past eras getting in trouble for smoking cigarettes, next to photos of women in the present smoking proudly. So, to a large extent such ads are "about" rebellion; they glamorize rebellion for women as a means of countering all those people who are still telling women they shouldn't smoke. In order to read what the ad is about in this way, we have to make explicit the cultural assumptions about the role of women, women's independence, etc., that the ad plays on—since these seem to be its most significant social contexts.

Remember that regardless of the subject you select for your analysis, you should directly address not just "What does this say?" but also "What are we to make of it, and in what context?"

## Demonstrate the Representativeness of Your Example

> **Problem:** generalizing on the basis of too little and unrepresentative evidence
>
> **Solution:** survey the available evidence and argue overtly for the representativeness of the examples on which you focus

One significant advantage of concentrating on your single best example is its economy: you can cut quickly to the heart of a subject. But with this advantage comes a danger: that the example you select will not in fact be representative. Thus, it's not enough just to select an example you think is representative. You also need to overtly demonstrate its representativeness. In other words, you must *show that your example is part of a larger pattern of similar evidence and not just an isolated instance.*

In logic terms, the problem of generalizing from too little and unrepresentative evidence is known as an *unwarranted inductive leap*. That is, the writer leaps from one or two instances to a broad claim about an entire class or category. For example, just because an economics professor and a biology professor wear corduroy jackets, you should not leap to the conclusion that all professors wear corduroy jackets.

The surest way you can guard against the problem of unwarranted inductive leaps is by reviewing the range of possible examples to make certain that the ones you choose to focus on are representative. If you were writing about faith as it is portrayed in the book of Exodus, for example, you might suggest the general trend by briefly mentioning instances in which the Israelites have difficulty believing in an unseen God. Then you could concentrate on the best example.

Not all illogical leaps are easy to spot. Here is a brief example from a writer who makes an unwarranted inductive leap:

> Some people feel that rock music videos are purely sexist propaganda and that they stereotype women as sex objects. I feel this is a generalization and far from the truth. Many types of videos exist, a lot of which show no women in them at all. Others do contain women and could be considered sexist only if you choose to look at them from that point of view.

The writer of this paragraph next offers three examples in support of her generalization that rock videos do not stereotype women as sex objects. One video consists entirely of concert footage. In another, the lead singer hugs and kisses his mother. The third shows a female passenger in a Jaguar trying to get the attention of the male singer, who is driving—a scenario that leads the writer to assert, "If anyone is being presented as the sex object, it is he."

Clearly, this writer is trying to correct the overgeneralization that all rock videos are sexist in their depiction of women, but her argument falls prey to the same kind of overgeneralization. Her *sample is too small.* Three examples of videos that do not depict women as sex objects constitute too small a sample to dismiss the charge of sexism. Her sample is also *too selective.* It does not confront examples that would challenge her point of view, examples that an opponent might use to prove that videos do stereotype women as sex objects. In other words, she avoids the difficult evidence, deliberately picking videos that may well be exceptions to the rule and then arguing that they are the rule.

Most of the time, unwarranted leaps result from making too large a claim and avoiding examples that might contradict it. As a rule, you should *deliberately seek out the single piece of evidence that might most effectively oppose your point of view and address it.* Doing so will prompt you to test the representativeness of your evidence and, in many cases, to qualify the claims you have made for it. The writer of the rock video example, for instance, can argue on the basis of three videos for a *more limited* version of her claim—that the representation of men and their relationship to women in rock videos is more varied and complex than the charge of sexism has allowed. In sum, if you select more complicated examples, or actively search out complication in evidence that at first seems simple and obvious, then you will be less likely to use unrepresentative examples to arrive at a claim that does not respond to the full range of relevant evidence.

## 10 on 1 and Disciplinary Conventions

In some cases, the conventions of a discipline would appear to discourage 10 on 1. The social sciences in particular tend to require a larger set of analogous examples to prove a hypothesis (tentative claim). Especially in certain kinds of research, the focus of inquiry rests on discerning broad statistical trends over a wide range of evidence. The inexperienced writer is likely to obey this disciplinary convention by providing a list of unanalyzed examples. But some trends deserve more attention than others, and some statistics similarly merit more interpretation than others. The best writers learn to choose examples carefully—each one for a reason—and to concentrate on developing the most revealing ones in depth; the interpretive and statistical models for analyzing evidence are not necessarily opposed to one another.

For instance, proving that tax laws are prejudiced in particularly subtle ways against unmarried people might require a number of analogous cases, along with a statistical summary of the evidence. But even with a subject such as this, you could still concentrate on some examples more than others. Rather than moving through each example as a separate case, you could use your analyses of these primary examples as *lenses* for investigating other evidence.

## Looking for Difference within Similarity: A Sample Essay with Revision

The following student paper, about the recurrence of flood stories in religious texts and myth, shows what happens when a writer falls into doing 1 on 10.

That is, rather than using in-depth analysis of a representative example to test and refine his ideas, he merely attaches the same underdeveloped point to each of his examples. What is good about this draft, however, is that the writer is using various analytical moves (as discussed in Chapter 1 and further developed in this chapter). As you will see, for example, he does locate a pattern of like detail and tries to make the implicit explicit (see Moves 3 and 4 in Chapter 1). He also offers evidence for his claims, rather than leaving them unsupported. What the writer does not yet do, and what he will want to do in revision, is to:

1. Look more closely at his evidence (10 on 1), drawing out more of its possible meanings, remembering that evidence can almost always be interpreted in more than one way
2. Look for contrasts and anomalies, deliberately attending to things that seem not to fit the pattern of like detail (another of the analytical moves described in Chapter 1)

This process for getting beyond 1 on 10 we call *looking for difference within similarity.* The phrase "difference within similarity" is to remind you that once you have started your thinking by locating apparent similarities, you can usually refine that thinking by pursuing significant, though often less obvious, distinctions among the similar things. Keep the idea of looking for difference within similarity in mind as you read the student paper on flood stories so you can consider how the method could be used to revise the paper.

## EXTENDED ANALYSIS

### FLOOD STORIES

In the essay that follows, we have used boldface to track the one point— the as-yet-underdeveloped thesis idea—that the writer has attached to each of his examples (1 on 10). Brackets and ellipses ([. . .]) indicate where we have abridged the essay.

### FLOOD STORIES

1 **The role of people**, as reflected in Genesis, Ovid's *Metamorphoses*, and the *Epic of Gilgamesh*, **is solely to please the gods.** People, as the gods' subordinates, exist to do right in the gods' eyes **and make them feel more like gods**; because without people, whom could the gods be gods of? [. . .]

2 In Genesis, for example, God created humans in his own image or likeness, and **when they displeased Him, He destroyed them.** If God could see wickedness in His creations, perhaps it was like seeing wickedness in himself. Further, the idea of having evidence of God's being able to create an imperfect, "wicked" race of humans may have been a point God wasn't willing to deal with.

*(continued)*

✳

> The Lord saw that the wickedness of man was great in the earth, and that every imagination of the thoughts of his heart was only evil continually. And the Lord was sorry that he had made man on the earth and it grieved him to his heart.

It seems as though **God had become unhappy with His creations,** so they were to be destroyed. Like a toy a child no longer has use for, humankind was to be wasted.

3 Similarly, in Ovid's *Metamorphoses,* the gods made humanity and "fashioned it into the image of the all-governing gods." Again here, humans were made in the gods' image to serve as an everlasting monument of their glorification, to honor them and do good by them. In other words, humans spent less time **making the gods happy** and therefore made them unhappy. Some humans even questioned the gods' existence and the strength of their power. Lyacon, for example, had a driving tendency to try to belittle the gods and make them look like fools. **The gods were very displeased** with this trend, and now the entire race had to be destroyed. A flood would be sent to wipe out the race of humans.

4 [The writer summarizes several examples in which the wicked are destroyed and a few upstanding citizens are preserved and arrives at the following conclusion:] Thus, the justification of yet another flood **to appease the gods' egos.**

5 Further evidence of **man as being a mere whim of the gods to make them happy** lies in the flood story in the *Epic of Gilgamesh.* It is obvious **the gods weren't concerned with humankind, but rather with their own comfort.** As the story goes, Enlil, the god of earth, wind, and air, couldn't bear the noise that humans were making while he tried to sleep, so he gathered all the gods together, and thus they jointly decided to solve the problem of having all the humans around by destroying them. Ea [the god of wisdom], however, warned one man (Utnapishtim) of the flood to come. He told him to build a boat for himself and his wife and for the "seeds of all living creatures." [. . .]

6 Enlil later repented the harshness of his actions, deified Utnapishtim and his wife, and then had the two live far away "on the distance of the mouths' rivers." It possibly **could have been belittling** to have Utnapishtim and his wife speaking to the new race of humans in terms of how rash and mindlessly the gods were capable of acting, so he immortalized them and had them live far out of the reach of human ears—"the secret of the gods."

7 It seems that **the main objective of the gods was to remain gods, because that is what made them happy. And humanity's role, then, was as the gods' stepping-stone to their happiness.** [. . .] Witnessing the fall

*(continued)*

\*　　　　　　　　　　　　　　　　　　　　　　　　　　　　　

of humankind, for the gods, was like witnessing imperfection in themselves, and thus their fall; anything causing these feelings didn't do the
gods any good and therefore could be terminated without a second
thought. **It was the job of human beings to make the gods happy,** and
upon failure at this task, they could be "fired" (death), only to be replaced
later. It wasn't a position that the gods could hold vacant for long. Thus
were the great flood stories.

The writer of the flood stories essay has already accomplished a lot. He has
discerned a pattern common to several flood stories, articulated a set of
shared characteristics (such as the use of the floods to destroy human beings),
and drafted a general explanation (the destructions were motivated by the
gods' self-serving reactions). Stopping at this point, however, left him blinded
by similarity and proving an overly general point. As the boldfacings in the
essay illustrate, the writer returns again and again to versions of his original
claim—that people exist "solely to please the gods." The result is a 1 on 10
paper in which the writer sees, in effect, only what he wants to see—opportunities to repeatedly match the evidence to his one governing claim.

What's wrong, you might ask, with showing how the evidence fits the
claim? Isn't this what writers are supposed to do? The answer is that you
do want to use evidence to show that your claims have validity, but not in
so general and redundant a way. As the final sentence of the essay demonstrates ("Thus were the great flood stories"), the writer never really arrives
at a conclusion. To develop his central claim, the writer needs to devote
much less space to repeating that claim and much more to actually looking at his evidence with an eye to variation within the general pattern.

In his second paragraph, for example, the writer makes a claim about
the God of Genesis that overlooks significant evidence. The claim is:

> God had become unhappy with His creations, so they were to be de-
> stroyed. Like a toy a child no longer has use for, humankind was to be
> wasted.

It is here that the writer allows the 1 on 10 pattern to rush his thinking
and distract him from his evidence. The depiction of God as one who treats
humans like toys may accurately describe Enlil, the god in *Gilgamesh* who,
as we are later told, decides to get rid of humans because they make too
much noise. But it does not so easily fit the God of Genesis, about whom
the writer has just told us that "the wickedness of man . . . grieved him to
his heart." Doesn't the grief that this evidence mentions suggest that God's
decision to flood the earth was possibly ethical rather than childishly selfish and rash? And the statement from Genesis that "every imagination of
the thoughts of [man's] heart was only evil continually" would seem to indicate not simply that humans were victims of divine prerogative, but
rather that they deserved punishment.

In short, the writer has not really taken the time and care to explain the evidence he has quoted. Instead, he has attempted to squeeze that evidence into a pattern he has apparently superimposed from *Gilgamesh*, thereby neglecting potentially significant differences among his examples.

So, how might the writer make better use of the evidence he has collected, using the principle of looking for difference within similarity?

---

**Revision Strategy 1:** *Assume that what you took for an answer (your conclusion about the evidence) does not yet go far enough.* Rather than having to throw out his thinking, the writer should consider, as is almost always the case in revision, that he hasn't refined his initial idea enough. As an interpretation of the evidence, it leaves too much unaccounted for.

**Revision Strategy 2:** *Find a "1" to use with 10 on 1—a piece of the evidence sufficiently revealing to be analyzed in more detail.* In the case of the writer of "Flood Stories," that "1" might be a single story, which he could examine in more detail. He would then need to test his claims about this story through comparison and contrast with the other stories. In the existing draft, the writer has not used comparison and contrast to refine his conclusion—he has just imposed the same conclusion on the other stories. Alternatively, the "1" might be the single most interesting feature that the three stories share.

**Revision Strategy 3:** *To find the most revealing piece or feature of the evidence, keep asking yourself, "What can I say with some certainty about the evidence?"* This question will induce you to rehearse the facts in order to keep your first ideas from "contaminating" or distorting your consideration of subsequent evidence.

If the writer of the flood stories paper were to apply these strategies, he might have a conversation with himself that sounded something like this:

"What can I say with some certainty about my evidence?"
"Well, in all three of these stories, a first civilization created by a god is destroyed by the same means—a flood."

Notice that this is a factual reporting of the evidence rather than a speculation about it. You are always better off to state the facts in your evidence carefully and fully before moving to conclusions:

"What else is certain about the evidence?"
"In each case the gods leave a surviving pair to rebuild the civilization rather than just wiping everybody out and inventing a new kind of being. Interestingly, the gods begin again by choosing from the same stock that failed the first time around."

Mulling over the evidence in this way, taking care to lay out the facts and distinguish them from speculation, will help you decide what evidence to concentrate on.

**Revision Strategy 4:** *Examine the evidence closely enough to see what questions the details imply and what other patterns they reveal.* So far, the writer of the flood stories paper has worked mostly from two quite general questions: why did the gods decide to wipe out their creations? And why do the gods need human beings? But there are other questions his evidence presses him to ask. In each story, for example, the gods are disappointed by humankind, and yet they don't invent submissive robots who will dedicate their lives to making the deities feel good about themselves. Why not? This question might cause the writer to uncover a shared feature of his examples (a pattern) that he has thus far not considered—the surviving pairs.

**Revision Strategy 5:** *Use the implications to develop your interpretation further.* Having selected the surviving pairs for more detailed examination, what might the writer conclude about them? One interesting fact that the surviving pairs reveal is that the flood stories are not only descriptions of the end of a world but also creation accounts, since they also tell us how a new civilization, the existing one, got started.

At this point, the writer might apply the principle of looking for difference within similarity to the survival pairs. Given the recurrence of the survival pairs in the three stories, where might the writer locate a significant difference? One potentially significant difference involves the survival pair in the story of *Gilgamesh,* who are segregated from the new world and granted immortality. Perhaps this separation suggests that the new civilization will not be haunted by the painful memory of a higher power's intervention, leaving humans less fearful of what might happen in the future. This distinction could focus the argument in the essay; it does not distract from the writer's overall generalization but rather develops it.

Notice how the hypothetical revision that we've been producing has made use of looking for difference within similarity. Instead of repeatedly concluding that the gods destroy humans when humans fail make to them happy, the writer is now on his way to a thesis about the relative optimism or skepticism of the way that the flood stories represent change. Such a thesis might be, for example, that the flood stories propose the view that real change is necessarily apocalyptic rather than evolutionary. Or, the thesis might be that the flood stories present qualified optimism about the possibility of new starts. And so forth.

## Evidence and Logic: Three Common Errors

Is using evidence like brushing your teeth? If you spend so much time analyzing evidence that you forget to brush your teeth, can we say that analyzing evidence causes tooth decay? The answer to the first question is "in some ways, but not really," and the answer to the second is "probably not." Both questions are examples of common logic errors in the use of evidence. The first is a *false analogy;* the second is an example of attributing a *simple cause* to a *complex effect* (it takes more than work habits to cause tooth decay).

APPLICATION:

## DESCRIBING EVIDENCE

Have a conversation with yourself (on paper) about some piece of evidence you are studying. Start with the question we proposed for the student writer of the flood stories essay: "What can be said with some certainty about this evidence?" What, in other words, is clearly true of the data? What can be reported about it as fact without going on to interpretation of the facts?

This *distinction between fact and interpretation* can be a tricky one, but it is also essential, because if you can't keep your data separate from what you've begun to think about it, you risk losing sight of the data all together. Press yourself to keep answering the same question—"What can be said with some certainty about this evidence?" or a variant of the question, such as "What's clearly true of this evidence is . . ."

You may find it helpful to do this exercise with a partner or in a small group. If you work in a small group, have one member of the group record the results as these emerge. And/or you might try this exercise as a freewrite (see the Application in Chapter 6 entitled "Passage-based Focused Freewriting" and the section in Chapter 1 on prewriting), and then share your results with others by reading aloud or putting your list of facts on a blackboard along with other people's results. Once you've assembled a list of what can fairly be stated as fact about your evidence, you are ready to start on some version of the question "What do these facts suggest?" or "What features of these data seem most to invite/require interpretation?"

Both false analogy and simple cause/complex effect interfere with the interpretation of evidence, and they share the same fundamental flaw: they oversimplify.

**Simple cause/complex effect**. One of the most common problems of thinking, the fallacy of simple cause/complex effect involves assigning a single cause to a complex phenomenon that cannot be so easily explained. A widespread version of this fallacy is seen in arguments that blame individual figures for broad historical events, for example, "Eisenhower caused America to be involved in the Vietnam War." Such a claim ignores the Cold War ethos, the long history of colonialism in Southeast Asia, and a multitude of other factors.

When you offer a simple cause for a complex effect—or assign a simple effect to a complex cause—you will virtually always be wrong. The writer of the flood stories essay falls prey to this kind of thinking error when he reduces a complex sequence of events (the various flood stories) to a simple and single cause: that humans had failed at the one task the gods assigned them—keeping the gods happy.

**False cause**. Another common cause/effect thinking error, false cause is produced by assuming that two events are causally connected when such causal connection does not necessarily exist. One of the most common forms of this fallacy—known as **post hoc, ergo propter hoc** (Latin for "after this, therefore because of this")—assumes that because *A* precedes *B* in time, *A* causes *B*. For example, it was once thought that the sun shining on a pile of garbage caused the garbage to conceive flies.

One version of this kind of error is the stuff that superstition is made of. "I walked under a ladder, and then I got hit by a car" becomes "Because I walked under a ladder I got hit by a car." Because one action precedes a second one in time, the first action is assumed to be the cause of the second. A more dangerous form of this error goes like this:

> **Evidence:** a new neighbor moved in downstairs on Saturday. My television disappeared on Sunday.
>
> **Conclusion:** the new neighbor stole my TV.

As this example also illustrates, *typically in false cause some significant alternative has not been considered,* such as the presence of flies' eggs in the garbage. Similarly, it does not follow that if a person watches television and then commits a crime, television-watching necessarily causes crime; there are other causes to be considered.

**Analogy and false analogy**. An analogy is a device for understanding something that is relatively foreign in terms of something that is more familiar. When you argue by analogy you are saying that what is true for one thing will necessarily be true for another thing that it in some way resembles. The famous poetic line "my love is like a red, red rose" is actually an argument by analogy. At first glance, this rather clichéd comparison seems too far-fetched to be reasonable. But is it a false analogy, or a potentially enabling one? Past users of this analogy have thought the thorns, the early fading, the beauty, and so forth sufficient to argue from the comparison. Similarly, you might glance back to the first paragraph of the Tienanmen Square essay, in which the writer's deft use of an extended analogy opens up his subject analytically. Analogies, in short, are not bad or illogical in themselves. In fact, they can be incredibly useful, depending on how you handle them.

The danger that arguing analogically can pose is that an inaccurate comparison, usually one that oversimplifies, prevents you from looking at the evidence. Flying to the moon is like flying a kite? Well, it's a little bit like that, but . . . This kind of oversimplification is what happens in the flood stories essay when the writer hits on the comparison of God and humans with a child and a toy the child no longer has use for. The problem is that the God/child analogy is essentially false. It doesn't fit the facts.

Another way that an analogy can become false is when it becomes overextended: there is a point of resemblance at one juncture, but the writer then goes on to assume that the two items compared will necessarily resemble each other in most other respects. To what extent is balancing your checkbook really like juggling? On the other hand, an analogy that first appears overextended may not be: how far, for example, could you reasonably go in comparing a presidential election to a sales campaign, or an enclosed shopping mall to a village main street?

Let's examine one more false analogy, from a recent ad campaign: "You choose the president; why not choose your cable company?" What's wrong with this comparison? For one thing, each of us is not entitled to our choice of president. If we were, there would be a lot of presidents. And second, the rules and circumstances covering what is best in the nation's communication network are not necessarily the same as the rules and circumstances covering the structure of our federal government. So the analogy doesn't work very well. What is true for one side of the comparison is not necessarily true for the other side; the differences are greater than the similarities.

The first questions to ask yourself when you find yourself reasoning by analogy are:

- *Are the basic similarities greater and more significant than the obvious differences?*
- *Am I overrelying on surface similarities and ignoring more essential differences?*

## What Counts as Evidence?

Thus far this chapter has concentrated on how to use evidence after you've assembled it. You also need in many cases to consider a more basic and often hidden question before you begin collecting data: what counts as evidence?

This question raises two related concerns:

*Relevance:* in what ways does the evidence bear on the claim or problem that you are addressing? Do the facts really apply in this particular case, and if so, how?

*Framing assumptions:* in what ways is the evidence colored by the point of view that designated it as evidence? At what point do these assumptions limit its authority or reliability?

To raise the issue of framing assumptions is not to imply that all evidence is *merely* subjective, somebody's impressionistic opinion. We are implying, however, that even the most apparently neutral evidence is the product of *some way of seeing* that qualifies the evidence as evidence in the first place. In some cases, this way of seeing is embedded in the established procedure of particular disciplines. In the natural sciences, for example, the actual data that go into the results section of a lab report or formal paper are the product of a highly controlled experimental procedure. As its name suggests, the section presents the *results* of seeing in a particular way.

The same kind of control is present in various quantitative operations in the social sciences, in which the evidence is usually framed in the language of statistics. And in somewhat less systematic but nonetheless similar ways, evidence in the humanities and some projects in the social sciences is always conditioned by methodological assumptions. A literature student cannot assume, for example, that a particular fate befalls a character in a story *because* of events in the author's life (it is a given of literary study that biography may inform but does not explain a work of art). As the professors' comments that pervade this section of the chapter make clear, evidence is never just some free-floating, absolutely reliable, objective entity for the casual observer to sample at random. It is always a product of certain starting assumptions and procedures that readers must take into account.

## VOICES FROM ACROSS THE CURRICULUM

### QUESTIONS OF RELEVANCE AND METHODOLOGY

What counts as evidence? I try to impress upon students that they need to substantiate their claims with evidence. Most have little trouble with this. However, when I tell them that evidence itself is dependent upon *methodology*—that it's not just a question of gathering "information," but also a question of *how* it was gathered—their eyes glaze over. Can we trust the source of information? What biases may exist in the way questions are posed in an opinion poll? Who counts as an authority on a subject? (No, Rush Limbaugh cannot be considered an authority on women's issues, or the environment, or, for that matter, anything else!) Is your evidence out of date? (In politics, books on electoral behavior have a shelf life only up to the next election. After two years, they may have severe limitations.)

Methodological concerns also determine the *relevance* of evidence. Some models of, say, democratic participation define as irrelevant certain kinds of evidence that other models might view as crucial. For instance, a pluralist view of democracy, which emphasizes the dominant role of competitive elites, views the evidence of low voter turnout and citizen apathy as a minor concern. More participatory models, in contrast, interpret the same evidence as an indication of the crisis afflicting contemporary democratic practices.

In addition to this question of relevance, methodology makes explicit the game plan of research: how did the student conduct his or her research? Why did he or she consider some information more relevant than others? Are there any gaps in the information? Does the writer distinguish cases in which evidence *strongly supports* a claim from evidence that is *suggestive* or *speculative?*

Finally, students need to be aware of the possible ideological nature of evidence. For instance, Americans typically seek to explain such problems as poverty in individualistic terms, a view consistent with our liberal heritage, rather than in terms of class structure, as a Marxist would. Seeking the roots of poverty in individual behavior simply produces a particular kind of evidence different from that which would be produced if we began with the assumption that class structure plays a decisive influence in shaping individual behavior.

—**JACK GAMBINO,** *Professor of Political Science*

As this professor's comments suggest, it is always useful to try to figure out the methodological *how* behind the *what,* since methodology is always based in certain assumptions as opposed to others. A useful example for thinking about evidence-gathering in this context is Werner Heisenberg's famous for-mulation, the Uncertainty Principle. A theoretical physicist, Heisenberg hy-pothesized a subatomic particle orbiting the nucleus of an atom that could be observed only when it passes through a concentrated beam of light. At the in-stant of its illumination, however, the direction of the particle would necessar-ily be skewed by the beam. From this model, Heisenberg concluded that the act of observation invariably alters whatever is observed. This insight has made its way across the academic disciplines. In anthropology, for example, Clifford Geertz has written extensively on the ways that researchers into other cultures not only impose their own cultural assumptions onto their subjects, but also, by their very presence, cause change in the behavior of the people they are observing.

The challenge of determining what counts as evidence is also at issue when you start with a given problem or question and then must decide what you should look at. Say you are looking into the causes of child abuse. How do you decide what to look at? How do you even define what it is you are studying, since what conceivably constitutes child abuse now might have been consid-ered normal child-rearing practices in the past? If you are searching for causes, what is the important evidence? In the past, the physical environment lay out-side what sociologists usually considered, but what if the height of buildings in which child abuse occurs provides better data than the size of families? As this hypothetical example suggests, the relationship between cause and effect is always slippery, and the assumptions about what is and isn't evidence are potentially blinding.

The preferences of different disciplines for certain kinds of evidence

## APPLICATION:

### OBSERVING ANALOGIES

We observed at the beginning of this book that one of the best ways of improving your thinking is to become more aware of yourself doing it. To put this observation into practice, here's something you might try. Keep a record during the course of a single day of the number of times you or oth-ers around you (in conversation, in the newspaper, on the radio, at work, in the classroom, etc.) make use of analogy. In some cases a single word will re-veal that a common phrase, like "nuclear family" is actually an analogy. At the end of the day, look over your list and isolate the most appropriate and insightful analogy as well as the most distorting one. If possible, share these with someone else (or a small group) who has been doing the same thing.

You might profitably spend another day doing this same exercise looking for examples of simple cause/complex effect and *post hoc ergo propter hoc*. (If you don't find an astonishing number of these, listen harder!)

notwithstanding, most professors share the conviction that the evidence you choose to present should not be one-sided.

## Kinds of Evidence: Some Examples

As we have been suggesting for most of this chapter, evidence is virtually never simply a matter of "the facts." It is no accident that one often hears the phrase "questions of evidence," because evidence is perennially subject to question—for its accuracy, its veracity, and so forth. When we hear that mellifluous voice-over in the TV commercial assuring us that "three out of four dentists recommend a fluoride toothpaste," how are we to take that remark? Why are lie detector tests "inadmissible as evidence" in some cases?

Nor is established practice a guarantee that the evidence is reliable. About fifteen years ago, the sportswriter Bill James levied a savage attack on the accepted way of providing data for assessing a baseball player's fielding—the fielding average, which was a ratio of the total number of balls hit to a fielder (his or her "chances") as against his or her errors. James pointed out that fielding percentage didn't take into account the greater number of balls that a superior fielder might get to in the first place, adding that the more difficult the chance, the more likely the player was to make an error. So the number of errors was not a reliable index of a player's proficiency. Consequently, James invented a new statistical measure, the range factor, which more heavily weights the number of chances and devalues the number of errors. In effect, he redefines the pool of evidence.

We are, to a significant degree, a society obsessed with evidence—from UFO freaks to conspiracy theorists to those who avidly follow the latest leaks in the press about the peccadilloes of the famous. And if we step back and think about the range of contexts in which evidence matters, we can conclude only that there are as many contexts for evidence as there are things to think about or questions to ask.

Following are some passages from student and professional writing, each of which illustrates a different kind of evidence. The list is not comprehensive, but we have tried to select a few of the most common kinds. Each of the samples contains what we consider effective use of evidence; we have interpolated in boldface brief commentary about that use.

### Statistical Evidence

Statistics are a primary tool—a virtual language—for those writing in the natural and especially the social sciences. They have the advantage of greater objectivity, and, in the social sciences, of offering a broad view of a subject. Remember, though, that like other forms of evidence, statistics do not speak for themselves; their significance must be overtly elucidated. And, as the fielding average example suggests, it should never simply be assumed that statistics are valid representations of the reality they purport to measure.

### EXCERPT FROM "MANDATE FOR THE STATUS QUO"

A statistical study of congressional and gubernatorial races supports the notion of a status quo election. *[general claim]* In 1996, eleven states held gubernatorial elections ("Victory by the Numbers" 40-1). Of those eleven states, only two underwent a change in partisanship: West Virginia elected a Republican governor, and New Hampshire elected a Democratic governor. The remaining nine states voted against change. And, considering that the changes in West Virginia and New Hampshire cancel each other (because the Republicans gain a seat and the Democrats gain a seat), it is not an exaggeration to say that Democrats and Republicans neither gained nor lost gubernatorial seats in 1996. *[begins with strongest data, then moves to supporting data]*

In Congress, changes were minimal as well. When compared to the so-called Republican Revolution in 1994, the 1996 elections resulted in almost no change. In both the House of Representatives and the Senate, Republicans maintained a majority. Republicans in the 105th Congress will not enjoy the same majority as their previous counterpart because the Democrats managed to win back a handful of congressional seats. *[Reasoning based on the evidence begins with the next sentence and continues for the rest of the paragraph. Writer interprets what the numbers mean; notice writer's caution in articulating what the statistics might prove.]* Considering the increasingly negative opinion of Newt Gingrich and his Republican counterparts, it is remarkable that the Republicans were able to maintain their majority. Also remarkable was the inability of Bill Clinton, with all of his success in office, to sweep fellow Democrats into office. One explanation is that voters still feel distrust for Clinton. In a *Los Angeles Times* exit poll, only three percent of Clinton voters said that they liked him because he possessed honesty and integrity ("Poll Update"). In 1992, voter distrust of Clinton was high as well, and many experts believe that this fact led to the election of a Republican Congress in 1994. *[Note how writer keeps returning to the evidence and expanding its significance.]* The poll indicates that voters still distrust Clinton. Perhaps this distrust again led to the election of a Republican-controlled Congress. If this is the case, voters reflected their status quo opinions by voting for a status quo Congress.

## VOICES FROM ACROSS THE CURRICULUM

### INTERPRETING THE NUMBERS

The most important advice we offer our psychology students about statistical evidence is to look at it critically. We teach them that it is easy to misrepresent statistics and that you really need to evaluate the evidence provided. Students need to learn to think about what the numbers actually mean. Where did the numbers come from? What are the implications of the numbers?

In my statistics course, I emphasize that it is not enough just to get the "correct" answer mathematically. Students need to be able to interpret the numbers and the implications of the numbers. For example, if students are rating satisfaction with the textbook on a scale of 1 (not at all satisfied) to 7 (highly satisfied), and we get a class average of 2.38, it is not enough to report that number. You must interpret the number (the class was generally not satisfied) and again explain the implications (time to choose a new textbook).

Students need to look at the actual numbers. Let's say I do an experiment using two different stat textbooks. Text A costs $67, and Text B costs $32. I give one class Text A and one class Text B, and at the end of the semester I find that the class using Text A did statistically significantly better than the class using Text B. Most students at this point would want to switch to the more expensive Text A. However, I can show them an example where the class using Text A had an average test grade of 87 and the class with Text B had an average test grade of 85 (which can be a statistically significant difference): students see the point that even though it is a statistical difference, practically speaking it is not worth double the money to improve the class average by only two points.

So much is written about the advantages and limitations of empirical information that I hardly know where to begin. Briefly, if it is empirical, there is no guesswork or opinion (Skinner said, "The organism is always right"—that is, the data are always right). The limitations are that the collection and/or interpretation can be fraught with biases and error. For example, if I want to know if women still feel that there is gender discrimination in the workplace, I do not have to guess or intuit this (my own experiences are highly likely to bias my guesses): I can do a survey. The survey should tell me what women think (whether I like the answer or not). The limitations occur in how I conduct the survey and how I interpret the results. You might remember the controversy over the *Hite Report* on sexual activities (whom did she sample, and what kind of people answer those kinds of questions, and do they do so honestly?).

Despite the controversy over the problems of relying on empirical data in psychology, I think that it is the only way to find answers to many fascinating questions about humans. The patterns of data can tell us things that we have no other access to without empirical research. It is critically important for people to be aware of the limitations and problems, but then to go on and collect the data.

—**LAURA SNODGRASS,** *Professor of Psychology*

### Anecdotal Evidence

An anecdote is a little story (a narrative), a piece of experience. The word comes from a Greek term meaning "things unpublished." Anecdotal evidence involves the close examination of particular instances; often it includes the writer/researcher's own experience with whatever he or she is studying. So, for example, a historian wishing to understand the origins and development of the Latino community in a small East Coast American city might use as a large part of her evidence interviews that she has conducted with local Latino residents.

Anecdotal evidence is in some ways at the opposite extreme from statistical evidence. Statistical research often attempts to locate broad trends and patterns by surveying large numbers of instances and tries to arrive at reliable information by deliberately controlling the kind and amount of questions it asks. In fact, one of the most important tasks for someone using statistical research is the careful crafting of the questions to guarantee that they don't, for example, predispose the respondent to choose a particular response. By contrast, the kind of thinking based on anecdotal evidence is less concerned with verifiable trends and patterns than with a more detailed and up-close presentation of particular instances.

Given the difficulty of claiming that a single case (anecdote) is representative of the whole, researchers using anecdotal evidence tend to achieve authority through a large number of small instances, which begin to suggest a trend. Authority can also be acquired through the audience's sense of the analytical ability of the researcher, her skill, for example, at convincingly connecting the evidence with the claim. This is to say that an audience's assessment of the reasonableness of an argument is often influenced by its sense of the reasonableness of the arguer.

Sometimes statistical and anecdotal evidence operate hand-in-hand; they tend to need each other. For example, a certain number of closely examined particular instances may be necessary in order to determine what questions to ask for a larger statistical survey. Statistical evidence is occasionally seen as incomplete and can even be misleading without more in-depth examination. Thus, for example, one of the most popular research tools in both business and the academic world is the combining of a questionnaire with follow-up discussion by what is known as a "focus group." The focus group usually consists of a representative sample of respondents to a questionnaire who are selected for a more detailed follow-up discussion of the questions than the statistical format could ever allow. Often the researcher will learn from the focus group that the questionnaire was asking the wrong questions or that respondents had been generally misunderstanding the questions.

Although a central claim of this book is that evidence cannot and should not be expected to speak for itself, and thus needs analysis, there is another side to this argument, especially in certain kinds of research. Historians, for example, are especially sensitive to the problem of distorting evidence by offering too much interpretation of it before they have rightly presented it—in effect, filtering it prematurely though their own conclusions. Although they take care to frame the evidence in a context that makes its range of meanings apparent, they try not to put too much of themselves between the reader and the data, so as to avoid competing with the eloquence of the evidence itself. Rather than speaking for their subjects, such historians give them a space to speak. Here is an example from the historian mentioned earlier, in which she presents the experience of a representative individual, one of the first Puerto Rican immigrants to Allentown, Pennsylvania. Note that she allows us to hear his "voice"—his experience—more than hers, although, if you look for it, you will see her presence as well.

**EXCERPT FROM** *HIDDEN FROM HISTORY: THE LATINO COMMUNITY OF ALLENTOWN, Pa.,* **by Anna Adams**

Jesus Ramos, the oldest of nine children of a Puerto Rican migrant worker, came to New Jersey in the early 1950s to pick fruit. He worked in the fields for two summers, returning to Puerto Rico for the winters. After visiting a Puerto Rican friend who had settled in Allentown, Ramos decided to move there himself. He recalls that by the late 1950s there were approximately 500 Latinos living in Allentown with no place to buy Spanish foods. *[The writer uses her interviewee as statistical source.]* Ramos and Juan Acevedo opened La Famosa grocery store where he sold Goya products upstairs and had pool tables in the basement. When Puerto Ricans began to congregate and socialize in the store, the police accused them of loitering and arrested Mr. Ramos for running a gambling establishment. *[The writer here embeds narrative of racism without commenting on it; notice that she sticks to the vividly evoked facts.]* After clearing himself of those charges, he went to work in the cutoff department of the Greif/Genesco Corporation where he stayed for twenty-eight years. He and his wife Carmen have raised nine children in Allentown. As one of the pioneers of the Puerto Rican community, Jesus tried to smooth the way for others. *[Here the writer generalizes about her subject, turning him into a representative figure.]* He lobbied for Genesco to hire more Spanish speaking people and was one of the founders of Casa Guadalupe. *[a community center dispensing social services]* Despite his efforts, things weren't always easy. "As long as you spoke Spanish, they looked at you different, and you had to work three times harder than the others," he says in fluent, heavily accented English. *[Notice the implied commentary in the fact that after forty years Ramos continues to sound Puerto Rican but also to speak his new language fluently: he inhabits two worlds, whether out of reluctance to deny his Puerto Rican heritage or inability to do so.]* He recalls one occasion when a subordinate co-worker quit rather than take orders from a Puerto Rican. *[Although*

---

**APPLICATION:**

## FINDING KINDS OF EVIDENCE

Find and examine a piece of writing that makes use of anecdotal evidence. Such evidence can take the form of stories or brief story-like examples in which the writer reports his or her own or others' experience and observations. You might look for examples of this kind of evidence in a magazine like *The New Yorker,* in a feature article of a newspaper's Sunday magazine section, in a chapter from a nonfiction book on some feature of contemporary life and culture, in a historical account (because history-writing often makes use of anecdotal evidence), in a transcript of a radio interview such as the kind Terry Gross conducts in her program *Fresh Air* on public radio, and so forth.

You could also look at a textbook you are using or seek out a textbook on economics or sociology or anthropology. Try to determine what in a given section of the book might be categorized as anecdotal evidence. Also try to name and categorize the other kinds of evidence that the book uses.

Remember that there are more kinds of evidence than we have named and illustrated in this chapter. Start getting into the habit of asking yourself, "What kind of evidence is this, and how is it used?"

---

use of the word "recalls" tells us that the whole account was told to the writer by Ramos, she is selective about what she actually quotes and exerts her influence in this way.]

### Authorities as Evidence and Empirical Evidence

A common way of establishing support for a claim is to invoke an authority— to call in as evidence the thinking of an expert in the subject area you are writing about. The practice of invoking authorities as evidence can be heard in TV advertising ("three out of four doctors recommend . . .," etc.) as well as in scholarly books and articles, where a writer may offer as partial support for a claim the thinking of a better-known writer.

Later in this book we devote a whole chapter to the matter of using authorities as evidence (Chapter 7, "Using Secondary Sources"). In that chapter we explain how to *use*—rather than just include and agree with—other writers on your subject. In the meantime, we offer the following passage from a student paper on ancient art. In it you will see how the writer calls on the authority of his sources, putting them into evidence for his case, but also how he offers alternatives to their claims on the basis of his own review of the primary evidence (the art objects themselves).

In addition, note that he does not import only his sources' claims but their evidence as well. Calling in the support of an authority, an expert witness, can be very useful, but it's no substitute for logic: the fact that somebody has gotten a claim printed doesn't mean it's a good conclusion. *Sharing the source's evidence and reasoning with your readers will help them to understand your use of the source.*

What we are calling "empirical" evidence in this student paper can be seen in those places where he reasons from observations about concrete data. Notice as you read, for example, the use the writer makes of the observable features of the figures he is studying, such as their all having ears and all being naked females. (The word *empirical* means "capable of being observed, available to the senses"; the word comes from the Greek word for *experience*.)

The paper from which we took the following excerpt is a study of a group of white marble statues from the Cycladic Islands in the Aegean Sea. Designated as part of the "Early Spedos" stylistic group, the statues date from 2700–2500 BC. After a careful description of the statues themselves, the writer uses a blend of his own analysis and theories by art history authorities to speculate about the significance of the statues.

### EXCERPT FROM "EARLY SPEDOS CYCLADIC IDOLS"

In his book, Thimme suggests that the statues were conceived as images of divine beings and specifically intended for the grave: the female figures represent a divine mistress of life and death who will secure for the deceased rebirth in another world (42).

The occurrence of female figures in both women's and men's graves best suits Thimme's hypothesis that the figures represent a being quite independent of the deceased, a divine or demonic being (Thimme 43). *[Writer cites empirical evidence to support one of his authority's claims.]* Fitton offers some words on the attractive possibility of the female deity theory:

> A female deity, perhaps with worshippers represented in her own image, is an attractive possibility. While the once-fashionable assumption that the prehistoric Aegean peoples worshipped a 'Great Mother' goddess is demonstrably simplistic, there can be no doubt that some explanation is needed to account for the fact that the majority of Cycladic figures are in the form of a naked female, and a female deity remains a possible identification. (69) *[includes not just another authority's claim but also the supporting evidence]*

The theories put forth by Fitton and Thimme seem to be the most plausible, because other interpretations, including substitute mother, nurse mother, concubine, and magical midwife, are weakened by our knowledge that, for the first two mother theories, there was a rarity of child tombs and, with the last two sexual/procreative theories, the inclusion of figurines in graves occurred irrespective of the individual's sex. *[Writer uses empirical evidence to dismiss claims of authorities conflicting with those he is advocating.]* In respect to the particular statues examined earlier, the presence of ears suggests a divine being who was designed to listen to prayers, a point to reinforce the validity of a female mother goddess theory. *[Writer uses more empirical evidence to justify chosen claim.]*

### Textual Evidence

All of the examples we've presented are in some sense textual—they consist of words on the page. We are using the term *textual evidence* to designate *instances in which the language itself is of fundamental importance,* in which the emphasis lies on how things are worded. A primary assumption in analyzing textual evidence is that the meanings of words are never simple and unambiguous. That is, the meanings of particular words cannot be assumed; they must be explained, and those explanations must be argued for. Insofar as the actual language of a document counts, you are in the domain of textual evidence.

It's a mistaken assumption that only people in literary studies do textual analysis. Perhaps the profession that most commonly uses textual evidence is the law, which involves interpreting the language of contracts, wills, statutes, statements of intention, and so forth. Similarly, diplomats, accountants, people in business—all those who must rely on written documents to guarantee understanding—need to be adept at textual analysis. People in such fields as media studies, communications, even public relations also engage in textual analysis when they examine visual images, because the images themselves matter and mean in the same ways that words do in a verbal text.

### Experimental Evidence

Experimental evidence is a form of empirical evidence (capable of being observed). It is usefully distinguished from other forms of evidence by the careful attention to procedure it requires. Evidence in the sciences is usually recorded in particular predetermined formats, both because methodology is important and because the primary test of validity in the sciences is that the experiment must be repeatable, so that another experimenter can follow the same procedure and achieve the same results.

The concern with procedure is present throughout writing in the sciences, though, not just in the "Methods" section of a lab report. Scientific writing constantly begins by asking the question, "How do we know what we think we know?" And, since experiments inevitably take a scientist into the unknown, it then asks, "On the basis of what we know, what else might be true, and how can we find out?" *The concern with procedure in scientific writing*

## APPLICATION:

# USING TEXTUAL EVIDENCE

Study the excerpt below from a student paper entitled "Women and Nature in Lessing and Chopin" and answer the following questions. Where do we see the writer's general claim about the evidence? Where does she select the feature of the text she wants to focus on? How does the cited evidence organize her thinking—on what pattern or organizing contrast?

> Chopin also applies the imagery of birds to her heroine, symbolically alluding to Edna's wish to fly, in a sense, from all of her responsibilities. Edna refers to her new home as the "pigeon house," a place where she thinks she has evaded her husband and children. She asserts her independence in this new dwelling, throwing parties and working on her art. Perhaps the greatest reference to Edna's tie to birds occurs right before she kills herself. Chopin portrays the scene on page 108, "A bird with a broken wing was beating the air above, reeling, fluttering, circling disabled down, down to the water." This bird comes to represent everything Edna has endured up until her breakdown, her suicide "down, down to the water." Edna can never reconcile her natural sexual instincts, her "broken wing," with the civilized world she inhabits; society will not let her merge the two domains, and so she resolves to die.

*is ultimately, then, a matter of clearly articulating the means of verifying and explaining what we think we know.*

The treatment of evidence in the following example of scientific writing, a review of existing research on a given phenomenon, has much in common with the treatment of authority and empirical evidence in the paper on ancient art discussed earlier. As in the review of available thinking in virtually any discipline, here the writer explores the adequacy of competing hypotheses by analyzing the theorists' evidence and reasoning. Notice that this analysis includes the writer's thinking on what the hypotheses *imply*.

### EXCERPT FROM "HYPOTHESES ABOUT REV FUNCTION"

Two major hypotheses for Rev function have been proposed. One is that Rev may inhibit splicing or interfere with the assembly of the spliceosome. This hypothesis would imply that inhibiting spliceosome activity would release pre-mRNA for transport to the cytoplasm (Fischer et al. 1995). The other hypothesis is that Rev might directly target viral pre-mRNA to the cytoplasm through the interaction of its domains with cellular cofactors. *[states hypotheses and their implications]* Although there is evidence to support both hypotheses, there seems to be stronger support in favor of the second hypothesis. The finding that functional inactivation of the Rev activation domain always resulted in the inability of the protein to exit the nucleus provides significant evidence that the activation domain is a nuclear export signal (NES) and Rev is indeed actively involved in the direct transport of viral mRNAs (Meyer et al. 1996). *[offers as rationale for preferred hypothesis that it better explains evidence]* Additionally, Rev was able to directly promote nuclear export of RRE-containing mRNAs after nuclear injection into Xenopus oocytes independently of the presence of introns in these RNAs and thus presumably in the absence of spliceosome formation (Fischer et al. 1994). *[adds additional evidence from second source to support preferred hypothesis]*

## Using What You Have

We've just talked about the different kinds of evidence, many of them distinguished by disciplinary community, but ultimately, the basic elements of argument and evidence always apply. Beneath the varieties of evidence, in other words, lie certain fundamental principles of application, principles that have occupied the bulk of this chapter.

It is time to return explicitly to an underlying principle first suggested, as a question, in the chapter's initial "Voices" box: "Does the writer distinguish cases in which evidence *strongly supports* a claim from evidence that is *suggestive* or *speculative?*" Underneath this question lurks a messier one. Given that, depending on what you're trying to accomplish, there are different kinds of evidence, and different audiences to whom it is presented, *how do you know if your evidence legitimately supports your claims?*

A simple, but not very helpful, answer is that you don't. Nor should you really expect definitive assurance on this question. It is helpful to realize, though, that evidence is usually *suggestive* rather than *conclusive.* In the realm of analysis, there are precious few smoking guns and absolutely reliable eyewitnesses. (When there are, you have an open-and-shut case that probably does not need to be argued.) So you want to avoid thinking that a particular use of evidence is strong and good because the evidence is clearly true and factual, whereas another use of evidence is weak and inadequate because it's clearly untrue and not factual. Most analytical uses of evidence are a matter of making inferences, rather than arriving at obviously true claims from clearly factual information.

Most of the areas in which we dwell on evidence are those where the issue is not what is and isn't a fact, but rather *what can fairly be made of the facts.* Once we've proven a claim with a fact, we are not necessarily at a stopping point (which is the drawback of 1 on 10). So, for example, if you discover a mess on your rug with your dog nearby, the only dog in the house, chances are that she made the mess. But this simple move from fact to claim is probably not what will concern you most. You will quickly move on to more hypothetical questions about the facts, such as "Did she make the mess because she's lonely or inadequately trained or ill or . . .?" or "Why do dogs always choose the rug?" Questions of this kind and the hypotheses (tentative theories) we produce in answer to them are what most of our real thinking is about. Finding solid evidence—the facts—is only part of the problem. The larger question is always: so what do the facts really tell us? But this question is the subject of the next several chapters.

We've argued in this chapter that there are different kinds of evidence. And we've argued that *the really interesting and important questions, at least for analytical writing, are to be found not in the facts but in our hypotheses about what the facts mean.* Given these considerations, how do you know what kind of evidence to use and when you've done it right?

To a significant extent, the question of appropriateness depends on the kind of claim you are making (how broad, for example, and how conclusive) and the genre you are writing in. What could be appropriate and valid for writing a magazine profile of residents trying to rebuild a poor urban neighborhood might not be appropriate and valid for supporting policy decisions or sociological theories about people in such neighborhoods. The strength of such a profile, however, should not be underestimated, because it may be rich in suggestion, in questions and angles of approach for further research.

Finally, whatever kind of evidence you're using, the emphasis rests on *how you use what you have:* how you articulate what it means and how carefully you link the evidence to your claims. When you find yourself asking, "How good is my argument?" here are two working criteria from the chapter:

1. Am I oversimplifying the implications of my evidence?
2. Does my use of evidence go beyond mere corroboration of an overly general claim? Do I, in other words, get beyond 1 on 10?

Another and final guiding principle, perhaps the chapter's most important point, is: *don't leave the evidence behind as you cast for what it means.* Rather, think with the evidence; always keep it before you. Here is a good rule of thumb in this regard: if you find that as much as a paragraph has gone by with no reference to your evidence, you can suspect that you are moving off into a perhaps ungrounded and overly abstract discussion.

Your thoughts about the evidence should launch you into broader conceptualizations, but if you start to move too far afield, remember to return repeatedly to the source, to the evidence itself, in order to refresh your thinking and keep it honest.

## VOICES FROM ACROSS THE CURRICULUM

### KEEPING THE EVIDENCE BEFORE YOU

In dance the majority of my work is getting students to locate evidence in the movement itself and in the theatrical accompaniments enhancing the work (sets, costumes, music, narrative, lights, etc.). This involves developing viewing skills and recognizing how dance communicates. I actually do many movement exercises with the students to help them see how a choreographer's manipulation of time, space, and energy creates "meaning."

Because dance is often abstract and purposely open to multiple interpretations, students are usually terrified at the prospect of finding and interpreting evidence in support of a thesis. Typical first responses to analysis include: "I enjoy watching dance, but I have never looked for meaning or message." "I don't know enough about dance to understand it."

My responses include: Sit back, relax, and enjoy the dance—save analysis for later. Start your analysis by pretending you are discussing the performance with a friend who did not see it. As you tell him or her about the performance, you will naturally begin to gather evidence and analyze.

—**KAREN DEARBORN**, *Professor of Dance*

❖ ❖ ❖

A wonderful feature of "doing history" is that everything counts as evidence in uncovering lives, landscapes, institutions, and cultures of the past. The rings of an oak tree can play into a historical argument with as great a resonance as the crown jewels. The literary romance, the census record, the portrait, the peasant's stone bench are all matter for the historian. What, then, the student of history has to hone is the ability to distinguish types of evidence and to assess when and why certain categories of evidence are of legitimate use. [. . .] Students (and professional historians) sometimes prejudge too quickly the purview of a body of evidence and move away from it before the sources have yielded all they have to tell. Again, the qualities of patience and tenacity are crucial here. When a text does not immediately unveil a startling discovery, the tendency can sometimes be to cast a wider and wider net, lapsing into generalization or abstraction. Here is where a close summary of the nature of the evidence, the context for its production or presence (sometimes absence), and its audience can open the way to a lively and perceptive historical essay.

—**ELLEN POTEET**, *Professor of History*

## Key Words (in order of appearance)

| | |
|---|---|
| claim | abstract and concrete |
| unsubstantiated | circular argument |
| thesis | self-evident truth |
| corroborate | qualifying a generalization |

| | |
|---|---|
| syllogism | hypothesis |
| premise | analogy and false analogy |
| warrant | simple cause/complex effect |
| backing (for a warrant) | anecdotal evidence |
| unwarranted inductive leap | empirical evidence |

## Guidelines for Analyzing Evidence

1. Learn to recognize unsubstantiated assertions, rather than treating claims as self-evident truths. Whenever you make a claim, offer your readers the evidence that led you to it.
2. Make details speak. Explain how evidence confirms or qualifies your claim, and offer your reasons for believing the evidence means what you say it does.
3. Say more about less rather than less about more, allowing a carefully analyzed part of your subject to provide perspective on the whole.
4. It is generally better to make ten points on a representative issue or example than to make the same basic point about ten related issues or examples.
5. Argue overtly that the evidence on which you choose to focus is representative. Be careful not to generalize on the basis of too little or unrepresentative evidence.
6. Use your best example as a lens through which to examine other evidence. Analyze subsequent examples to test and develop your conclusions, rather than just confirming that you are right.
7. Look for difference within similarity. Rather than repeating the same overly general claim, use significant variation within the general pattern to better develop your claim.
8. To find the most revealing piece or feature of the evidence, keep asking yourself, "What can I say with some certainty about the evidence?" If you continually rehearse the facts, you are less likely to let an early idea blind you to subsequent evidence.
9. Whatever kind of evidence you're using, the emphasis rests on how you use what you have: on articulating what the evidence means and carefully linking it to your claims.

CHAPTER 3

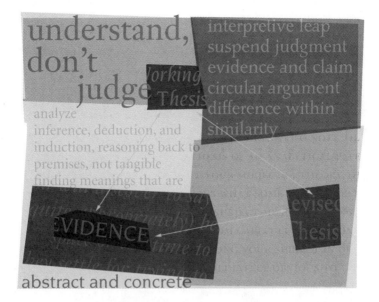

# RECOGNIZING AND FIXING WEAK THESIS STATEMENTS

As we've been defining it so far, *a thesis is a paper's major claim.* This chapter will explain in more detail what a thesis is by showing you how to convert weak thesis statements into stronger ones. Then, in the next chapter, we will illustrate how writers go about finding and evolving strong theses and discuss how different disciplines define and use them.

## Five Kinds of Weak Theses and How to Fix Them

A *strong thesis* makes a claim that (1) requires proof and (2) offers some point about the significance of your evidence that would not have been immediately obvious to your readers. By contrast, a *weak thesis* either makes no claim or makes a claim that does not need proving, such as a statement of fact or an opinion with which virtually all of your readers would most likely agree before reading your paper (for example, exercise is good for you).

Weak thesis statements take various forms. Often they contain clichéd, obvious, or overly general ideas and so don't need or are not worth proving. Other kinds of weak theses substitute for analysis either a global value judgment (for

77

example, individualism is good) or a personal like or dislike (for example, shopping malls are wonderful places).

The five kinds of weak thesis statements are ones that:

1. Make no claim
2. Are obviously true or a statement of fact
3. Restate conventional wisdom
4. Offer personal conviction as the basis for the claim
5. Make an overly broad claim

What all five weak thesis types have in common is that they are not ideas. *A thesis is an idea.*

## What It Means to Have an Idea

What does it mean to have an idea? Must an idea be something that is entirely "original"? Must it revamp the way you understand yourself or your stance toward the world?

Such expectations are unreasonably grand. Clearly, a writer in the early stages of learning about a subject can't be expected to arrive at an idea so original that, like a Ph.D. thesis, it revises complex concepts in a discipline. Nor should you count as ideas only those that lead to some kind of self-revelation.

What, then, does it mean to have an idea? We can probably best understand what ideas are by considering what ideas do and where they can be found. Here is a partial list:

An idea answers a question; it explains something that needs to be explained.

An idea usually starts with an observation that is puzzling, with something that you want to figure out rather than something that you think you already understand.

An idea may be the discovery of a question where there seemed not to be one.

An idea may make explicit and explore the meaning of something implicit—an unstated assumption upon which an argument rests, or a logical consequence of a given position.

An idea may connect elements of a subject and explain the significance of that connection.

An idea often accounts for some *dissonance*—that is, something that seems not to fit together.

*Most strong analytical theses launch you in a process of resolving problems and bringing competing ideas into some kind of alignment.* They put you in a position where there is something to negotiate, where you are required not just to list answers but also to ask questions, make choices, and engage in reasoning about the significance of your evidence.

We now turn to examples of five types of weak thesis statements——actual excerpts from student papers—and show how they can be reworded in ways that will promote analysis.

## Weak Thesis Type 1: The Thesis Makes No Claim

The following statements are not productive theses, because they do not advance an idea about the topics the papers will explore.

### Problem Examples

- I'm going to write about Darwin's concerns with evolution in *The Origin of Species*.
- This paper will address the characteristics of a good corporate manager.

The problem examples name a subject and link it to the intention to write about it, but they don't make any claim about the subject. As a result, they direct neither the writer nor the reader toward some position or plan of attack. The second problem example begins to move toward a point of view through the use of the value judgment "good," but there is still no assertion—no framework for analysis. The statement-of-intention thesis invites a list: one paragraph for each quality the writer chooses to call "good." Even if the thesis were rephrased as "This paper will address why a good corporate manager needs to learn to delegate responsibility," the thesis would not adequately suggest why such a claim would need to be argued or defended. *There is, in short, nothing at stake, no issue to be resolved.* (This is not to say that the overt statement of intention necessarily encourages a writer to avoid making a claim. For discussion of statements of procedure and intention in some disciplines, see Chapter 5, "Matters of Form.")

### Solution

Raise specific issues for the essay to explore.

### Solution Examples

- Darwin's concern with survival of the fittest in *The Origin of Species* leads him to neglect a potentially conflicting aspect of his theory of evolution—survival as a matter of interdependence.
- The very trait that makes for an effective corporate manager—the drive to succeed—can also make the leader domineering and therefore ineffective.

It should be noted that some disciplines expect writers to offer a statement of method and/or intention in their papers' openings. Generally, however, these openings also make a claim: for example, "In this paper I will examine how congressional Republicans undermined the attempts of the

Democratic administration to legislate a fiscally responsible health-care policy for the elderly," *not* "In this paper I will discuss America's treatment of the
elderly."

## Weak Thesis Type 2:
## The Thesis Is Obviously True or Is a Statement of Fact

The following statements are not productive theses, because they do not require proof. A thesis needs to be an assertion with which it would be possible
for readers to disagree.

### Problem Examples

- The jean industry targets its advertisements to appeal to young adults.
- The flight from teaching to research and publishing in higher education
  is a controversial issue in the academic world. I will show different
  views and aspects concerning this problem.

If few people would disagree with the claim that a thesis makes, there is
no point in writing an analytical paper on it. Though one might deliver an inspirational speech on a position that virtually everyone would support (such
as the value of tolerance), endorsements and appreciations don't usually lead
to analysis; they merely invite people to feel good about their convictions.

In the second preceding problem example, few readers would disagree with
the fact that the issue is "controversial." In the second sentence of that example,
the writer has begun to identify a point of view—that the flight from teaching is
a "problem"—but her next declaration, that she will "show different views and
aspects," is a statement of fact, not an idea. The phrasing of the claim is non-
committal and so broad that it prevents the writer from formulating a workable
thesis.

### Solution

Find some avenue of *inquiry*—a question about the facts or an issue raised by
them. Make an assertion with which it would be possible for readers to disagree.

### Solution Examples

- By inventing new terms, such as "loose fit" and "relaxed fit," the jean
  industry has attempted to normalize, even glorify, its product for an
  older and fatter generation.
- The "flight from teaching" to research and publishing in higher education is a controversial issue in the academic world. As I will attempt
  to show, the controversy is based to a significant degree on a false assumption: that doing research necessarily leads teachers away from the
  classroom.

## Weak Thesis Type 3:
## The Thesis Restates Conventional Wisdom

Restatement of one of the many clichés that constitute a culture's conventional wisdom is not a productive thesis unless you have something to say about it that hasn't been said many times before.

### Problem Examples

- An important part of one's college education is learning to better understand others' points of view.
- From cartoons in the morning to adventure shows at night, there is too much violence on television.
- "I was supposed to bring the coolers; *you* were supposed to bring the chips!" exclaimed ex-Beatle Ringo Starr, who appeared on TV commercials for wine coolers a few years ago. By using rock music to sell a wide range of products, the advertising agencies, in league with corporate giants such as Pepsi, Michelob, and Ford, have corrupted the spirit of rock and roll.

All of these problem theses say nothing worth proving because they are clichés. (*Conventional wisdom* is a polite term for *clichés*.) Most clichés were fresh ideas once, but over time they have become trite, prefabricated forms of nonthinking. Faced with a phenomenon that requires a response, many inexperienced writers rely on a knee-jerk reaction: they resort to a small set of culturally approved "answers." So commonly accepted that most people nod to them without thinking, statements of conventional wisdom make people feel a comfortable sense of agreement with one another. The problem with this kind of packaged solution is that conventional wisdom is so general and so conventional that it doesn't teach anybody—including the writer—anything. Worse, because the cliché appears to be an idea, it prevents the writer from engaging in a fresh, open-minded exploration of his or her subject.

There is, of course, some truth in all of the preceding problem examples. None of them, however, *complicates* its position. A thoughtful reader could, for example, respond to the claim that advertising has corrupted the spirit of rock and roll by suggesting that rock and roll was highly commercial long before it colonized the airwaves. The conventional wisdom that rock and roll is somehow pure and honest whereas advertising is phony and exploitative in fact invites the savvy writer to formulate a thesis that overturns these clichés. As our solution example demonstrates, one could argue that rock actually has improved advertising, not that advertising has ruined rock—or alternatively, that rock has shrewdly marketed idealism to a gullible populace, at least since the "love generation" captured the national imagination in the late sixties. At the least, a writer deeply committed to the original thesis would do better to examine what it was that Ringo was selling—what he stands for in this particular case—than to discuss rock and advertising in such general terms.

### Solution

Seek to complicate—see more than one point of view on—your subject. Avoid conventional wisdom unless you can qualify it or introduce a fresh perspective on it.

### Solution Examples

- Although an important part of one's college education is learning to better understand others' points of view, a persistent danger is that students will be required simply to substitute the teacher's answers for the ones they grew up uncritically believing.
- Although some might argue that the presence of rock-and-roll soundtracks in TV commercials has corrupted rock's spirit, this point of view not only falsifies the history of rock but also blinds us to the ways that the music has improved the quality of television advertising.

## Weak Thesis Type 4: The Thesis Offers
## Personal Conviction as the Basis for the Claim

A statement of one's personal convictions or one's likes or dislikes does not alone supply sufficient grounds for a productive thesis.

### Problem Examples

- The songs of the punk rock group Minor Threat relate to the feelings of individuals who dare to be different. The group's songs are composed of pure emotion. Pure emotion is very important in music, because it serves as a vehicle to convey the important message of individuality. Minor Threat's songs are meaningful to me because I can identify with them.
- Sir Thomas More's *Utopia* proposes an unworkable set of solutions to society's problems because, like communist Russia, it suppresses individualism.
- Although I agree with Jeane Kirkpatrick's argument that environmentalists and business should work together to ensure the ecological future of the world and that this cooperation is beneficial for both sides, the indisputable fact is that environmental considerations should always be a part of any decision that is made. Any individual, if he looks deeply enough into his soul, knows what is right and what is wrong. The environment should be protected because it is the right thing to do, not because someone is forcing you to do it.

Like conventional wisdom, personal likes and dislikes can lead inexperienced writers into knee-jerk reactions of approval or disapproval, often expressed in a moralistic tone. The writers of the preceding problem examples assume that their primary job is to judge their subjects or testify to their worth, not to evaluate them analytically. As a result, such writers lack critical detachment, not only from their topics but also, crucially, from their own assumptions and biases. They have taken personal opinions for self-evident truths. You can test a thesis for this problem by asking if the writer's response to questions about the thesis would be "because I think so."

The most blatant version of this tendency occurs in the third problem example, which asserts, "Any individual, if he looks deeply enough into his soul, knows what is right and what is wrong. The environment should be protected because it is the right thing to do." Translation (only slightly exaggerated): "Any individual who thinks about the subject will obviously agree with me because my feelings and convictions feel right to me and therefore they must be universally and self-evidently true." The problem is that this writer is not distinguishing between his own likes and dislikes (or private convictions) and what he takes to be "right," "real," or "true" for everyone else. *Testing an idea against your own feelings and experience is not an adequate means of establishing whether something is accurate or true.*

### Solution

Try on other points of view honestly and dispassionately; treat your ideas as hypotheses to be tested rather than as obvious truths. In the following solution examples, we have replaced opinions (in the form of self-evident truths) with ideas—theories about the meaning and significance of their subjects that could be supported with evidence.

### Solution Examples

- Sir Thomas More's *Utopia* treats individualism as a serious but remediable social problem. His radical treatment of what we might now call "socialization" attempts to redefine the meaning and origin of individual identity.
- Although I agree with Jeane Kirkpatrick's argument that environmentalists and business should work together to ensure the ecological future of the world, her argument undervalues the necessity of pressuring businesses to attend to environmental concerns that may not benefit them in the short run.

It is fine, of course, to write about what you believe and to consult your feelings as you formulate an idea. But the risk you run in arguing from your unexamined feelings and convictions is that you will prematurely dismiss from consideration anything that is unfamiliar or does not immediately conform to what you already believe. The less willing you are to test these established and habitual convictions, the less chance you will have to refine or expand the ways in which you think. You will continue to play the same small set of tunes in response to everything you hear. And without the ability to think from multiple perspectives, you will be less able to defend your convictions against the ideas that challenge them, because you won't really have examined the logic of your own beliefs—you just believe them.

At the root of this problem lurks an antianalytical bias that predisposes many writers to regard as the enemy any challenge to their habitual ways of thinking and to view those who would raise this challenge as cynics who don't believe in anything. Such writers often feel personally attacked, when in fact the conviction they are defending is not really so personal after all. Consider, for example, the first two preceding problem examples, in which both writers take individualism to be an incontestable value. Where does this conviction come from? Neither of the writers arrived at the thesis independent of the particular culture in which he or she was raised, permeated as it is by the "rugged individualism" of John Wayne and Sylvester Stallone movies.

In other words, individualism as an undefined blanket term verges on *cultural cliché*. That it is always "good" or "positive" is a piece of conventional wisdom. But part of becoming educated is to take a look at such global and undefined ideas that one has uncritically assimilated. Clearly, the needs and rights of the individual in contemporary American culture are consistently being weighed and balanced against the rights of other individuals and the necessity of cooperation in groups. Look at the recent nationwide concerns with health maintenance organizations (HMOs), which control health costs but constrain the individual prerogative of the physician, or with the rights of crime victims who are banding together to seek support from a government they believe is protecting the individual rights of the criminal at the expense of the individual rights of the victim.

In light of these considerations, the writers of the first two problem examples would have to question the extent to which they can attack a book or support a rock band merely on the basis of whether or not each honors individualism. If the author of the second problem example had been willing to explore how Thomas More conceives of and critiques individualism, he or she might have been able to arrive at a revealing analysis of the tension between the individual and the collective rather than merely dismissing the entire book.

This is not to suggest that the first requirement of analytical writing is that you abandon all conviction or argue for a position that you do not believe. But we are suggesting that the risk of remaining trapped within a limited set of culturally inherited opinions is greater than the risk that you will run by submerging your personal likes or dislikes and instead honestly and dispassionately trying on different points of view. *The energy of analytical writing comes not from rehearsing your convictions, but rather from treating them as hypotheses to be tested, as scientists do*—finding the boundaries of your ideas, reshaping parts of them, seeing connections you have not seen before.

*An idea is not the same thing as an opinion.* The two are closely related, since both, in theory, are based on reasoning. Opinions, however, often take the form of judgments, the reflections of your personal attitudes and beliefs. Although having ideas necessarily involves your attitudes and beliefs, it is a more disinterested process than opinion-making. The formulation of ideas, which is one of the primary aims of analysis, involves questioning; by contrast, opinions are often habitual responses, mental reflexes like the jerk your knee makes when someone taps it lightly with a hammer.

When a writing assignment asks for your ideas about a subject, it is usually not asking for your opinion, what you think *of* the subject, but rather for your reasoning on what and how the subject means. The following observations from a political science professor explain why and how he warns student writers to be wary of opinions:

---

**VOICES FROM ACROSS THE CURRICULUM**

**IDEAS VERSUS OPINIONS**

Writers need to be aware of the distinction between an argument that seeks support from evidence and mere opinions and assertions. Many students taking political science courses often come with the assumption that in politics one opinion is as good as another. (Tocqueville thought this to be a peculiarly democratic disease.) From this perspective any position a political science professor may take on controversial issues is simply his or her opinion to be accepted or rejected by students according to their own beliefs/prejudices. The key task, therefore, is not so much substituting knowledge for opinions, but rather substituting well-constructed arguments for unexamined opinions.

What is an argument, and how might it be distinguished from opinions? Several things need to be stressed: (1) The thesis should be linked to evidence drawn from relevant sources: polling data, interviews, historical material, and so forth. (2) The thesis should make as explicit as possible its own ideological assumptions. (3) A thesis, in contrast to mere statement of opinion, is committed to making an argument, which means that it presupposes a willingness to engage with others. To the extent that writers operate on the assumption that everything is an opinion, they have no reason to construct arguments; they are locked into an opinion.

—**JACK GAMBINO,** *Professor of Political Science*

---

## Weak Thesis Type 5:
## The Thesis Makes an Overly Broad Claim

An overly general claim is not a productive thesis, because it oversimplifies and is too broad to direct development. Such claims usually lead either to "say-nothing" theses or to reductive categorical thinking (see "Working with Categorical Thinking" later in the chapter).

### Problem Examples

- Violent revolutions have had both positive and negative results.
- There are many similarities and differences between the Carolingian and the Burgundian Renaissances.

- *Othello* is a play about love and jealousy.
- It is important to understand why leaders act in a leadership role. What is the driving force? Is it an internal drive for the business or group to succeed, or is it an internal drive for the leader to dominate others?

Overly generalized theses avoid complexity. At their worst, as in our first three examples, they settle for assertions broad enough to fit almost any subject and thus say nothing in particular about the subject at hand. A writer in the early stages of his or her drafting process might begin working from a general idea, such as what is positive and negative about violent revolutions or how two historical periods are like and unlike, but these formulations are not specific enough to guide the development of a paper. Such broad categories are likely to generate listing, not thinking. We can, for example, predict that the third of the preceding theses will prompt the writer to produce a couple of paragraphs demonstrating that *Othello* is about love and then a couple of paragraphs demonstrating that *Othello* is about jealousy, without analyzing what the play says about either.

Our fourth problem example, inquiring into the motivation of leaders in business, demonstrates how the desire to generalize can drive writers into logical errors. Because this thesis overtly offers readers two possible answers to its central question, it appears to avoid the problem of oversimplifying a complex subject. But this appearance of complexity is deceptive, because the writer has reduced the possibilities to only two answers—an either/or choice: is "the driving force" of leadership a desire for group success or a desire to dominate others? Readers can only be frustrated by being asked to choose between two such options when the more logical answer probably lies somewhere in between or somewhere else altogether.

The best way to avoid the problem evident in the first three examples is to sensitize yourself to the characteristic phrasing of such theses: "both positive and negative," "many similarities and differences," "both pros and cons." Virtually everything from meatloaf to taxes can be both positive and negative.

### Solution

Convert broad categories and generic (fits anything) claims to more specific assertions; find ways to bring out the complexity of your subject. As we will demonstrate, *rethinking is to a significant degree a matter of rephrasing.*

### Solution Examples

- The differences between the Carolingian and Burgundian Renaissances outweigh the similarities.
- Although *Othello* appears to attack jealousy, it also supports the skepticism of the jealous characters over the naïveté of the lovers.
- Although violent revolutions begin to redress long-standing social inequities, they often do so at the cost of long-term economic dysfunction and the suffering that attends it.

### How to Rephrase Thesis Statements: Specify and Subordinate

Clear symptoms of an overly generalized thesis can be found by looking at its grammar. Each of the first three preceding problem examples, for instance, relies mostly on nouns rather than verbs; the nouns announce a broad heading, but the verbs don't do anything with or to the nouns. In grammatical terms, these thesis statements don't *predicate* (affirm or assert something about the subject of a proposition). Instead, they rely on anemic verbs like *is* or *are,* which function as equal signs, linking general nouns with general adjectives, rather than specifying more complex relationships.

By replacing the equal sign with a more active verb, you can force yourself to advance some sort of claim, as in one of our preceding solutions, for example: "The differences between the Carolingian and Burgundian Renaissances *outweigh* the similarities." Although this reformulation remains quite general, it at least begins to direct the writer along a more particular line of argument. Replacing the *is* or *are* equal sign with a stronger verb will usually impel you to rank ideas in some order of importance and to assert some conceptual relation between them.

In other words, the best way to remedy the problem of overgeneralization is to *move toward specificity in word choice, in sentence structure, and in idea.* If you find yourself writing "The economic situation is bad," consider revising it to "The tax policies of the current administration threaten to reduce the tax burden on the middle class by sacrificing education and health-care programs for everyone":

| Broad Noun | + | Weak Verb | + Vague, Evaluative Adjective |
|---|---|---|---|
| The economic situation | | is | bad |

| Specific Noun | + | Active Verb | + | Specific Modifiers |
|---|---|---|---|---|
| (The) tax policies (of the current administration) | | threaten to reduce (the tax burden on the middle class) | | by sacrificing education and health-care programs for everyone. |

By eliminating the weak thesis formula—broad noun + *is* + vague evaluative adjective—a writer is compelled to qualify, or define carefully, each of the terms in the original proposition, arriving at a more particular and conceptually rich assertion.

A second way to rephrase overly broad thesis statements, in tandem with adding specificity, is to subordinate one part of the statement to another. The both-positive-and-negative, both-similarity-and-difference formulas are recipes for say-nothing theses, because they encourage pointless comparisons. Given that it is worthwhile to notice both strengths and weaknesses—that your subject is not all one way or all another way—what, then, can you do to convert the thesis from a say-nothing to a say-something claim? Generally, there are two strategies for this purpose that operate together. The first we have already discussed:

- *Specify:* replace the overly abstract terms—in this case, positive and negative (or similarity and difference, etc.)—with something specific; *name* something that is positive and something that is negative instead.

Once you have begun to specify, usually you will also need to:

- *Subordinate:* rank one of the two items in the pairing underneath the other. When you subordinate, you put the most important, pressing, revealing side of the comparison in what is known as the "main clause," and the less important side in what is known as the "subordinate clause," introducing it with a word like *while* or *although*. (See Chapter 8, "Editing for Correctness," for more discussion of main and subordinate clauses.)

In short, specify to focus the claim and subordinate to qualify (further focus) the claim still more. This strategy has produced the remedies to both the *Othello* and the violent revolution examples. As evidence of the refocusing work that fairly simple rephrasing accomplishes, consider the following version of the violent revolution example, in which we have merely inverted the ranking of the two items in the pair.

- Although violent revolutions often cause long-term economic dysfunction and the suffering that attends it, such revolutions at least begin to redress long-standing social inequities.

---

## VOICES FROM ACROSS THE CURRICULUM

### MAKING THE THESIS SPECIFIC

*Good thesis:* "While Graham and Wigman seem different, their ideas on inner expression (specifically subjectivism versus objectivism) and the incorporation of their respective countries' surge of nationalism bring them much closer than they appear.

*Not so good thesis/question:* "What were Humphrey's and Weidman's reasons behind the setting of *With My Red Fires,* and of what importance were the set and costume design to the piece as a whole?"

What I like about the good thesis is that it moves beyond the standard "they are different, but alike" (which can be said about anything) to actually tell the reader what specific areas the paper will explore. I can also tell that the subject is narrow enough for a fairly thorough examination of one small slice of these two major choreographers' work rather than some overgeneralized treatment of these two historic figures. I would probably encourage the writer of the not so good thesis to search for a better thesis with the question: How does the costume design of *With My Red Fires* support this story of young lovers and their revolt against the family Matriarch?

—**KAREN DEARBORN**, *Professor of Dance*

### Another Note on the Phrasing of Thesis Statements: Questions

The following question is frequently asked about thesis statements: is it okay to phrase a thesis as a question? The answer is both yes and no. Phrasing a thesis as a question makes it more difficult for both the writer and the reader to be sure of the direction the paper will take, because a question doesn't make an overt claim. Questions, however, can clearly imply claims. And many writers, especially in the early, exploratory stages of drafting, will begin with a question. As we've noted in the discussion of "What It Means to Have an Idea," an idea answers a question; it explains something that needs to be explained.

As a general rule, use thesis questions cautiously, especially in final drafts. Although they often function well to spark a writer's thinking, they can too often muddy the thinking by leaving the area of consideration too broad. Just make sure that you do not let the thesis-question approach allow you to evade the responsibility of making some kind of claim. Especially in the drafting stage, a question posed overtly by the writer can provide focus, but only if he or she then proceeds to answer it with what would become a first statement of thesis.

---

## APPLICATION:

## DIAGNOSING AND FIXING WEAK THESIS STATEMENTS

What follows is a list of thesis statements to analyze and revise. Each is followed by questions and focused review from the chapter. In cases where we provide more than a sentence, it helps to know that thesis statements often emerge near the end of the first paragraph. The revising will require you to add information (as we have done in the preceding solution examples).

1. In this paper I will discuss police procedures in recent domestic violence cases.

This is an example of which of the five weak thesis types? Start revising it by asking yourself what questions this thesis requires the writer to answer. Using the chapter's discussion on the syntax of thesis statements, try querying and then shrinking the individual terms in the statement itself—"police procedures," for example, or "recent." Having generated some thinking in this way, try to produce a thesis that would give a paper on this subject more direction.

2. The way that the media portrayed the events of April 30, 1975, when Saigon fell, greatly influenced the final perspectives of the American people toward the end result of the Vietnam War.

How would you categorize this weak thesis? How would you fix it?

(continued)

3. From cartoons in the morning to adventure shows at night, there is too much violence on television.

You will recognize this assertion as one of the problem examples from Weak Thesis Type 3, "The Thesis Restates Conventional Wisdom." Presumably, most readers would agree with this assertion, but what will the writer *do* with it? Try rewriting the thesis in a way that would give the writer something more specific and something less clichéd to prove in his or her paper. Might you propose a thesis in which you focus on a particular type of television violence and how it has changed over time, or how it characterizes a particular group, for example? Try, in other words, to come up with some interesting claims that most readers would not already have thought of to develop the subject of television violence.

4. The songs of the punk rock group Minor Threat relate to the feelings of individuals who dare to be different. The group's songs are composed of just pure emotion. Pure emotion is very important in music, because it serves as a vehicle to convey the important message of individuality. Minor Threat's songs are meaningful to me because I can identify with them.

Here is the first problem example from Weak Thesis Type 4, "The Thesis Offers Personal Conviction as the Basis for the Claim." Pinpoint the places in the paragraph in which the writer asks readers to accept assertions only on the basis of personal conviction. What other features of the example seem to you to raise problems? After answering these questions, produce a couple of sentences that predict the kind of paper that the paragraph is likely to produce (this is a good test for the adequacy of any thesis).

Then, draft a strong thesis (one requiring proof and offering some point not immediately obvious) about any artist or type or piece of contemporary music that you particularly like or dislike. Remember that your goal is to get beyond statements of likes and dislikes to an assertion that will lead to analysis.

5. Regarding the promotion of women into executive positions, they are continually losing the race because of a corporate view that women are too compassionate to keep up with the competitiveness of a powerful firm.

What is potentially strong, and what is potentially weak about this thesis? What would it require the writer to prove? What pitfalls might the writer have to be wary of if he or she decided to go with this thesis as worded?

Having worked on these sample thesis statements, you might try working either as a class or in small groups at formulating and troubleshooting thesis statements for an upcoming paper.

# Working with Categorical Thinking: How to Improve the Logic of Your Thesis Statements

Categorical thinking is an unavoidable and distinctive feature of how all human beings go about analyzing a subject. It is also extremely useful: in order to generalize from particular experiences, we try to put those experiences into meaningful categories. When we contract an illness, doctors diagnose it by type. When we study personality theory, different behaviors are grouped by personality type. Subject areas in school are categorized into divisions: the natural sciences, the social sciences, the humanities. Analytical thought is quite unthinkable without categories.

But categorical thinking can also be dangerous. It can mislead us into oversimplification when the categories are too broad or too simply connected. This is especially the case with the either/or choices to which categorical thinking is prone: approve/disapprove, real/unreal, accurate/inaccurate, believable/unbelievable. Such either/or thinking often provokes thinkers into a premature and overly narrow decision either to support the subject or to denounce it (the problem discussed in Chapter 1 in relation to "debate-style" argument). This rush to value judgment can so dominate a writer's attention that he or she fails to examine not only the values upon which the judgment is based, but also the subject itself.

If you look back over the examples in "Five Kinds of Weak Theses," you will notice that a number of them engage in the dangerous side of categorical thinking. That is, they are overly global—inclined to all-or-nothing claims. The writer who evaluates leadership in terms of its selflessness/selfishness, for example, needs to pause to consider why we should evaluate leadership in these terms in the first place.

Many weak theses are the result of oversimplified categorical thinking. The writer puts everything into big, undifferentiated categories, labeled all black or all white, with nothing in between. The trick is to use categorical thinking in a way that allows you to make careful distinctions. To that end, we will now focus on how to use one of the most common forms of categorical thinking as a tool rather than letting it trap you into overly dichotomized positions.

## Refocus Binaries

In human—and computerized—thinking, a binary is a pair of elements, usually in opposition to each other, as in off/on, yes/no, right/wrong, agree/disagree, and so on. Many ideas begin with a writer's noticing some kind of opposition or tension or choice within a subject—capital punishment either does or does not deter crime; a character in a novel is either a courageous rebel or a fool; a new environmental policy is either visionary or blind. *A major advantage of looking for and using binaries is that they help you determine*

*what issues are at stake in your subject, because binaries position you among com-
peting choices.*

There is an old joke to the effect that there are two kinds of people—those
who like binary thinking and those who do not. Part of the humor here seems
to lie in the recognition that we cannot help but think in binary terms. As the
philosopher Herbert Marcuse says, "We understand that which is in terms of
that which is not": light is that which is not dark; masculine is that which is
not feminine; civilized is that which is not primitive. Creating opposing categories is fundamental to defining things. But as these examples may suggest,
binaries are also dangerous because they can perpetuate what is called *reductive
thinking,* especially if applied uncritically.

Reductive thinking oversimplifies a subject, eliminating alternatives between two extremes—that, for example, women are either virgins or whores,
that teachers either instill a love of learning in students or alienate them from
their feelings. As these examples suggest, if you restrict yourself to thinking in
binary terms, you can run into two problems. First, most subjects cannot be
adequately considered in terms of only two options—either this or that, with
nothing in between. Second, binaries often conceal value judgments: the category "primitive," as opposed to "civilized," is not a neutral description but (in
most cases) a devaluation.

In sum, *it is useful to begin by constructing binaries but dangerous to stay
with them too long,* because you run the risk of ignoring the more complex
gray area in between. Often there are more than two alternatives, or both alternatives have some truth to them: a new environmental policy may be
both visionary and blind, some combination of the two. We have all encountered paper topics framed in binary terms—"Was the Civil War fought
over slavery or economics?"—but you should keep in mind that such questions often seek to stimulate your thinking. They are not necessarily pressing you to choose one side of the binary over the other as the absolute answer (that economics caused the war and that slavery had nothing to do
with it, or vice versa).

The agree/disagree binary, like either/or, can lead to reductive thinking.
Let us briefly consider two agree/disagree thesis statements: (1) "I agree/dis-
agree with the way that Charles Bovary treats his wife in the novel *Madame
Bovary.*" (2) "I agree/disagree with Eisenhower's foreign policy decisions during the Cold War." The problem with both claims is that they invite oversimplified good/bad or yes/no responses that don't respect the complexity of the
subject.

A writer's feelings about a fictional character (Bovary) will be important in
an analysis only when connected to an argument about the meaning of the
novel; the writer would do better to focus on the question "How does the novel
predispose readers to judge Bovary's treatment of his wife—and why?" The
wording of the question about Eisenhower's foreign policy similarly invites
quick and overly broad judgment (consulting one's prejudices): the writer's
task is not to approve or disapprove of Eisenhower, but rather to analyze his
decisions.

### Strategies for Using Binaries Analytically

#### STRATEGY 1: LOCATE A RANGE OF OPPOSING CATEGORIES

The first step in using binaries analytically is to locate and distinguish them carefully. Consider, for example, the binaries contained in the following question: "Does the model of management known as Total Quality Management (TQM) that is widely used in Japan work in the American automotive industry?" The most obvious binary in this question is work versus not work. But there are also other binaries in the question—Japanese versus American, for example, and TQM versus more traditional and more traditionally American models of management. These binaries imply further binaries. Insofar as TQM is acknowledged to be a team-oriented, collaborative management model, the question requires a writer to consider the accuracy and relative suitability of particular traits commonly ascribed to Japanese versus American workers, such as communal and cooperative versus individualistic and competitive.

#### STRATEGY 2: ANALYZE AND DEFINE THE OPPOSING TERMS

Having located the various binaries, you should begin to analyze and define terms. What, for example, does it mean to ask whether TQM *works* in the American automotive industry? Does *work* mean "make a substantial profit"? Does *work* mean "produce more cars more quickly"? Does *work* mean "improve employee morale"? You would probably find yourself drowning in vagueness unless you carefully argued for the appropriateness of your definition of this key term.

#### STRATEGY 3: QUESTION THE ACCURACY OF THE BINARY

Having begun to analyze and define your terms, you would next need to determine how accurately they define the issues raised by your subject. You might consider, for example, the extent to which American management styles actually differ from the Japanese version of TQM. In the process of trying to determine if there are significant differences, you could start to locate particular traits in these management styles and in Japanese versus American culture that might help you to formulate your binary more precisely. Think of the binary as a starting point—a kind of deliberate overgeneralization—that allows you to set up positions you can then test in order to refine.

#### STRATEGY 4: CHANGE "EITHER/OR" TO "THE EXTENT TO WHICH" ("TO WHAT EXTENT?")

The best strategy in using binaries analytically is usually to locate arguments on both sides of the either/or choice that the binary poses. So, in answer to the question we mentioned earlier, "Was the Civil War fought over slavery or economics?," you would attempt to determine *the extent to which* each side of the binary—slavery and economics—could reasonably be credited as the cause of the war. To do so, you would first rephrase the question, "To what extent did economics, rather than slavery, cause the Civil War?" Rephrasing in this way might also enable you to see problems with the original binary formulation.

Making this move would not release you from the responsibility of taking a stand and arguing for it. But by analyzing the terms of the binary, you would come to question it and ultimately to arrive at a more complex and qualified position to write about. For example, you might ultimately decide that economics rather than slavery was the primary cause of the Civil War, but in so doing, you would also be inclined to acknowledge that slavery is itself an economic issue as well as a moral one.

In short, using "to what extent?" as a formula for rephrasing stark either/or binaries can help you to:

1. Weight one side of your binary more heavily than the other, rather than seeing the issue as all or nothing (all of one and nothing of the other)
2. Discover that the two terms of your binary are not really so separate and opposed after all, but rather part of one complex phenomenon or issue
3. Discover that you have not adequately named the binary; another opposition would be more accurate

To make one quick application, let's consider what might happen if you were to select the following binary: was the poet Emily Dickinson psychotic, or was she a poetic genius? This is a useful if overstated starting point for prompting thinking. You might decide that she was thirty percent psychotic and seventy percent genius. Or you might decide that poetic genius is a form of insanity. Or you might decide that insanity versus poetic genius is not really the issue and that you need to find another, more revealing opposition to start the process of analysis again (for example, Dickinson as unconventional and truly eccentric versus Dickinson as much more conventional and in sync with her time than is generally acknowledged).

Admittedly, in reorienting your thinking from the obvious and clear-cut choices that either/or formulations provide to the murkier waters of "the extent to which," your decision process will be made more difficult. The gain, however, is that "the extent to which" mind-set, by predisposing you to assess multiple and potentially conflicting points of view, will enable you to address more fairly and accurately the issues raised by your subject.

Where might you end up if you approached our earlier sample topic (whether or not TQM works in the American automotive industry) by asking *to what extent* one side of the binary better suits available evidence, rather than arguing that one side is clearly the right choice and the other entirely wrong? You would still be arguing that one position on TQM in American industry is more accurate than the other, but you would inevitably arrive at more carefully *qualified* conclusions than the question might otherwise have led you to. You would most likely take care, for example, to suggest the danger of assuming that all American workers are rugged individualists whereas all Japanese workers are communal bees.

## APPLICATION:

## REFOCUSING BINARIES

Apply the "Strategies for Using Binaries Analytically" to revise the following thesis statements and questions, as we did with the TQM example. This does not mean that you must proceed step-by-step through the strategies, but, at the least, for each thesis statement or question you should:

1. List all of the binaries you can find, both implicit and explicit, in each example.

2. Isolate the one or two key terms that reveal what is at issue for each writer, and determine what they mean. You should write out the implied definitions.

We have suggested some of the key terms with boldfacing. Notice that such key terms often involve the writer's evaluation of the subject. So, in Statement b, for example, the key binary appears to be "first-world" versus "third-world," but even more important for defining the writer's thinking is arguably what he or she means by "good."

3. Even if the original formulation looks okay to you, assume that it is an overgeneralization that needs to be refined and rephrased. On the basis of your list of oppositions and definitions of key terms, rewrite the thesis statement in a more qualified and accurate form.

In proposing your revised thesis, you might try substituting "to what extent?" for either/or (which will press you to limit the claims that binary formulations are prone to overstate).

a. It is important to understand why leaders act in a leadership role. What is the driving force? Is it an internal drive for the business or group to succeed, or is it an internal drive for the leader to dominate others?

This example comes from our discussion of Weak Thesis Type 5, "The Thesis Makes an Overly Broad Claim." Its binary formulation is part of what makes it problematically broad. In this case, a significant part of the problem is that the binary—succeed versus dominate—offers too narrow a range of options for explaining a very complex and individualized motivation. At the very least, how would you rewrite the paragraph to include more options, more possible oppositions?

b. Is nationalism **good** for emerging third-world countries?

c. The private lives of public figures should not **matter** in the way they are assessed by the public. What matters is how competently they do their jobs.

d. The Seattle sound of rock and roll known as Grunge is not **original**; it's just a **rehash** of Punk and New Wave elements.

## Qualify Your Claims and Check for Unstated Assumptions

We will refer to the following two examples to illustrate how to strengthen the logic of your thesis statements by qualifying your claims and checking for the unstated assumptions upon which your claims depend. Both of these strategies were also at work in the process of refocusing binaries in the TQM example, wherein we needed to limit the scope of the claim and locate the unacknowledged binaries lurking beneath it.

### EXAMPLE 1

> I think that there are many things shown on TV that are damaging for people to see. But there is no need for censorship. No network is going to show violence without the approval of the public, obviously for financial reasons. What must be remembered is that the public majority will see what it wants to see in our mass society.

### EXAMPLE 2

> Some members of our society feel that [the televised cartoon series] *The Simpsons* promotes wrong morals and values for our society. Other members find it funny and entertaining. I feel that *The Simpsons* has a more positive effect than a negative one. In relation to a real-life marriage, Marge and Homer's marriage is pretty accurate. The problems they deal with are not very large or intense. As for the family relationships, the Simpsons are very close and love each other.

### Qualifying Overextended Claims

The main problem with Example 1 is the writer's failure to qualify his ideas, a problem that causes him to generalize to the point of oversimplification. Note the writer's habit of stating his claims absolutely:

> "there is *no* need for censorship"
> "*no* network is going to show violence without"
> "*obviously* for financial reasons"
> "what *must* be remembered"
> "the majority *will* see"

We have italicized the words that make these claims unqualified.

Broad, pronouncement-like claims are difficult to support fairly. The solution is for the writer to more carefully limit his claims, especially his key premise about public approval. The assertion that a commercial television industry will, for financial reasons, give the public "what it wants" is true *to an extent*. But, as with the "extent to which" strategy for refocusing binaries, the solution here is to modify this claim as well as to consider other possibilities. Couldn't it also be argued, for example, that given the power of television to shape people's tastes and opinions, the public sees not just what it wants but what it has been taught to want? This necessary complication of the writer's argument about public approval seriously undermines the credibility of his global assertion that "there is no need for censorship." The remedy lies with qualifying his thesis. Simply reversing it to "there is a need for censorship" would not solve the problem, because the need for defining and limiting the writer's position will be just as great on the other side of the issue.

Example 2 would appear to be more qualified than Example 1 (because it acknowledges the possibility of at least two points of view). The writer opens by attempting to acknowledge the existence of more than one point of view on the show; and rather than broadly asserting that the show is positive and accurate, she tempers these claims (as italics show): "I *feel* that *The Simpsons* has a *more* positive effect *than* a negative one"; Marge and Homer's marriage is *pretty* accurate." These qualifications, however, are superficial. Although "pretty" would seem to admit that the show is not entirely accurate, the statements that follow the accuracy claim do not pursue this qualification. The writer does not explore what "accurate" means. Instead, she assumes the standard of accuracy (that an accurate show is a good show) as a given.

## Checking for Unstated Assumptions

Before she could convince us to approve of *The Simpsons* for its accuracy in depicting marriage, the writer of Example 2 would have to convince us that accuracy is a reasonable criterion for evaluating TV shows (especially cartoons) rather than simply accepting it as an unstated assumption. One could certainly argue against her unstated premise. Would an accurate depiction of the life of a serial killer, for example, necessarily make for a "positive" show? Similarly, if a fantasy show has no interest in accuracy, is it necessarily "negative" and without moral value?

When writers present a debatable premise as if it were self-evidently true, the conclusions built upon it cannot stand. At the least, the writer of Example 2 needs to *recognize her debatable premise, articulate it, and make an argument in support of it.* She also needs to precede her judgment about the show with more analysis. Before deciding that the show is "more positive than negative" and thus does not promote "wrong morals and values for our society," she needs to more deeply analyze what the show has to say about marriage, how it goes about making this statement, and why (in response to what?).

Likewise, if the writer of Example 1 had looked at his own claims rather than rushing to argue an absolute position on censorship, he would have noticed how much of the thinking that underlies them remains unarticulated and thus unexamined. His argument that "there is no need for censorship," for example, depends on the validity of another of his assertions: that "no network is going to show violence without the approval of the public, obviously for financial reasons."

The writer's argument depends on readers' accepting a position that he asserts ("obviously") as though it were too clearly true to need defending.

# Developing a Thesis by Reasoning Back to Premises

All arguments ultimately rest on fundamental assumptions called *givens*—positions not in need of argument because you assume the reader will "give" them to you as true. Often, however, these assumptions need first to be acknowledged and then argued, or at least tested. You cannot assume that their truth is self-evident (as the authors of the *Simpsons* and censorship examples have done). The failure to locate and examine unacknowledged assumptions (premises) is the downfall of many essays. The problem occurs because our categories—the mental boxes we've created over time—have become so fixed, so unquestioned, that we cease to be fully aware of them.

---

### VOICES FROM ACROSS THE CURRICULUM

#### WHAT'S BENEATH THE QUESTION?

On some occasions, students find that they have confronted an issue that cannot be resolved by the deductive method. This can be exciting for them. Will cutting marginal tax rates cause people to work more? The answer is yes or no, depending on the premises underlying the work-leisure preferences incorporated into your model.
—JAMES MARSHALL, *Professor of Economics*

---

As Marshall implies, the very shape and direction of a thesis ultimately depend on a writer's awareness of the underlying premises. The danger of categorical thinking is not just that it overstates issues reductively, but worse, that it can leave an argument's operating assumptions concealed. The "real" category is so unquestioned that it is not even mentioned when the writer makes his or her claims. As a result, the ideas that would galvanize the formation of a good thesis remain hidden. As the following example illustrates, it is crucial for you to reason backward in a chain far enough to recognize your premises and the givens that underlie them.

## Reasoning Back to Premises: A Brief Example

Consider the rather fuzzy but not hopelessly overgeneral thesis "tax laws benefit the wealthy." No matter how you might develop this claim (moving it forward), you would get into trouble if you didn't also move backward to uncover the premises embedded in this thesis about the purpose of tax laws. The wording of the thesis seems to conceal an egalitarian premise: the assumption that tax laws should not benefit anyone, or, at least, that they should benefit everyone equally. But what is the purpose of tax laws? Should they redress economic inequities? Should they spur the economy by rewarding those who generate capital? You might go to the U.S. Constitution and/or legal precedents to resolve such questions, but our point here is that you would need to move your thesis back to this point and test the validity of the assumptions upon which it rests.

Regardless of the position you adopt as your thesis—attacking tax laws, defending them, showing how they actually benefit everyone, or whatever—you would risk arguing blindly if you failed to question what the purpose of tax law is in the first place. This testing of assumptions would, at the least, cause you to qualify and refine your thesis. (See Figure 3.1.)

Making deliberate and systematic use of the questioning of your own ideas and assertions as a means of evolving your thesis is the subject of the book's next chapter. We would like to anticipate that chapter here by demonstrating how reasoning back to premises—as a means of recognizing and fixing weak thesis statements—is also a means of finding and developing a thesis. This process that we've been describing as a corrective, in other words, is also an excellent way to generate and evolve ideas. In the sample essay that follows, notice how the writer's use of reasoning back to premises for the purpose of attacking what he sees as other writers' weak theses also generates his own argument at the same time.

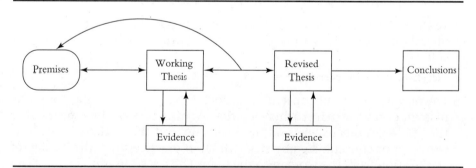

**FIGURE 3.1**

**Reasoning Back to Premises.**

A writer makes the thesis evolve by reasoning not only forward to conclusions but also backward to underlying assumptions (premises).

## EXTENDED
**ANALYSIS**

### A SAMPLE ESSAY: REASONING BACK TO PREMISES

Because the following essay originally appeared as a newspaper editorial, it is less expository (explanatory) than is much academic analytical writing. We have included it because it so clearly illustrates how a writer reasons forward to conclusions by reasoning backward to premises. The essay also illustrates how the strategies of refocusing binaries and qualifying claims operate in a finished piece of writing. As we noted earlier, these strategies, which are so useful for recognizing and fixing problems in writing, are equally useful for producing ideas.

As you read this editorial on the controversial rules established at Antioch College to govern sexual conduct among its students, try to focus not only on the content of the argument, but also on its form, that is, how the writer moves from one phase of his thinking to the next. Toward this end, we have added our own summaries of what each paragraph of the editorial accomplishes. At the end of the editorial we sum up the writer's primary developmental strategies in a form you can apply to your own writing.

#### PLAYING BY THE ANTIOCH RULES, BY ERIC FASSIN

**1** A good consensus is hard to find—especially on sexual politics. But the infamous rules instituted last year by Antioch College, which require students to obtain explicit verbal consent before so much as a kiss is exchanged, have created just that. They have provoked indignation (this is a serious threat to individual freedom!) as well as ridicule (can this be serious?). Sexual correctness thus proves a worthy successor to political correctness as a target of public debate.

*[Writer names the issue: the complaint that rules threaten individual freedom.]*

**2** Yet this consensus against the rules reveals shared assumptions among liberals, conservatives and even radicals about the nature of sex in our culture.

*[Writer identifies members of unlikely consensus.]*

**3** The new definition of consent at Antioch is based on a "liberal" premise: it assumes that sexual partners are free agents and that they mean what they say—yes means yes, and no means no. But the initiator must now obtain prior consent, step by step, which in practice shifts the burden of clarification from the woman to the man. The question is no longer "Did she say no?" but "Did she say yes?" Silence does not indicate consent, and it becomes his responsibility to dispel any ambiguity.

*[Writer identifies "freedom" premise underlying rules.]*

**4** The novelty of the rules, however, is not as great as it seems. Antioch will not exert more control over its students; there are no sexual police. In practice, you still do what you want—as long as your partner does not complain . . . the morning after. If this is censorship, it intervenes ex post facto, not a priori.

*[Writer questions premise that rules will actually control individual freedom more than do present norms.]*

**5** In fact, the "threat" to individual freedom for most critics is not the invasion of privacy through the imposition of sexual codes, but the very existence of rules. Hence the success of polemicists like Katie Roiphe or Camille Paglia, who argue that feminism in recent years has betrayed its origins by embracing old-style regulations, paradoxically choosing the rigid 1950s over the liberating 1960s. Their advice is simply to let women manage on their own, and individuals devise their own rules. This individualist critique of feminism finds resonance with liberals, but also, strangely, with conservatives, who belatedly discover the perils of regulating sexuality.

*[Writer locates "antiregulatory" (laissez-faire) premise beneath "freedom" premise.]*

**6** But sexual laissez-faire, with its own implicit set of rules, does not seem to have worked very well recently. Since the collapse of established social codes, people play the same game with different rules. If more women are complaining of sexual violence, while more men are worrying that their words and actions might be misconstrued, who benefits from the absence of regulation?

*[Writer attacks "laissez-faire" premise for ineffectiveness.]*

**7** A laissez-faire philosophy toward relationships assumes that sexuality is a game that can (and must) be played without rules, or rather that the invention of rules should be left to individual spontaneity and creativity, despite rising evidence that the rule of one's own often leads to misunderstandings. When acted out, individual fantasy always plays within preordained social rules. These rules conflict with the assumption in this culture that sex is subject to the reign of nature, not artifice, that it is the province of the individual, not of society.

*[Writer uncovers premise beneath "laissez faire": that sex is "natural" and thus outside social rules.]*

**8** Those who believe that society's constraints should have nothing to do with sex also agree that sex should not be bound by the social conventions of language. Indeed, this rebellion against the idea of social constraints probably accounts for the controversy over explicit verbal consent—from George Will, deriding "sex amidst semicolons," to Camille Paglia railing, "As if sex occurs in the verbal realm." As if sexuality were incompatible with words. As if the only language of sex were silence. For *The New Yorker*, "the [Antioch] rules don't get rid of the problem of unwanted sex at all; they just shift the advantage from the muscle-bound frat boy to the honey-tongued French major."

*[Writer develops linguistic implications of "natural" premise and questions assumption that sex is incompatible with language.]*

**9** This is not very different from the radical feminist position, which holds that verbal persuasion is no better than physical coercion. In this view, sexuality cannot be entrusted to rhetoric. The seduction of words is inherently violent, and seduction itself is an object of suspicion. (If this is true, Marvell's invitation "To His Coy Mistress" is indeed a form of sexual harassment, as some campus feminists have claimed.)

*[Writer develops further implications: attack on rules masks fear of language's power to seduce; writer questions equation of seduction with harassment.]*

**10** What the consensus against the Antioch rules betrays is a common vision of sexuality which crosses the lines dividing conservatives, liberals, and radicals. So many of the arguments start from a conventional situation, perceived and presented as natural: a heterosexual encounter with the man as the initiator, and the woman as gatekeeper—hence the focus on consent.

*[Writer redefines consensus as sharing unacknowledged premise that conventional sex roles are natural.]*

**11** The outcry largely results from the fact that the rules undermine this traditional erotic model. Not so much by proscribing (legally), but by prescribing (socially). The new model, in which language becomes a normal form of erotic communication, underlines the conventional nature of the old one.

*[Writer reformulates thesis about anti-rules consensus: rules undermine attempts to pass off traditional sex roles as natural.]*

**12** By encouraging women out of their "natural" reserve, these rules point to a new definition of sexual roles. "Yes" could be more than a way to make explicit the absence of "no"; "yes" can also be a cry of desire. Women may express demands, and not only grant favors. If the legal "yes" opened the ground for an erotic "yes," if the contract gave way to desire, and if consent led to demand, we would indeed enter a brave new erotic world.

*[Writer extends implications of thesis: rules could make sex more erotic rather than less free.]*

**13** New rules are like new shoes: they hurt a little at first, but they may fit tomorrow. The only question about the Antioch rules is not really whether we like them, but whether they improve the situation between men and women. All rules are artificial, but, in the absence of generally agreed-upon social conventions, any new prescription must feel artificial. And isn't regulation needed precisely when there is an absence of cultural consensus?

*[Writer questions standard by which we evaluate rules; proposes shift in terms from artificial versus natural to whether or not rules will improve gender relations.]*

**14** Whether we support or oppose the Antioch rules, at least they force us to acknowledge that the choice is not between regulation and freedom, but between different sets of rules, implicit or explicit. They help dispel the illusion that sexuality is a state of nature individuals must experience outside the social contract, and that eroticism cannot exist within the conventions of language. As Antioch reminds us, there is more in eroticism and sexuality than is dreamt of in this culture.

*[Writer culminates thesis: Antioch rules are good because they force us to acknowledge as a harmful illusion the idea that sex operates outside social conventions.]*

Despite its brevity, this editorial covers a daunting amount of ground—an examination of "shared assumptions among liberals, conservatives, and even radicals about the nature of sex in our culture" (Paragraph 2). The writer, given his audience (readers of the Sunday *New York Times*), allows himself more breadth in both his topic and his claims than he would if he were writing an article on the same subject in an academic setting, where he would narrow his focus in order to supply more analysis of issues and evidence. The aim of editorials like this one is not only to inform or persuade but also to provoke and entertain. Nevertheless, the strategies that direct the thinking in this piece are, with some minor exceptions, the same as they would be in a more extended analytical piece. They are central strategies that you can apply to many sorts of writing situations as a means of finding and developing your ideas.

## Strategies for Developing the Thesis by Reasoning Back to Premises

1. *Set up a claim but delay passing judgment on it.* In the concluding sentence of Paragraph 1, the word "target" suggests that the essay might attack Antioch's policy. In Paragraph 2, however, the writer does not go on to demonstrate what is threatening and potentially ridiculous about Antioch's sexual contract, but neither does he yet offer his own conclusion on whether the views he has thus far described are right or wrong. Instead, he slows down the forward momentum toward judgment and begins to analyze what the consensus against the Antioch rules might mean—the "shared assumptions" it reveals "among liberals, conservatives, and even radicals about the nature of sex in our culture." In fact, the writer spends the first three-quarters of the essay trying on various answers to this question of meaning.

(Note: A careful reader would recognize by tonal signals such as the exclamation mark in "serious threat to individual freedom!" that the opening paragraph has, in fact, begun to announce its position, albeit not overtly, by subtly overstating its opposite. It is not until later in the editor-ial, however, that we can clearly recognize that the writer is employing a common introductory strategy—defining the position you plan to argue against.)

2. *Decide what is really at issue by reasoning back to premises.* Rather than proceeding directly to a judgment on whether or not the Antioch rules threaten individual freedom, the writer carefully searches out the assump-tions—the premises and givens—underlying the attacks on the rules. (This is a key step missing from most inadequately developed analyses and argu-ments.) He proposes, for example, that underneath the consensus' attack on the rules and its defense of individual freedom lies a basic premise about sex and society—that sexuality should not be governed by rules because it is natural rather than cultural: "These rules conflict with the assumption in this culture that sex is subject to the reign of nature, not artifice, that it is the province of the individual, not of society."

3. *Be alert for terms that create false dichotomies.* As we discussed earlier in this chapter, a *false dichotomy* (sometimes called a *false binary*) inaccu-rately divides possible views on a subject into two opposing camps, forc-ing a choice between black and white, when some shade of gray might be fairer and more accurate. When reading, or when writing an argument of your own, it is a good strategy to question any either/or dichotomy. Con-sider whether its opposing terms define the issue fairly and accurately be-fore accepting an argument in favor of one side or the other.

Consider, too, how you might reject both choices offered by an either/or opposition in order to construct an alternative approach that is truer to the issues at hand. This is what the writer of the editorial does. He outlines and then rejects as a false dichotomy the consensus view that sexual behavior either is a province of individual freedom or is regulated by society:

| FALSE | Freedom versus regulation |
|---|---|
| DICHOTOMIES | Natural versus artificial |
| | No rules versus rules |

The writer argues instead that much of what we perceive to be natural is in fact governed by social rules and conventions, such as the notion of men as sexual initiators and women as no-sayers and gatekeepers. He pro-poses that what is really at stake is a different dichotomy, a choice between two sets of rules, one implicit and one explicit:

| REFORMULATED | Rules versus other rules |
|---|---|
| DICHOTOMIES | Implicit versus explicit |
| | Not working versus might work |
| | Based on "no" versus based on "yes" |

The editorial concludes that we need to decide questions of sexual be-havior—at Antioch and in the culture at large—by recognizing and evaluat-ing the relative merits of the two sets of rules rather than by creating a false dichotomy between rules and no rules, between regulation and freedom.

**4.** *In your conclusion, return to the position that you set out to explore and restate it in the more carefully qualified way you arrived at in the body of your essay:* "The choice is not between regulation and freedom, but between different sets of rules." Clearly, the essay's conclusion does not simply repeat the essay's introductory claims, but it does respond to the way in which the essay began. Notice that virtually the entire essay has consisted of reasoning back to premises as a way of arriving at new ways of thinking. This strategy is not a prelude to revision—it is the revision itself. This matter of sharing your thinking with readers as you develop and qualify your thesis is the primary subject of the next chapter.

In conclusion, this chapter has dealt with two distinct yet related problems that beset the construction of thesis statements: claims that advance no ideas and claims that advance ideas too sloppily. The solutions we have offered—to be skeptical of global generalizations, either/or formulations, and unexamined premises—may sound timid and even indecisive compared with the insistent pronouncements of daytime talk shows and televised political debates. But the effort you put into carefully formulating your ideas by checking for unstated assumptions and qualifying your claims will make you a stronger writer and thinker.

---

### APPLICATION:

## REASONING BACK TO PREMISES

1. In the following excerpt from a student paper, the writer advances various claims based on premises that are not articulated. Find the places in the paragraph where her operating assumptions—what she takes as givens—are left unsaid, and compile a list of these. First, try to find the premises that are articulated. On what premises, for example, does the writer base her argument that self-interest contributes to the health and growth of the economy as a whole?

In all levels of trade, including individual, local, domestic, and international, both buyers and sellers are essentially concerned with their own welfare. This self-interest, however, actually contributes to the health and growth of the economy as a whole. Each country benefits by exporting those goods in which it has an advantage and importing goods in which it does not. Importing and exporting allow countries to focus on producing those goods that they can generate most efficiently. As a result of specializing in certain products and then trading them, self-interest leads to efficient trade, which leads to consumer satisfaction.

Here is a fairly flexible procedure for reasoning back to premises in what you read.

*(continued)*

*Reasoning Back to Premises (continued)*

First, *paraphrase to rehearse the claim.* We would paraphrase the first two sentences as follows: self-interest motivates trade for all parties at all levels, and in this way self-interest serves not just individuals but also the good of the whole.

Next, *try on an oppositional stance* in order to gain some critical distance, regardless of how you feel about the subject. Assume, in other words, for the sake of argument, that the writer is wrong, and ask yourself, "Can I think of any exceptions to this claim?" How about a company that provides an essential service—like electricity or telephone lines—serving its self-interest by limiting its trade to people from whom it could expect the maximum return for the minimum investment? Would it help the health of the economy as a whole to have only people in urban areas served by phones and electricity, given that outlying areas are more expensive for the companies to serve?

Next, *determine how the writer is defining her key terms and then, again, assume that these definitions might be wrong* or at least incomplete, that there might be other ways of seeing the same thing. Your paraphrasing process and oppositional stance will help you to see these key terms—key concepts—upon which the argument depends. What are the various ways, for example, that the writer's key term, "self-interest," might be defined? Should she, for example, distinguish between long- and short-term self-interest? Does the question of self-interest change significantly if we are to assume either the existence or lack of government regulations? A small loss in cost effectiveness might be nothing compared with an expensive legal battle with the government.

What we are trying to do here is to imagine/reinvent the process of thinking by which a writer has arrived at a position (or alternatively, she may have leapt to this position without much thinking). It is incredibly useful in formulating and understanding arguments and positions to be able to "think backward" from either your own or another's position.

What we have attempted to do with the first two sentences of this paragraph you should now try to do with the three remaining sentences: paraphrase, assume something's wrong, define, and again assume something's wrong. *The result of this process should be a list of the premises upon which the writer's argument operates that have not been made sufficiently clear.*

Here are a few hints to get you started. The thinking in these last three sentences is quite abstract, so try assuming your oppositional stance by coming up with some concrete examples that would unsettle the writer's claims. What if the goods a country has are less valuable than the goods a country needs? Also pay attention to key terms, such as "advantage" and "consumer satisfaction."

2. In the following paragraph the writer has made her premises quite clear but has not acknowledged the possible validity of competing

*(continued)*

*(continued)*

premises. (It is this same neglect of other possible positions that Fassin makes the substance of his editorial against the detractors of the Antioch rules; use him as a model). If the writer could become more self-conscious of reasoning back to premises, she would be more likely to discover these competing claims and either qualify her argument or overtly counter these competing claims.

Field hockey is a sport that can be played by either men or women. All sports should be made available for members of both sexes. As long as women are allowed to participate on male teams in sports such as football and wrestling, men should be allowed to participate on female teams in sports such as field hockey and lacrosse. If women press for and receive equal opportunity in all sports, then it is only fair that men be given the same opportunity. If women object to this type of equal opportunity, then they are promoting reverse discrimination.

*First,* examine the paragraph and *lay out the writer's premises in your own words.* That is, find at least two key assumptions that she wishes us to accept. Hint: the writer assumes, for example, that fairness ought to take precedence over other possible values in the selection of athletic teams. More generally, think about how she is defining other of her key terms.

*Then lay out at least two competing premises*—the basis upon which a counterargument might be built.

## Key Words (in order of appearance)

| | |
|---|---|
| strong thesis | binary thinking |
| weak thesis | reductive thinking |
| dissonance | qualified claim |
| conventional wisdom | a given |
| cultural cliché | unacknowledged assumption |
| generic claims | reasoning back to premises |
| predicate | false dichotomy |
| categorical thinking | |

## Guidelines for Recognizing and Fixing Weak Thesis Statements

1.  Your thesis should make a claim with which it would be possible for readers to disagree. Find some avenue of inquiry rather than defending statements your readers would accept as obviously true.

2. Be skeptical of your first (often semiautomatic) response to a subject. It will often be a cliché or too broad. Avoid conventional wisdom unless you can qualify it or introduce a fresh perspective on it.

3. Convert broad categories and generic (fits anything) claims to more specific assertions. Find ways to bring out the complexity of your subject.

4. Submit the wording of your thesis to this grammatical test: if it follows the "abstract noun + *is* + evaluative adjective" formula ("the economic situation is bad"), substitute a more specific noun and an active verb that will force you to predicate something about a focused subject ("tax laws benefit the rich").

5. Examine and question your own terms and categories rather than simply accepting them.

6. Always work to uncover and make explicit the unstated assumptions (premises) underlying your thesis. Don't treat debatable premises as givens.

7. As a rule, be suspicious of thesis statements that depend on words such as *real, accurate, believable, right,* and *good.* These words usually signal that you are offering personal opinions—what "feels" right to you—as self-evident truths for everybody.

8. One way to assess the adequacy of a thesis statement is to ask yourself where the writer would need to go next to develop his or her idea. If you can't answer that question, then the thesis is still too weak.

9. Reason forward to conclusions by reasoning backward to premises.

# CHAPTER 4

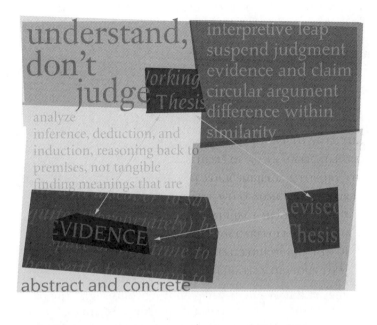

# MAKING THE THESIS EVOLVE

This chapter is the heart of the book. Let's begin it by rehearsing three key definitions from the preceding chapter:

- The *thesis* of an analytical paper is an idea about your subject, a theory that explains what some feature or features of your subject mean.
- A *strong thesis* comes from carefully examining and questioning your subject in order to arrive at some point about its meaning that would not have been immediately obvious to your readers.
- A *weak thesis* either makes no claim or makes a claim that does not need proving, such as a statement of fact or an opinion with which virtually all of your readers would most likely agree before reading your paper (for example, "exercise is good for you").

There are two key concepts that this chapter will add to the discussions of evidence and thesis that occupied Chapters 2 and 3:

First, a strong thesis moves, or in the language of this chapter's title, it *evolves*. By contrast, a weak thesis is *static* (fixed, unchanging). To say that a thesis evolves is to say that it changes as a paper progresses; it is progressively reformulated.

Second, the changes in the thesis are galvanized by its repeated encounters with evidence. Your ability to discover ideas and improve on them in revision, as we've argued in the preceding chapters, depends largely on your attitude toward evidence—on your ability to use it as a means of testing and developing your ideas rather than just (statically) confirming and reasserting them.

## Developing a Thesis Is More Than Repeating an Idea

Perhaps the most common misunderstanding about the thesis is that it must appear throughout the paper in essentially the same form. In fact, this absence of change is the primary trait of a weak thesis. Like an *inert* (unreactive) material, a weak thesis neither affects nor is affected by the evidence that surrounds it. By contrast, in nearly all good writing the thesis evolves by gaining in complexity and, thus, in accuracy as the paper progresses.

Even in cases where, for disciplinary reasons, the thesis itself cannot change, there is still movement between the beginning of the paper and the end. In the report format of the natural and social sciences, for example, the hypothesis as initially worded must be either confirmed or denied, but it still undergoes much conceptual development. Rather than simply being confirmed or rejected, its adequacy is considered from various angles, and alternatives are often proposed, along with alternative methodologies for testing the original hypothesis again. (A later section of this chapter, "The Evolving Thesis and the Final Draft," will discuss the differences but especially the similarities in the ways various disciplines locate and use thesis statements.)

Weak thesis statements (poorly formulated and inadequately developed) are most easily detected not only by their repetitiveness but also by their predictability. The writer says the same thing again and again, drawing the same overgeneralized conclusion from each piece of evidence ("and so, once again we see that . . ."). As the discussion of the 1 on 10 approach to evidence in Chapter 2 illustrated, a thesis that functions as an inert formula closes down a writer's thinking rather than guiding and stimulating it.

Inert thesis statements are, at least in part, products of a writer's adhering to an overly rigid and mechanical organizational scheme. Such schemes have the advantage of guaranteeing order, which they achieve by arranging everything under some single unifying point. Any data that do not conform, however, remains unnoticed or are studiously ignored. Thus, a thesis such as "government welfare programs stifle initiative" will tend to exclude welfare success stories, and a thesis such as "Marlowe's *Doctor Faustus* is a play about greed" will tend to screen out the main character's moments of generosity.

Where do writers get the idea in the first place that a thesis should be static? As the next section will discuss, in most cases they learned it early in their writing careers as part of a stubbornly inflexible organizational scheme known as five-paragraph form.

# What's Wrong with Five-Paragraph Form?

Perhaps the best introduction to what's wrong with five-paragraph form can be found in Greek mythology. On his way to Athens, the hero Theseus encounters a particularly surly host, Procrustes, who offers wayfarers a bed for the night, but with a catch. If they do not fit his bed exactly, he either stretches them or lops off their extremities until they do. This story has given us the word *procrustean,* which the dictionary defines as "tending to produce conformity by violent or arbitrary means."

Five-paragraph form is a procrustean formula that most students learn in high school. Although it has the advantage of providing a mechanical format that will give virtually any subject the appearance of order, it usually lops off a writer's ideas before they have the chance to form, or stretches a single idea to the breaking point. In other words, this simplistic scheme blocks writers' ability to think deeply or logically, restricting rather than encouraging the development of complex ideas.

A complex idea is one that has many sides. To treat such ideas intelligently, writers need a form that will not require them to cut off all of those sides except the one that most easily fits the bed. Most of you will find the basic five-paragraph form familiar:

1. An introduction that announces the writer's main idea, about which he or she lists three points
2. A paragraph on each of the three points
3. A conclusion beginning "Thus, we see" or "In conclusion" that essentially repeats the introduction

Here is an example in outline form:

Introduction: *The food in the school cafeteria is bad. It lacks variety, it's unhealthy, and it is always overcooked. In this essay I will discuss these three characteristics.*

Paragraph 2: *The first reason cafeteria food is bad is that there is no variety.* (Plus one or two examples—no salad bar, mostly fried food, etc.)

Paragraph 3: *Another reason cafeteria food is bad is that it is not healthy.* (Plus a few reasons—high cholesterol, too many hot dogs, too much sugar, etc.)

Paragraph 4: *In addition, the food is always overcooked.* (Plus some examples—the vegetables are mushy, the "mystery" meat is difficult to recognize, etc.)

Conclusion: *Thus, we see* (plus a restatement of the introductory paragraph).

Most high school students write dozens of themes using this basic formula. They are taught to use five-paragraph form because it seems to provide the greatest good—a certain minimal clarity—for the greatest number of students. But the form does not promote logically tight and intellectually aggressive writing. It is a meat grinder that can turn any content into sausage. The two major problems it typically creates are easy to see.

**1.** The introduction reduces the remainder of the essay to *redundancy:* The first paragraph tells readers, in an overly general and listlike way, what they're going to hear; the succeeding three paragraphs tell readers the same thing again in more detail, carrying the overly general main idea along inertly; and the conclusion repeats what the readers have just been told (twice). The cause of all this redundancy lies with the thesis. As in the preceding example, the thesis (cafeteria food is "bad") is too broad—an unqualified and obvious generalization—and substitutes a simple list of predictable points for a complex statement of idea.

**2.** The form arbitrarily divides content: why are there three points (or examples or reasons) instead of five or one? A quick look at the three categories in our example reveals how arbitrarily the form has divided the subject. Isn't overcooked food unhealthy? Isn't a lack of variety unhealthy? The format invites writers to list rather than to analyze, to plug supporting examples into categories without examining them or how they are related. Five-paragraph form, as is evident in our example's transitions ("first," "second," "in addition"), counts things off but doesn't make logical connections. At its worst, the form prompts the writer to simply append evidence to generalizations without saying anything about it.

The subject, on the other hand, is not as unpromising as the format makes it appear. It could easily be redirected along a more productive pathway. (If the food is bad, what are the underlying causes of the problem? Are students getting what they ask for? Is the problem one of cost? Is the faculty cafeteria better? Why or why not?)

Now let's look briefly at the introductory paragraph from a student's essay on a more academic subject. Here we can see a remarkable feature of five-paragraph form—its capacity to produce the same kind of say-nothing prose on almost any subject.

Throughout the film, *The Tempest,* a version of Shakespeare's play, *The Tempest,* there were a total of seven characters. These characters were Calibano, Alonso, Antonio, Aretha, Freddy, the doctor, and Dolores. Each character in the film represented a person in Shakespeare's play, but there were four people who were greatly similar to those in Shakespeare and who played a role in symbolizing aspects of forgiveness, love, and power.

The final sentence of the paragraph reveals the writer's addiction to five-paragraph form. It signals that the writer will proceed in a purely mechanical and superficial way, producing a paragraph on forgiveness, a paragraph on love, a paragraph on power, and a conclusion stating again that the film's characters resemble Shakespeare's in these three aspects. The writer is so busy demonstrating that the characters are concerned with forgiveness, love, and power that she misses the opportunity to analyze the significance of her own observations. Instead, readers are drawn wearily to a conclusion; they get no place except back where they began. Further, the demonstration mode prevents the writer from analyzing connections among the categories. The writer might consider, for example:

- How the play and the film differ in resolving the conflict between power and forgiveness
- To what extent the film and the play agree about which is the most important of the three aspects

These more analytical approaches lie concealed in the writer's introduction, but they never get discovered because the five-paragraph form militates against analytical thinking. Its division of the subject into parts, which is only one part of analysis, has become an end unto itself. The procrustean formula insists upon a tripartite list in which each of the three parts is separate, equal, and, above all, *inert.*

Here are two *quick checks* for whether a paper of yours has closed down your thinking through a scheme such as five-paragraph form:

1. *Look at the paragraph openings.* If these read like a list, each beginning with an additive transition like "another" followed by a more or less exact repetition of your central point ("another example is . . . ," "yet another example is. . ."), you should suspect that you are not adequately developing your ideas.
2. *Compare the wording in the last statement of the paper's thesis (in the conclusion) with the first statement of it in the introduction.* If the wording at these two locations is virtually the same, you will know that your thesis has not responded adequately to your evidence.

## Developing a Thesis through Successive Complications

The first step in finding a thesis is to recognize that one will not appear to you, ready-made, in the material you are analyzing. In other words, summarizing may help you to find an analytical thesis, but a restatement of some idea that is already clearly stated in your subject is not itself a thesis. The process of finding a thesis—an idea about the facts and ideas in your subject—begins only when you start to ask questions about the material, deliberately looking for a place where you detect some kind of problem to be solved.

More often than not, when inexperienced writers face a situation in which evidence seems to be unclear or contradictory, they tend to make one of two unproductive moves: they either ignore the conflicting evidence, or they abandon the problem altogether and look for something more clear-cut to write about. Faced with evidence that complicates your thesis, the one thing not to do is run away. The "problem" you have discovered offers *an opportunity to make your thesis evolve,* as the following example shows.

## Making a Thesis Evolve: A Brief Example

The savvy writer will actively seek out complicating evidence, taking advantage of opportunities to make apparent complications explicit in order to make the thesis more fully responsive to evidence. Let's revisit a sample thesis from the last chapter, "tax laws benefit the wealthy." If you were to seek out evidence that would complicate this overstated claim, evidence would press you to make some distinctions that the initial formulation of this claim leaves obscure. You would need, for example, to distinguish different sources of wealth and then to determine whether all or just some wealthy taxpayers are benefited by tax laws.

Do people whose wealth comes primarily from investments benefit less (or more) than those whose wealth comes from high wages? Evidence might also lead you to consider whether tax laws, by benefiting the wealthy, also benefit other people indirectly. Both of these considerations would necessitate some reformulation of the thesis. By the end of the paper, the claim that tax laws benefit the wealthy should have evolved into a more carefully defined and qualified statement that reflects the thinking you have done in your analysis of evidence. This is what good concluding paragraphs do—they reflect back on and reformulate your paper's initial position in light of the thinking you have done about it. (See Figure 4.1.)

But, you might ask, isn't this reformulating of the thesis something a writer does before he or she writes the essay? Certainly some of it is accomplished in your prewriting phase—the exploratory drafting and note-taking you do before you begin to compose the first draft of the essay. But your finished essay will necessarily be more than a list of conclusions. To an extent, all good writing reenacts the chains of thought that led you to your conclusions. Your revision process will have weeded out various false starts and dead ends that you may have wandered into on the way to your finished ideas, but the main routes of your movement from a tentative idea to a refined and substantiated theory should remain visible for readers to follow. (See "The Evolving Thesis and the

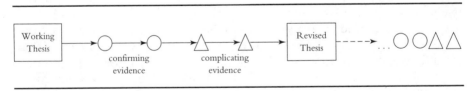

## FIGURE 4.1

### The Evolving Thesis.

A strong thesis evolves as it confronts and assimilates evidence. Depending on the evidence, the evolved thesis may expand or restrict the original claim. The dotted line after the revised thesis indicates that the process may need to be repeated a number of times.

---

**APPLICATION:**

## QUALIFYING OVERSTATED CLAIMS

Using the model of inquiry in the treatment of the example, "tax laws bene-fit the wealthy," seek out complications in three of the overstated claims in the following list. On the basis of these complications, restate each claim in a more carefully defined and qualified way.

Either alone or working in groups, list as many complications as you can think of. These complications might include conflicting evidence (which you should specify), and questions about the meaning or appropriateness of key terms. Then reformulate the claim in language that is more carefully qualified and accurate.

This process of making assertions, seeking out conflicting evidence and problems in terminology, and then using these conflicts and problems to re-vise the assertion is a primary movement of the mind in analytical writing.

Welfare encourages recipients not to work.

Religious people are more moral than those who are not.

Good defense beats good offense.

School gets in the way of education.

Herbal remedies are better than pharmaceutical ones.

Women are more sensitive than men.

Those who are not part of the solution are part of the problem.

The book is always better than the film.

We learn from the lessons of history.

Always start a paper by outlining.

Only standard English should be taught in the schools.

---

Final Draft" later in this chapter for a more extensive discussion of how much thesis evolution to include in your final draft.)

## The Reciprocal Relationship between Thesis and Evidence: The Thesis as Camera Lens

What we have said so far about the thesis does not mean that all repetition is bad or that a writer's concluding paragraph should have no reference to the way the paper began. One function of the thesis is to provide the connective tissue, so to speak, that holds together a paper's three main parts—beginning, middle, and end. Periodic reminders of your paper's thesis, its unifying idea, are essential for keeping both you and your readers on track.

But, as we've also argued, developing an idea requires more than repetition. It is in light of this fact that the analogy of thesis to connective tissue proves inadequate. A better way of envisioning how a thesis operates is to think of it as a camera lens. This analogy more accurately describes the relationship between the thesis and the subject it seeks to explain: while the lens affects how we see the subject (what evidence we select, what questions we ask about that evidence), the subject we are looking at also affects how we adjust the lens.

Here is the principle that the camera lens analogy allows us to see: the relationship between thesis and subject is *reciprocal*. In good analytical writing, especially in the early, investigatory stages of writing and thinking, *not only does the thesis direct the writer's way of looking at evidence; but also the analysis of evidence should direct and redirect (bring about revision of) the thesis.* Even in a final draft, writers are usually fine-tuning their governing idea in response to their analysis of evidence. (See Figure 4.2.)

The enemy of good analytical writing is the fuzzy lens—imprecisely worded thesis statements. Very broad thesis statements, those that are made up of imprecise (fuzzy) terms, make bad camera lenses. They blur everything together and muddy important distinctions. If your lens is insufficiently sharp, you are not likely to see much in your evidence. If you say, for example, that the economic situation today is bad, you will at least have some sense of direction, but the imprecise terms "bad" and "economic situation" don't provide you with a focus clear enough to distinguish significant detail in your evidence. Without significant detail to analyze, you can't develop your thesis, either by showing readers what the thesis is good for (what it allows us to understand and explain) or by clarifying its terms.

A writer's thesis is usually fuzzier in a paper's opening than it is in the conclusion. As we argued in our critique of five-paragraph form, a paper ending with a claim worded almost exactly as it was in the beginning has not made its thesis adequately responsive to evidence. The body of the paper should not only substantiate the thesis by demonstrating its value in selecting and explaining evidence, but also bring the opening version of the thesis into better focus.

## Six Steps for Making the Thesis Evolve

This section of the chapter presents an extended example that illustrates how the initial formulation of a thesis might evolve—through a series of complica-

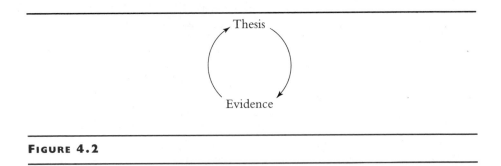

FIGURE 4.2

tions—over the course of a draft. Later in the chapter you will also find an extended example illustrating how to revise an exploratory draft in order to focus and develop a thesis.

The procedure for evolving a thesis can be described in the following steps:

1. *Formulate an idea about your subject.* This *working thesis* should be some claim about the meaning of your evidence that is good enough to get you started.
2. *See how far you can make this thesis go in accounting for evidence.* Use the thesis to explain as much of your evidence as it reasonably can. Try it on.
3. *Locate evidence that is not adequately accounted for by the thesis.* You will need to look actively for such evidence because the initial version of the thesis will incline you to see only what fits and not to notice the evidence that doesn't fit.
4. *Make explicit the apparent mismatch between the thesis and selected evidence.* Explain how and why some pieces of evidence do not fit the thesis.
5. *Reshape your claim to accommodate the evidence that hasn't fit.* This will mean rewording your thesis to resolve or explain apparent contradictions.
6. *Repeat Steps 2, 3, 4, and 5 several times.* Repeat them until you are satisfied that the thesis statement accounts for your evidence as fully and accurately as possible. This is to say that the procedure for making a thesis evolve is *recursive:* it requires you to go over the same ground repeatedly, formulating successive versions of the thesis that are increasingly accurate in wording and idea.

**As an overarching guideline, acknowledge the questions that each new formulation of the thesis prompts you to ask.** Remember that the thesis develops through successive complications. Allowing your thesis to run up against potentially conflicting evidence ("but what about this?") enables you to build upon your initial idea, extending the range of evidence it can accurately account for by clarifying and qualifying its key terms.

**EXTENDED**
**ANALYSIS**

### MAKING AN ESSAY EVOLVE THROUGH SUCCESSIVE COMPLICATIONS: AN EXAMPLE APPLYING THE SIX STEPS

Let's consider the stages you might go through within a more finished draft to evolve a thesis about a film. In *Educating Rita,* a working-class English hairdresser (Rita) wants to change her life by taking courses from a professor (Frank) at the local university, even though this move threatens her relationship with her husband (Denny), who burns her books and puts pressure on her to quit school and get pregnant. Frank, she discovers, has his own problems: he's a divorced alcoholic who is bored with his life, bored with his privileged and complacent students, and bent on self-destruction. The film follows the growth of Frank and Rita's friendship and the changes it brings about in their lives. By the end of the film, each has left a limiting way of life behind and has set off in a seemingly more promising direction. She leaves her constricting marriage, passes her university examinations with honors, and begins to view her life in terms of choices; he stops drinking and sets off, determined but sad, to make a new start as a teacher in Australia.

1. **Formulate an idea about your subject.**

> **Working thesis: "*Educating Rita* celebrates the liberating potential of education."** The film's relatively happy ending and the presence of the word "Educating" in the film's title make this thesis a reasonable opening claim.

2. **See how far you can make this thesis go in accounting for evidence.** The tentative thesis seems compatible, for example, with Rita's achievement of greater self-awareness and independence. You would go on to locate more data like this that would support the idea that education is potentially liberating. She becomes more articulate, allowing her to free herself from otherwise disabling situations. She starts to think about other kinds of work she might do, rather than assuming that she must continue in the one job she has always done. She travels, first elsewhere in England and then to the Continent. So, the thesis checks out as viable: there is enough of a match with evidence to make it worth pursuing.

3. **Locate evidence that is not adequately accounted for by the thesis.**

4. **Make explicit the apparent mismatch between the thesis and selected evidence.**
Other evidence troubles the adequacy of the working thesis, however: Rita's education causes her to become alienated from her husband, her parents, and her social class; at the end of the film she is alone and unsure about her direction in life. In Frank's case, the thesis runs into even more problems. His boredom, drinking, and alienation seem to have been caused, at least in part, by his education rather than by his lack of it. He sees his book-lined study as a prison. Moreover, his profound knowledge of literature has not helped him to control his life: he comes to class drunk, fails to notice or care that his girlfriend is having an affair with one of his colleagues, and asks his classes whether it is worth gaining all of literature if it means losing one's soul.

5. **Reshape your claim to accommodate the evidence that hasn't fit.**
*Question: what are you to do?* You cannot convincingly argue that the film celebrates the liberating potential of education, because that thesis ignores such a significant amount of the evidence. Nor can you "switch sides" and argue that the film attacks education as life-denying and disabling, because this thesis is also only partially true.

*What not to do.* Faced with evidence that complicates your thesis, you should not assume that it is worthless and that you need to start over from scratch. View the "problem" you have discovered as an opportunity to modify your thesis rather than abandon it. After all, the thesis still fits a lot of significant evidence. Rita is arguably better off at the end of the film than at the beginning: we are not left to believe that she should have remained resistant to education, like her husband Denny, whose world doesn't extend much beyond the corner pub.

*What to do.* Make apparent complications—the film's seemingly contra-dictory attitudes about education—explicit and then modify the wording of your thesis in a way that might resolve or explain these contradictions. You might, for example, be able to resolve an apparent contradiction be-tween your initial thesis (the film celebrates the liberating potential of ed-ucation) and the evidence by proposing that there is more than one ver-sion of education depicted in the film. You would, in short, start qualifying and clarifying the meaning of key terms in your thesis.

In this case, you could divide education as represented by the film into two kinds: enabling and stultifying. Then the next step in the develop-ment of your thesis would be to elaborate on how the film seeks to distin-guish true and enabling forms of education from false and stultifying ones (as represented by the self-satisfied and status-conscious behavior of the supposedly educated people at Frank's university).

> **Revised thesis:** *"Educating Rita* celebrates the liberating potential of enabling—in contrast to stultifying—education."

6. **Repeat Steps 2, 3, 4, and 5 several times.**
Having refined your thesis in this way, you would then repeat the step of see-ing what the new wording allows you to account for in your evidence. The re-vised thesis might, for example, explain Frank's problems as being less a prod-uct of his education than of the cynical and pretentious versions of education that surround him in his university life. You could posit further that, with Rita as inspiration, Frank rediscovers at least some of his idealism about education.

What about Frank's immigration to Australia? If we can take Australia to stand for a newer world, one where education would be less likely to be-come the stale and exclusive property of a self-satisfied elite, then the re-fined version of the thesis would seem to be working well. In fact, given the possible thematic connection between Rita's working-class identity and Australia (associated, as a former frontier and English penal colony, with lower-class vitality as opposed to the complacency bred of class privilege), the thesis about the film's celebration of the contrast between enabling and stultifying forms of education could be sharpened further. You might propose, for example, that the film presents institutional education as des-perately in need of frequent doses of "real life" (as represented by Rita and Australia)—infusions of lower-class pragmatism, energy, and optimism—if it is to remain healthy and open, as opposed to becoming the oppressive property of a privileged social class. This is to say that the film arguably ex-ploits stereotypical assumptions about social class.

> **Revised thesis:** *"Educating Rita* celebrates the liberating potential of enabling education, defined as that which remains open to healthy doses of working-class, real-world infusions."

Similarly, you can make your supporting ideas (those on which your thesis depends) more accurate and less susceptible to oversimplification by seeking evidence that might challenge their key terms. *Sharpening the language of your supporting assertions will help you develop your thesis.*

Consider, for example, the wording of the supporting idea that Ed-ucating Rita has a happy ending. Some qualification of this idea through consideration of possibly conflicting evidence could produce an adjustment in the first part of the working thesis, that the film cele-brates education and presents it as liberating. At the end of the film, Frank and Rita walk off in opposite directions down long, empty air-port corridors. Though promising to remain friends, the two do not become a couple. This closing emphasis on Frank's and Rita's alien-ation from their respective cultures, and the film's apparent insistence on the necessity of their each going on alone, significantly qualifies the happiness of the "happy ending."

Once you have complicated your interpretation of the ending, you will again need to modify your thesis in accord with your new observations. Does the film simply celebrate education if it also presents education as being, to some degree, incompatible with conventional forms of happiness? By emphasiz-ing the necessity of having Frank and Rita each go on alone, the film may be suggesting that in order to be truly liberating, education—as opposed to its less honest and more comfortable substitutes—inevitably produces and even requires a certain amount of loneliness and alienation.

> **Final version of thesis: "*Educating Rita* celebrates the liberating po-tential of enabling education (kept open to real-world, working-class energy) but also acknowledges its potential costs in loneliness and alienation."(See Figure 4.3.)**

## APPLICATION:

## FINDING AND TRACKING A THESIS

You can improve your handling of a thesis in your own writing by training yourself to become more aware of how the thesis operates in material you read. Choose a piece of reading, perhaps for a course, preferably an essay or article rather than an excerpt from a textbook. Then do the following:

1. Highlight all appearances of the paper's central claim (thesis) as these occur throughout. Be sure to make special note of the first and last appearances of the thesis. (For examples of how to do this, you may wish to look ahead in this chapter to the student essay in the section "Revising the Thesis in an Exploratory Draft," where the evolving claim is boldfaced throughout.)
2. Describe the evolution of the thesis—how it changes from paragraph to paragraph. (For a model, see the italicized restatements inserted at the ends of paragraphs in the essay "Playing by the Antioch Rules" near the end of Chapter 3.)

After you have gained some skill at finding and tracking a thesis, try this exer-cise with your own writing and in small groups. You can do this either late in the rough draft stage or, perhaps most usefully, at the point that you are prepar-ing to revise for formal resubmission a paper you had already "completed."

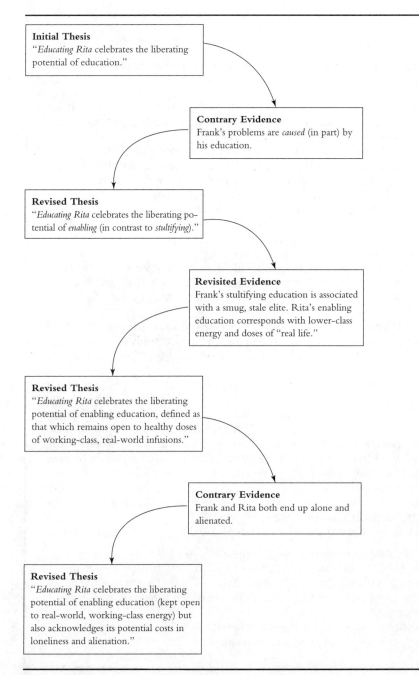

**Initial Thesis**
"*Educating Rita* celebrates the liberating potential of education."

**Contrary Evidence**
Frank's problems are *caused* (in part) by his education.

**Revised Thesis**
"*Educating Rita* celebrates the liberating potential of *enabling* (in contrast to *stultifying*)."

**Revisited Evidence**
Frank's stultifying education is associated with a smug, stale elite. Rita's enabling education corresponds with lower-class energy and doses of "real life."

**Revised Thesis**
"*Educating Rita* celebrates the liberating potential of enabling education, defined as that which remains open to healthy doses of working-class, real-world infusions."

**Contrary Evidence**
Frank and Rita both end up alone and alienated.

**Revised Thesis**
"*Educating Rita* celebrates the liberating potential of enabling education (kept open to real-world, working-class energy) but also acknowledges its potential costs in loneliness and alienation."

**FIGURE 4.3**

**Successive Revisions of a Thesis.**

An initial thesis about *Educating Rita* evolves through successive complications as it reexamines evidence in the film.

APPLICATION:

## TAKING A TRIAL THESIS THROUGH THE SIX STEPS

Having followed the evolution of a thesis through successive complications on the film *Educating Rita,* you should experiment with the process in writing and/or discussion with others.

You can do this exercise on your own or in the context of class or small group discussion. There are several possible sequences. You might start the exercise in writing and then complete it in discussion with others; or you might start the exercise in discussion and take it to completion in writing. Talking your way through the successive complications of an idea is useful, given that good analytical writing can be thought of as *dialogic:* it involves a conversation of sorts (a dialogue) that you have with yourself and with the views you assume your readers might have.

You can more easily learn to operate dialogically in writing by doing some "writing" out loud in dialogue with others. (In point of fact, it is virtually always a good idea to "talk your paper out" to somebody else while you are engaged in writing it.)

**The assignment:** formulate and evolve a thesis on a film or painting. Alternatively, you might use an episode of a television show or an advertisement. (Visual material is sometimes easier than print for groups to examine collaboratively.)

*First,* begin by formulating a variety of possible statements about the film or painting that could serve as a working thesis. These might be in answer to the question, "What is the film/painting about?" or "What does it 'say'?" Or you might return to the five critical moves introduced in Chapter 1, and formulate a thesis to explain a pattern of repetition or contrast you have observed. In any case, you shouldn't worry that these initial attempts will inevitably be overstated and thus only partially true—you have to start somewhere.

*Then,* discuss these statements with others in your class or group, and agree on one that seems good enough to serve as a working (tentative, trial) thesis. At this point you will have completed Step 1.

*Next,* follow the remainder of the six steps, listed again here for convenience:

1. Formulate an idea about your subject.
2. See how far you can make this thesis go in accounting for evidence.
3. Locate evidence that is not adequately accounted for by the thesis.
4. Make explicit the apparent mismatch between the thesis and selected evidence.
5. Reshape your claim to accommodate the evidence that hasn't fit.
6. Repeat Steps 2, 3, 4, and 5 several times.

## The Evolving Thesis and the Final Draft

Having achieved a final version of a thesis, *what next?* How and where do you locate the fully evolved thesis in the final draft? Why, for example, wouldn't a writer just offer this last statement of the thesis in his or her first paragraph, and then prove it?

## Placing the Thesis in the Final Draft

One answer to this last question has to do with the reader. The position articulated in the fully evolved thesis is in most cases too complex and too dependent on the various considerations that preceded it to be stated intelligibly and concisely in the introduction. By the time you get to drafting the final or close-to-final version of the essay, you will be writing with a reasonably secure sense of how you will conclude, but even then it is not always possible or desirable to try to encapsulate in an essay's first couple of sentences what it will actually take the whole essay to explain.

Another answer has to do with the writer: writing is a matter not just of communicating with and persuading readers but also of communicating with and persuading yourself. The evolution of a thesis involves the discovery of new ways of thinking brought about by successive confrontations with evidence. *The history of your various changes in thinking is, in many ways, the thesis of the essay (and in some cases, the essay itself).*

A fuller answer to the questions of where to locate the fully evolved thesis in a final draft and how much of its evolution to include involves two separate but related issues:

1. The location of the thesis statement in relation to the conventional shapes of argument—induction and deduction
2. The customary location of the thesis according to the protocols (ways of proceeding) of different disciplines

## The Evolving Thesis and Common Thought Patterns: Deduction and Induction

Put most simply, in a deductive paper a fairly full-fledged version of the thesis appears at the beginning; in an inductive paper, it appears at the end.

The standard definition of *deduction* is "based on inference from accepted principles" or "the process of drawing a conclusion from something known or assumed." A deductive argument draws out the implications—infers the consequences—of a position you already agree to. As a thought process, deduction reasons from the general to the particular.

For example, a deductive paper might state in its first paragraph that attitudes toward and rules governing sexuality in a given culture can be seen, at least in part, to have economic causes. The paper might then apply this principle, already assumed to be true, to the codes governing sexual behavior in several cultures or several kinds of sexual behavior in a single culture. The writer's aim would be to use the general principle as a means of explaining selected features of particular cases. (She or he would, it should be added, thereby articulate what is implicit in the general principle as well.)

A deductive paper will thus state at or near its beginning the general principle governing its examination of evidence. *It is important to note that the general principle stated at the beginning of the paper and the idea stated as the paper's conclusion are usually not the same.* Rather, the conclusion presents the idea that the writer has arrived at through the application of the principle.

An inductively organized paper typically begins not with a principle already assumed to be true, but rather with particular data for which it seeks to generate some explanatory principle. Whereas deduction moves by applying a generalization to particular cases in point, induction moves from the observation of individual cases to the formation of a general principle.

Ideally, the principle arrived at through inductive reasoning is not deemed a workable theory until the writer has examined all possible instances (every left-handed person, for example, if you wish to theorize that left-handed people are better at spatial thinking than right-handers). But because this comprehensiveness is usually impossible, the thesis of an inductive paper (principle or theory arrived at through the examination of particulars) is generally deemed acceptable if a writer can demonstrate that the theory is based on a reasonably sized sampling of representative instances. This matter of a writer's establishing the representativeness of his or her examples was taken up in detail in Chapter 2, "Analyzing Evidence." For present purposes, suffice it to say that a child who arrives at the thesis that all orange food tastes bad on the basis of squash and carrots has not based that theory on an adequate sampling of available evidence.

We have been arguing in this chapter that a thesis—the governing idea of an analysis—evolves through successive confrontations with evidence. *This evolution occurs, we now wish to add, whether the paper is primarily deductive or inductive.* Because the full version of the thesis statement doesn't emerge until the end in our "Six Steps for Making the Thesis Evolve," it might appear that the procedure will work only if you are thinking inductively. But in fact, as the *Educating Rita* example illustrates, in most cases induction and deduction operate in tandem. (See Figure 4.4.)

It's true that in some disciplines (philosophy, for example) something close to an entirely deductive pattern of argument prevails. But writers using this thought pattern still, for the most part, repeatedly rearticulate and develop their deductive claims through a series of smaller, essentially inductive moves. In other words, the examination of particular cases that constitute a writer's evidence will be both deductive and inductive—clearly reflective of the general principle but also leading to new formulations that will in various ways modify the general principle.

*There is some danger, then, in conceiving of deduction and induction as essentially separate and alternative ways of proceeding.* Whether the overall shape of the argument—its mode of progression—is primarily inductive or deductive, it will still gain in complexity from beginning to end. The statement with which you begin is not also the end.

## The Evolving Thesis as Hypothesis and Conclusion in the Natural and Social Sciences

It is important to note that the way a thesis functions in a paper—how fully it must be stated at the outset, for example, and what happens to it between

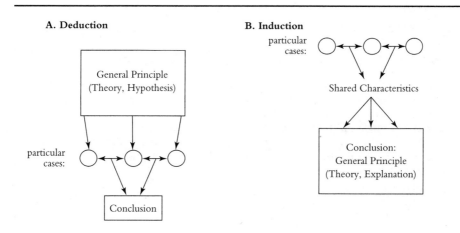

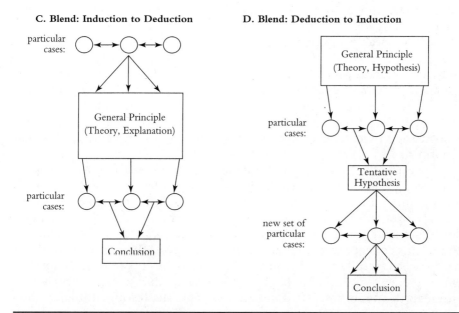

## FIGURE 4.4

### Deduction and Induction.

Deductive reasoning (A) uses particular cases to exemplify general principles and analyze their implications. Inductive reasoning (B) constructs general principles from the analysis of particular cases. In practice, analytical thinking and writing blend deduction and induction, starting either with particular cases (C) or a general principle (D).

**APPLICATION:**

**INDUCTION AND DEDUCTION EXERCISE**

Study a group of like things inductively. You might, for example, use greeting cards aimed at women versus greeting cards aimed at men; a group of poems by one author, ads created for one kind of product (jeans) or aimed at one target group (teenage girls). Make note of significant details you observe about the items in the group until you arrive at a generalization that you think is interesting and accurate. This generalization is your inductive principle.

Then use it to examine more data of the same kind deductively. That is, you will be using your claim not only to explain the pool of data but also to articulate more fully all that is implicit in the claim.

the beginning of the paper and the end—is not the same for all disciplines. Disciplinary differences appear largest as you move back and forth between courses in the humanities and courses in the natural and certain of the social sciences.

Broadly speaking, papers in the humanities are inclined to proceed inductively, and papers in the natural and social sciences deductively. The natural and social sciences generally use a pair of terms, *hypothesis* and *conclusion,* for the single term *thesis.* Because writing in the sciences is patterned according to the scientific method, writers in disciplines such as biology and psychology must report how the original thesis (hypothesis) was tested against empirical evidence and then conclude on this basis whether or not the hypothesis was confirmed.

The gap between this way of thinking about the thesis and the concept of an evolving thesis is not as large as it may seem. In fact, one of the chapter's main points—if not *the* main point—is that something must happen to the thesis between the introduction and the conclusion so that the conclusion does more than just reassert what had already been asserted in the beginning. To put this concept in the language of the sciences, the paper's hypothesis needs to be carefully tested against evidence, the results of which allow the writer to draw conclusions about the hypothesis's validity. So, in the sciences, although the hypothesis itself does not change, the testing of it and subsequent interpretation of those results produce commentary on and often qualifications of the paper's central claim.

So, in the sciences, successive reformulations of the thesis are less likely to be recorded and may not even be expressly articulated. But, as in all disciplines, the primary analytical activity in the sciences is to repeatedly reconsider the assumptions upon which a conclusion is based. (For an example of a paper using the scientific format, see "Formats in the Natural and Social Sciences" in Chapter 5, "Matters of Form.")

## VOICES FROM ACROSS THE CURRICULUM

### THE HYPOTHESIS IN THE SCIENCES

It should go without saying that if the empirical evidence doesn't confirm your hypothesis, you rethink your hypothesis; but it's a complex issue. Researchers whose hypotheses are not confirmed in fact often question their *method* ("if I had more subjects," or "a better manipulation of the experimental group," or "a better test of intelligence," etc.) as much as their hypothesis. And that's often legitimate. Part of the challenge of psychological research is its reliance on a long array of assumptions. Failure to confirm a hypothesis could mean a problem in any of that long array of assumptions. So failure to confirm your hypothesis is often difficult to interpret.

—**ALAN TJELTVEIT,** *Professor of Psychology*

❖ ❖ ❖

The thesis is usually presented in the abstract and then again at the end of the introduction. Probably the most frequent writing error is not providing a thesis at all. Sometimes this is because the student doesn't *have* a thesis; other times it is because the student wants to maintain a sense of mystery about the paper, as if driving toward a dramatic conclusion. This actually makes it harder to read. The best papers are clear and up front about what their point is, then use evidence and argument to support and evaluate the thesis. I encourage students to have a sentence immediately following their discussion of the background on the subject that can be as explicit as: "In this paper I will argue that although research on toxic effects of methyl bromide provides troubling evidence for severe physiological effects, conclusive proof of a significant environmental hazard is lacking at this time."

I am careful in my courses about my use of the term "hypothesis." I think it can mislead students into assuming that scientists always *start* with an idea about how something works. Frequently, that is not the case. Some of the best science starts with observation. Darwin's work on finches is a classic example. His ideas about adaptation probably derived *from* the observation.

—**BRUCE WIGHTMAN,** *Professor of Biology*

## The Evolving Thesis and Introductory and Concluding Paragraphs

When you are not using the hypothesis/conclusion format, final drafts often begin by predicting the evolution of their theses. Thus, the *Rita* paper might open with the claim that *at first glance* the film seems to celebrate the liberating potential of education. You could then lay out the evidence for this view and proceed to complicate it in the ways we've discussed.

What typically happens is that you lead (usually at the end of the first paragraph or at the beginning of the second) with the best version of your thesis that you can come up with that will be understandable to your readers without a lengthy preamble. If you find yourself writing a page-long introductory paragraph in order to get to your initial statement of thesis, try settling for a simpler articulation of your central idea in its first appearance. As you move through the paper, substantiate, elaborate on, test, and qualify your paper's opening gambit.

The most important thing to do in the introductory paragraph of an analytical paper is to lay out a *genuine issue,* which is to say, something that seems to be *at stake* in whatever it is you are studying. Preferably, you should select a complex issue—one not easily resolved, seeming to have some truth on both sides—and not an overly general one. Otherwise you run the risk of writing a paper that proves the obvious or radically oversimplifies.

Set up this issue as quickly and concretely as you can, avoiding generic (fits anything) comments, throat-clearing, and review-style evaluations. As a general rule, you should assume that readers of your essay will need to know on page 1—preferably by the end of your first paragraph—what your paper is attempting to resolve or negotiate.

The first paragraph does not need to—and usually can't—offer your conclusion; it will take the body of your paper to accomplish that. It should, however, provide a quick look at particular details that set up the issue. Use these details to generate a tentative *theory, a working hypothesis* about whatever it is you think is at stake in the material. The rest of the paper will test and develop this theory.

Your concluding paragraph will offer the more carefully qualified and evolved version of your thesis that the body of your paper has allowed you to arrive at. Rather than just summarize and restate what you said in your introduction, the concluding paragraph should leave readers with what you take to be your single best insight, and it should put what you have had to say into some kind of *perspective.* (See Chapter 5, "Matters of Form," for a more extended discussion of introductions and conclusions.)

## The Evolving Thesis and the Revision Process: Pursuing Implications by Asking "So What?"

The thinking process that allows a writer to arrive at and substantiate a supportable idea (thesis) about the meaning of evidence is markedly similar from discipline to discipline (even though the forms of final products in the various disciplines differ). The governing principle is that *the thesis evolves through a series of careful reformulations in light of the writer's analysis of evidence.*

Because the writing process is a way not just of recording but also of discovering ideas, writers often set out with one idea or direction in mind and then, in the process of writing, happen upon a potentially better idea that emerges in the draft. These emerging thoughts may lead to a markedly different thesis, or they may provide the means of extending your paper's original thesis well beyond the point you'd settled for in your exploratory draft.

Writers undertake this kind of conceptual revision in different ways. Some rely on repeatedly revising as they work their way through a first draft (which,

---

## VOICES FROM ACROSS THE CURRICULUM

### RECOGNIZING YOUR THESIS

For an analytical or interpretive historical essay, "thesis" is a conventional term and one of much value. The thesis usually is that point of departure from the surfaces of evidence to the underlying significance, or problems, that a given set of sources reveals to the reader and writer. In most cases, the thesis is best positioned up front, so that the writer's audience has a sense of what lies ahead and why it is worth reading on. I say "usually" and "in most cases" because the hard and fast rule should not take precedence over the inspirational manner in which a thesis can be presented. But the inspiration is not to be sought after at the price of the thesis itself. It is my experience, in fact, that if inspiration strikes, one realizes it only after the fact.

Recognizing a thesis can be extremely difficult. It can often be a lot easier to talk "about" what one is writing than to say succinctly what the thrust of one's discussion is. I sometimes ask students to draw a line at the end of a paper and then write one, at most two, sentences stating what they most want to tell their readers. My comment on that postscript frequently is: "Great statement of your thesis. Just move it up to your first paragraph."

—**ELLEN POTEET,** *Professor of History*

---

when finished, will be close to a final draft). Others move quickly through the first draft without much revision and then comprehensively rethink and restructure their work (sometimes two, three, or more times). Whatever mode of revision works best for you, the thinking processes we here define and demonstrate are the common denominators of the various stages of the writing process.

## EXTENDED
### ANALYSIS

#### REVISING AN ESSAY BY ASKING "SO WHAT?": AN EXAMPLE

Our previous extended example in this chapter, the analysis of the film *Educating Rita,* demonstrated how to formulate a thesis in your initial draft. Now we turn to a related task: how to focus and improve the thesis in an existing draft.

As you will see, we will be offering you a procedure resembling the "Six Steps for Making the Thesis Evolve" but now adapted to revision. A perennial problem of early drafts is that *they usually contain more than one potential thesis,* often without the writer's recognition. Often these competing theses are in fact partial reformulations of the writer's known thesis; they are further assertions that could help the writer make his or her thesis evolve if they could be recognized as such. Because they usually remain unrecognized, however, they are not adequately incorporated into the thesis.

The writer instead keeps going back to the same overly general claim, in effect ignoring his or her own additional observations.

The solution to this problem is contained in the overarching guideline we defined at the end of the "Six Steps": *recognize and articulate the ques-*

**FIGURE 4.5**

Diego Velázquez, *Las Meninas*, 1656. Approximately 10'5" x 9'. Museo del Prado, Madrid.

*tions that each new formulation of the thesis prompts you to ask.* The method for doing this is to ask *"So what?"* The key in revision is to ask this question not just of the evidence but also of your own observations. "So what?" is shorthand for questions such as "Where does this get me?," "What am I getting at here?," and "What (and what else) might I conclude about this feature of my evidence?"

Our means of demonstrating how writers focus and improve the thesis in an existing draft is to take you through the steps a writer would follow in revising a draft of an actual paper, in this case a student paper on a painting, *Las Meninas (The Ladies in Waiting)*, by the seventeenth-century painter Diego Velázquez. (See Figure 4.5.) As you read the draft, watch how the writer develops the claim made at the end of her first paragraph—that, despite the painting's complexity, it clearly reveals at least some of the painter's intentions (referred to elsewhere in the paper as what the painting is saying, what it suggests, or what the painter wants). We have highlighted each appearance of this claim in the text of the paper to make the writer's development of her central idea easier to follow.

## Velázquez's Intentions in *Las Meninas*

1 Velázquez has been noted as being one of the best Spanish artists of all time. It seems that as Velázquez got older, his paintings became better. Toward the end of his life, he painted his masterpiece, *Las Meninas*. Out of all of his works, *Las Meninas* is the only known self-portrait of Velázquez. There is much to be said about *Las Meninas*. **The painting is very complex, but some of the intentions that Velázquez had in painting *Las Meninas* are very clear.**

2 First, we must look at the painting as a whole. The question that must be answered is "Who is in the painting?" The people are all members of the Royal Court of the Spanish monarch, Philip IV. In the center is the daughter of the king who would eventually become empress of Spain. Around her are her *meninas* or ladies in waiting. These *meninas* are all daughters of influential men. To the right of the *meninas* are dwarfs, who are servants, and the family dog, who looks fierce but is easily tamed by the foot of the little dwarf. The more unique people in the painting are Velázquez himself, who stands to the left in front of a large canvas, the king and queen, whose faces are captured in the obscure mirror, the man in the doorway, and the nun and man behind the *meninas*. **To analyze this painting further, the relationship between characters must be understood.**

3 Where is this scene occurring? Well, most likely it is in the palace. But, why is there no visible furniture? **Is it because Velázquez didn't want the viewers to become distracted from his true intentions? I believe it is to show that this is not just a painting of an actual event.** This is an event out of his imagination.

4 Now, let us become better acquainted with the characters. The child in the center is the most visible. All the light is shining on her. **Maybe**

**Velázquez is suggesting that she is the next light for Spain and that even God has approved her by shining all the available light on her.** Back in those days there was a belief in the divine right of kings, so this just might be what Velázquez is saying.

5 The next people of interest are the ones behind the *meninas*. The woman in the habit might be a nun and the man a priest.

6 The king and queen are the next group of interesting people. They are in the mirror, which is to suggest they are present, but they are not as visible as they might be. Velázquez suggests that they are not always at the center where everyone would expect them to be.

7 The last person and the most interesting is Velázquez. He dominates the painting along with the little girl. He takes up the whole left side along with his gigantic easel. But what is he painting? As I previously said, he might be painting the king and queen. But I also think he could be pretending to paint us, the viewers. The easel really gives this portrait an air of mystery because Velázquez knows that we, the viewers, want to know what he is painting.

8 The appearance of Velázquez is also interesting. His eyes are focused out here. They are not focused on what is going on around him. It is a steady stare. Also interesting is his confident stance. He was confident enough to place himself in the painting of the royal court. **I think that Velázquez wants the king to give him the recognition he deserves by including him in the "family."** And the symbol on his vest is the symbol given to a painter by the king to **show that his status and brilliance have been appreciated by the monarch.** It is unknown how it got there. It is unlikely that Velázquez put it there himself. That would be too outright, and Velázquez was the type to give his messages subtly. Some say that after Velázquez's death, King Philip IV himself painted it to finally give Velázquez **the credit he deserved for being a loyal friend and servant.**

9 I believe that Velázquez was very ingenious by putting his thoughts and feelings into a painting. He didn't want to offend the king who had done so much for him. It paid off for Velázquez because he did finally get what he wanted, even if it was after he died.

---

Although its thinking is still underdeveloped, this version of the student's paper is a good exploratory draft. The writer has begun to interpret details and draw plausible conclusions from what she sees, rather than just describing (summarizing) the scene depicted on the canvas or responding loosely to it with her unanalyzed impressions.

The paper is typical of an early draft in several ways:

- It is written more for the writer—as a form of inquiry—than for readers. The writer reports her thoughts as they occur, but she doesn't always explain how she arrived at them or how they connect to each other.

- A recognizable thesis doesn't emerge until near the end (in Paragraph 8), probably at the point where the writer became able to formulate the idea her evidence has directed her to.
- The paper contains more than one potential thesis, ideas that are related but still inadequately connected. The writer appears not to be sufficiently aware that there are different ideas competing for control of the paper.
- The paper ignores the conflict between its various theses and some of its evidence.
- The writer tends to end paragraphs with promising observations and then walk away, leaving the observations undeveloped. Rather than draw out the implications of her observations, she halts her thinking too soon in order to move on to the next piece of evidence. As we will illustrate later, the writer can remedy this problem by querying her observations with the question "So what?".
- Typically, first drafts have undeveloped observations because they are not organized in a way that allows for development. See, for example, this writer's repeated return to paragraph openings using "next" and "also," which traps her into listing parallel examples rather than building connections among them. As a rule, the use of these terms (and "another") at points of transition traps writers in repetition, preventing them from seeing opportunities to advance their ideas. (See "What's Wrong with Five-Paragraph Form?" earlier in this chapter.)

## Revising the Thesis in an Exploratory Draft: Applying the Six Steps

In the following analysis of the *Las Meninas* essay, we use a version of the "Six Steps for Making the Thesis Evolve" that are modified slightly to demonstrate how they would work in revising a draft rather than arriving at one. We here offer them together in list form, and then apply them one by one to the essay.

As you read through our description of the revision process, remember that the primary activity of conceptual revision (as opposed to correcting and editing) is to make the thesis more fully responsive to evidence, either by formulating a mostly new thesis and beginning again or by modifying the existing thesis.

**Step 1:** check for multiple (often competing) theses.

**Step 2:** see how far you can make the theses go in accounting for evidence.

**Step 3:** locate evidence that is not adequately accounted for by each thesis.

**Step 4:** make explicit the apparent mismatch between the thesis and selected evidence.

**Step 5:** choose the claim that seems to account for the most evidence, and then reshape that claim to better accommodate evidence that doesn't fit.

**Step 6:** repeat Steps 2 through 5 as necessary.

### Step 1: Check for Multiple (Often Competing) Theses

*As a general rule, you should assume the presence of other theses or potential theses (in addition to the one you recognize) that you haven't yet seen.* In the *Las Meninas* paper, as is often the case in early drafts, no single idea emerges clearly as the thesis. Instead, we get three related but not entirely compatible ideas vying for control of the paper (all in Paragraph 8):

"I think that Velázquez wants the king to . . ."

**Thesis 1:** give Velázquez "the recognition he deserves by including him in the 'family'."

**Thesis 2:** "show that his [Velázquez's] status and brilliance have been appreciated."

**Thesis 3:** give Velázquez "the credit he deserved for being a loyal friend and servant."

These three ideas about the painter's intentions could be made to work together, but at present the writer is left with an uneasy fit among them.

### Step 2: See How Far You Can Make Each Thesis Go in Accounting for Evidence

Each of the three potential thesis ideas explains some of the evidence. The writer should try on each one to see what it helps to explain.

**Thesis 1:** painting as bid for inclusion in the family

| **Evidence explained:** | the painter's inclusion of himself with the family—the king, queen, and princess—in a fairly domestic scene |
|---|---|

**Thesis 2:** painting as bid for appreciation of status and brilliance

| **Evidence explained:** | prominence of easel and brush as well as painter's own prominence in the painting; painter's confident stare and the apparent decentering of king and queen; painting set in artist's studio—his space |
|---|---|

**Thesis 3:** painting as bid for credit for being loyal friend and servant

| **Evidence explained:** | painter's location of himself among other loyal servants at court (ladies in waiting, dog, and large dwarf) |
|---|---|

### Step 3: Locate Evidence That Is Not Adequately Accounted for by Each Thesis

### Step 4: Make Explicit the Apparent Mismatch between the Thesis and Selected Evidence

What happens when the writer begins to search for evidence that doesn't seem to be adequately accounted for by her various thesis formulations?

**Thesis 1:** painting as bid for inclusion in the family

| Evidence mismatches: | presence of painter among servants; foregrounding of servants in image and in painting's title (The Ladies in Waiting)—painter's large size (larger than king and queen) does not go with the idea of "inclusion," and emphasis on servants does not go with inclusion in royal family |

**Thesis 2:** painting as bid for appreciation of status and brilliance

| Evidence mismatches: | prominence of other servants in the painting; emphasis on family as much as or more than on artist himself—if bidding for status, painter would not present himself as just one of the servants, nor might he give so much attention to the princess (and the king and queen's regard for her) |

**Thesis 3:** painting as bid for credit for being loyal friend and servant

| Evidence mismatches: | painter's prominence; his confident stare; prominence of easel and brush; small size of king and queen (smaller than servants)—if painter wished to emphasize loyalty and service, his subordinate relationship to the more powerful at court, he would have made himself and the tools of his trade less important |

If you notice various mismatches of this sort in your draft—between thesis and evidence as well as among possible theses—your key revision strategy should be to view these inconsistencies as opportunities rather than faults. In an exploratory draft, varying interpretations of evidence are your raw material, records of your thinking that can be refined and developed in the next draft. The challenge is to recognize when an idea you've arrived at is a starting point rather than an end to the writing process.

### Step 5: Choose the Claim That Seems to Account for the Most Evidence, and Then Reshape That Claim to Better Accommodate Evidence That Doesn't Fit

When you've found conflicting or inadequately explained evidence, try using it to evolve your existing thesis rather than beating a too-hasty retreat. Although throwing out the old thesis and starting over may be what is needed, you should first try to use evidence that is not accounted for by your current thesis as a means of evolving it further.

To an extent, the writer of the *Las Meninas* paper has already begun the process of testing her thesis against evidence that seems not to fit and then using that evidence to reformulate her thesis. In Paragraph 4, for example, the writer comes up with a thought that might have become her thesis—that the painting was Velázquez's way of endorsing the divine right of kings. But evidence that the writer includes in Paragraphs 6 and 7 (the decentering of the king and queen as well as the prominence and confident stare of the painter) apparently caused her to drop the thought about divine right.

The direction in which the writer's thinking is moving—that the painting asks for someone's strengths to be recognized—is not an entirely new start, however. The shift she is apparently making but not yet overtly articulating is from the painting as showcase of royal power to the painting as showcase of the painter's own power.

The writer needs to press herself to be more aware of implications—both in her observations and in the evidence itself. She can do this by pushing her thinking with the question "So what?"

**Here are two of the "So what?" questions the writer's own draft should invite her to ask:**

- So what that the king and queen are small, but the painter, princess, and dwarf (another servant) are all large and fairly equal in size and/or prominence?
- So what that there are size differences in the painting? What might large or small size mean?

**Here are various possible answers to the "So what?" questions:**

- Perhaps the relative size and/or prominence of figures in the painting can be read as indicators of their importance or of what the painter wants to say about their importance.
- Perhaps the king and queen have been reduced so that Velázquez can showcase their daughter, the princess.
- Perhaps the size and physical prominence of the king and queen are relatively unimportant. In that case, what matters is that they are a presence, always overseeing events (an idea implied but not developed by the writer in Paragraph 6).
- Perhaps the painter is demonstrating his own ability to make the king and queen any size—any level of importance—he chooses. Although the writer does not overtly say so, the king and queen are among the smallest as well as the least visible figures.

Given these answers to the "So what?" questions, the writer should probably choose Thesis 2—that the painting is a bid for recognition of the painter's status and brilliance—because this thesis explains more of the evidence than anything else the writer has come up with so far. It explains, for example, the painter's prominence and the relative insignificance of the monarchs: that the painter, in effect, creates their stature (size, power) in the world through his paintings. Framed in a mirror and appearing to hang on the wall, the king and queen are, arguably, suspended among the painter's paintings, mere reflections of themselves—or, rather, the painter's reflection of them.

### Step 6: Repeat Steps 2 through 5 as Necessary

Repeat the steps until you are satisfied that the thesis statement accounts for your evidence as fully and accurately as possible. In the case of the *Las Meninas* essay, given the amount of rethinking that has already gone into it, the writer would probably want to concentrate most on repeating Step 2, seeing how far she can go in making her revised thesis account for additional evidence.

*Additional evidence explained by the thesis:* the presence of the large dwarf in the right-hand foreground. Positioned in a way that links him with the painter, the dwarf arguably furthers the painting's message and does so, like much else in the painting, in the form of a loaded joke: the small ("dwarfed" by the power of others) are brought forward and made big.

As you locate additional evidence that the thesis explains, it will continue to evolve, but only slightly. For example, if (as the writer has said) the painter is demonstrating that he can make the members of the royal family any size he wants, then the painting not only is a bid for recognition, but also can be seen as a playful though not-so-subtle threat: be aware of my power and treat me well, or else suffer the consequences. As artist, the painter decides how the royal family will be seen. The king and queen depend on the painter, as they do in a different way on the princess, with whom Velázquez makes himself equal in prominence, to extend and perpetuate their power.

*More evidence that fits the thesis:* in subverting viewers' expectations both by decentering the monarchs and concealing what is on the easel, the painter again emphasizes his power, in this case, over the viewers (among whom might be the king and queen if their images on the back wall are mirror reflections of them standing, like us, in front of the painting). He is not bound by their expectations and in fact appears to use those expectations to manipulate the viewers: he can make them wish to see something he has the power to withhold.

We emphasize before leaving this example that the version of the thesis that we have just proposed is not necessarily the "right" answer. Looked at in a different context, the painting might have been explained primarily as a demonstration of the painter's mastery of the tools of his trade—light, for example, and perspective. But our proposed revision of the thesis for the *Las Meninas* paper meets two important criteria for evaluating thesis statements:

1. It unifies the observations the writer has made.
2. It is capable of accounting for a wide range of evidence.

## Knowing When to Stop: How Much Revising Is Enough?

How do you know when you've done enough reformulating of your thesis? You can't know for sure when you've arrived at the best possible idea about your evidence unless you are working in a field in which your thesis can be tested against irrefutable evidence (carefully controlled experiments and statistical data, for example—though even these are rarely irrefutable). Getting the thesis to account for (respond to) all rather than just some of your evidence does not mean that you need to discuss every detail of the subject. Writers (rather like trial lawyers) must take care not to ignore important evidence, especially if it would alter their "case," but no analysis can address everything—nor should it. Your job as a writer is to select those features of your subject that seem most significant and to argue for their significance. An analysis says to readers, in effect, "These are the details that best reveal the nature and meaning of my subject, or at least the part of the subject that I am trying to address."

## Facing the Fear

As this chapter began by suggesting, your ability to formulate productive thesis statements and to improve on them in revision depends largely on your attitude toward evidence. And so we've demonstrated throughout the chapter how to use evidence as a means of testing and developing your thesis rather than just confirming the same static point again and again. What we have not yet fully acknowledged is a fear that writers sometimes express about making the thesis evolve by confronting significant differences and potential contradictions in the evidence. This fear commonly takes two forms:

1. The fear that including potentially contradictory evidence might encourage readers to reject or lose track of the writer's main idea
2. The fear that recognizing contradictions and complications in the evidence might cancel out all of a writer's potential ideas, leaving him or her with nothing to say

The "Organizational Scheme" and the "Guidelines" at the end of the chapter provide quick advice for negotiating these quite reasonable fears, but there are no easy antidotes.

In regard to quelling the first fear, you need to realize that avoiding evidence that doesn't easily fit with your thesis will not make that evidence go away. If your readers know of evidence that might challenge your thesis, but you fail to address it, the credibility of your argument will be damaged far more than if you had brought up that awkward evidence yourself and tried to account for it.

In regard to quelling the second fear, if you are worried that acknowledging complications in your evidence will cancel out your ideas, you need to understand that qualifying or limiting your claim is an advantage, not a liability. The resulting thesis, though smaller in scope, will be more accurate and therefore stronger.

Think of evidence as stars and of analysis as the means by which those stars may be connected into constellations. Thesis statements are the lines that allow us to see the constellations rather than just the separate stars. Writers are invariably constellating evidence, and the challenge, given that a star can be a part of more than one constellation, comes in drawing the lines—formulating the thesis—that connect the stars.

In any case, if you make a point of substantiating your claims, of showing the logic by which you moved from the evidence to the claim, and of acknowledging the possibility of other explanations, you will almost surely arrive at a plausible thesis. Your readers may not agree with you, but they will be able neither to dismiss your point nor to attack your method.

## The Evolving Thesis and Logic: Three Common Errors

The approach taken in this chapter to finding and developing a thesis emphasizes the importance of word choice—of carefully casting and recasting the language with which you categorize and name your ideas. Therefore, we've elected to define in this short section on logic errors a few thinking problems that stem from sloppy use of words, especially of those words that function as key terms in a thesis. (See Chapter 3, "Recognizing and Fixing Weak Thesis Statements," for more examples of thinking problems that weaken thesis statements.)

**Equivocation.** Equivocation confuses an argument by slipping between two different meanings for a single word or phrase. For example: "Only man is capable of religious faith. No woman is a man. Therefore, no woman is capable of religious faith." Here the first use of "man" is generic, intended to be gender neutral, whereas the second use is decidedly masculine. One specialized form of equivocation results in what are sometimes called **weasel words.** A weasel word is one that has been used so loosely that it ceases to have much of any meaning (the term derives from the weasel's reputed practice of sucking the contents from an egg without destroying the shell). The word *natural,* for example, can mean "good, pure, and unsullied," but it can also refer to the ways of nature (flora and fauna). Such terms—*love, reality,* and *experience* are others—invite equivocation because they mean so many different things to different people.

**Begging the question.** To beg the question is to argue in a circle by asking readers to accept without argument a point that is actually at stake. This kind of fallacious argument hides its conclusion among its assumptions. For example, "*Huckleberry Finn* should be banned from school libraries as obscene because it uses obscene language" begs the question by presenting as obviously true issues that are actually in question: the definition of *obscenity* and the assumption that the obscene should be banned because it is obscene.

**Overgeneralization.** An overgeneralization is an inadequately qualified claim. It may be true that some heavy drinkers are alcoholics, but it would not be fair to claim that all heavy drinking is or leads to alcoholism. As a rule, be wary of "totalizing" or global pronouncements; the bigger the generalization, the more likely it will admit of exceptions. See for example the process of qualifying a claim illustrated in the discussion of *Educating Rita.*

One particular form of overgeneralization, the **sweeping generalization,** occurs when a writer overextends the reach of the claim. The claim itself may be adequately qualified, but the problem comes in an overly broad application of that generalization, suggesting that it applies in every case when it applies only in some.

When you move prematurely from too little evidence to a broad conclusion, you have fallen into **hasty generalization.** Much of this book addresses ways of avoiding this problem, also known as an *unwarranted leap*. See "Demonstrate the Representativeness of Your Example" in Chapter 2.

# An "All-Purpose" Organizational Scheme

Although there is some mention of organization in this chapter in the section about locating a thesis in the final draft, we do not there offer an organizational scheme to replace the mechanical ones like five-paragraph form you may have become accustomed to using. The next chapter is all about ways to organize the various kinds of writing that assignments (topics) call for. But, before we leave this chapter, we offer the following all-purpose organizational scheme—a template—that you can adapt to many kinds of analytical writing.

1. Begin analytical papers by defining some issue, question, problem, or phenomenon that the paper will address. The initial version of your thesis—the working thesis—which usually appears somewhere in the paper's first or second paragraph (depending on the conventions of the discipline you are writing in), should offer a tentative explanation, answer, or solution that the body of your paper will go on to apply and develop (clarify, extend, substantiate, qualify, and so on).

2. Move into the body of your paper by querying your working thesis and other opening observations with the question "So what?," which is shorthand for questions like "What does this observation mean?" and "Where does this thesis get me in my attempts to explain my subject?"

3. Test the adequacy of your working thesis (initial claim) by seeing how much of the available evidence it can honestly account for. Expect to encounter evidence that doesn't fit your initial formulation of the thesis.

4. When you encounter obstacles, try other ways of responding to your subject and other terms for talking about it. This is how a thesis evolves, by assimilating obstacles and refining terms.

5. Arrive at a conclusion in which you reflect on and reformulate your paper's opening position in light of the thinking that your analysis of evidence has caused you to do. Culminate rather than merely restate your paper's main idea in the concluding paragraph. Do this by getting your conclusion to again answer the question "So what?," which, in the conclusion, is shorthand for questions like "Where does it get us to view the subject in this way?" or "What are the possible implications or consequences of the position the paper has arrived at?"

APPLICATION:

## APPLYING THE SCHEME

Examine the essay entitled "Playing by the Antioch Rules" at the end of Chapter 3 in light of the all-purpose organizational scheme.

How and to what extent does it follow this five-step thought pattern?

How does the introduction define the issue that is at stake? What is the working thesis?

How does the writer test the adequacy of the working thesis? How does he use apparent obstacles—evidence that seemingly contradicts his position—to evolve his idea?

How, finally, does the writer culminate (rather than just restate) his main idea? How does this conclusion answer the question "So what?"?

## Key Words (in order of appearance)

| | |
|---|---|
| evolving thesis | working thesis |
| static thesis | recursive |
| inert | dialogic |
| procrustean | deduction and induction |
| complex idea | hypothesis |
| redundancy | "So what?" |
| tripartite thesis | equivocation |
| additive transition | begging the question |
| reciprocal relationship | |

## Guidelines for Finding and Developing a Thesis

1. A thesis is an idea that you formulate and reformulate about your subject. It should offer a theory about the meaning of evidence that would not have been immediately obvious to your readers.
2. Look for a thesis by focusing on an area of your subject that is open to opposing viewpoints or multiple interpretations. Rather than attempting to locate a single right answer, search for something that raises questions.
3. Treat your thesis as a hypothesis to be tested rather than an obvious truth.
4. The body of your paper should serve not only to substantiate the thesis by demonstrating its value in selecting and explaining evidence, but also to bring the opening version of the thesis into better focus.

5. Evolve your thesis—move it forward—by seeing the questions that each new formulation of it prompts you to ask.

6. Develop the implications of your evidence and of your observations as fully as you can by repeatedly asking, "So what?"

7. When you encounter potentially conflicting evidence (or interpretations of that evidence), don't simply abandon your thesis. Take advantage of the complications to expand, qualify, and refine your thesis until you arrive at the most accurate explanation of the evidence that you can manage.

8. Arrive at the final version of your thesis by returning to your initial formulation—the position you set out to explore—and restating it in the more carefully qualified way you have arrived at through the body of your paper.

9. To check that your thesis has evolved, locate and compare the various versions of it throughout the draft. Have you done more than demonstrate the general validity of an unqualified claim?

CHAPTER 5

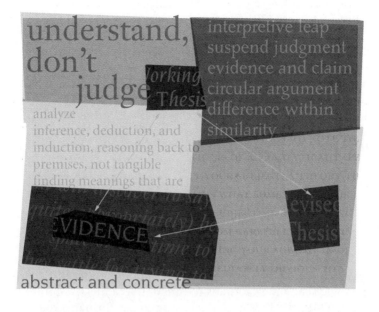

# MATTERS OF FORM

This is a chapter about form, about the way writers structure their ideas. We concluded the last chapter by offering what we termed an "all-purpose" organizational scheme for analytical writing. In this chapter we will consider the matter of organization and presentation in more detail and with more attention to the rules governing the forms of finished papers in the various disciplines.

The chapter is divided into three parts:

1. *Disciplinary formats,* along with underlying similarities among them
2. *Rhetoric:* how a writer's awareness of an audience's attitudes and needs affects the shape of her or his writing
3. *Introductions and conclusions,* two particularly important and challenging parts of virtually all organizational schemes

In our discussions of form we will also be using a more specialized term, *format,* to distinguish the organizational schemes to which the members of the various academic disciplines conform in their scholarly and professional writing. In biology and psychology, for example, formal papers and reports generally follow an explicitly prescribed pattern of presentation. Some other disciplines are less uniform and less explicit about their reliance on formats, but writers in these fields—economics, for example, or political science—usually operate within fairly established forms as well. Thus, we will also use the term *format* for organizational schemes that, although not rigidly discipline-specific, are often treated as formats in writing assignments, laying out the form of prospective papers in a series of steps.

Given the disciplinary emphasis in this chapter, you will be encountering a significant number of "Voices from Across the Curriculum" boxes that provide advice from faculty members in the natural and social sciences. This chapter is ultimately less concerned, however, with teaching you particular formats than with teaching you ways of thinking about and putting to the best use whatever formats you are asked to write in.

# The Two Functions of Formats: Product and Process

A problem for many writers when learning to use formats is that they see only the emphasis on the form of a final product and remain too little aware of the underlying logic that allows formats to function as a means of finding and exploring ideas. Thus, the first step in learning to use formats productively is to recognize that they have two related but separate functions: product and process.

- *As sets of rules for organizing a final product,* formats make communication among members of a discipline easier and more efficient. By standardizing the means of displaying thinking in a discipline, the format enables readers to compare more readily one writer's work to that of others in the field, because readers will know where to look for particular kinds of information—the writer's methodology, for example, or his or her hypothesis or conclusions.
- *As guides and stimulants to the writing process,* formats offer writers a means of finding and exploring ideas. The procedures that formats contain seek to guide the writer's thinking process in a disciplined manner, prompting systematic and efficient examination of a subject. The notion of formats functioning as aids to invention—idea generation—goes back at least as far as Aristotle, whose *Rhetoric* defined twenty-eight general "topics" (such as considering causes and effects or dividing a subject into parts) that speakers might pursue in order to invent arguments.

Most of the writing (and thinking) we do is generated by some kind of format, even if we are not aware of it. Writers virtually never write in the absence of any instructions. Accordingly, you should not regard most of the formats that you encounter simply as *prescriptive* (that is, strictly required) sets of artificial rules. Rather, think of them as descriptive accounts of the various *heuristics*—sets of questions and categories—that humans typically use to guide and stimulate their thinking.

Perhaps the biggest problem that formats can create for writers is a premature emphasis on product—on the form of the finished paper at the expense of process. In effect, the format can rush the writer through the successive steps, inhibiting his or her ways of generating the thinking that the finished product will present. In other words, the concept of formats as lines of inquiry (what Aristotle and other classical rhetoricians called the *topics of invention*) has become partially lost in the concept of formats as methods of arranging a finished piece of writing—imposing shape on a final product.

The primary goal of this first section of the chapter is to suggest the heuristic potential of formats. The conventional format of the scientific paper, for example, stimulates rather than merely containing thought. By stipulating the inclusion of a review of prior research, for instance, this format induces the writer to arrive at thoughtful connections between his or her work and earlier experiments. Nor is the process aspect of formats limited to the sciences. Poets, for example, have continued to write sonnets, one of the most highly structured poetic formats, for hundreds of years because the form has heuristic value. It guides the writer down certain pathways that provoke thought. The sonnet form itself—typically, fourteen lines of rhymed iambic pentameter, moving in one logical and/or emotional direction for eight lines and then shifting direction in the final six—lends itself to the production of certain kinds of thinking, such as putting ideas into dialogue with each other, establishing complex logical relationships.

Clearly, formats can both stimulate the writing process and organize the final product, but not when writers think of formats primarily as packaging and thus concern themselves with rigid adherence to form at the expense of more thoughtful exploration of content. At its worst, this *slot-filler approach* to formats can mislead writers into being more concerned with merely filling the slots than with analyzing the material they are filling them with. This was the primary problem we diagnosed in our critique of five-paragraph form in Chapter 4, "Making the Thesis Evolve." (Typically, this format has a three-part thesis, an example supporting each part, and a concluding paragraph that repeats the thesis from the introduction verbatim.)

Unlike five-paragraph form, most of the formats you encounter in college are roomier. They are not as rigidly overspecified, and they usually leave the writer space for more complex development of ideas. Generally speaking, formats provide a logic for dividing a subject into manageable parts and a logical order for dealing with each of these parts. To develop ideas in depth, writers need some means of deciding what to talk about when. Unlike more mechanical organizational schemes, good formats help you to order your thinking sequentially, according to relatively distinct phases.

## Using Formats Heuristically: An Example

As we observed in our discussion of formats as process and product, it is possible to lose sight of the heuristic value of formats and instead become concerned with formats primarily as disciplinary etiquette. The solution to this problem probably sounds easier than it is: you need to *find the space in a format that will allow it to work as a heuristic.* Consider how you might go about using even a highly specified organizational scheme like the following.

1. State the problem.
2. Develop criteria of adequacy for a solution.
3. Explore at least two inadequate solutions.
4. Explicate the proposed solution.
5. Evaluate the proposed solution.
6. Reply to anticipated criticisms.

The comforting feature of this format is that it appears to tell you exactly what to do. Thinking, however, especially in the early stages of the writing process, is rarely as linear as the six numbered steps in this example imply. As Chapter 4 was dedicated to illustrating, only by testing the adequacy of various solutions (Step 3), for example, is one likely to arrive at a clear statement of the problem (Step 1). And what if the problem has no solution or has several possible solutions, depending on the details of the problem? And couldn't the exploration of inadequate solutions (Step 3) be the best means of discovering criteria of adequacy (standards for determining the acceptability of a solution in Step 2)?

Our questions about the preceding format, however, also reveal your best means of using one like it:

- In the early stages of drafting, allow yourself to move freely among the steps in the order that best sparks your thinking. There will be time later to reassemble your results in the required order.
- Recognize that few formats insist on the writer's devoting exactly the same amount of space and attention to each of its steps or phases. If, for example, the relative inadequacy of any solution seems to you the most pressing thing you have to say, you should be able to place your emphasis accordingly.

This advice doesn't mean that you can select from the format the steps you wish to attend to and ignore the others. You can, however, lean more heavily on one of the steps and build your paper around it.

The best reason not to ignore any of the six steps in this problem/solution format we've been looking at is that *the format does have a logic,* although it leaves that logic unstated. The purpose of including at least two inadequate solutions (Step 3), for example, is to protect the writer against moving to a conclusion too quickly on the basis of too little evidence. The requirements that the writer evaluate the solution and reply to criticisms (Steps 5 and 6) are there to press the writer toward complexity, to prevent a one-sided and uncritical answer. In short, heuristic value in the format is there for a writer to use if he or she doesn't allow a premature concern with matters of form to take precedence over thinking.

## Formats in the Natural and Social Sciences

In some disciplines, especially in the natural sciences and psychology, the pattern of presentation for formal papers and reports is explicitly prescribed and usually mandatory. The American Psychological Association (APA), for example, issues a disciplinary style guide (now in its fourth edition) to which all writers seeking to publish in the field must adhere. In other disciplines, especially in the humanities and other of the social sciences, the accepted patterns of organization are less rigidly defined. Nonetheless, writers in these fields also operate to a significant extent within established forms, such as those set forth by the Modern Language Association (MLA) handbook. See the Appendix of this textbook for a guide to citation and reference lists in APA and MLA styles.

Because formats offer a means not only of displaying thinking in a discipline but also of shaping (in the sense of creating) it, the format that a discipline tacitly or overtly requires conditions its members to think in particular ways. Learning to use the format that scientists use predisposes you to think like a scientist. Learning the differences among the various disciplines' formats can help you recognize differences in *epistemology* (ways of knowing). As we stress elsewhere in this book, how you say something is always a part of what you say; the two can't be easily separated. Although knowing the required steps of a discipline's writing format won't write your papers for you, not knowing how writers in that discipline characteristically proceed can keep you from being read.

But by concentrating on apparent differences in the surface features of writing in the disciplines, it is possible to overemphasize difference and to underestimate the amount of common ground that the disciplines share. *The various formats across the disciplines,* the skeletons that both shape and display thinking in those disciplines, are actually quite similar. They usually contain most of the same elements, although these elements might be called by different names and arranged in slightly different orders. A science paper and a history paper, for example, both *advance a hypothesis, provide context for it, specify methodology, and support their claims by carefully weighing the evidence.*

You should note that the observations in the following "Voices" box apply to much but certainly not all of the writing that goes on in the sciences. In the following contribution, a professor of biology concentrates on the logic of the scientific format, but he also stresses its relative *flexibility*. That is, the distinctions among the various parts are not always as clear-cut as some students may think they are.

## VOICES FROM ACROSS THE CURRICULUM

## USING THE SCIENTIFIC FORMAT

There are firm rules in organizing scientific writing. Papers are usually divided into four major sections:

1. Introduction: provides context and states the question asked and the hypothesis tested in the study
2. Methodology: accurately describes experimental procedure
3. Results: states the results obtained
4. Discussion: analyzes and interprets results with respect to the original hypothesis; discusses implications of the results

As this organizational model should make clear, scientific papers are largely deductive with a shift to inductive reasoning in the discussion when the writer usually attempts to generalize or extend conclusions to broader circumstances.

Scientific papers also include an abstract, which is placed on the page following the title page. The abstract summarizes the question being investigated in the paper, the methods used in the experiment, the results, and the conclusions drawn. The reader should be able to determine the major topics in the paper without reading the entire paper. Compose the abstract after the paper is completed.

—**RICHARD NIESENBAUM,** *Professor of Biology*

❖ ❖ ❖

In writing in the social sciences, there is a standard plot with three alternative endings. The "Introduction" (a standard section of APA style) sets forth the problem, which the "Methods" section promises to address. The "Results" section "factually" reports the outcome of the study, with the "Discussion" section interpreting the results. "The data" are given the starring role in determining which ending is discussed in the "Discussion" section: hypothesis confirmed, hypothesis rejected, or hard to say. (I would say "which ending the author chooses" versus "which ending is discussed," but the data are supposed to be determinative, and the role of the author/investigator neutral.) Analytical thinking comes in setting up the problem and making sense of the results in conjunction with existing literature on the subject.

—**ALAN TJELTVEIT,** *Professor of Psychology*

❖ ❖ ❖

Experimental Psychology uses a very rigid format. I explain to the students the functions of the different sections for the reader. Once students start to read journal articles themselves, the functions of the sections become clear. Readers do not always want to read or reread the whole article. If I want to

*(continued)*

*(continued)*

replicate someone's research, I may read just the "Methods" section to get the technical details I need. I may read just the "Results" section to get a sense of the numerical results I might expect. On the other hand, I may not care about the details of how the experiment was run. I might just want to know if it worked, in which case I would read the first few sentences of the "Discussion" section. The format lets me know exactly where to find whatever I might be looking for, without having to read through the whole article.

—LAURA SNODGRASS, *Professor of Psychology*

## VOICES FROM ACROSS THE CURRICULUM

### TREATING THE FORMAT FLEXIBLY

Scientific format appears highly formulaic at first glance. Papers are generally broken into four sections: "Introduction" (What is this all about, what do we already know, why do we care?), "Experimental Procedures" (What did you actually do?), "Results" (What happened in your experiments?), and "Discussion" (What do you think it means, what are the remaining questions?). This breakdown is useful because it emphasizes the process of argument (introduction and results), providing evidence (results), and analysis (discussion). However, although this may seem different from writing in other disciplines, I think of it as a codification of basic analytical writing that is common in most disciplines.

A common mistake made by beginning and intermediate students is taking this breakdown too literally. In order to be comprehensible, the rules must be broken periodically. For example, results frequently must be referred to in the "Experimental Procedures" section in order to understand *why* the next procedure was performed. Similarly, the "Results" section frequently must include some discussion, so that the reader understands the immediate significance of the results, if not the broader implications. For example, the following sentences might appear in a "Results" section: "These data suggest that the p53 protein may function in repressing cell division in potential cancer cells. In order to test this possibility, we overexpressed p53 protein in a transformed cell line." The first sentence provides an interpretation to the results that is necessary to understand why the next experiment was performed.

—BRUCE WIGHTMAN, *Professor of Biology*

APPLICATION:

## FINDING THE PARTS IN THE SCIENTIFIC FORMAT

The four sections of the scientific report can be understood as responses to questions.

*Introduction:*    what is this all about? What do we already know? Why do we care?

*Methodology:*    what did you actually do?

*Results:*    what happened in your experiments?

*Discussion:*    what do you think it means? What are the remaining questions?

Find the places in each section of the following paper where the writer most clearly answers these questions. In the introduction, for example, find the sentences that seem to you to most clearly answer the question "Why do we care?" Underline or otherwise designate specific sentences in the report that answer each of the preceding questions.

---

### THE EFFECTS OF SEROTONIN AND SOCIAL EXPERIENCE ON THE TAIL FLIP RESPONSE OF THE CRAYFISH *CAMBARUS BARTONI*

INTRODUCTION

For the common crayfish *Cambarus bartoni,* the battle to establish and maintain dominance is of utmost importance to survival. Being at the top of the social hierarchy means getting first opportunity at food, access to shelter for protection, and an overall increased probability to survive long enough to procreate. When encountering a sufficiently large threat, the best defense for crayfish is to escape the situation and seek protection. The most common and effective mechanism for a quick escape is the tail flip—a quick and powerful reflex that whisks the crayfish away from possible danger. Thus, the ability to execute a strong and well-timed tail flip is advantageous and of inherent survival value. Because dominant crayfish possess certain survival advantages, one could also speculate upon the effect of social status on the tail flip response: that is, does the social standing of a particular creature affect the tail flip mechanism? As it turns out, dominant creatures *are* better at tail-flipping than subordinate creatures, according to previously conducted studies (Yeh & Edwards, 1996). The nature of the tail flip difference seems to be a question of sensitivity. Dominant crayfish are more sensitive to stimuli that initiate a tail flip, whereas subordinate crayfish are less sensitive. This reaction makes sense in terms of survival ability, because a dominant creature will have a better chance to detect and respond to possible or actual threats.

*(continued)*

*(continued)*

If there indeed is a difference in tail flip responses between organisms of different social experience, what could the underlying physiological cause of such a difference be? The architecture of the nervous system is relatively static in adult organisms, and so it seems improbable that social standing can affect the gross structure of the crayfish in terms of rewiring nerves and axons. However, the use of neurotransmitters and manipulation of neurotransmitter response allow a much more flexible and feasible mechanism for change. Previous studies looked at this issue and studied how the crayfish nervous system responds to serotonin under varying social constraints (Yeh et al., 1996).

Serotonin is a neurotransmitter found in the nervous system of many organisms, including *Procambarus clarkii*. Derived from tryptophan, this monoamine does not directly cause the opening of ionic channels in the postsynaptic membrane, but does create an excitatory postsynaptic potential (EPSP) through the use of secondary messengers (Fox, 1996, p. 166). The binding of the serotonin molecule to the proper serotonin receptor activates the secondary messenger system, and so the correct molecule/receptor interaction is vital in serotonin response.

Furthermore, Yeh et al. had discovered that there exist two different serotonin receptors in the crayfish: one that is excitatory in terms of tail flip response, and the other inhibitory in nature. A logical explanation of this tail flip variation may be that in dominant animals more excitatory receptors are being produced, whereas in subordinate animals inhibitory receptors are being produced. This would cause an observed increase and decrease in sensitivity to tail flip stimuli, respectively. If this is true, then dominant crayfish should express a lower threshold for the tail flip response, whereas subordinate crayfish should express a higher threshold for the same action.

## MATERIALS AND METHODS

Two adult crayfish were marked with paint and placed in a small aquarium containing only one rock shelter. After a short period of hierarchical determination (about one hour), the dominant crayfish claimed the area under the rock, whereas the subordinate crayfish remained exposed in the tank, avoiding the dominant crayfish. This pair was maintained for two weeks in this environment—every few days some of the fresh water was changed, and the animals were fed liver pieces. At the end of the two-week period, the animals were then prepared for sacrifice and experimentation. After being anesthetized on ice for a few minutes, the tail of the animal was removed just below the last pair of legs. The tail was then dissected dorsally to expose the ventral nerve cord. Exposed areas were kept wet with 5% Ringer's Solution to prevent ionic imbalance. Micromanipulators were then used to position small electrodes alongside the nerve cord in order to deliver electrical stimulation. After recording the minimal threshold stimulus that would elicit a tail flip response of a qualitative magnitude under normal conditions, approximately 1–2 mL of serotonin solution (5ug/mL) was applied to the nerve.

*(continued)*

*Finding the Parts in the Scientific Format (continued)*

Following a short bathing period, the new threshold stimulus that elicited a response of similar magnitude was recorded. The animal was then washed with saline; the procedure was repeated once more.

RESULTS

### TABLE 1.

Effect of serotonin on tail flipping behavior in *Cambarus bartoni* with respect to dominant and subordinate social status.

| SAMPLE GROUP 1 DOMINANT | | NUMBER OF SAMPLE 2 VALUES LESS THAN SAMPLE 1 | SAMPLE GROUP 2 SUBORDINATE | |
|---|---|---|---|---|
| 1. | 2.00 | 10 | 1. | 1.00 |
| 2. | 0.50 | 0 | 2. | 2.20 |
| 3. | 1.40 | 5 | 3. | 1.20 |
| 4. | 0.20 | 0 | 4. | 0.60 |
| 5. | 1.33 | 4.5 | 5. | 1.25 |
| 6. | 0.33 | 0 | 6. | 1.66 |
| 7. | 0.88 | 1 | 7. | 5.20 |
| 8. | 0.40 | 0 | 8. | 1.50 |
| 9. | 0.25 | 0 | 9. | 1.80 |
| 10. | 0.79 | 1 | 10. | 1.33 |
| 11. | 0.83 | 1 | 11. | 1.50 |
| 12. | 0.50 | 0 | 12. | 1.50 |
| 13. | 0.66 | 1 | 13. | 3.00 |
| 14. | 0.50 | 0 | 14. | 3.60 |
| C=23.5 | | | | |

Data is the percent change in strength of stimulus required to invoke tail-flipping after adding serotonin compared to before adding serotonin:

threshold voltage after adding serotonin

threshold voltage before adding serotonin

*Mann-Whitney U-test*

$$U_s \text{ (Mann-Whitney Statistic)} = 72.5$$

$$U_s > U_{.001[14,14]}$$

*(continued)*

*(continued)*

According to the Mann-Whitney U-test, the two samples are significantly different at P>.001.

### DISCUSSION

According to the Mann-Whitney U-test for the two data samples, there is a significant difference between dominant and subordinate threshold stimulus values at P=.001. The hypothesis tested was whether social experience can affect the tail flip response in crayfish. Dominant crayfish are better at tail-flipping than their subordinate counterparts in terms of sensitivity, and this phenomenon is thought to be regulated by serotonin's effect on the nervous system. At least two different types of serotonin receptors are present in the crayfish: one that responds to serotonin by enhancing the tail flip action, and one that inhibits it. Dominant animals are thought to express a higher amount of serotonin-enhancing receptors, whereas subordinates are thought to express more of the inhibiting receptors. If this is true, then in dominant creatures the minimum threshold stimulus level for a tail flip response should be lower than the threshold level for subordinates when serotonin is applied.

In order to eliminate voltage differences between data collection groups and equipment, a ratio of the threshold voltage after and before serotonin exposure was calculated. In dominant crayfish, this ratio should be less than one (serotonin lowered the threshold level). In subordinate crayfish, this ratio should be greater than one, indicating that exposure to serotonin increased the threshold voltage. The results of the statistical analysis suggest that the two sample groups are indeed different, supporting the preceding hypothesis.

### REFERENCES

Fox, S. I. (1996). *Human Physiology.* 158–172.

Preiser, R. (1996). Animal Watch: Chemistry and status. *Discover.* July, 34.

Yeh, S., Fricke, R., & Edwards, D. (1996). The effect of social experience on serotonergic modulation of the escape circuit of crayfish. *Science.* 271, 366–369.

## The Psychology of Form

Thus far in this book we have talked about form in relation to the search for meaning. We've demonstrated that some forms of arranging ideas (five-paragraph form, for example) have the effect of interfering with a writer's ability to have ideas in the first place. Whatever form one uses, we've argued, has to be flexible enough to allow ideas to evolve. The point is that there are various factors influencing a writer's decisions about forms and formats. These include both the demands of the subject itself and those of the discourse community within which the writing seeks to communicate.

We now wish to expand upon the role that a writer's sense of his or her *audience* plays in determining the formal presentation of ideas. We have entitled this section "The Psychology of Form" to emphasize the effects that a chosen form has on an audience—on its receptiveness to a writer's ideas, for example.

Since classical times, there have been numerous studies of this subject, known as *rhetoric*. The study of rhetoric is primarily concerned with the various means at a writer's (or speaker's) disposal for influencing the views of an audience. In early rhetorics, Greek and Roman writers divided these means into three large categories: *ethos, logos,* and *pathos.* We'll use these categories for organizing what we wish to say about the relationship between formal structures and audience.

1. *Ethos.* The category of ethos has to do with the character of the speaker or writer. The basic idea of ethos is that if an audience perceives a speaker to be ethical and rational, it will be inclined to perceive her or his argument as ethical and rational too. Thus, writers attend to the kind of *persona* they become on the page, the personality conveyed by the words and the tone of the words. In classical orations—the grandparent of virtually all speech and essay formats—the first section was always allotted to particular means of establishing an appealing persona, one that an audience would want to listen to and believe.

Although there are many ways of talking about ethos, this book has been implicitly recommending essentially the same kind of writer's persona throughout: one that is emotionally neutral and primarily interested in understanding a subject and conveying that understanding. Such a persona assumes a relationship of mutual interest with his or her audience and avoids a defensive posture toward the material or the audience.

2. *Logos.* This category has to do with the character of the thinking itself, which has been our emphasis throughout this book—the rational component, evident in the presence and development of the ideas.

3. *Pathos.* This category includes appeals to the audience's emotions—which writing does all of the time, whether a writer wants it to or not. It is possible to think of the form of a paper in terms of how it might negotiate, for example, the likes and dislikes, the hopes and fears, of its assumed audience. If, for instance, you were to present an argument in favor of a position with which you knew in advance that your audience was predisposed to disagree, you would probably choose to delay making a case for this position until you had found various ways of earning that audience's trust. By contrast, when presenting an argument to an audience of like-minded people, you would be much more likely to start out with the position you planned to advance.

In any piece of writing, there are always issues of authority. And so, as a writer you need to concern yourself with using language in a way that will incline readers to credit what you say. We have been advancing as the best source of authority your ability to show others why and how you take the evidence to mean what you say it does. A premise of this book is that rather than spend a lot of time cultivating a set of rhetorical strategies for defeating opponents, writers should find ways to make their thinking about evidence clear, and convincing in its clarity.

## How to Locate Concessions and Refutations

In the language of argument you *concede* whenever you acknowledge that a position at odds with your own does indeed have merit, even though you continue to believe that your position is the more reasonable one. A central idea of the preceding chapter, in fact, was that one option for dealing with views that conflict with your own is to use these to evolve your own position, thereby assimilating them. Another option is to argue against these views so as to *refute* their reasonableness.

There are several guidelines for locating concessions and refutations in an argument. It is a rule of thumb, for example, not to make your readers wait too long before you concede or refute a view that you can assume will already have occurred to them. To delay too long is to suggest that you are either unaware of the competing view or that you are afraid to bring it up.

In the case of short and easily managed concessions and refutations, writers often house these within the first several paragraphs, in this way clearing a space for the position they wish to promote. In the case of more complicated and potentially more threatening alternative arguments, writers take care to get their own positions clearly and convincingly expressed first, before addressing the alternatives. But to avoid the rhetorical problem of appearing to ignore substantive opposing arguments, writers will often give these a nod in brief, telling readers that they will return to a fuller discussion of these once they have laid out their own position in some detail.

Here are some more specific guidelines:

- Don't end on a concession. If you do include a concession in your concluding paragraph, be sure to return to your own position in the final sentences.
- If you state an opposing argument in your introduction, you should be sure that it can be accurately presented in the brief form that introductory paragraphs require. You need to be careful about turning the opposing view into a straw man—an easily knocked-down version of the opposing view. (We take up this subject in more detail in Chapter 7, "Using Secondary Sources.")
- One means of making sure you don't treat an opposing argument unfairly but also don't inadvertently convince your readers that this argument is better than your own is to concede the merits of this opposing view, but then argue that, in the particular context you are addressing, your argument is more important, more appropriate, and so forth.
- The placement of arguments has much to do with their relative complexity. Reasonably straightforward and easily explained concessions

and refutations can often all be grouped in one place, perhaps as early as the second or third paragraph of a paper. The approach to concession and refutation in more complex arguments does not allow for such grouping. For each part of your argument, you will probably need to concede and refute as necessary, before moving to the next part of your argument and repeating the procedure.

## Application:

## Locating Concessions and Refutations

The following passage is the second part of an introductory paragraph for an essay on the relation between gender inequality and language. The first half of the paragraph (only partly included) sets up the issue: whether or not the elimination of sexism in language (the use of male pronouns and words like *mankind,* for example, in circumstances applying to both men and women) through the use of generic pronouns (those that do not indicate gender, such as *they* rather than *he*) can help to eliminate gender exclusion in the culture. The paragraph names the two sides of the issue and moves from there to a tentative thesis.

What in the paragraph seems to you to be concession? Where do you find refutation? To be a concession, a writer's acknowledgment of a competing point of view should not be completely taken away by refutation. What, if any, language in the concession marks it as a position the writer is willing to acknowledge as creditable—rather than only seemingly creditable until he or she lays out a means of opposing it?

Refutations typically operate not just by revealing poor thinking or inadequate evidence in a competing point of view, but also by proposing the greater value of adopting another position. This is to say that refutations often concede an opposing argument's merits but refute their importance in favor of a position that seems to hold more promise under a given set of circumstances. What part of a competing argument is the refutation in the following passage still willing to concede? How is the refutation that the writer offers different from the position to which he concedes?

### Gender Inequality and Linguistic Bias

The more conservative side on this issue questions whether the elimination of generic pronouns can, in fact, change attitudes and whether intentionally changing language is even possible. The reformist side believes that the elimination of generic pronouns is necessary for women's liberation from oppression and that reshaping the use of male pronouns as generic is both possible and effective. Although the answer to the debate over the direct link between a change in language and a change in society is not certain, it is certain that the

*(continued)*

*(continued)*

attitudes and behaviors of societies are inseparable from language. Language conditions what we feel and think. The act of using *they* to refer to all people rather than the generic *he* will not automatically change collective attitudes toward women. These generic pronouns should be changed, however, because (1) the struggle itself increases awareness and discussion of the sexual inequalities in society, and, subsequently, this awareness will transform attitudes and language and because (2) the power of linguistic usage has been mainly controlled by and reserved for men. Solely by participating in linguistic reform, women have begun to appropriate some of the power for themselves.

## Organizing Comparisons and Contrasts

The first decision a writer has to make when arranging comparisons and contrasts is whether to address the two items being compared and contrasted sequentially in blocks or point by point. So, for example, if you are comparing Subject A with Subject B, you might first make all the points you wish to make about *A* and then make points about *B* by explicitly referring back to *A* as you go. The advantage of this format is that it is easier to use in early drafts when you're not yet sure what your major points will be. Writing about first one subject and then the other will allow you to use comparing and contrasting to figure out what you wish to say.

The disadvantage of this "Subject-A-then-Subject-B" format is that it can easily lose focus. If you don't manage to keep the points you raise about each side of your comparison parallel, you may end up with a paper comprised of two loosely connected halves. The solution is to make your comparisons and contrasts in the second half of the paper connect explicitly with what you said in the first half. What you say about Subject A, in other words, should set the subtopics and terms for discussion of Subject B.

The alternative pattern of organization for comparisons and contrasts is to organize by topic—not *A* then *B*, but *A1 B1, A2 B2, A3 B3*, and so forth. That is, you talk about both *A* and *B* under a series of subtopics. If, for example, you were comparing two films, you might organize your work under such headings as directing, script, acting, special effects, and so forth.

The advantage of this format is that it better focuses the comparisons, pressing you to use them to think with. The disadvantage is that organizing in this way is sometimes difficult to manage until you've already done quite a bit of thinking about the two items you're comparing. The solution, particularly in longer papers, is sometimes to use both formats. You begin by looking at each of your subjects separately to make the big links and distinctions apparent, and then focus what you've said by further pursuing selected comparisons one topic at a time.

Regardless of which format you adopt, the comparison/contrast will not really begin to take shape until you have done enough preliminary drafting to discover what the most significant similarities and differences are, and beyond that, whether the similarities or the differences are most important—whether, that is, your primary goal is to compare or to contrast. At this point, you can begin to operate according to the principle we will discuss next: climactic order. (See Chapter 6, "Making Your Response to Topics More Analytical," for further discussion of comparison and contrast.)

## Climactic Order

Climactic order has to do with arranging the elements in a list from least important to most important. The idea is to build to your best points, rather than leading with them and thereby allowing the paper to trail off from your more minor and less interesting observations.

But what are your best points? A frequent mistake that writers commit in arranging their points climactically—and one that has much to do with the psychology of form—is to assume that the best point is the most obvious, the one with the most data attached to it and the one least likely to produce disagreement with readers. Such writers end up giving more space than they should to ideas that really don't need much development because they are already evident to most readers.

A better strategy is to define as your best points those that are *most revealing, most thought-provoking, and often, at first glance, least obvious.* In such cases, if you followed the principle of climactic order, you would begin with the most obvious and predictable points—and ones that, psychologically speaking, would get readers assenting—and then build to the more revealing and less obvious ones. So, for example, if the comparisons between Film A and Film B are fairly mundane, but the contrasts are really provocative, you'd get the comparisons out of the way first and build to the contrasts.

Note that the principle of climactic order works with all kinds of organizational schemes, not just with comparison and contrast. If, for example, there are three important reasons for banning snowmobiling in your town, you might choose to place the most compelling one last. If you were to put it first, you might draw your readers in quickly (a principle used by news stories) but then lose them as your argument seemed to trail off into less interesting rationales. Similarly, if you have four examples for a point you wish to make, you might use the first three to pave the way for the one you take to be the best and most revealing.

One of the reasons that thesis statements, as we will discuss shortly, often contain subordinate clauses ("although there are many reasons to believe $x$, the most compelling reason is . . .") is that this sentence structure allows the reader to predict the paper's use of climactic order.

## How Thesis Shapes Predict the Shape of the Paper

Many thesis statements begin with a grammatically subordinate idea that they go on to replace or outweigh with a more pressing claim: "Although $x$ appears to account for $z$, $y$ accounts for it better." The paper then proceeds by following the pattern predicted by the order of clauses in the thesis statement, so that the first part of the paper would deal with the claims for *x*, and then move to a fuller embrace of *y* (usually in overt relation to *x*). (See Chapter 8, "Editing for Correctness," for a discussion of grammatical subordination.)

The advantage of this subordinate construction (and the reason that so many theses are set up this way) is that the subordinate idea helps you to define your own position by giving you something to define it against. It should at this point be evident that the thesis shape containing subordination and the paper that follows from it are both versions of climactic order.

In practice, using this shape will often lead you to arrive at some compromise position between the claims of both *x* and *y*. To use language that we explain elsewhere in this book, what appeared to be a *binary opposition*—"not *x*, but *y*"—emerges as a complex combination of the two.

Sometimes this combination is already evident in a thesis shape related to the subordination model: "not only *x*, but also *y*." Here the emphasis predicts that you will make *additional* claims, probably less obvious ones (*y*), after you have discussed *x*.

As you will see in our discussion of introductory paragraphs, one of the most important things to accomplish in an introduction is to locate an issue, question, or problem—something that is at stake—and then place it in an explanatory context. The subordinate clause of a thesis helps you to demonstrate that there is in fact an issue involved—that is, more than one possible explanation for the evidence you are considering—and thus a reason to be writing the paper in the first place.

Another thesis shape that can predict the shape of a paper is the *list*. This shape, in which a writer might offer three points and then devote a section to each, often leads to sloppier thinking than thesis statements containing both subordinate and independent clauses, because the list often does not sufficiently specify the connections among its various components. As a result, it fails to assert a relationship among ideas. The list is in fact the shape used by five-paragraph form—a form that (in Chapter 4) we conceded achieves considerable clarity of organization but at the (very high) cost of oversimplifying and derailing analysis.

---

### APPLICATION:

## THESIS SHAPES

As discussed earlier, thesis statements often contain more than one part, but, unlike the multiple parts of the thesis that merely lists, productive thesis statements arrange the parts in some sort of overt relation to each other. When you look at such a thesis statement, you can easily see the shape of the paper that will follow from it. What shape, for example, might a paper governed by the following thesis take? What will probably be discussed first,

*(continued)*

---

◥  *Thesis Shapes (continued)*

what second, and why? Which words in the thesis are especially predictive of the shape the paper will take?

Joinville paints, though indirectly, a picture of military, social, and political gain having very little to do with religion and more to do with race hatred and the acquisition of material wealth.

What paper shape (ordering of parts) does the following thesis predict? What are the various options the writer would have for ordering his or her follow-through on this thesis shape? With which part, for example, might the writer begin?

The reforms in education, created to alleviate the problems of previous reforms, have served only to magnify the very problems they were meant to solve.

---

## The Shaping Force of Transitions

The preceding critique of the list as an overly loose organizational format also applies to the connective tissue among the parts of an essay. Transitional wording like "another example of" or "also" at the beginning of paragraphs does tell readers that a new but related point or example will follow. But the organizational model at work in these sorts of additive schemes is again the list.

Instead, transitional wording should indicate more precisely the nature of the relationship with what has gone before in the paper. Language such as "similarly" and "by contrast" can sometimes serve this purpose. In many cases, however, fuller restatement of what has been said and its relation to what will come next is called for. Relatively inexperienced writers tend to underestimate the amount of productive restating that goes on in papers, often because they fail to see that the restatement is not just repetition. It is a "saying again" in different language for the purpose of advancing the writer's thinking further. *A good transition reaches backward, telling where you've been, as the grounds for making a subsequent move forward.*

Often this kind of transitional thinking will require you to concentrate on articulating how what has preceded connects to what will follow—the logical links. This is especially the case in the evolving rather than static model of thesis development advocated in Chapter 4, wherein the writer needs to keep updating the thesis as it moves through evidence.

**APPLICATION:**

## TRACKING TRANSITIONS

A good way to improve your use of transitions is to become more aware of them, not only in your own writing, but also in everything you read. In order to see how the transitions work as a skeleton for something you are reading, look at the openings of paragraphs. How do they typically begin? To what extent do the transitions move beyond being merely additive (as in "Another example of *x* is . . .")?

Read for words—both at the beginnings of and within paragraphs—that are directional indicators. *And,* for example, is a plus sign. It indicates that the writer will add something on, essentially continuing in the same direction. The words *but, yet, nevertheless,* and *however* are among the many transitional words that alert readers to a change in the direction of the writer's thinking. They might indicate, for example, the introduction of a qualification, a potentially contradictory piece of evidence, an alternative point of view, and so forth. Some additive transitions do more work than *also* or *another.* The word *moreover* is an additive transition, but it adds emphasis to the added point. The transitional sequence *not only . . . but also* restates and then adds information in a way that clarifies what has gone before. You can learn much about the shape of a writer's thinking and his or her method of connecting and advancing ideas by circling or underlining all of these directional indicators.

It is also instructive to underline or copy out paragraph openings as a means of seeing the paper's overall shape at a glance. Try this with some of your own recent work, or trade papers with other writers in a small group and do this with pieces of each other's writing. What, for example, does the following essay "skeleton" reveal about the way the writer is connecting her ideas?

Sexual harassment is evident among peers in two television shows.
In another show, *Martin,* there was additional evidence of harassment and exploitation by peers.
On television, sexual harassment and exploitation are also apparent in the workplace.
*Married with Children* also demonstrated sexual harassment in the workplace.
Although *Happy Days, Martin, The Mary Tyler Moore Show,* and *Married with Children* were produced for different audiences during various time periods, their depiction of women is quite similar. Each show clearly demonstrated sexual harassment and exploitation of women.

What might this writer do to improve these transitions in a final draft?
A good way to improve transitions at paragraph opening is to make them reach backward before moving forward, as in the following example: "The lack of convenience or awkwardness of using *he* over *they* is not the real issue for reformers. They worry that women are excluded from language and opportunity."

## Bringing It All Together

At the end of Chapter 4 we offered what we called an "all-purpose organizational scheme." The shape of this scheme was premised on the necessity of moving in steps through the analysis of evidence, but not simply additive steps. To briefly revisit the scheme, it involves:

> First, trying on an idea for its potential adequacy in explaining evidence, carrying that idea as far as you think it can go
>
> Next, deliberately confronting your idea with evidence that it cannot so easily account for
>
> Then, through repeated modification of the wording and shape of your idea, making it evolve—that is, making it grow and change as you bring it into contact with potentially conflicting data

This model of organizing your thinking requires a different kind of introduction and conclusion than you may have been taught to write. The next section of this chapter—on beginnings and endings—tells you what to do in introductory paragraphs once you accept that the introduction usually should not and cannot preview the paper's entire argument.

As you will see, disciplines vary in the kind and amount of concluding that writers are expected to provide up front. The philosophy paper, for example, usually locates the thesis—the paper's central claim—in the paper's first sentence and explains in the rest of the opening paragraph how the claim will be proved. Yet even this model of beginning, strictly deductive and conclusion-oriented, normally devotes more space to showing readers the issues that the rest of the paper will address than to dwelling on the answers. *Thus, all disciplines tend to agree that introductions raise issues rather than settle them.*

---

> ### APPLICATION:
>
> ### INFERRING THE FORMAT OF A PUBLISHED ARTICLE
>
> Often the format governing the organization of a published piece is not immediately evident. That is, it is not subdivided according to conventional disciplinary categories that are obeyed by all members of a given discourse community. Especially if you are studying a discipline in which the writing does not follow an explicitly prescribed format, such as history or literature or economics, you may find it illuminating to examine representative articles or essays in that discipline, looking for an implicit format. In other words, you can usually discern some underlying pattern of organization: the formal conventions, rules that are being followed even when these are not highlighted.
>
> *(continued)*

*(continued)*

You can do the following exercise either working alone or in groups. First you need to assemble several articles from the same or a similar kind of journal or magazine. "Journal" is the name given to publications aimed at specialized, usually scholarly, audiences, as opposed to general or popular audiences. *Time, Newsweek,* and the *New Yorker* are called *magazines* rather than *journals* because they are aimed at a broader general audience. *Shakespeare Quarterly* is a journal; *Psychology Today* is a magazine.

Having found at least three journal or magazine articles, study them in order to focus on the following question: *insofar as there appears to be a format that articles in this journal adhere to, what are its parts?*

How, for example, does an article in this journal or magazine typically begin and end? Does there seem to be a relatively uniform place in which these articles include opposing arguments? You will, in other words, be analyzing the articles inductively (reasoning from particular details to general principles—see Chapter 4 on induction): begin with the product and reason backward to the skeleton beneath the skin.

Note: if you are working with magazines rather than journals, you should probably further narrow the focus—to the *Time* cover story or to *The New Yorker*'s "Letter from [the name of a city]" or another such recurring feature story. Even gossip columns and letters of advice to the lovelorn in teen magazines adhere to certain visible though not explicitly marked-out formats.

Present your findings, individually or as a group (it could be an oral report or a paper or both). Cite particular language from at least two articles in support of your claims about the implicit format.

In presenting your evidence, keep the focus on the underlying form, showing how the different articles proceed in the same or similar ways. Don't let yourself get too distracted by the articles' content, even though there may be similarities here as well. Instead, work toward formulating a rationale for the format—what you take to be its psychology of form. In other words, you will need (for example) both to lay out the typical form of the introduction and to account for its taking that typical form.

## Introductions and Conclusions: An Overview

You have probably noticed that it is difficult to read attentively and do something else at the same time. Imagine, for instance, trying to read a book while playing a guitar. Depending on the difficulty of the reading matter and your powers of concentration, you might not be able even to listen to a guitar and read at the same time. When you read, you enter a world created of written language—a textual world—and to varying degrees, you leave the world "out there." Even if other people are around, we all read in relative isolation; our attention is diverted from the social and physical world upon which the full range of our senses normally operates.

In this context, now place yourself in the position of the writer, rather than a reader, and consider the functions that the introduction and conclusion provide for a piece of writing. Your introduction takes the reader from a sensory world and submerges him or her into a textual one. And your conclusion returns the reader to his or her nonwritten reality. Introductions and conclusions *mediate*—they carry the reader from one way of being to another. They function as the most *social* parts of any written communication, the passageways in which you need to be most keenly aware of your reader.

At both sites, there is a lot at stake. The introduction gives the reader his or her first impression, and we all know how indelible that can be. The conclusion leaves the reader with a last—and potentially lasting—impression of the written world you have constructed.

Most of the difficulties in composing introductions and conclusions arise in deciding how you should deal with the thesis. How much of it should you put into the introduction? Should your conclusion summarize the thesis or extend it? To an extent, as the first section of this chapter has argued, the formats or conventions of a particular academic discipline may arbitrate such questions. As with other aspects of writing analytically, there are no absolute rules for writing introductions and conclusions, but insofar as disciplinary conventions permit, *in introductions, play an ace but not your whole hand; and in conclusions, don't just summarize—culminate.*

## The Function of Introductions

As the Latin roots of the word suggest—*intro*, "within" + *ducere*, "to lead or bring"—an introduction brings the reader into a subject. Its length varies, depending on the scope of the writing project. An introduction may take a paragraph, a few paragraphs, a few pages, a chapter, or even a book. In most academic writing that you will do, one or two paragraphs is a standard length. In that space you should try to accomplish some or all of the following objectives:

- Define your topic—the issue, question, or problem—and say why it matters.
- Indicate your method of approach to the topic.
- Provide necessary background or context.
- Offer the working thesis (hypothesis) that your paper will develop.

An objective missing from this list that you might expect to find there is the admonition to engage the reader. Clearly, all introductions need to engage the reader, but this admonition is too often misinterpreted as a directive to be entertaining or cute. In academic writing, you don't need a gimmick to engage your readers; you can assume they care about the subject. You will engage them if you can articulate why your topic matters, doing so in terms of existing thinking in the field.

Especially in a first draft, the objectives just listed are not so easily achieved, which is why many writers defer writing a polished version of the introduction until they have completed at least one draft of the paper. At that point, you will usually have a clearer notion of why your subject matters and which aspect of your thesis to place first. Often the conclusion of a first draft becomes the introduction to the second draft. Other writers find that they can't proceed on a draft until they have arrived at an introduction that clearly defines the question or problem they plan to write about and its significance. For these writers, crafting an approach to the topic in the introduction is a key part of their planning phase, even though they also expect to revise the introduction based on what happens in their initial drafts.

In any case, the standard shape of an introduction is a *funnel*. It starts wide, providing background and generalization, and then narrows the subject to a particular issue or topic. Here is a typical example from a student paper:

> People have a way of making the most important obligations perfunctory, even trivial, by the steps they take to observe them. For many people traditions and rituals become actuality; the form overshadows the substance. They lose sight of the underlying truths and what these should mean in their lives, and they tend to believe that observing the formalities fulfills their obligation. This is true of professional ethics as they relate to the practice of examining and reporting on financial data—the primary role of the auditor.

The paragraph begins with a generalization in the first sentence (about making even important obligations perfunctory) and funnels it down in the last sentence to a working thesis (about the ethics of an auditor's report on financial data).

## Putting an Issue or Question in Context

In the following "Voices from Across the Curriculum" boxes, notice that implicit in all of the professors' accounts is some concept of the funnel. Rather than leaping immediately to the paper's issue, question, or problem, most effective introductions provide some broader context to indicate why the issue matters.

Although the various models we offer here differ in small ways from discipline to discipline, the essential characteristics that they share suggest that most professors across the curriculum want the same things in an introduction: *the locating of a problem or question within a context that provides background and rationale, culminating in a working thesis.*

## VOICES FROM ACROSS THE CURRICULUM

### PROVIDING AN INTRODUCTORY CONTEXT

Although some expression of the main idea should find its way into the opening paragraph, that paragraph is also an opportunity to draw the reader in, to convince the reader to read on. What's the point of your paper? Why is the issue important? Is it a theoretical issue? A policy issue? What's the historical context? Is this a question that represents a part of a larger question?

—JAMES MARSHALL, *Professor of Economics*

❖ ❖ ❖

I think it is important to understand that an introduction is not simply the statement of a thesis but also the place where the student needs to set a context, a framework that makes such a thesis statement interesting, timely, or in some other way important. It is common to see papers in political science begin by pointing out a discrepancy between conventional wisdom (what the pundits say) and recent political developments, between popular opinion and empirical evidence, or between theoretical frameworks and particular test cases. Papers, in other words, often begin by presenting *anomalies.*

I encourage students to write opening paragraphs that attempt to elucidate such anomalies by:

1. Stating the specific point of departure: are they taking issue with a bit of conventional wisdom? Popular opinions? A theoretical perspective? This provides the context in which a student is able to "frame" a particular problem, issue, and so forth. Students then need to indicate:

2. Why the wisdom/opinion/theory has become problematic or controversial by focusing on a particular issue, event, test case, or empirical evidence. (Here the students' choice of topic becomes important, because topics must be both relevant to the specific point of departure as well as to some degree controversial.) I would also expect in the opening paragraph(s):

3. A brief statement of the tentative thesis/position to be pursued in the paper. This can take several forms, including the revising of conventional wisdom/theory/opinion, discarding it in favor of alternative conceptions, or calling for redefinition of an issue and question. In papers directed toward current political practices (for instance, an analysis of a particular environmental policy or of a proposal to reform political parties), the thesis statement may be stated by indicating (a) hidden or flawed assumptions in current practices or (b) alternative reforms and/or policy proposals.

—JACK GAMBINO, *Professor of Political Science*

## Introductions of Reports in the Sciences

Earlier in this chapter we saw that formats control fairly strictly the overall form of standard writing projects in the natural sciences and psychology. The same is true for the standard form of introductions in these fields. The professors quoted in the "Voices" boxes to follow emphasize the importance of isolating a specific question or issue and locating it within a wider context. Notice, as you read these "Voices," how *little* the model for an introduction changes in moving from a social science (psychology) to the natural sciences of biology and physics.

### VOICES FROM ACROSS THE CURRICULUM

### INTRODUCTIONS IN THE SCIENCES

A paper usually starts by making some general observation or a description of known phenomena and by providing the reader with some background information. The first paragraphs should illustrate an understanding of the issues at hand and should present an argument for why the research should be done. In other words, a context or framework is established for the entire paper. This background information must lead to a clear statement of the objectives of the paper and the hypothesis that will be experimentally tested. This movement from broad ideas and observations to a specific question or test starts the deductive scientific process.

—**RICHARD NIESENBAUM,** *Professor of Biology*

In the sciences, the introduction is an especially important and also somewhat challenging section of the report for writers, because it requires writers *not merely to assemble but also to assimilate* the background of information and ideas that frame the writers' hypothesis.

### VOICES FROM ACROSS THE CURRICULUM

### ASSIMILATING PRIOR RESEARCH

The introduction is one of the hardest sections to write. In the introduction, students must summarize, analyze, and integrate the work of numerous other authors and use that to build their own argument.

*(continued)*

*Assimilating Prior Research (continued)*

Students frequently have trouble writing the introduction. They tend to just list the conclusions of previous authors. So-and-So said this, and So-and-So said this, and on and on in a list format. Usually, they *quote* the concluding statements from an article. But the task is really to read the article and *summarize* it in your own words. The key is to analyze rather than just repeat material from the articles so as to make clear the connections among them. (It is important to note that experimental psychologists almost never use direct quotes in their writing. Many of my students have been trained to use direct quotation for their other classes, and so I have to spend time explaining how to summarize without directly quoting or plagiarizing the work that they have read.)

Finally, in the introduction the students must show explicitly how the articles they have summarized lead to the hypothesis they have devised. Many times the students see the connection as implicitly obvious, but I require that they explicitly state the relationships between what they read and what they plan to do.

—**LAURA SNODGRASS,** *Professor of Psychology*

One distinctive feature of scientific papers is that they stipulate a separate prefatory section called the *abstract* that precedes the introduction. Authors also produce abstracts for papers in many other disciplines, but these are usually published separately—for example, in a bibliography, in a journal's table of contents, and so forth.

## VOICES FROM ACROSS THE CURRICULUM

## WRITING ABSTRACTS

The publishable paper in physics begins with an abstract, which briefly describes the experiment, gives the conclusion, and the significance of the work, all in three or four sentences. In the opening paragraph of the main body of the paper, the writer tries to put the work to be described into some larger context. This context usually includes reference to the following:

- similar experiments, which may, or may not, have shown similar results; and
- theoretical work suggesting the importance of the experiment, the scientific or technological significance of the work.

—**ROBERT MILLIGAN,** *Professor of Physics*

## Using Procedural Openings

In the interests of clear organization, some professors require students to include in the introduction an explanation of how their paper will proceed. Such general statements of method and/or intention are known as *procedural openings*. The discipline in which you are most likely to find this format is philosophy. It is also common in political science and sociology.

---

### VOICES FROM ACROSS THE CURRICULUM

#### PROCEDURAL OPENINGS

I encourage students to provide a "road map" paragraph early in the paper, perhaps the second or third paragraph. (This is a common practice in the professional journals.) The "road map" tells the reader the basic outline of the argument. Something like the following: "In the first part of my paper I will present a brief history of the issue. . . . This will be followed by an account of the current controversy. . . . Part III will spell out my alternative account and evidence. . . . I then conclude. . . ." I think such a paragraph becomes more necessary with longer papers.
    —**JACK GAMBINO,** *Professor of Political Science*

❖ ❖ ❖

I address the issue of an opening paragraph by having the students conceive of an opening section (or introduction) that tells the uninformed reader what's about to happen. I'll say, "Assume I know next to nothing about what lies ahead; so let me, the reader, know. 'My paper's about boom. In it, I'll do boom, boom. I chose this topic for the following reasons: boom, boom, boom.' Then get on with it."
    —**FREDERICK NORLING,** *Professor of Business*

---

As the professor of political science observes, the procedural opening is particularly useful in longer papers, where it can provide a condensed version of what's to come as a guide for readers. Also note that he advises placing it early in the essay but not in the first paragraph, which, as seen in his earlier contribution to this chapter, he reserves for "presenting anomalies." In other words, he seems to value the introduction primarily as a site for the writer's idea, "stating the specific point of departure," and, that taken care of, only secondarily as a place for forecasting the plan of the paper. These priorities bear mentioning because they imply *a potential danger in relying too heavily on procedural openings: that the writer will avoid making a claim at all.*

As Chapter 3 ("Recognizing and Fixing Weak Thesis Statements") argued, the statement of a paper's plan is not the same thing as its thesis, because the plan need not contain an idea about the topic that the paper will explore and defend. Consider the deficiencies of the following procedural opening:

> In this paper I will first discuss the strong points and weak points in America's treatment of the elderly. Then I will compare this treatment with that in other industrial nations in the West. Finally, I will evaluate the various proposals for reform that have been advanced here and abroad.

As an introduction, this paragraph does not fare well in achieving the four objectives listed on page 164. It identifies the subject, but it neither addresses why the subject matters nor suggests the writer's approach. Nor does it provide background to the topic or suggest a hypothesis that the paper will pursue. Even though a procedural opening is built into the conventions of report writing, these conventions also stipulate that the writer include some clear statement of the hypothesis, counteracting the danger that the writer won't make any claim at all.

## How Much to Introduce Up Front

A big problem with introductions lies with the amount of work that needs to get done in a limited space. To specify a thesis and locate it within a larger context, to suggest the plan or outline of the entire paper, and to negotiate first relations with a reader—that's a lot to pack into a paragraph or two. In deciding how much to introduce up front, you must make a series of difficult choices. We list some of these choices next, phrased as questions you can ask yourself:

- How much can I assume that my readers know about my subject?
- Which parts of the research and/or the background are sufficiently pertinent to warrant inclusion?
- How much of my thesis do I include, and which particular part or parts should I begin with?
- What is the proper balance between background and foreground?
- Which are the essential parts of my plan or road map to include?

### Typical Problems That Are Symptoms of Doing Too Much

If you consider the preceding questions, you can avoid writing introductions that try to do too much. When you try to do too much—to turn an introduction into a miniature essay—a variety of problems can result. In this context, consider the three problems discussed next as symptoms of overcompression, telltale signs that you need to reconceive, and probably reduce, your introduction.

#### Digression

*Digression* results when you try to include too much background. If, for example, you plan to write about a recent innovation in video technology, you'll need to monitor the amount and kind of technical information you include in your opening paragraphs. You'll also want to avoid starting at a point that is too far away from your immediate concerns, as in "From the beginning of time humans have needed to communicate."

The standardized formats that govern procedural openings in some disciplines can help you to avoid digressing endlessly. There is a given sequence of steps to follow for a psychology report of an empirical study, for instance. Nonetheless, these disciplinary conventions still leave plenty of room for you to lose your focus. You still must choose which contexts are sufficiently relevant to be included up front.

In those disciplines that expect you to include context but do not stipulate a specific manner of doing so, the number of choices is greater, and so is the danger that you will get sidetracked into paragraphs of background that bury your thesis and frustrate your readers. One reason that many writers fall into this kind of digression in introductions is that they misjudge how much their audience needs to know. As a general rule in academic writing, *don't assume that your readers know little or nothing about the subject.* Instead, use the social potential of the introduction to negotiate your audience, setting up your relationship with your readers and making clear what you are assuming they do and do not know.

### Incoherence

*Incoherence* results when you try to preview too much of your paper's conclusion. Incoherent introductions move in too many directions at once, usually because the writer is trying to conclude before going through the discussion that will make the conclusion comprehensible. The language you are compelled to use in such cases tends to be too dense, and the connections between the sentences tend to get left out, because there isn't enough room to include them. After having read the entire paper, your readers may be able to make sense of the introduction, but in that case, the introduction has not done its job.

The following introductory paragraph is incoherent, primarily because it tries to include too much. It neither adequately connects its ideas nor defines its terms.

> Twinship is a symbol in many religious traditions. The significance of twinship will be discussed and explored in the Native American, Japanese Shinto, and Christian religions. Twinship can be either in opposing or common forces in the form of deities or mortals. There are several forms of twinship that show duality of order versus chaos, good versus evil, and creation versus destruction. The significance of twinship is to set moral codes for society and to explain the inexplicable.

### Prejudgment

*Prejudgment* results when you appear to have already settled the question to be pursued in the rest of the paper. The problem here is logical. In the effort to preview your paper's conclusion at the outset, you risk appearing to assume something as true that your paper will in fact need to test. In most papers in the humanities and social sciences, where the thesis evolves in specificity and complexity between the introduction and conclusion, writers and readers can find such assumptions prejudicial. Opening in this way, at any event, can make the rest of the paper seem redundant. Even in the sciences, where a concise statement of objectives, plan of attack, and hypothesis are usually required up front, a separate "Results" section is reserved for the conclusion.

The following introductory paragraph *prejudges,* which is to say that it offers a series of conclusions already assumed to be true without introducing the necessary background issues and questions that would allow the writer to adequately explore these conclusions. As you may recall, this same paragraph first appeared in Chapter 3, "Recognizing and Fixing Weak Thesis Statements," as an example of writing that contains unstated assumptions. Prejudgment is in fact a case of assuming too much up front.

> Field hockey is a sport that can be played by either men or women. All sports should be made available for members of both sexes. As long as women are allowed to participate on male teams in sports such as football and wrestling, men should be allowed to participate on female teams in sports such as field hockey and lacrosse. If women press for and receive equal opportunity in all sports, then it is only fair that men be given the same opportunity. If women object to this type of equal opportunity, then they are promoting reverse discrimination.

The following advice also addresses the problem of prejudging—of making strong claims too early.

---

### VOICES FROM ACROSS THE CURRICULUM

#### AVOIDING STRONG CLAIMS IN THE INTRODUCTION

I might be careful about how tentative conclusions should play in the opening paragraph, because this can easily slide into a prejudging of the question at hand. I would be more comfortable with a clear statement of the prevailing views held by others. For example, a student could write on the question, "Was Franklin Delano Roosevelt a Keynesian?" What purpose would it serve in an opening paragraph to reveal without any supporting discussion that FDR was or was not a Keynesian? What might be better would be to say that in the public mind FDR is regarded as the original big spender, that some people commonly associate New Deal policies with general conceptions of Keynesianism, but that there may be some surprises in store as that common notion is examined.

In sum, I would discourage students from making strong claims at or near the beginning of a paper. Let's see the evidence first. We should all have respect for the evidence. Strong assertions, bordering on conclusions, too early on are inappropriate.

—**JAMES MARSHALL,** *Professor of Economics*

## Opening Gambits: Five Good Ways to Begin

The primary challenge in writing introductions, it should now be evident, lies in occupying the middle ground between overasserted prejudgment and avoidance of taking any position. There are a number of fairly common opening gambits that can help you to achieve an effective middle ground. An opening gambit in games such as chess is the initial move—not an announcement of the entire game plan.

### Gambit 1: Challenge a Commonly Held View

One of the best opening gambits is to *challenge a commonly held view.* This is what the economics professor advises when he suggests that rather than announcing up front the answer to the question at which the paper arrives, you convey that "there may be some surprises in store as that common notion is examined." This move has several advantages. Most important, it provides you with a framework *against* which to reply; it allows you to begin by *reacting.* Moreover, because you are responding to a known position, you have a ready way of integrating context into your paper. As the professor notes of the FDR example, until we understand why it matters whether or not FDR was a Keynesian, it is pointless to answer the question.

### Gambit 2: Begin with a Definition

In the case of the FDR example, a writer would probably include another common introductory gambit, *defining* Keynesianism. Beginning with a definition is a reliable way to introduce a topic, so long as that definition has some significance for the discussion to follow. If the definition doesn't do any conceptual work in the introduction, the definition gambit becomes a pointless cliché.

### Gambit 3: Offer a Working Hypothesis

But, you may be wondering, where is the thesis in the FDR example? As the economics professor suggests, you are often better off introducing a *working hypothesis*—an opening claim, sometimes in the form of a question, that stimulates the analytical process—instead of offering some full declaration of the conclusion. The introduction he envisions, for example, implies that the question of FDR's Keynesianism is not as simple as is commonly thought, further implying that the common association of "New Deal policies with general conceptions of Keynesianism" is, to some extent, false.

### Gambit 4: Lead with Your Second-Best Example

Another versatile opening gambit, where disciplinary conventions allow, is to *use your second-best example to set up the issue or question* that you later develop in depth with your best example. This gambit is especially useful in papers that proceed inductively on the strength of representative examples. As you are assembling evidence in the outlining and prewriting stage, in many cases you will accumulate a number of examples that illustrate the same basic point. For example, several battles might illustrate a particular general's military strategy; several primaries might exemplify how a particular candidate tailors his or her speeches to appeal to the religious right; several scenes might show how a particular playwright romanticizes the working class, and so on.

Save the best example to receive the most analytical attention in your paper. If you were to present this example in the introduction, you would risk making the rest of the essay vaguely repetitive. A quick close-up of another example will strengthen your argument or interpretation. By using a different example to raise the issues, you suggest that the phenomenon exemplified is not an isolated case and that the major example you will eventually concentrate upon is indeed representative.

What kind of example should you choose? By calling it "second best," we mean to suggest only that it should be another resonant instance of whatever issue or question you have chosen to focus upon. Given its location up front and its function to introduce the larger issues to which it points, you should handle it more simply than subsequent examples. That way your readers can get their bearings before you take them into a more in-depth analysis of your best example in the body of your paper.

### Gambit 5: Exemplify the Topic with a Narrative

One more opening gambit that is common in the humanities and social sciences is the *narrative opening*. The narrative introduces a short, pertinent, and vivid story or anecdote that exemplifies a key aspect of your topic. Although generally not permissible in formal reports of the natural and social sciences, narrative openings are common across the curriculum in virtually all other kinds of writing. Here is an example from a student paper in psychology:

> In the past fifteen years, issues surrounding AIDS have incited many people to examine their thoughts and feelings about homosexuality. As a result, instances of prejudice and discrimination toward gays, lesbians, and bisexuals have risen recently (Herek 1989). Although some instances are sufficiently damaging to warrant criminal charges, other less serious instances of prejudice occur every day. Nonetheless, they demonstrate a problem with our society that needs to be addressed. I witnessed one of these subtle demonstrations of prejudice in a social psychology class. The topic of the class was love and relationships, how they develop, endure, and deteriorate. Although the professor had not specifically stated it previously, the information being presented was relevant to homosexual relationships as well as heterosexual ones. At one point during her lecture, the professor was presenting an example using a hypothetical sorority member. The professor, in passing, referred to the sorority member's love relationship partner as a "she." This reference to a homosexual relationship did not seem intentional on the professor's part. However, many in the class noticed and reacted with silence at first, then glances at neighbors, which led finally to nervous laughter. After this disruption ended, a student explained to the professor what had been said that caused the disruption. And in response the professor promptly explained that the theories for love and relationships also apply to homosexual relationships.

In that moment of nervous laughter, many in the class displayed prejudice against homosexual relationships. In particular, they were displaying
a commonly held belief that homosexual relationships are not founded
on the same emotions, thoughts, and feelings that heterosexual relationships are. The main causes of prejudice displayed in class against homo-
sexuality include social categorization and social learning.

As this introduction funnels down to its thesis, the readers have received a
graphic sense of the issue the writer will now develop nonnarratively. Such
nonnarrative treatment is necessary, because by itself, anecdotal evidence can
be seen as merely personal. Story-telling is suggestive but rarely constitutes
sufficient proof; it needs to be corroborated. In the preceding paragraph the
writer has strengthened his credibility by focusing not on his personal responses but rather on the lesson to be drawn from his experience—a lesson
that other people might also draw from it. (For a fuller discussion—and defense—of anecdotal evidence, see "What Counts as Evidence?" in Chapter 2.)

Like challenging a commonly held view or using a second-best example, a
narrative opening will also help to safeguard you from trying to do too much
up front. All three gambits enable you to play an ace, establishing your authority with your reader, without having to play your whole hand. In other words,
when disciplinary conventions permit, introductions set up a starting position;
they don't necessarily offer a miniature version of the essay. As a general rule,
an effective introduction will pose one problem and offer one enigmatic example—seeking in some way to engage the reader in the thought process that the
writer is beginning to unfold. *The introduction seeks to raise the issue, not settle it.*

---

## Application:

## Writing Introductions

1. A good way to learn about introductions is to gather some sample
   introductory paragraphs and, working on your own or in a small
   group, figure out how each one works, what it accomplishes. Here
   are some particular questions you might pose:

   - Why does the writer start in this way—what is accomplished?
   - What kind of relationship does this opening establish with the audi-
     ence, and to what ends?
   - How does the writer let readers know why the writing they are about
     to read is called for, useful, and necessary?
   - Where and by what logic does the introduction funnel?

   *(continued)*

Writing Introductions (continued)

2. Rewrite the paragraph on gender inequality in sports (p. 172), which the text has offered as an example of prejudgment, using one or more of the offered strategies for writing introductions. You should be guided in your revision by the chapter's key point about introductions, that they typically seek to raise the issue, not settle it. How might the introduction be rewritten to use the strategy of "challenging a commonly held view"?

   Consider which of the five introductory strategies discussed in the "Opening Gambits" section would be the most appropriate. Before rewriting the paragraph, list some reasons supporting your choice. How might you defend that the best choice for rewriting the paragraph would be to begin with definition, for example? If you think another of the gambits would be more suited to the paragraph's particular subject matter, on what grounds?

   Obviously, this exercise can be adapted to any introductory paragraph that you encounter either in your own work or in the work of others. It also could provide an effective small group revision exercise in which you exchange first drafts.

3. This last application will give you an opportunity to think about how a writer's assessment of his or her audience influences the choice of opening. Compare and contrast introductory paragraphs from a popular magazine with those from journals aimed at a more specialized audience. Analyze each to determine what its authors assume the audience knows. Where in each paragraph are these assumptions most evident?

# The Function of Conclusions

Like introductions, conclusions have a key social function: they escort the readers out of the paper, just as the introduction has escorted them in. What do readers want as they leave the textual world you have taken them through? Although the form and length of the conclusion depend on the purpose and disciplinary conventions of the particular paper, it is possible to generalize a set of shared expectations for conclusions across the curriculum. In some combination most readers want three things: a judgment, a culmination, and a send-off.

## Judgment

The conclusion is the site for final judgment on whatever question or issue or problem the paper has focused upon. In most cases, this judgment occurs in overt connection with the introduction, often repeating some of its key terms. The conclusion normally reconsiders the question raised by the opening hypothesis, and, however tentatively, rules yea or nay. It also explicitly revisits the introductory claim for why the topic matters.

## Culmination

More than simply summarizing what has preceded or reasserting your main point, the conclusion needs to culminate. The word *culminate* is derived from the Latin *columen,* meaning "top or summit." To culminate is to reach the highest point, and it implies a mountain (in this case, of information and analysis) that you have scaled. When you culminate a paper in a conclusion, you bring things together and ascend to one final statement of your thinking.

## Send-Off

The climactic effects of judgment and culmination provide the basis for the send-off. The send-off is both social and conceptual, a final opening out of the topic that leads the reader out of the paper with something further to think about. As is suggested by most of the following "Voices from Across the Curriculum" boxes, the conclusion needs to move beyond the close analysis of data that has occupied the body of the paper into a kind of speculation that the writer has earned the right to formulate.

Here is an example of a conclusion that contains a final judgment, a culmination, and a send-off. The paper, a student's account of what she learned about science from doing research in biology, opens by claiming that, to the apprentice, "science assumes an impressive air of complete reliability, especially to its distant human acquaintances." Having been attracted to science by the popular view that it proceeds infallibly, she arrives at quite a different final assessment:

> All I truly know from my research is that the infinite number of factors that can cause an experiment to go wrong make tinkering a lab skill just as necessary as reading a buret. A scientist can eventually figure out a way to collect the data she wants if she has the patience to repeatedly recombine her materials and tools in slightly different ways. A researcher's success, then, often depends largely on her being lucky enough to locate, among all the possibilities, the one procedure that works.
>
> Aided more by persistence and fortune than by formal training, I evolved a method that produced credible results. But, like the tests from which it derived, the success of that method is probably also highly specific to a certain experimental environment and so is valid only for research involving borosilicate melts treated with hydrofluoric and boric acids. I've discovered a principle, but it's hardly a universal one: reality is too complex to allow much scientific generalization. Science may appear to sit firmly on all-encompassing truths, but the bulk of its weight actually rests on countless little rules tailored for particular situations.

This writer deftly interweaves the original claim from her introduction—that "science assumes an impressive air of complete reliability"—into a final *judgment* of her topic, delivered in the last sentence. This judgment is also a *culmination,* as it moves from her account of doing borosilicate melts to the small but acute generalization that "little rules tailored for particular situations," rather than "all-encompassing truths," are the mainstay of scientific research. Notice that *a culmination does not need to make a grand claim in order to be effective*. In fact, the relative smallness of the final claim, especially in contrast to the sweeping introductory position about scientific infallibility, ultimately provides a *send-off* made effective by its unexpected understatement.

## Ways of Concluding

The three professors quoted next all advise some version of the judgment/culmination/send-off combination. The first "Voices" box stresses the send-off:

---

### VOICES FROM ACROSS THE CURRICULUM

#### EXPANDING POSSIBILITIES IN THE CONCLUSION

I tell my students that too many papers "just end," as if the last page or so were missing. I tell them the importance of ending a work. One could summarize main points, but I tell them this is not heavy lifting. They could raise issues not addressed (but hinted at) in the main body: "given this, one could consider that." I tell them that a good place for reflection might be a concluding section in which they take the ball and run: react, critique, agree, disagree, recommend, suggest, or predict.

I help them by asking, "Where does the paper seem to go *after* it ends on paper?" That is, I want the paper to live on even though the five pages are filled. I don't want to suddenly stop thinking or reacting just because I've read the last word on the bottom of page 5. I want an experience, as if the paper is still with me.

I believe the ending should be an expansion on or explosion of possibilities, sort of like an introduction to some much larger "mental" paper out there. I sometimes encourage students to see the concluding section as an option to introduce ideas that can't be dealt with now. Sort of a "Having done this, I would want to explore boom, boom, boom if I were to continue further." Here the students can critique and recommend ("Having seen 'this,' one wonders 'that'").

—**FREDERICK NORLING**, *Professor of Business*

❖ ❖ ❖

There must be a summation. What part did the stock market crash of 1929 play in the onset of the Great Depression? Let's hear that conclusion one more time. Again, but now in an abbreviated form, what's the evidence? What are the main ambiguities that remain? Has your paper raised any new questions for future research? Are there any other broader ramifications following in the wake of your paper?

—**JAMES MARSHALL**, *Professor of Economics*

Although it is true that the conclusion is the place for "broader ramifications," this phrase should not be understood as a call for a global generalization. As the next quotation suggests, often the culmination represents a final limiting of a paper's original claim.

---

**VOICES FROM ACROSS THE CURRICULUM**

### LIMITING CLAIMS IN THE CONCLUSION

In the professional journals, conclusions typically appear as a refined version of a paper's thesis—that is, as a more qualified statement of the main claim. An author might take pains to point out how this claim is limited or problematic, given the adequacy of available evidence (particularly in the case of papers dependent on current empirical research, opinion polls, etc.). The conclusion also may indicate the implications of current or new evidence on conventional wisdom/theory—how the theory needs to be revised, discarded, and so forth. Conclusions of papers that deal with contemporary issues or trends usually consider the practical consequences or the expectations for the future.

The conclusion does not appear simply as a restatement of a thesis, but rather as an attempt to draw out its implications and significance (the "So what?"). This is what I usually try to impress upon students. For instance, if a student is writing on a particular proposal for party reform, I would expect the concluding paragraph to consider both the significance of the reform and its practicality.

I should note that professional papers often indicate the tentativeness of their conclusions by stressing the need for future research and indicating what these research needs might be. Although I haven't tried this, maybe it would be useful to have students conclude papers with a section entitled "For Further Consideration" in which they would indicate those things that they would have liked to have known but couldn't, given their time constraints, the availability of information, and lack of methodological sophistication. This would serve as a reminder of the tentativeness of conclusions and the need to revisit and revise arguments in the future (which, after all, is a good scholarly habit).

—JACK GAMBINO, *Professor of Political Science*

---

## Discussion Sections of Reports in the Sciences

As is the case with introductions, the conclusions of reports written in the natural sciences and psychology are regulated by formalized disciplinary formats. Conclusions, for example, occur in a section entitled "Discussion." As the next three "Voices" demonstrate, the organization and contents of "Discussion" sections vary little from discipline to discipline. For that matter, the imperatives that guide "Discussion" sections share essential traits with conclusions across the curriculum. Look for these similarities in the three comments that follow.

## VOICES FROM ACROSS THE CURRICULUM

## WRITING CONCLUSIONS IN THE SCIENCES

The conclusion occurs in a section labeled "Discussion" and, as quoted from the *Publication Manual of the American Psychological Association* (4th ed., Washington, DC, 1994), is guided by the following questions:

- What have I contributed here?
- How has my study helped to resolve the original problem?
- What conclusions and theoretical implications can I draw from my study? (p. 19)

In a broad sense, one particular research report should be seen as but one moment in a broader research tradition that *preceded* the particular study being written about and that will *continue after* this study is published. And so the conclusion should tie this particular study into both previous research considering implications for the theory guiding this study and (when applicable) practical implications of this study. One of the great challenges of writing a research report is thus to place this particular study within that broader research tradition. That's an analytical task.

—**ALAN TJELTVEIT,** *Professor of Psychology*

❖ ❖ ❖

Papers are concluded with a "Discussion" section in which conclusions are analyzed and qualified and in which ultimately their implications for the "bigger picture" are presented. The conclusion of the paper often represents the move from the deductive to the inductive aspect of science. The specific results first are interpreted (but not restated), and their implications and limitations are then discussed. The original question should be rephrased and discussed in light of the results presented. Conclusions should be qualified, and alternative explanations should be considered. Finally, conservative generalizations and new questions are posed.

—**RICHARD NIESENBAUM,** *Professor of Biology*

❖ ❖ ❖

In the "Discussion" section, students must critically evaluate the extent to which the empirical evidence they have collected supports the hypothesis they put forth in the introduction. If the data does not support their hypothesis, they need to explain why. The reasons typically are either that there was something wrong with the hypothesis or something wrong with the experiment. Interestingly, students usually find it easier to write the "Discussion" section if their hypothesis was not supported than if it was—to guess what went wrong—because it is difficult to integrate new results into existing theory.

—**LAURA SNODGRASS,** *Professor of Psychology*

## Three Strategies for Writing Effective Conclusions

There is striking overlap in the advice offered by the preceding cross-disciplinary "Voices" boxes. All caution that the conclusion should provide more than a restatement of what you've already said. All suggest that the conclusion should, in effect, serve as the introduction to some "larger mental paper out there" (as one professor puts it), beyond the confines of your own paper. By consensus, the professors make three recommendations for conclusions:

1. *Pursue implications.* Reason inductively from your particular study to consider broader issues, such as the study's practical consequences or applications, or future-oriented issues, such as avenues for further research. To unfold implications in this way is to broaden the view from the here-and-now of your paper by looking outward to the wider world and forward to the future.
2. *Come full circle.* Unify your paper by interpreting the results of your analysis in light of the context you established in your introduction.
3. *Identify limitations.* Acknowledge restrictions of method or focus in your analysis, and qualify your conclusion (and its implications) accordingly.

---

### APPLICATION:

### LOCATING THE THREE STRATEGIES

The following example provides the concluding paragraphs of the paper from which we earlier quoted the introduction as an example of a narrative opening. That opening anecdote, you may recall, introduced the problems of social categorization and social learning as causes of homophobia in the academic environment.

First reread the writer's introduction (see pp. 174–75).

Then locate the sentences in the following paragraphs where the writer begins to accomplish each of the three strategies for concluding effectively—unfolding implications, coming full circle, and limiting claims.

Finally, describe how the writer has implemented these strategies. What, for example, does he repeat of the claims made in the introduction? How does he change the context in which these claims are now to be viewed? What words does he use to qualify both the final summary of evidence and his concluding claim?

> There are many other instances of prejudice, stereotyping, and discrimination against homosexuals. These range from beliefs that homosexual partners cannot be adequate parents, to exclusion from the military, to bias (hate) crimes resulting in murder. But in recent decades, attempts have been made

*(continued)*

to help end these discriminations. One of the first occurred in 1973 when the American Psychological Association changed its policy so that homosexuals were no longer regarded as mentally ill (Melton, 1989). Thus the stigma that homosexuals are not able to fully contribute to society was partially lifted.

Other ways that have been suggested to reduce prejudice regarding homosexuals include increasing intergroup contact. In this way, each group may come to recognize similarities and encounter counterstereotypical information. Herek (1989) also suggests that education in elementary through high schools about diversity and tolerance of it—for students as well as teachers—may help prevent stereotypes, prejudice, and hate crimes. And if people are made aware of their schemas and stereotypes, they may consider information they would have ignored based on their schemas. We may never be able to eliminate the process of social categorization, but perhaps we may be able to teach that all out-groups are not necessarily "bad."

## Solving Typical Problems in Conclusions

The primary challenge in writing conclusions, it should now be evident, lies in finding a way to culminate your analysis without claiming either too little or too much. There are a number of fairly common problems to guard against if you are to avoid either of these two extremes.

### Redundancy

In Chapter 4, "Making the Thesis Evolve," we lampooned an exaggerated example of the five-paragraph form for constructing its conclusion by stating "Thus, we see" and then repeating the introduction verbatim. The result is *redundancy.* As you've seen, it's a good idea to refer back to the opening, but don't reinsert it mechanically. Instead, reevaluate what you said there in light of where you've ended up, repeating only key words or phrases from the introduction. This kind of *selective repetition* is a desirable way of achieving unity and will keep you from either of two opposite mistakes—either repeating too much or bringing up a totally new point in the conclusion.

### Raising a Totally New Point

Raising a totally new point can distract or bewilder a reader. This problem often arises out of a writer's praiseworthy desire to avoid repetition. As a rule, you can guard against the problem by making sure that you have clearly expressed the conceptual link between your central conclusion and any implications you may draw. *An implication is not a totally new point, but rather one that follows from the position you have been analyzing.*

Similarly, although a capping judgment or send-off may appear for the first time in your concluding paragraph, it should have been *anticipated* by the body of your paper. Conclusions often indicate where you think you (or an interested reader) may need to go next, but you don't actually go there. In a paper on the economist Milton Friedman, for example, if you think that another economist offers a useful way of critiquing him, you probably should not introduce this person for the first time in your conclusion.

## Overstatement

Many writers are confused over how much they should claim in their conclusion. Out of the understandable (but mistaken) desire for a grand (rather than a modest and qualified) culmination, writers sometimes *overstate* the case. That is, they assert more than their evidence has proven, or even suggested. Must a conclusion arrive at some comprehensive and final answer to the question that your paper has analyzed? Depending on the question and the disciplinary conventions, you may need to come down exclusively on one side or another. In a great many cases, however, the answers with which you conclude can be more moderate. Especially in the humanities, good analytical writing seeks to unfold successive layers of implication, so it's not even reasonable for you to expect neat closure. In such cases, you are usually better off qualifying your final judgment, drawing the line at a point of relative stability.

## Anticlimax

It makes a difference precisely where in the final paragraph(s) you qualify your concluding claim. The end of the conclusion is a "charged" site, because it gives the reader a last impression of your paper. As was noted in this chapter's discussion of "The Psychology of Form," if you end with a concession—on a note that detracts from your fundamental thesis—you risk leaving the reader unsettled and possibly confused. The term for this kind of letdown from the significant to the inconsequential is *anticlimax*. In most cases, you will flub the send-off if you depart the paper on an anticlimax.

There are many forms of anticlimax besides ending with a concession. If your conclusion peters out in a random list or an apparent afterthought or a last-minute qualification of your claims, the effect is anticlimactic. And for many readers, *if your final answer comes from quoting an authority in place of establishing your own, that, too, is an anticlimax.*

At the beginning of this section we suggested that a useful rule for introductions is to play an ace but not your whole hand. In the context of this card game analogy, it is similarly effective to *save an ace for the conclusion.* In most cases, this high card will provide an answer to some culminating "So what?" question—a last view of the implications or consequences of your analysis.

**APPLICATION:**

## COLLECTING INTRODUCTIONS AND CONCLUSIONS

One of the best ways to learn about matters of form is to make a conscious effort to ask not just "What does this or that part of the reading say?" but also "What does each part do?". Try spending one week in which you consciously attend to introductions and conclusions—to how various kinds of writing (and speaking) characteristically begin and end. Collect at least a half dozen examples of introductions and conclusions that you find interesting and analyze them for presentation to a class or small group. Name and describe each introduction's opening gambit, a number of which are discussed in this chapter, such as "challenging a commonly held view."

You should also examine how the issues or questions and the working hypothesis framed in the introduction reemerge in the concluding paragraph. What echo or echoes of the introduction, if any, do you find in the conclusion? Which sentence or sentences restate the hypothesis (in its evolved form)? Where and how in the paragraph does the writer get beyond summary to culmination and send-off?

## Key Words (in order of appearance)

| | |
|---|---|
| disciplinary format | climactic order |
| prescriptive | subordinate construction |
| heuristics | transition |
| epistemology | additive transition |
| rhetoric | the abstract |
| topics of invention | procedural opening |
| ethos | prejudgment |
| to culminate | persona |
| logos | send-off |
| pathos | redundancy |
| concession | overstatement |
| refutation | anticlimax |

## Guidelines for Attending to Matters of Form

1. Find the space in a format that will allow it to work as a *heuristic,* a set of steps designed not just to organize but also to stimulate and guide your thinking. Avoid the slot-filler mentality.
2. Look for and expect to find the common denominators among the various formats you learn to use across the curriculum. You can master—and

benefit from—virtually any format if you approach it not as a set of arbitrary and rigid rules, but rather as a formalized way of thinking.

3. Don't make your readers wait too long before you concede or refute a view that you can assume will already have occurred to them. Otherwise, they may assume you are unaware of the competing view or afraid to bring it up.

4. Always treat opposing views fairly. A good strategy is to concede their merits but argue that, in the particular context you are addressing, your position is more important or appropriate.

5. Use climactic order to organize your points, building to your best ones. The best ones are usually the most revealing and thought-provoking, not the most obvious or commonly agreed upon.

6. Phrasing your thesis to include a subordinate construction—"although $x$ appears to account for $z$, $y$ accounts for it better"—will give your paper a ready-made organizational shape, along with giving you something to define your own position against.

7. A good transition reaches backward, telling where you've been, as the grounds for making a subsequent move forward. Opt for "similarly" and "by contrast," for example, which specify connections for your readers, rather than merely additive transitions such as "another" and "also."

8. The introduction seeks to raise the issue, not settle it. Articulate why, in the context of existing thinking on the subject, your topic matters.

9. Especially in longer papers, you can use a procedural opening to forecast the organization clearly, but don't let it distract you from also stating your claim.

10. In writing conclusions, don't just summarize; culminate. Offer your most fully evolved statement of the thesis or your final judgment on the question posed in the introduction.

11. Come full circle in your conclusion. Revisit the introductory hypothesis and context. This strategy will unify your paper and help locate it within scholarly conversation on your topic.

12. Your conclusion should not assert more than your evidence has established, but it should attempt to leave the reader with implications or speculations to think about further (a send-off). Avoid closing the conclusion with a concession.

## CHAPTER 6

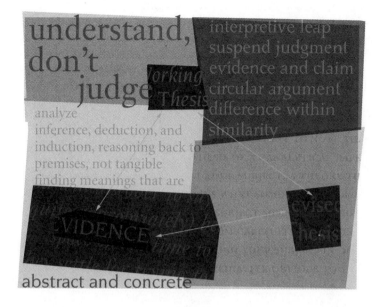

# MAKING YOUR RESPONSE TO TOPICS MORE ANALYTICAL

By the time you reach college, you will have learned to recognize certain kinds of instructions that topics characteristically contain: compare and contrast, define, agree or disagree. The key words of a topic trigger different kinds of writing. Some topics call for *argument*—for taking a firm stand on one side of an issue and making a case for that stand. Some call for *summary*—for restating ideas and information in a focused and concise way. Some call for *personal response*—for testing an idea or attitude or question against your own life experience.

It is the case, however, that far fewer writing assignments call for these kinds of writing—argument, summary, personal response—than most students seem to think. The most commonly called-for kind of writing in college courses—and beyond college—is analysis. Analytical topics, rather than inviting the writer to take a stand or to relate to the material, aim at extending the writer's understanding.

As we discussed in Chapter 1, although analysis appears in most other kinds of writing, it has its own characteristic methods and aims. An analytical topic, one asking you to consider what some feature of a subject means or how it functions, requires a different approach from a topic asking you to summarize or to take a firm and persuasive stand, as you might in a debate.

If you are not accustomed to writing analytically, you will need to learn how to see when a topic calls for analysis and how to design such topics for yourself. This chapter will show you how to make your responses to common kinds of topics more analytical.

## The Two Functions of Topics and How They Are Commonly Misunderstood

In some respects, the standard kinds of assignments closely resemble formats: they aim to focus, shape, and stimulate a writer's thinking. The key to dealing productively with topics, as is the case with formats, is to learn to use them as tools, not just as containers—to recognize that they offer a way of thinking, not just a way of arranging the thoughts you already have.

Virtually all topics—that is, all kinds of writing assignments—have two functions:

1. To get students to demonstrate their control of the information
2. To get students to acquire experience with the *epistemology* (the ways of knowing) particular to the context or the discipline

Students often assume that topics are mainly concerned with the former (demonstrating control of information) and not with the latter (showing that you have learned how to think in the ways that the discipline expects). Learning to think at the college level requires more than the mastery of information. At the heart of the problem is an underestimation of what it means "to learn the material."

Many students recognize that topics call for more than the mastery of information—that they are expected to engage it in some way—but they seem unsure how. Often they will either attempt to identify with the information ("this is like the way I feel" or "this isn't like the way I feel," etc.), or they will attempt to judge it ("I agree with/like this" or "I disagree with/don't like this"). Such students have the right impulse, but they take it in the wrong direction. The best papers are personally committed, but they are not personal in the sense of turning the topic into autobiography. Instead, the writer finds ways to invest himself or herself in the issues raised by the subject, finds ways to make them matter.

Many students seem to believe that if they are not to judge the subject and not to "relate to" it, then the teacher wants them to generalize about it. In fact, the other major obstacle to productive thinking about topics is vagueness and generality. *Learning the material is not equal to being able to generalize about it.* Indeed, premature generalization usually interferes with a person's ability to learn the material, especially when the goal is to learn to think with and about it. Thus, to say that the problem with third world economies is inefficiency or that a given poem is about love or death or rebirth is to speak so broadly that the offered generalizations could be applied to almost anything. The problem with generality, then, is that it leaves the material inert.

## Becoming Conversant

It is a reasonable expectation of any course that you should become *conversant* with the material. To become conversant means that:

1. After a significant amount of work with the material, you should be able to talk about it conversationally with other people and to answer questions about it without having to look everything up
2. You should be able to converse with the material—to be in some kind of dialogue with it, to see the questions the material asks, and to pose your own questions about it

It is this conversancy, and not inert generalizations, that most academic topics seek to elicit. Quite simply, you cannot expect to demonstrate your control of the information without getting closer to it than generalizations allow. One of the most crippling and frustrating circumstances for many students is to expect that, if they read through something once and then look away, they should be able either to accurately and productively restate it or to have an idea about it.

Few people are able to really understand things they read without making the language of that material in some way their own, actively engaging material rather than moving passively through it. This is why skills such as note-taking, paraphrasing, outlining—all forms of summary—are not just empty mechanical tasks. They are the mind's means of acquiring material, both the ideas and the language that make it possible to work with these ideas.

Consider, for example, the importance of *paraphrasing* in this respect. Meaning "to put one phrase next to another," *paraphrase*—wherein you recast the language of a passage into other words—gets you actually working with the language rather than veering away from it into some generality about it. Once you begin allowing yourself the time to paraphrase the language of the material, recasting it and, in various ways, assimilating it into your thinking, you will be able not only to demonstrate your mastery of the material but also to engage in and use its way of thinking.

This book has offered a number of formulations for ways of becoming more involved with the material, of thinking about it more concretely and substantively. As we have consistently tried to show, the time you devote to engaging material will inevitably lead to seeing the questions it invites you to ask, and thus to your having ideas. Here, in brief review, are some of the major strategies that the book has offered so far for engaging material:

*Chapter 1.* The five analytical moves: suspend judgment, define significant parts and how they are related, make the implicit explicit, look for patterns of repetition and contrast, keep asking questions

## APPLICATION:

### PARAPHRASING

Paraphrasing will increase your comprehension of virtually anything you read. If you paraphrase something that is difficult to understand, you will understand it better, and in some cases, you may discover that there is a problem—an unintentional ambiguity or confusion—in the passage itself (and that kind of observation is always valuable analytically). If you paraphrase something that seems easy to understand, you will often find that there is more in the words than you first thought. Regardless of what you paraphrase, remember this key: *recast the language repeatedly*. It is in successive recastings that the meaning grows in depth and variousness.

To hone your skills in paraphrasing, you can choose virtually any language you encounter—front page stories in a newspaper, a political speech, the directions on an income tax form. Here is a useful exercise:

Locate a central passage from any textbook you are reading—the kind of passage most likely to attract yellow highlighter—and paraphrase it several times. How do the recastings differ? Which is best, and why?

Poetry, which tends to select its words very carefully and often to compress and multiply meanings, provides a particularly rich field in which to cultivate paraphrasing skills. Try paraphrasing the following exchange from the opening of Shakespeare's play, *A Midsummer Night's Dream:*

> Theseus, Duke of Athens:
>> Now, fair Hippolyta, our nuptial hour
>> Draws on apace. Four happy days bring in
>> Another moon; but O, methinks, how slow
>> This old moon wanes! She lingers my desires,
>> Like to a stepdame or a dowager,
>> Long withering out a young man's revenue.
>
> Hippolyta, Queen of the Amazons, conquered by Theseus:
>> Four days will quickly steep themselves in night,
>> Four nights will quickly dream away the time;
>> And then the moon, like to a silver bow
>> New-bent in heaven, shall behold the night
>> Of our solemnities.

Once you have paraphrased both passages, answer the following questions:

- What does each of these speakers have to say about the moon?
- How do the tone and the implications of each speaker's language differ?

*Chapter 2.* Analyze evidence in depth by doing 10 on 1 rather than 1 on 10

*Chapter 3.* Recognize and fix weak theses by qualifying categorical thinking, reasoning back to premises, and using binaries analytically (questioning the accuracy of the terms of the binary and changing either/or to "the extent to which")

*Chapter 4.* Make your thesis evolve by using the following steps: formulate a tentative hypothesis, see how far you can make it work to explain the data, look actively to find data that does not fit, use that data to evolve the terms of your hypothesis, and then repeat these steps until the match between thesis and evidence is as comprehensive and precise as you can manage

*Chapter 5.* Use formats not just to organize final products but also to generate ideas

## Looking for Questions Rather Than Answers

The remainder of this chapter will give you more strategies for engaging material, organized in terms of the most frequently assigned kinds of topics. What all of our suggestions will have in common is the single requirement that you train yourself to look for questions rather than leaping too quickly to answers. It is this orientation toward topics that will move you beyond merely reporting information and lead you to think with and about it.

The best way to become more analytical in your response to topics is to actively search out an area of your subject where there are no clear and obvious answers—to look for something that needs explaining rather than reiterating the obvious.

## Assigned versus Open Topics

Most of the analytical writing you do for your college courses will be in response to one of two situations: (1) you are given a topic to write about, with varying degrees of specificity about how you should proceed, or (2) you are asked to locate a topic of your own within guidelines that also vary in their specificity. There are obviously some big differences between having a topic assigned to you and coming up with one on your own. Ultimately, though, assigned and open (self-designed) topics share underlying similarities that outweigh these differences.

Perhaps the most important thing to recognize in your treatment of topics is that the effectiveness of your response to the topic will depend on your ability to interpret the directions and recognize the kind of writing being called for. Consider, for example, an assignment to "discuss how a supply-side economist might respond to the idea of eliminating most tariffs on imported goods." How do you interpret the word "discuss"? Should you confine your response to summarizing (restating) the reading you've done on the subject? Should you analyze the reading, by drawing out its unstated assumptions or pointing to inconsistencies in its position? Should you write an argument about the reading, revealing the extent to which you agree or disagree with the supply-side view?

In answering such questions, you should keep in mind that a major aim of most topics is to challenge you to focus further within the assigned boundaries. In this sense, the professor constructs a topic that you construct some more, which makes virtually all assigned topics to some extent open.

By the same token, virtually all open or self-designed topics contain invisible limits. When you are told to "write a paper" on tariff legislation or the novel *Moby Dick* or the Franco-Prussian War, you recognize that you aren't really free in all sorts of fundamental ways. You know not to discuss the war in terms of last Sunday's football game, or the novel in terms of the Classics Illustrated comic book version, or the tariff in terms of biblical laws about usury. As you gain experience in a particular discipline, you come to know the more specific rules that govern how a given kind of topic may be approached in that discipline. An English major knows, for example, that biographical information about an author may be used in an analysis of that author's work as an informing context but not as proof of the author's intentions. A psychology major knows that a hypothesis must be subjected to empirical testing.

In assigned topics, a discipline's methodology and ways of limiting and defining evidence are often prescribed overtly. In open topics, these prescriptions are more often assumed or implied; the professor assumes that you either already know the rules of the game or will learn them by having to design the topic. In both cases, formulating and interpreting topics are crucial parts of the writing process, not just preludes to it.

## Six Rules of Thumb for Handling Complexity

As we have been suggesting, an analytical response to a topic involves you in explaining something that is not overtly explained for you in the subject matter you are studying. Such topics call on you, in other words, to *deliberately situate yourself among sites of potential ambiguity or conflict,* so that your writing can explore the complexity of your subject. In order to learn how to enter this uncertain space, you will first have to get over the fear that you are doing something wrong if you cannot arrive quickly at a clear and obvious answer. Many inexperienced writers deliberately avoid complexity—rejecting positions, for example, for which there is a possible counterargument—because of this fear.

If you want your education to teach you analytical skills and not just information, you need to resist the temptation to bail out when you encounter uncertainty and complexity. Although repeating material from lectures and readings can teach you ideas, it cannot teach you how to arrive at ideas. You can't learn to deduce the implications of President John F. Kennedy's foreign policy, for example, only by paraphrasing how someone else has drawn out those implications.

Virtually all writers feel discomfort when encountering complexity. But discomfort need not lead to avoidance or to verbal paralysis. The following rules of thumb can help you to discover and respond to the complexities of the topics that you encounter rather than oversimplifying or evading them.

### Rule 1: Reduce Scope

Whenever possible, reduce drastically the scope of your inquiry. Resist the temptation to include too much information. Even when an assignment calls for broad coverage of a subject, an effective and usually acceptable strategy is for you to begin with an overview and then analyze one or two key points in greater depth.

For example, if you were asked to write on President Franklin Roosevelt's New Deal, you would obviously have to open with some general observations, such as what it was and why it arose. But if you tried to stay on this general level throughout, your paper would have little direction or focus. You could achieve a focus, though, by moving quickly from the general to some much smaller and more specific part of the subject, such as attacks on the New Deal. You would then be able to limit the enormous range of possible evidence to a few representative figures, such as Huey Long, Father Coughlin, and Alf Landon. Once you began to compare the terms and legitimacy of their opposition to the New Deal, you would be much more likely to manage a complex analysis of the subject than if you had remained at the level of broad generalization. Typically you will find that some mixture of wide-angle coverage with more narrowly focused discussion is the best way to cover the ground without sacrificing depth.

## Rule 2: Study the Wording of Topics for Unstated Questions

Nearly all formulations of an assigned topic contain one or more overt questions but also other questions that are implied by the topic's wording. Taking the time to ponder the wording and to articulate the questions that wording implies is often the first step to having an idea—to finding an angle of approach.

Consider, for instance, a topic question such as "Is feminism good for Judaism?" The question itself seems to invite you simply to argue yes or no, but the wording implies preliminary questions that you would need to articulate and answer before you could address the larger issue. What, for example, does "good for Judaism" mean? That which allows the religion to evolve? That which conserves its tradition? The same kinds of questions, defining and contextualizing and laying out implications, might be asked of the term "feminism." And what of the possibility that feminism has no significant effect whatsoever?

As this example illustrates, even an apparently limited and straightforward question presses writers to make choices about how to engage it. So don't leap from the topic question to your plan of attack too quickly. One of the best tricks of the trade lies in smoking out and addressing the unstated *assumptions* implied by the wording of the topic. (See Chapter 3, the section entitled, "Checking for Unstated Assumptions.")

## Rule 3: Suspect Your First Responses

If you settle for your first response, the result is likely to be superficial, obvious, and overly general. A better strategy is to examine your first responses for ways in which they are inaccurate and then develop the implications of these overstatements (or errors) into a new formulation. In many cases, writers go

**APPLICATION:**

## ANALYZING A TOPIC

Analyze the following topic, taken from an actual standardized placement exam:

> In a well-written essay, evaluate the truth of the assertion that follows. Use evidence and examples from your reading or experience to make your argument convincing. "It is human nature to want patterns, standards, and a structure of behavior. A pattern to conform to is a kind of shelter."

As we began to do with "Is feminism good for Judaism?" earlier, make a list of all of the questions implicit in this topic. Which words, both in the directions given to students and in the quotation itself, require attention? When you have compiled your list, write a paragraph or two in which you explain, as specifically as possible, what the question is asking writers to do and how a writer might go about fulfilling these tasks.

---

through this process of proposing and rejecting ideas ten times or more before they arrive at an angle or approach that will sustain an essay.

A first response is okay for a start, as long as you don't stop there. For example, many people might agree, *at first glance,* that no one should be denied health care, or that a given film or novel that concludes with a marriage is a happy ending, or that the American government should not pass trade laws that might cause Americans to lose their jobs. On closer inspection, however, each of these responses begins to reveal its limitations. Given that there is a limited amount of money available, should everyone, regardless of age or physical condition, be accorded every medical treatment that might prolong life? And might not a novel or film that concludes in marriage signal that the society offers too few options, or more cynically, that the author is feeding the audience an implausible fantasy to blanket over problems raised earlier in the work? And couldn't trade laws resulting in short-term loss of jobs ultimately produce more jobs and a healthier economy?

As these examples suggest, first responses—usually pieces of conventional wisdom—can blind you to rival explanations. Try not to decide on an answer to questions too quickly. (See Chapter 3, the section entitled "Weak Thesis Type 3: The Thesis Restates Conventional Wisdom.")

## Rule 4: Begin with Questions, Not Answers

Whether you are focusing an assigned topic or devising one of your own, you are usually better off to begin with something that you don't understand very well and want to understand better. Begin by asking what kinds of questions

**APPLICATION:**

## "APPEARS TO BE ABOUT x BUT IS REALLY ABOUT y"

"The reading appears to be about *x* but is really about *y*" is a useful formula for quickly getting past your first responses. An alternative version of this formula is "Initially I thought *x* about the reading, but now I think *y*." Take any reading assignment you have been given for class, and, prior to the class meeting, write either formula at the top of a page, fill in the blanks, and then explain the statement for a few paragraphs. You might also try these formulae when you find yourself getting stuck while drafting a paper.

the material poses. So, for example, if you are convinced that Robinson Crusoe changes throughout Defoe's novel and you write a paper cataloguing those changes, you will essentially be composing a selective plot summary. If, by contrast, you wonder *why* Crusoe walls himself within a fortress after he discovers a footprint in the sand, you will be more likely to interpret the significance of events than just to report them.

### Rule 5: Expect to Become Interested

Writing gives you the opportunity to cultivate your curiosity by thinking exploratively. Rather than approaching topics in a mechanical way or putting them off to the last possible moment and doing the assignment grudgingly, try giving yourself and the topic the benefit of the doubt. If you can suspend judgment and start writing, you will often find yourself uncovering interests where you had not seen them before. In other words, accept the idea that interest is a product of writing—not a prerequisite.

### Rule 6: Write All of the Time about What You Are Studying

Because interest is so often a product and not a prerequisite of writing, it follows that writing informally about what you are studying while you are studying it is probably the single best preparation for developing interesting topics. By writing spontaneously about what you read, you will accustom yourself to being a less passive consumer of ideas and information, and you will have more ideas and information available to think actively with and about. In effect, you will be formulating possible topics long before an actual topic is assigned. In any case, you should not wait to start writing until you think you have an idea you can organize a paper around. Instead, use writing to get you *to* the idea.

There are various forms of informal writing, which go under the general heading of *prewriting*. We will discuss the most prevalent of these forms next.

# Using Prewriting to Find and Interpret Topics

For most writers, prewriting offers the best antidotes to superficial writing and to writer's block. It will also enable you to develop and organize your ideas when you begin drafting more formally because you already will have explored some of the possible paths you might travel and rejected others as dead ends.

All of the forms of prewriting are premised on the belief that the act of writing is not just a way of recording what you think but rather of discovering what you think. As the novelist E. M. Forster put it (in regard to the "tyranny" of prearrangement), "How can I tell what I think till I see what I say?" Unlike a finished essay, in which the sentences follow logically as you unfold your central idea, prewriting encourages you to leap *associatively* from idea to idea as these arise. One of the advantages of this less structured, less sequential kind of writing is that it reduces anxiety. Rather than worrying about what you can find to say, you start saying things. Not everything you come up with will be worthy of developing into a paper, but you will often be surprised at the connections you make and the workable starting points you discover when prewriting.

## Freewriting

Freewriting is the loosest form of prewriting, requiring only that you write more or less continuously—and usually without much premeditation—for a specified period of time (usually between ten and twenty minutes). Try to keep moving. Don't pause to edit or correct or bite your pen or stare into space; just write. The pressure of writing continuously will reduce your anxiety about being wrong and encourage you to switch tracks when you hit a dead end or when a new idea springs up. Although some freewrites unfold along a single line, more often they allow you to survey the range of your thinking on a subject. Whenever you feel yourself getting stuck, try finishing the sentence, "What I'm really trying to say is. . . ." Try finishing this sentence not just once but a half dozen times or more, and see what happens.

## Focused Freewriting

Focused freewriting follows the same procedure as freewriting, except that you attempt to stay within a more narrowly defined subject. Often you will take your best idea from a previous freewrite and then explore it on the page for ten minutes or so without stopping. Or you might put a single word or idea at the top of the page and write continuously about that.

Focused freewrites are an especially useful way to move from a broad topic to one that is more carefully directed and narrowed. Focused freewrites can also help you to notice more in your reading and to be better prepared for class discussion. Try preparing for class by doing one on a single question or passage from the reading. You can locate passages by asking yourself questions like,

---

### APPLICATION:

## PASSAGE-BASED FOCUSED FREEWRITING

1. Choose a single short passage taken from a text that you are studying, write it at the top of a page, and do a twenty-minute focused freewrite.

   This is one of the best analytical exercises you can do. You might choose the passage in answer to the question, "What is the one passage in the reading that needs to be discussed, that poses a question or a problem, or that seems, in some way perhaps difficult to pin down, anomalous or even just unclear?" You can vary this question infinitely, selecting the passage that you find most puzzling or most important or most dissonant, or whatever.

   One advantage of focused freewriting is that it forces you to articulate what you notice as you notice it, not delaying—or as is more common, simply avoiding—thinking in a persistent and relatively disciplined way about what you are reading. There is no set procedure for such writing, but it usually involves the following:

   - It selects out key phrases or terms in the passage and paraphrases them, trying to tease out the possible meanings of these words.

   - It addresses how the passage is representative of broader issues in the reading; perhaps it will refer to another, similar passage.

   - It attends, at least briefly, to the context surrounding the passage, identifying the larger section of which the passage is a part.

2. Type up the focused freewrite, revising and further freewriting until you have filled a page. Eventually, you can build up, through a process of accretion, the thinking for an entire paper in this way.

---

"Which part of the reading did I find the most interesting or significant or revealing or useful or unexpected or challenging?"

It's also a good idea to try both open and focused freewriting as soon as possible after a lecture or discussion as a way of consolidating, retaining, and thinking about what you have just learned. Try starting points like, "What I now understand about the subject is. . . ."

## Journals

Unlike keeping a personal diary in which you keep track of your day's activities and recount the feelings these occasioned, keeping a journal for a course is for generating and collecting ideas and for keeping track of your interactions with the material. The journal becomes, in effect, a collection of focused freewrites developed in response to the reading and lectures in a course.

The best way to get a journal to work for you is to experiment. You might try, for example, copying and commenting on statements from your reading or class meetings that you found potentially illuminating. Use the journal to write down the ideas, reactions, and germs of ideas that you had during a class discussion or that you found running around in your head after a late night's reading. Use the journal to retain your first impressions of books or films or music or performances, so that you can look back and trace the development of your thinking.

If possible, write in your journal every day. As with freewriting, the best way to get started is just to start, see what happens, and take it from there. The more you write, the more you'll find yourself noticing, and thus the more you'll have to say.

# Making Topics Analytical: Locating Areas of Uncertainty

Although disciplines vary in the kinds of questions they characteristically ask, every discipline is concerned with asking questions, exploring areas of uncertainty, and attempting to solve or at least clarify problems. As a general rule, you should seek out *live questions over inert answers.* Rather than leading you to a single or obvious answer, an analytical topic aims to define a space in which you can have ideas about (explore the questions in) what you've been learning.

Finding a space in which you can have an idea doesn't mean that you should pursue your own ideas while ignoring all other information, nor does it mean that you should merely report information with no reference to your own thinking. Instead, you need to find ways of formulating and interpreting topics that locate a middle ground between these two extremes.

The remainder of this chapter will offer specific strategies for making your responses to five of the most common kinds of topics more analytical. These topics are:

1. Summary
2. Personal response
3. Agree/disagree
4. Comparison and contrast
5. Definition

## The Summary Topic

All analytical topics require, as we have explained, a blend of two components: a thinking component and an information component. Summary provides the information component. Summarizing is basically a translation process, and as such, it is an essential part of learning. It is the way that not just facts and figures but also other people's theories and observations enter your writing.

An effective summary requires significant analytical skill. Although summaries at their worst may merely present a list of sentences paraphrased or
quoted randomly from a reading, effective summaries (as we suggested in the
"Analysis and Summary" section of Chapter 1) require you to determine which
parts of the information are important, as well as to figure out and articulate
how these parts connect.

There are two contexts in which summary is particularly valuable:

1. As a preliminary or prewriting assignment designed to help you assimilate information
2. As part of a larger analysis, providing information blended with or
   juxtaposed to your thinking about it

How does summary function as part of a larger analysis? In focusing a
topic, you are trying to discover the significance of a particular feature of your
subject. It is essential when doing so to *contextualize* your subject accurately—
to create a fair picture of what's there. If you don't take the time to get your
whole subject in perspective, you are more prone to misrepresenting it in your
analysis. Summary performs this contextualizing function.

Summarizing can become a problem, however, when you interpret the
wording of the topic as a call to summarize, when in fact it calls for you to analyze. Effective analytical topics, we've been saying, aim to give you something
to negotiate, which means that they necessarily require you to do more than
give back what you've been given. Too often, however, summarizing becomes
a way of avoiding analysis. In particular, the direction to "discuss" a topic creates the most ambiguity on the summarize/analyze borderline.

### Strategies for Using Summaries Analytically

#### STRATEGY 1: RANK THE ITEMS IN YOUR LIST

As we discussed in "The Psychology of Form" in Chapter 5, the list is the weak-
est form of logical organization because it omits the conceptual links among
ideas. Most ineffective summaries make no effort to establish these conceptual
links. The best ways to get beyond summaries that operate as inert lists are:

1. To emphasize the *logical structure,* the way the ideas are connected in
   the piece you are summarizing
2. To select the information that you wish to discuss on some principle
   other than general coverage of the material, and then *rank* these items
   in some order of importance (see "Climactic Order" in Chapter 5)

Let's say that you are assigned a paper on major changes in the tax law or on
recent developments in U.S. policy toward eastern Europe. Rather than simply
collecting the information, try to arrange it into hierarchies. What are the least or
most significant changes or developments, and why? Which are most overlooked
or most overrated or most controversial or most practical, and why?

A ranking goes beyond a summary because you are having to supply something that is not already evident in the reading—a series of decisions about the material and your rationales for them. And unlike writing a passive summary, *ranking encourages you to ask questions.* Say, for example, that you selected one of three changes in U.S. foreign policy toward eastern Europe as the most overlooked. You would then be prompted not only to provide your reasons for making this claim, but also to consider why and by whom this policy change has been overlooked, as well as what the significance of its being overlooked might be. As a result of ranking, perhaps three-quarters of your paper on policy changes toward eastern Europe might center on the significance of one change. Rather than covering the entire field of policy changes by listing them all, you would be able to reduce the scope drastically and narrow your summary into a good topic.

### STRATEGY 2: SHIFT THE FOCUS FROM "WHAT?" TO "HOW?" AND "WHY?"

Admittedly, it is more difficult to get beyond summary in some subjects than in others. The nature of course content sometimes seems to leave space for little more than repeating material from the reading. An effective means of making your response to summary topics more analytical is to redirect your attention from "What?" questions to "How?" questions.

For example, a question such as "What were the major discoveries that Darwin made on *The Beagle?*" could easily lead to passive listing. To incorporate analysis, you would need some principle of selection that would allow you to analyze Darwin's thinking rather than just describe his conclusions—to shift the critical focus from what Darwin says to how he proceeds.

You could choose to focus, for example, on Darwin's use of the scientific method, in which case you might locate passages where Darwin expresses uncertainty, examining how he builds, and in some cases, discards hypotheses. The method of ranking that we described in Strategy 1 works well when you are answering "How?" questions. You could select several passages that illustrate *how* Darwin proceeded from evidence to conclusion, and then *rank them in order of importance* to the overall theory, arguing for that ranking. Notice that although you would be shifting the emphasis from "What?" to "How?" and "Why?," you would not be excluding "What?" (the information component) from your discussion.

### STRATEGY 3: PURSUE ONLY SELECTED FEATURES OF YOUR SUBJECT

If your response to a topic can be organized into a list that arranges its elements in no particular order, then your response is still too broad. A question such as "What makes Chaucer's *Canterbury Tales* funny?" is likely to invite unanalyzed plot summary precisely because it is so general. But narrowing the question to "How does Chaucer's use of religious commentary contribute to the humor of 'The Wife of Bath's Tale'?" reduces the scope to a single tale and the humor to a single aspect of humor, which offers you a manageable space within which to analyze.

Similarly, an essay might address not why the American colonies rebelled against England, but how American and British history textbooks differ in their treatment of the Boston Tea Party. The broader version of this subject invites passive summary—a list of standard generalizations about the American Revolution. The narrower version creates a space for you to enter, analyze, and arrive at a formulation not contained in the text you are studying. Notice that it also addresses, though in much more focused form, the larger question of why the colonies rebelled.

Although the suggestions we've offered here for making a summary more analytical will inevitably involve some loss of breadth—you won't be able to cover everything—this is usually a trade-off worth making. Your ability to rank parts of your subject or to choose a particularly revealing feature to focus on will indicate that you are in control of the material, more than if you just reproduced what was in the text. Before narrowing the focus, you can still begin with a brief survey of major points to contextualize your topic. In short, refocusing summary questions in order to make them more analytical does not slight the importance of information.

---

## APPLICATION:

### SUMMARIZING TWO SUMMARIES OF THE SAME SOURCE

Read the following generally effective and well-written summaries of the same academic article. As you will see, they differ widely in their organizational strategies, choice of examples, and emphases.

1. Nina Auerbach argues in "Waiting Together: *Pride and Prejudice*" that the novel is about the absurdity and emptiness of early nineteenth-century society. She notes how Austen depicts the parlor as a place for the women of Longbourn to wait for a husband and how this ultimately "defines the female world" (337). The women of Longbourn are representative of the microcosm that is the Bennet family and the macrocosm that is England. The novel is set during the end of the Napoleonic wars, as are many of Austen's novels, illustrating in a metaphoric way the waiting these women do and extending the Longbourn women's issues into a critique of Austen's society.

Auerbach compares the women of Longbourn to Samuel Beckett's heroes in *Waiting for Godot,* not only because their existence depends on finding a husband, but also because it is their waiting that wholly defines them. The neighborhood acts as a place in which no secrets exist and sets up an unfeeling family existence that Auerbach correlates to the family's nonexistence. This nonexistence comes mainly from the family's lack of a son, which makes the survival of these women dependent on marriage, since the estate is subject to an "entail" stipulating that it go only to a male heir. The dialogue amongst the women shows their "joy of absence from Longbourn, not presence in it" (338.)

*(continued)*

Auerbach argues as well that Austen's novel's construction also shows the emptiness of these women's lives. She speaks of the "near-invisibility" (340) of the house, because the audience receives little description of the house's details or any material objects within. It is the presence of prospective husbands that brings "domestic substance" (341) to the description of Longbourn and ultimately to the prospective wives.

2. Nina Auerbach dedicates much of her essay "Waiting Together: *Pride and Prejudice*" to supporting her assertion that the novel serves to strengthen rather than weaken the conventional role of marriage as well as the patriarchal and male-empowered society described by Austen. Auerbach begins by citing instances within the novel where female characters "waited" for the presence of males—for example, the Bennet family waiting for a son. Auerbach goes on to say that "her England is in large part a country of women whose business it is to wait for the return of the men who have married them or may do so . . ." (337).

Auerbach then focuses on the Bennet family and its inner dynamics. Most criticized is the Bennet family's blatant lack of intimacy and adhesion. Auerbach brings readers' attention to the lack of scenes in which the family members are alone together and also to the desire of each married daughter to leave the family behind. Auerbach credits this lack of family adhesion to the "entail's overweening power" (339) and the family's lack of a past.

Auerbach then declares that it is the men who bring substance to the Bennet family: "it is not women but available men whose presence makes a house a house" (340). As opposed to the considerable lack of visual detail afforded to the Longbourn home, the description of Pemberley is saturated with details and description: "the descriptive energy of the novel [is] reserved for the homes the girls marry into . . ." (341). Based on this evidence, Auerbach states that "marriage and marriage alone gives the world contour" (342).

Auerbach moves on to describe the role of female power within the novel. According to Auerbach, all power given to a female within the novel is abused, and therefore *Pride and Prejudice* serves to support a male-dominated society. One example cited and explored is the character and role of Lady Catherine. Also, Auerbach reasons that, as opposed to the idiotic characters of Lady Catherine and Mrs. Bennet, Elizabeth accepts the male's dominance over the right to inheritance.

Auerbach then shifts to an exploration of Darcy's character and the power bestowed therein. Auerbach asserts that Elizabeth is attracted to Darcy's power and notes another flaw in the Bennet family hierarchy: Mr. Bennet's act of giving the power to Mrs. Bennet.

Therefore, according to Auerbach, *Pride and Prejudice* is far from a radical piece of art whose function is to question the established social order and behavior. Rather it is a novel that preaches the conventions of the time: first, marriage is the business of women; and second, men, and not women, should have the power and authority.

*(continued)*

*(continued)*

1. Summarize the summaries: allow yourself one sentence for each paragraph. This may seem daunting at first, because the paragraphs are already radically condensed. To do this task well, you will need either (a) to eliminate information or (b) to condense it further. If (a), you'll need to figure out, given the whole summary, which piece in each paragraph is most important. If (b), you will need to decide what the sentences have in common that you could generalize about in one sentence, without becoming so general that you eliminate everything substantive. Good summaries blend the general with the particular: without some of the particulars of the material you are summarizing, your generalizations about the material may not make useful sense to your readers.

2. Then generalize, preferably in one sentence for each summary, about how each proceeds—from what to what to what? How, in other words, does each summary move? On the basis of these two sentences, briefly answer the question, "What is each summary's organizational strategy?"

3. Compare the last paragraph of the second summary with the introductory paragraph of the first summary. Then answer the question, "What does the second summary make clear about Auerbach's article that the first summary does not?"

## APPLICATION:

## COVERAGE VERSUS RANKING

Write two summaries of the same article or book chapter. Make the first one *consecutive*—that is, try to cover the piece by essentially listing the key points as they appear. Aim to limit yourself to a typed page.

Then rewrite the summary, doing the following:

- Rank the items in order of importance *according to some principle that you designate,* and explain—make an argument for—your rationale.

- Eliminate the last few items on the list, or at most, give each a single sentence.

- Use the space you have saved to include more detail about the most important item or two.

The second summary will probably require close to two pages.

## The Personal Response Topic

How do you know when you are being asked for a personal response? And what does it mean to respond personally? When asked for your reactions to a particular subject, or for what you think is most important or interesting or revealing in it, *you are being asked to select your own starting point* for discussion, for the initial impressions that you will later analyze more systematically. You will often discover in such reactions the germ of an idea about the subject.

The biggest advantage of personal response topics is that they give you the freedom to explore where and how to engage your subject. Such topics often bring to the surface your emotional or intuitive response, allowing you to experiment with placing the subject in various contexts. You might, for example, offer your personal response to an article on the abuses of hazing in fraternity and sorority life in the context of your own experience. Or you might think about it in connection to some idea about in-groups and out-groups that you read about in a sociology course, or as it relates to what you read about cultural rituals in an anthropology course.

Another advantage of personal response questions is that they often allow you to get some distance on your first impressions, which can often be deceiving. If, as you reexamine your first reactions, you look for ways that they might not be accurate, you will often find places where you now disagree with yourself, in effect, stimulating you to think in new ways about the subject. In such cases, the first reaction has helped to clear the way to a second, and better, response.

Personal response becomes a problem, however, when it distracts you from analyzing the subject. In most cases, you will be misinterpreting the intent of a personal response topic if you view it as an invitation either to:

1.  Assert your personal opinions unreflectingly or
2.  Substitute narratives of your own experience for careful consideration of the subject

In a sense, all analysis involves your opinions, insofar as you are choosing what particular evidence and arguments to focus upon. But, at least in an academic setting, *an opinion is more than simply an expression of your beliefs—it's a conclusion that you earn the rights to through a careful examination of evidence.*

In most cases, when you are asked to respond personally, the professor is looking for more than your endorsement, appreciation, or denouncement of the subject. If you find yourself constructing a virtual list—"I agree with this point" or "I disagree with that point"—you are probably doing little more than matching your opinions with the points of view encountered in a reading. In such cases, you are simply reporting how well they fit with your own viewpoints, when you should be exploring the viewpoints in the material.

Similarly, when you substitute personal narrative for analysis, your own experiences and prejudices tend to become an unquestioned standard of value. Your own disastrous experience with a health maintenance organization (HMO) may predispose you to dismiss a plan for nationalized health care, but your writing needs to examine in detail the holes in the plan, not evoke the three hours you lingered in some doctor's waiting room. It is, however, okay to integrate some personal experience into a topic, provided that you have also analyzed the subject past the anecdotal stage to the point where you have become aware of the argument that is exemplified by your narrative.

### Strategies for Using Personal Responses Analytically

#### STRATEGY 1: TRACE YOUR RESPONSES BACK TO THEIR CAUSES

As the preceding discussion of problems with personal response topics suggests, *you need to bring your reactions back to the subject so that you can identify and analyze exactly what in the reading has produced your reaction, how, and why.* If you find an aspect of your subject irritating or interesting, disappointing or funny, you will be able to use rather than simply indulge such responses if you then examine a particular piece of evidence that has provoked them.

Let's say, for example, that you are assigned to respond to an article on ways of increasing the numbers of registered voters in urban precincts. You find the article irritating; your personal experience working with political campaigns has taught you that getting out the vote is not as easy as this writer makes it seem. From that starting point, you might analyze one (to you) overly enthusiastic passage, concentrating on how the writer has not only overestimated what campaign workers can actually do but also condescended to those who don't register—assuming, perhaps, that they are ignorant rather than indifferent or disillusioned.

Once you get down to analyzing evidence, you will often find that you no longer agree with your original response. The attack you planned on the article for its naïveté might instead become an explanation for the differences between the article's and your point of view. Perhaps the writer's enthusiasm was not founded so much on an oversimplification of the problem of getting out the vote as on another way of viewing the situation. Having opened this possibility, you might discover that the writer has in mind a much more long-term effect or that urban models differ significantly from the suburban ones of your experience. A common result of tracing your responses back to their causes is a revision of your responses—not surprisingly, because you will inevitably be shifting the focus from your reactions to the material itself.

Another example: say that you are assigned to respond to a play that you found funny, such as J. M. Synge's *The Playboy of the Western World*. Your best strategy would be to locate one line that made you laugh—such as the playboy's declaration at the end of Act I that if he had known how popular with the women he would become by killing his father, he'd have done it long ago. You could then ask yourself where the humor lies in this remark, what it suggests (for example) about the attitudes of rural Irish culture toward fathers, and the significance of the fact that the playwright uses the line to end the act on a comic note.

### STRATEGY 2: ASSUME THAT YOU MAY HAVE MISSED THE POINT

It's difficult to see the logic of someone else's position if you are too preoccupied with your own. Similarly, it is difficult to see the logic, or illogic, of your own position if you already assume it to be true. Because you have assumed that something is obviously true or false, you cease to think about it and quickly forget where your view came from in the first place.

Although an evaluative response (approve/disapprove) can sometimes spur analysis, it can also lead you to prejudge the case. If, however, you question the validity of your own point of view as a matter of course, you will sometimes recognize the possibility of an alternative point of view, as was the case in the voter registration example. See Figure 6.1.

### STRATEGY 3: ACHIEVE CRITICAL DETACHMENT

Especially in cases where your primary response is emotional (anger, moral indignation, fear), you run the risk of getting so caught up in expressing how you feel that you will not get around to examining the subject analytically. Paying too much attention to how a subject makes you feel or fits your experience of life can seduce you away from paying attention to how the subject itself operates. This problem is compounded in areas where there are few or no arguments in favor of an opposing point of view. Except in very limited cases, for example, you could not achieve critical detachment on the subject of racism by considering that it might be a good thing. In such cases, the aim of achieving critical detachment is not to get you to change your mind or even

**FIGURE 6.1** Making Personal Response More Analytical.

---

**Evaluative Personal Response:** *"The article was irritating."* This response is too broad and dismissively judgmental. Make it more analytical by tracing the response back to the evidence that triggered it.

**A More Analytical Evaluative Response:** *"The author of the article oversimplifies the problem by assuming the cause of low voter registration to be voters' ignorance rather than voters' indifference."* Although still primarily an evaluative response, this observation is more analytical. It takes the writer's initial response ("irritating") to a specific cause.

**A Non-Evaluative Analytical Response:** *"The author's emphasis on increased coverage of city politics in local/neighborhood forums such as the churches suggests that the author is interested in long-term effects of voter registration drives and not just in immediate increases."* Rather than simply reacting ("irritating") or leaping to evaluation ("oversimplifies the problem"), the writer here formulates a possible explanation for the difference between her point of view on voter registration drives and the article's.

---

to assess the value of alternative points of view, but rather *to allow you to disengage your emotions enough for you to look closely at your subject and, in so doing, come to understand more about it.*

In this context, consider how you might write about two vastly different treatments of racism: the charter of the Ku Klux Klan and *Black Boy,* Richard Wright's autobiographical account of racist brutality during his boyhood in the American South. If the racism in both documents left you so morally outraged that all you did was list examples of it and voice your disapproval, you would be able to write virtually the same personal response essay to both documents! In this respect, the documents themselves have become irrelevant.

How do you achieve critical detachment from your first responses in order to transform them into analysis? In the case of the KKK charter and *Black Boy,* for example, you could locate passages that provoked your reaction and carefully study their specific language. Question it. How do the passages you've selected reveal the writers' assumptions about the nature or causes of racism? Or you might focus on a part of the larger subject, such as the language of racism or the psychological effects of racism. What are the apparent intentions of the authors, and how does their use of language define or manipulate their intended audience? Whatever questions you ask, so long as they focus on the material rather than just your reactions to it, they can provide a very useful way of redirecting you from the merely personal and toward some more public and generalizable understanding.

### STRATEGY 4: LOCATE THE TOPIC WITHIN A LIMITING CONTEXT

Suppose you are asked to write about the topic "Define your religious beliefs." Although this topic would naturally lead you to think about your own experiences and beliefs, you would probably do best to approach the topic in some more limiting context. The reading in the course could provide this limit. Let's say that thus far you have read two modern religious thinkers, Martin Buber and Paul Tillich. Reflecting on these thinkers' ideas would not necessarily push you and your convictions out of your essay but could give you a means of bringing your own beliefs into clearer view. "What do I believe?" would become "How does my response to Buber and Tillich illuminate my own assumptions about the nature of religious faith?" An advantage of this move, beyond making your argument less general, is that it would help you to get perspective on your own position.

Another way of limiting your context is to consider how one author or recognizable point of view that you have encountered in the course might respond to a single statement from another author or point of view. If you used this strategy to respond to the topic "Does God exist?," you might arrive at a formulation such as "How would Martin Buber critique Paul Tillich's definition of God?" Although this topic appears to exclude personal response entirely, it in fact does not. Your opinion would necessarily enter because you would be actively formulating something that is not already evident in the reading (how Buber might respond to Tillich).

## APPLICATION:

## MAKING PERSONAL RESPONSE ANALYTICAL

One common impressionistic response to something read is that it is "interesting"—a word that actually says little about what was read, because it begs such questions as "What in particular was interesting?" and "Why was it interesting?"

A similar response, and one that is easier to get analytical about, is that something read is "odd." Write a page about something that you found odd. Be as specific as possible about the data that led you to this impression. It could be the plot of a TV show, the outcome of a sporting event, the behavior of a friend in a given circumstance, or, of course, something you have read. Bring to bear especially the first and third strategies offered earlier for making personal response more analytical: trace your responses back to their causes, and try to maintain critical detachment on your subject. One good tip for making personal response analytical is to think of your responses as those that any reasonable person might have, as opposed to those that depend upon your particular attitudes and experience.

### The Agree/Disagree Topic

We offer here only a brief recap of this kind of topic, because it is discussed at length in an earlier chapter. Topics are frequently worded this way, especially on essay exams, but the wording is potentially misleading, because you are rarely being asked for as unqualified an opinion as agree or disagree.

Creating opposing categories (binary oppositions) is fundamental to defining things. But binaries are also dangerous because they can invite *reductive thinking*—oversimplifying a subject by eliminating alternatives between the two extremes.

Your best strategy in dealing with agree/disagree questions is to start not by choosing one side or the other and arguing for it, but rather by using some more expository (explanatory) mode, such as comparison and contrast or definition, that will help you to understand what is at stake on each side of the opposition. In most cases, if you take time to analyze the agree/disagree issue, you will come to question its terms and ultimately to arrive at a more complex and qualified position to write about. You should aim, in other words, at using the binary split to organize the issue, but then move beyond the generally oversimplified either/or format in order to discuss how both sides of the issue are related.

These matters are treated in considerable detail in Chapter 3, especially "Refocus Binaries" and "Strategies for Using Binaries Analytically." We offer here a brief review of these strategies:

Strategy 1: locate a range of opposing categories.

Strategy 2: analyze and define the opposing terms.

Strategy 3: question the accuracy of the binary.

Strategy 4: change "either/or" to "the extent to which" ("to what extent?").

Applying these strategies will usually cause you to do one or more of the following (repeated from Chapter 3):

1. Weight one side of your binary more heavily than the other, rather than seeing the issue as all or nothing (all of one and none of the other).
2. Discover that you have not adequately named the binary; another opposition would be more accurate.
3. Discover that the two terms of your binary are not really so separate and opposed after all, but actually part of one complex phenomenon or issue.

---

**APPLICATION:**

## WORKING THROUGH BINARIES

Using the strategies discussed in this section, write a page or two in which you analyze the familiar expression "School gets in the way of one's education."Resort to your personal experience insofar as it is pertinent, but keep the focus on working through the binary implicit in the quotation. What other terms would you align with "school" and with "education"? Your analysis should also question the accuracy of the claim. Although you may ultimately agree or disagree with its sentiments, you should assess to what extent, and in what ways, the expression is both true and false.

---

## Comparison/Contrast and Definition Topics

Among the most common topics are those that ask you to compare and/or contrast parts of a subject or to define its key concepts or terms. Like summary topics, these also call upon you to assemble and organize the information you have been acquiring in a course. We have chosen to treat comparison/contrast and definition topics together because both (1) organize the information into categories and (2) proceed on the basis of similarity and difference.

At first glance, the comparative nature of definitions may appear less obvious, but in defining, you first classify something as part of a group or category of comparable things and then you differentiate it from those other things.

A chair, for example, is a piece of furniture (classification) that one person can sit on, which differentiates it from other furniture, such as tables, which no one sits on, and from sofas, which several people can sit on.

The biggest advantage of comparison/contrast and definition topics, and the reason that they get assigned so frequently, is that they press you to understand different parts of your subject in relation to one another. As a result, you can:

1. Understand each part more clearly, because you will be considering what it has that another part does not, and what it lacks that another part contains.
2. Understand how the various parts of your subject are divided or connected.

At the beginning of Chapter 3, in a section entitled "What It Means to Have an Idea," we suggested that an idea may connect elements and explain the significance of the connection and that it may account for some dissonance, something that seems not to fit together. The tasks that comparison/contrast and definition topics ask you to do lead in these directions: the fundamental assumption from which they spring is that you can usually discover ideas about a subject much more easily when you are not viewing it in isolation.

When executed mechanically, however, without the writer pressing to understand the significance of a similarity or difference, comparison/contrast and definition topics can suffer from pointlessness. They are not by nature pointless, but they often produce results that, quite literally, lack any controlling purpose or point. The problem arises because such topics sometimes appear to invite you simply to present inert information. Although these topics are meant to invite analysis, they are too often treated as ends in themselves.

Comparison/contrast topics produce pointless essays if you allow them to turn into matching exercises—that is, if you match different parts of the subject or common features of two subjects, but don't get beyond the equation stage ($a, b, c = x, y, z$). Writers fall into this trap when they have no larger question or issue to explore and perhaps resolve by making the comparison. If, for example, you were to pursue the comparison of the representations of the Boston Tea Party in British and American history textbooks, you would begin by identifying similarities and differences. But simply presenting these and concluding that the two versions resemble and differ from each other in some ways would be pointless.

Like comparison/contrast topics, definition topics can produce pointless essays when you get no further than assembling pertinent information. In other words, *definition is meaningful only within some context:* you define "rhythm and blues" because it is essential to any further discussion of the evolution of rock-and-roll music, or because you need that definition in order to discuss the British Invasion spearheaded by groups such as the Beatles, the

Rolling Stones, and the Yardbirds in the late 1960s, or because you cannot classify John Lennon or Mick Jagger or Eric Clapton without it. Moreover, when you construct a summary of existing definitions with no clear sense of purpose, you tend to list definitions indiscriminately. As a result, you are likely to overlook conflicts among the various definitions and overemphasize their surface similarities.

### Strategies for Using Comparison/Contrast Analytically

Given that your response to comparison topics can suffer from an essential underlying problem—pointlessness—it is not surprising that there is a single underlying solution: *give the comparison a point.* In most cases, you can provide this solution by ranking the information, focusing it, and then asking and answering the question, "So what?" All of the more specific strategies that follow develop from this starting point. (For suggestions on ways of organizing comparison/contrast essays, see Chapter 5, the section entitled "Organizing Comparisons and Contrasts.")

#### STRATEGY 1: DISCUSS REVEALING SIMILARITIES AND DIFFERENCES

Perhaps the best way to press yourself beyond the pointless comparison is to *look at the categories you have assembled and ask yourself, "So what?"* In comparing the textbook treatments of the Boston Tea Party, you would probably first need to focus on particular matches that seem especially revealing—for example, that British and American textbooks trace the economic background of the incident in different ways. Then, in response to the "So what?" question, you would attempt to develop some explanation of what these differences reveal and why they are significant. You might, for example, decide that the British textbooks view the matter from a more global economic perspective, whereas American textbooks emphasize nationalism. (See Chapter 4, the section entitled "The Evolving Thesis and the Revision Process: Pursuing Implications by Asking "So What?")

#### STRATEGY 2: ARGUE FOR THE SIGNIFICANCE OF A KEY COMPARISON

Rather than simply covering a range of comparisons, focus on a key comparison. Although narrowing the focus might seem to eliminate other important areas of consideration, in fact it usually allows you to incorporate at least some of these other areas in a more tightly connected, less listlike fashion.

So, for example, a comparison of the burial rites of two cultures will probably reveal more about them than a much broader but more superficial list of cultural similarities and differences. And in developing this comparison, you would probably be able to bring in cultural attitudes toward religion, gender, family structure, the land, and so forth. In the majority of cases, covering less is covering more.

Implicit in this way of fixing the comparison topic is the method of *ranking* introduced in the advice for fixing summary topics. You are ranking whenever you designate one part of your topic as especially important or revealing. As a critical move, ranking induces you to convert summary into analysis. Let's consider one more example. Suppose you are asked to compare General Norman Schwarzkopf's strategy in the Persian Gulf War with General Douglas MacArthur's strategy in World War II. As a first move, you could limit the comparison to some revealing parallel, such as the way each man dealt with the media, and then argue for its significance above other similarities or differences. You might, for instance, claim that in their treatment of the media we get an especially clear or telling vantage point on the two generals' strategies. At this point you are on your way to an analytical point—for example, that because MacArthur was more effectively shielded from the media at a time when the media was a virtual instrument of propaganda, he could make choices that Schwarzkopf might have wanted to make but couldn't.

### STRATEGY 3: USE ONE SIDE OF THE COMPARISON TO ILLUMINATE THE OTHER

Usually it is not necessary to treat each part of the comparison equally. It's a common misconception that each side must be given equal space. In fact, the purpose of your comparison governs the amount of space you'll need to give to each part. Often, you will be using one side of the comparison primarily to illuminate the other. For example, in a course on contemporary military policy, the ratio between the two parts would probably be roughly seventy percent on Schwarzkopf to thirty percent on MacArthur rather than fifty percent on each.

### STRATEGY 4: IMAGINE HOW ONE SIDE OF YOUR COMPARISON MIGHT RESPOND TO THE OTHER

This strategy, a variant of the preceding one, is a particularly useful way of helping you to respond to comparison/contrast topics more purposefully. This strategy can be adapted to a wide variety of subjects. If you were asked to compare Sigmund Freud with one of his most important followers, Jacques Lacan, you would probably be better off focusing the broad question of how Lacan revises Freud by considering how and why he might critique Freud's interpretation of a particular dream in *The Interpretation of Dreams*. Similarly, in the case of the Persian Gulf War example, you could ask yourself how MacArthur might have handled some key decision in the Persian Gulf War and why. Or you might consider how he would have critiqued Schwarzkopf's handling of that decision and why.

### STRATEGY 5: FOCUS ON UNEXPECTED SIMILARITIES AND DIFFERENCES

The typical move when you are asked to compare two subjects is to collect a number of parallel examples and show how they are parallel. In the case of obvious similarities, you should move quickly to *significant differences within the similarity* and the implications of these differences. For example, the Carolingian and Burgundian Renaissances share an emphasis on education, but if you were asked to compare them, you could reveal the character of these two historical periods more effectively by concentrating on the different purposes and origins of this emphasis in education. A corollary of this tip is that you should

## APPLICATION:

### FINDING THE UNEXPECTED SIMILARITY OR DIFFERENCE

The strategies for using comparison and definition share a common goal: to prevent these topics from becoming inert summaries. You might try all of them in conjunction with reading you are doing in one of your courses. We have chosen an exercise based on those strategies that aim at getting you to rank your comparisons and contrasts by some principle—as the "Application" on summary invited you to do—as a means of getting beyond a pointless matching exercise.

The preceding discussion has offered several examples of kinds of topics that would offer good experience with making comparison and contrast more analytical, to which we add the following list:

Accounts of the same event from two different newspapers or magazines or textbooks

Courtship behavior as practiced by men and by women

Two CDs by the same artist or group

Two versions of the same song by different artists

Two ads for the same kind of product

Graffiti in men's restrooms versus graffiti in women's restrooms

The political campaigns of two opponents running for the same or similar office

Two breeds of dog

Two clothing styles as emblematic of a group or subgroup in your school, town, or workplace

Select one item from this list, and write a comparative essay. First, list as many similarities and differences as you can: go for coverage. Then go over your list, and select the two or three most revealing similarities and the two or three most revealing differences. At this point, you are ready to write an essay in which you argue for the significance of a key difference or similarity. In so doing, you may find it interesting to focus on an *unexpected* similarity or difference—one that other readers might not initially notice. (We recommend trying the "unexpected" gambit.)

focus on *unexpected similarity rather than obvious difference*. It is no surprise that President Bill Clinton's economic package differed from President Ronald Reagan's, but much could be written about the way that Clinton "out-Reaganed Bush" (as one political commentator put it) by appealing to voters with Reagan's brand of populist optimism.

### Strategies for Using Definition Analytically

As with interpreting comparison topics, so with revising definition topics: the key is to give them a point, which is usually a matter of examining and using definitions rather than simply including them.

#### STRATEGY 1: TEST THE DEFINITION AGAINST EVIDENCE

One common form of the definition topic asks you to apply a definition to a body of information. It is rare to find a perfect fit. Therefore, you should, as a general rule, use the data to assess the accuracy and the limitations of the definition, rather than simply imposing it on your data and ignoring or playing down the ways in which it does not fit.

Suppose you were given the assignment, "Define capitalism in the context of third world economies." You might begin by matching some standard definition of *capitalism* with specific examples from one or two third world economies, with the express purpose of detecting where the definition does and does not apply. In other words, you would respond to the definition topic by assaying the extent to which the definition provides a tool for making sense of the subject.

#### STRATEGY 2: EXPLORE COMPETING PARTS OF THE DEFINITION

Another common form of the definition topic focuses on the term itself—such as "What is capitalism?" Such topics generally aim to get you to achieve some perspective on the term, to understand its richness of implication. In such cases, you can avoid passive summary—simply listing definitions from a range of sources—by exploring competing parts or versions of the definition.

The definition of *capitalism* that you might take from Karl Marx, for example, will differ in its emphases from Adam Smith's. In this case, you would not only isolate the most important of these differences but also try to account for the fact that Marx's villain is Smith's hero. Such an accounting would probably lead you to consider how the definition has been shaped by each of these writers' political philosophies or by the culture in which each theory was composed.

When you respond to a definition topic by exploring competing parts of the definition, you are, in effect, *focusing on the significance of the difficulties of definition.* That is, your analysis achieves direction and purpose by problematizing the term—locating and then exploring the significance of the uncertainties and conflicts of definition.

#### STRATEGY 3: USE A DEFINITION FROM ONE SOURCE TO CRITIQUE ANOTHER

As a general rule, you should attempt to identify the points of view of the sources from which you take your definitions, rather than accepting them as uncontextualized "answers." If you can distinguish the particular slant, your treatment of definition topics will usually move beyond simply synthesizing lists of defining characteristics from your sources. Such synthesis is often a problem, because it tends to overlook the conflicting elements among various definitions of a key term.

A paper on alcoholism, for example, will lose focus if you use all of the definitions available. If, instead, you *convert the definition topic into a comparison and contrast of competing definitions,* you can more easily generate a point and purpose for your definition. By querying, for example, whether a given source's definition of *alcoholism* is moral or physiological or psychological, you can more easily problematize the issue of definition.

### STRATEGY 4: SHIFT FROM "WHAT?" TO "HOW?" AND "WHY?" QUESTIONS

It is no accident that we earlier offered the same strategy for making summary topics more analytical: like all productive analytical topics, those that require

---

## APPLICATION:

### DEFINING IN DEPTH

As the chapter has been arguing, weak use of definition simply applies a given definition to a body of material in a way that affects neither. Defining in depth is a process analogous to the one that this book advocated in its discussion of the relation between thesis and evidence in Chapter 4, "Making the Thesis Evolve." The definition should allow us to see things that don't fit, which, in turn, should lead us to revise the definition.

Using the example about alcoholism in the preceding Strategy 3, write a comparative definition in which you seek out different and potentially competing definitions of the same term or terms.

Begin with a dictionary such as the *Oxford English Dictionary* (popularly known as the *OED*, available in most library reference rooms) that contains both historically based definitions that track the term's evolution over time and etymological definitions that identify the linguistic origins of the term— what the words from which it came (in older languages) mean. Locate both the etymology and the historical evolution of the term or terms.

Then look up the term in one or preferably several specialized dictionaries. We offer a list of some of these in Chapter 7, "Using Secondary Sources," but you can also ask your reference librarian for pertinent titles. Generally speaking, different disciplines generate their own specialized dictionaries.

Summarize key differences and similarities among the ways the dictionaries have defined your term or terms. Then write a comparative essay in which you argue for the significance of a key similarity or difference, or an unexpected one.

Here is the list of words: *hysteria, ecstasy, enthusiasm, witchcraft, leisure, gossip, bachelor, spinster, romantic, instinct, punk, thug, pundit, dream, alcoholism, aristocracy, atom, ego, pornography, conservative, liberal, entropy, election, tariff.*

Some of these words are interesting to look at together, such as *ecstasy/ enthusiasm* or *liberal/ conservative* or *bachelor/spinster.* Feel free to write on a pair instead of a single word.

definition finally depend on "Why?" or "How?" questions, not "What?" questions. Because, like summary topics, definition topics appear at first glance to be asking a "What?" question, you need to be especially vigilant in resisting the temptation to do little more than gather information (in this case, uses of the term to be defined).

If, for example, you were confronted with the assignment to define the meaning of "darkness" in Joseph Conrad's *Heart of Darkness* and any two other modern British novels, you would do better to ask why the writers find "darkness" such a fertile term than simply to accumulate various examples of the term in the three novels. You might start by isolating the single best example from each of the works, preferably one that reveals important differences as well as similarities. Then, in analyzing how each writer uses the term, you could work toward some larger point that would unify the essay. You might show how the conflicts of definition within Conrad's metaphor evolve historically, get reshaped by woman novelists, change after World War I, and so forth.

## Key Words (in order of appearance)

| | |
|---|---|
| epistemology | focused freewriting |
| conversant | contextualizing |
| paraphrasing | reductive thinking |
| complexity | binaries |
| ambiguity | dissonance |
| freewriting | problematize |

## Guidelines for Making Your Response to Topics More Analytical

1. Start with questions rather than preconceived or obvious answers. Don't settle for your first response or idea.
2. Experiment with prewriting. Find out what you think by seeing what you say.
3. Analyze the topic by uncovering unstated assumptions and questioning key terms. What, for example, does "good" mean in the question "Is feminism good for Judaism?"
4. Seek out uncertainty and complexity. Look for multiple and competing possibilities to negotiate rather than a single "right" answer.
5. Drastically reduce scope. Concentrate on—rank—what seems the most important or revealing part of your subject rather than trying to cover everything.
6. Develop your observations by asking yourself, "So what?" Why is what you have noticed significant?
7. Complicate binaries: get past either/or formulations.

8. Avoid turning comparisons into pointless matching exercises. Set up similarities and differences only to discuss the significance of that comparison.
9. Rather than answering a question of definition with inert summary, test the definition against evidence and/or explore its competing parts.

## CHAPTER 7

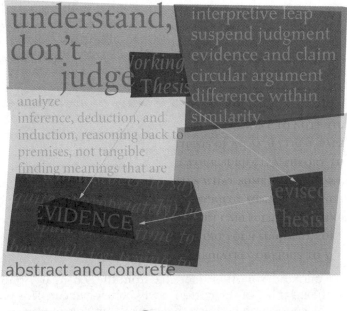

# USING SECONDARY SOURCES

There are three characteristic problems that writers can have with incorporating research into their writing:

1. Leaving quotations and paraphrases to speak for themselves
2. Not differentiating themselves from their sources (ventriloquizing)
3. Resorting to overly global agreeing and disagreeing as their only means of response other than summary

This chapter is built around a concept we call *conversing with sources*—an alternative to letting them speak for you or ignoring them altogether. The chapter will also address such matters as finding and evaluating sources, citing sources (see also the "Appendix" on documentation), integrating quotations into one's own prose, and organizing a research paper.

Note: we will use the terms *source* and *secondary source* interchangeably to designate ideas and information about your subject that you find in the work of other writers. Distinctions can be made between these terms: if you were writing a paper on the philosopher Nietzsche, his writing would be your *primary source,* and critical commentaries on his work would be your secondary sources. If, however, you were writing on the poet Yeats, who read and was influenced by Nietzsche, a work of Nietzsche's philosophy would become a secondary source of yours on your primary source, Yeats's poetry. Chapter 2 of this book, "Analyzing Evidence," is essentially about primary sources. This chapter is about how to analyze and incorporate the secondary sources you use to understand your primary sources.

## Secondary Sources Are a Form of Evidence

Because the use of secondary sources is a special case of the use of evidence, the strategies for analyzing them resemble those we offered in Chapter 2, "Analyzing Evidence." First and foremost, you cannot expect secondary sources to speak for themselves. Rather, you need to *clarify the meaning of the material you have quoted or paraphrased or summarized and explain its significance* in light of your evolving thesis.

A problem in using secondary sources emerges when a writer leaves the experts he or she cites to speak for themselves. In this situation, the writer characteristically makes a generalization in his or her own words, then juxtaposes it to a quotation or other reference from the secondary source and assumes that the meaning of the reference will be self-evident. This practice not only leaves the connection between the writer's thinking and his or her source material unstated, but also substitutes mere repetition of someone else's viewpoint for a more active interpretation. The source has been allowed to have the final word, with the effect that it stops the discussion and the writer's thinking.

### "Source Anxiety" and What to Do about It

The risk of using sources uncritically does not mean that you should ignore them altogether. *A writer needs to find the middle ground between developing an idea that is entirely independent of what experts have written on a subject and producing a paper that does nothing but repeat other people's ideas.* If you don't consult what others have said, you run at least two risks:

1. You will waste your time reinventing the wheel.
2. You will undermine your analysis (or at least leave it incomplete) by not considering information or acknowledging positions that are commonly discussed in the field.

By remaining unaware of existing thinking, you choose, in effect, to stand outside of the conversation that others interested in the subject are having. Standing in this sort of intellectual vacuum sometimes appeals to writers who fear that consulting sources will leave them with nothing to say. But it is possible, as this chapter shows, to learn what others have had to say without allowing your sources to do all of your thinking for you. A little research—even if it's only an hour's browse in the reference collection of the library—will virtually always raise the level of what you have to say above what it would have been if you had consulted only the information and opinions that you carry around in your head.

A fear that some writers express is that using secondary sources will cause them to lose track of their own ideas. Confronted with the seasoned views of experts in a discipline, you may well feel that there is nothing left for you to say because it has all been said before, or, at least, it has been said by people who greatly outweigh you in reputation and experience. This anxiety explains why so many writers surrender to the role of conduit for the voices of the experts, providing conjunctions between quotations.

A good rule of thumb for coping with this anxiety is to formulate a tentative position on your topic before you consult secondary sources. In other words, give yourself time to do some preliminary thinking. Try prewriting about the topic, analyzing some piece of pertinent information already at your disposal. That way you will have in writing your initial responses to weigh against what others have said. Prewriting of this sort also helps you to select what to look at in the sources you eventually consult.

## The Conversation Analogy

The first step in using sources effectively—neither discounting nor overrelying on them—is to *reject the assumption that sources provide final and complete answers.* If they did, there would be no reason for others to continue writing on the subject. As in conversation, we raise ideas for others to respond to. Accepting that no source has the final word does not mean, however, that you should shift from unquestioning approval to the opposite pole and necessarily assume an antagonistic position toward all sources. Indeed, a habitually antagonistic response to others' ideas is just as likely to bring your conversation with your sources to a halt as is the habit of always assuming that the source must have the final word.

Most people would probably agree on the attributes of a really good conversation. There is room for agreement and disagreement, for give and take, among a variety of viewpoints. Generally, people don't deliberately misunderstand each other, but a significant amount of the discussion may go into clarifying one's own as well as others' positions. Such conversations construct a genuinely collaborative *chain* of thinking: Karl builds on what David has said, which induces Jill to respond to Karl's comment, and so forth.

There are, of course, obvious differences between conversing aloud with friends and conversing on paper with sources. As a writer, you must construct the chain of thinking, orchestrate the exchange of views with and among your sources, and give the conversation direction and point. A good place to begin in using sources is to recognize that you need not respond to everything another writer says, nor do you need to come up with an entirely original point of view—one that completely revises or refutes the source. You are using sources analytically, for example, when you note that two experiments (or historical accounts, or whatever) are similar but have different priorities, or that they ask similar questions in different ways. Building from this kind of observation, you could then analyze what these differences imply.

There are, in any case, many ways of approaching secondary sources, but they generally share a common goal: *to use the source as a point of departure.* Here is a brief list of ways to do that:

- Make as many points as you can about a single representative passage from your source, and then branch out from this center to analyze other passages that "speak" to it in some way. (See Chapter 2, the section "10 on 1 vs. 1 on 10.")
- Build upon the source's point of view, extending its implications.
- Apply the idea in the source to another subject.
- Agree with most of what the source says, but take issue with one small part that you want to modify.
- Identify a contradiction in the source, and explore its implications, without necessarily arriving at a solution.

If you quote with the aim of conversing with your sources rather than allowing them to do your thinking for you, you will discover that sources can promote rather than stifle your analysis. In short, think of sources not as answers but as voices inviting you into a community of interpretation, discussion, and debate.

---

### VOICES FROM ACROSS THE CURRICULUM

### REPORTING VERSUS ANALYZING IN SCIENTIFIC EXPERIMENTS

There is a big difference between simply reporting on what has been done in a scientific venture and analyzing and evaluating the venture. One of the problems with trying to *read* critical analyses of scientific work is that few scientists want to be in print criticizing their colleagues. That is, for political reasons scientists who write reviews are likely to soften their criticism or even avoid it entirely by reporting the findings of others simply and directly. However, by definition such a review is not critical. That author stakes out no particular point of view and thus does not have to defend anything.

What I want from students in molecular biology is a critical analysis of the work they have researched. This can take several forms.

First, *analyze* what was done. What were the assumptions (hypotheses) going into the experiment? What was the logic of the experimental design? What were the results?

Second, *evaluate* the results and conclusions. Here, it's even appropriate to use the first person. *You* are commenting on the field. Foremost, how well do the results support the conclusions? What alternative interpretations are there? What additional experiments could be done to strengthen or refute

*(continued)*

*(continued)*

their argument? This is hard, no doubt, but it is what you should be doing every time you read anything in science or otherwise.

Third, *synthesize* the results and interpretations of a given experiment in the context of the field. How does this study inform other studies? Even though practicing scientists are hesitant to do this in print, everyone does it informally in journal clubs held usually on a weekly basis in every lab all over the world. When I publish something, I know that all over the United States, Canada, Japan, and Europe, there are scientists sitting around in little rooms ripping my paper to shreds.

—**Bruce Wightman,** *Professor of Biology*

## Six Strategies for Critical Analysis of Sources

### Strategy 1: Make Your Sources Speak

Quote, paraphrase, or summarize *in order to* analyze. You should not assume that either the meaning of the source material or your reason for including it is self-evident. You should also avoid just stringing together citations for which you provide little more than conjunctions. Instead, explain to your readers what the quotation or paraphrase or summary of the source means. What elements of it do you want to emphasize? How does it relate to your evolving thesis?

In making a source speak, focus on articulating how the source has led to the conclusion you draw from it. Beware of simply putting a generalization and a quotation next to each other (juxtaposing them) without explaining the connection. Consider this problem in the following paragraph from a student's paper on political conservatism:

> Edmund Burke's philosophy evolved into contemporary American conservative ideology. There is an important distinction between philosophy and political ideology: philosophy is "the knowledge of general principles that explain facts and existences." Political ideology, on the other hand, is "an overarching conception of society, a stance that is reflected in numerous sectors of social life" (Edwards 22). Therefore, conservatism should be regarded as an ideology rather than a philosophy.

The final sentence offers the writer's conclusion—what the source information has led him to—but how did it get him there? The word "therefore" indicates to the reader that the conclusion is the result of a process of logical reasoning, but this reasoning has been omitted. Instead, the writer assumes that the reader will be able to connect the quotations with his conclusion. The writer needs to make the quotation speak by analyzing its key terms more closely. What is "an overarching conception of society," and how does it differ from "knowledge of general principles"? More importantly, what is the ratio-nale for categorizing conservatism as either an ideology or a philosophy?

Here, by contrast, is a writer who makes her sources speak. Note how she integrates analysis with quotation:

> Stephen Greenblatt uses the phrase "self-fashioning" to refer to an idea he believes developed during the Renaissance—the idea that one's iden-tity is not created or born but rather shaped, both by one's self and by others. The idea of self-fashioning is incorporated into an attitude to-ward literature that has as its ideal what Greenblatt calls "poetics of cul-ture." A text is examined with three elements in mind: the author's own self, the cultural self-fashioning process that created that self, and the author's reaction to that process. Because our selves, like texts, are "fash-ioned," an author's life is just as open to interpretation as that of a liter-ary character.
>
> If this is so, then biography does not provide a repository of unshake-able facts from which to interpret an author's work. Greenblatt criticizes the fact that the methods of literary interpretation are applied just to art and not to life. As he observes, "We wall off literary symbolism from the symbolic structures operative elsewhere, as if art alone were a human cre-ation" (Begley 37). If the line between art and life is indeed blurred, then we need a more complex model for understanding the relationship be-tween the life and work of an author.

In this example, we can see how the writer's thinking has been stimu-lated by the source. At the end of the first paragraph and the beginning of the second, for example, she not only specifies what she takes to be the meaning of the quotation but also draws a conclusion about its implications (that the facts of an author's life, like his or her art, require interpretation). And this manner of proceeding is habitual: the writer repeats the pattern in the second paragraph, *moving beyond what the quotation says to explore what its logic suggests.*

## Strategy 2: Use Your Sources to Ask Questions, Not Just to Provide Answers

Use your selections from sources as a means of raising issues and questions. Avoid the temptation to plug in such selections as "answers" that require no further commentary or elaboration. In other words, in your source reading you will no doubt find viewpoints you believe to be valid, but it is not enough to drop these "answers" from the source into your own writing at the appropriate spots. You need to *do* something with the secondary material, even with those sources that seem to have said what you want to say.

As long as you consider only the source in isolation, you may not discover much to say about it. Once you begin considering it in other contexts and with other sources, you may begin to see aspects of your subject that your source *problematizing* does not adequately address. Having recognized that the source does not answer all questions, you should not conclude that the source is "wrong"—only that it is limited in some ways. Discovering such limitations is in fact advantageous, because it can lead you to identify a place from which to launch your own analysis.

It does not necessarily follow that you will then provide your own answer in place of one offered by a source. Often—in fact, far more often than many writers suspect—it is enough to discover an issue or problem and raise it clearly. Phrasing *explicitly* the issues and questions that remain *implicit* in a source is an important part of what analytical writers do, especially with cases in which there is no solution, or at least none that can be presented in a relatively short paper. Here, for example, is how the writer on Stephen Greenblatt's concept of "self-fashioning" concludes her essay:

> It is not only the author whose role is complicated by New Historicism; the critic also is subject to some of the same qualifications and restrictions. According to Adam Begley, "it is the essence of the new-historicist project to uncover the moments at which works of art absorb and refashion social energy, an endless process of circulation and exchange" (39). In other words, the work is both affected by and affects the culture. But if this is so, how then can we decide which elements of culture (and text) are causes and which are effects? If we add the critic to this picture, the process does indeed appear endless. The New Historicists' relationship with their culture infuses itself into their assessment of the Renaissance, and this assessment may in turn become part of their own self-fashioning process, which will affect their interpretations, and so forth. . . .

Notice that this writer *incorporates the quotation into her own chain of thinking.* By paraphrasing the quotation ("In other words"), she arrives at a question ("how then") that follows as a logical consequence of accepting its position ("but if this is so"). Note, however, that she does not then label the quotation right or wrong. Instead, she tries to figure out *to what position it might lead* and to what possible problems.

By contrast, the writer of the following excerpt, from a paper comparing two films aimed at teenagers, settles for plugging in sources as answers and consequently does not pursue the questions implicit in her quotations:

> In both films, the adults are one-dimensional caricatures, evil beings whose only goal in life is to make the kids' lives a living hell. In *Risky Business,* director Paul Brickman's solution to all of Joel's problems is to have him hire a prostitute and then turn his house into a whorehouse. Of course, as one critic observes, "the prostitutes who make themselves available to his pimply faced buddies are all centerfold beauties: elegant, svelte, benign and unquestionably healthy (after all, what does V.D. have to do with prostitutes?)" (Gould 41)—not exactly a realistic or legal solution.

Allan Moyle, the director of *Pump Up the Volume,* provides an equally unrealistic solution to Mark's problem. According to David Denby, Moyle "offers self-expression as the cure to adolescent funk. Everyone should start his own radio station and talk about his feelings" (59). Like Brickman, Moyle offers solutions that are neither realistic nor legal.

This writer is having a hard time figuring out what to do with sources that offer well-phrased and seemingly accurate answers ("self-expression as the cure to adolescent funk"). Her analysis of both quotations leads her to settle for the bland and undeveloped conclusion that films aimed at teenagers are "not realistic"—an observation that most readers would already recognize as true. But unlike the writer of the previous example, she does not ask herself, *"If this is true, then what follows?"* Had she done so, she might, for example, have inquired how the illegality of the solutions is related to their unrealistic quality. (So what, for example, that the main characters in both films are not marginalized as criminals and made to suffer for their illegal actions, but rather are celebrated as heroes? What different kinds of illegality do the two films apparently condone, and how might these be related to the different decades in which each film was produced?) Rather than use her sources to think with, in order to clarify or complicate the issues, the writer has simply used them to confirm an obvious generalization.

## Strategy 3: Put Your Sources into Conversation with One Another

Rather than limiting yourself to agreeing or disagreeing with your sources, aim for conversation with and among them. Although it is not "wrong" to agree or disagree with your sources, it is wrong to see these as your only possible moves. You should also understand that although it is sometimes useful and perhaps even necessary to agree and disagree, these judgments should (1) always be *qualified* and (2) occur only *in certain contexts.*

Especially near the beginning of a paper, for example, a source can be extraordinarily helpful in orienting your readers for the discussion to follow. This practice of *framing the discussion* typically locates the writer either for or against some well-known point of view or frame of reference. That is, a source can succinctly summarize a position that you plan to develop, or it can present a series of statements that you can challenge. This latter strategy—sometimes known as a *straw man,* because you construct a "dummy" position specifically in order to knock it down—can stimulate you to formulate a point of view, especially if you are not accustomed to responding critically to sources.

As this boxing analogy suggests, however, setting up a straw man can be a dangerous game. If you do not fairly represent and put into context the straw man's argument, you risk encouraging readers to dismiss your counterargument as a cheap shot and to dismiss you for being *reductive.* On the other hand, if you spend a great deal of time detailing the straw man's position, you risk losing momentum in developing your own point of view. In any case, if you are citing a source in order to frame the discussion, the more reasonable move is both to agree *and* disagree with it. First, identify shared premises; give the source some credit. Then distinguish the part of what you have cited that you intend to develop or complicate or dispute. This method of proceeding is obviously less combative than the typically blunt straw man approach; it verges on conversation.

In the following passages from a student's paper on Darwin's theory of evolution, the student clearly recognizes that he needs to do more than summarize what Darwin says, but he seems not to know any way of conversing with his source other than indicating his agreement and disagreement with it.

> The struggle for existence also includes the dependence of one being on another being to survive. Darwin also believes that all organic beings tend to increase. I do not fully agree with Darwin's belief here. I cannot conceive of the fact of all beings increasing in number. Darwin goes on to explain that food, competition, climate, and the location of a certain species contribute to its survival and existence in nature. I believe that this statement is very valid and that it could be very easily understood through experimentation in nature.

This writer's use of the word "here" in his third sentence is revealing. He is tagging summaries of Darwin with what he seems to feel is an obligatory response—a polite shake or nod of the head: I can't fully agree with you there, Darwin, but here I think you might have a point. The writer's tentative language lets us see how uncomfortable, even embarrassed, he feels about venturing these judgments on a subject that is too complex for this kind of response. It's as though the writer moves along, talking about Darwin's theory for a while, and then says to himself, "Time for a response," and lets a particular summary sentence trigger a yes/no switch. Having pressed that switch, which he does periodically, the writer resumes his summary, having registered but not analyzed his own interjections. There is no reasoning in a chain from his own observations, just random insertions of unanalyzed agree/disagree responses.

Here, by contrast, is the introduction of an essay that frames the conversation that the writer is preparing to have with her source:

> In *Renaissance Thought: The Classic, Scholastic and Humanist Strains,* Paul Kristeller responds to two problems that he perceives in Renaissance scholarship. The first is the haze of cultural meaning surrounding the word "humanism": he seeks to clarify the word and its origins, as well as to explain the apparent lack of religious concern in humanism. Kristeller also reacts to the notion of humanism as an improvement upon medieval Aristotelian scholasticism.

Rather than leading with her own beliefs about the source, the writer emphasizes the issues and problems she believes are central in it. Although the writer's position on her source is apparently neutral, she is not summarizing passively. In addition to making choices about what is especially significant in the source, she has also located it within the conversation that Kristeller was having with his own sources—other practitioners of Renaissance scholarship who have developed a widely accepted view of humanism he wants to revise ("Kristeller responds to two problems"). Further on in the paper, the writer achieves a clearer picture of Kristeller's point of view by putting it into conversation with another source:

> Unlike Kristeller, Tillyard [in *The Elizabethan World Picture*] also tries to place the seeds of individualism in the minds of the medievals. "Those who know most about the Middle Ages," he claims, "now assure us that humanism and a belief in the present life were powerful by the 12th century" (30). Kristeller would undoubtedly reply that it was scholasticism, lacking the humanist emphasis on individualism, that was powerful in the Middle Ages. True humanism was not evident in the Middle Ages.
>
> In Kristeller's view, Tillyard's attempts to assign humanism to medievals are not only unwarranted, but also counterproductive. Kristeller ends his chapter on "Humanism and Scholasticism" with an exhortation to "develop a kind of historical pluralism. It is easy to praise everything in the past that appears to resemble certain favorable ideas of our own time, or to ridicule and minimize everything that disagrees with them. This method is neither fair nor helpful" (174). Tillyard, in trying to locate humanism within the medieval world, allows the value of humanism to supersede the worth of medieval scholarship. Kristeller argues that there is inherent worth in every intellectual movement, not simply in the ones that we find most agreeable.
>
> Kristeller's work is valuable to us primarily for its forthright definition of humanism. Tillyard has cleverly avoided this undertaking: he provides many textual references, usually with the companion comment that "this is an example of Renaissance humanism," but he never overtly and fully formulates the definition in the way that Kristeller does.

As this excerpt makes evident, the writer has found something to say about her source by putting it into conversation with another source ("Kristeller would undoubtedly reply") with which she believes Kristeller would disagree. Although it seems obvious that the writer prefers Kristeller to Tillyard, her agreement with him is not the main point of her analysis. She focuses instead on foregrounding the problem that Kristeller is trying to solve and on relating that problem to different attitudes toward history. In so doing, she is deftly orchestrating the conversation between her sources. Her next step would be to distinguish her position from Kristeller's. Having used Kristeller to get perspective on Tillyard, she now needs somehow to get perspective on Kristeller. The next strategy will address this issue.

**APPLICATION:**

## MAKING ONE SOURCE SPEAK TO ANOTHER

This exercise requires you to filter one source through another, speculating (imagining) how each source would respond to the other's position. Choose two articles or book chapters by different authors or by the same author at different points in his or her career. The overriding aim of the exercise is to give you practice in getting beyond merely reacting and generalizing, and instead, to participate in the *thinking* of your sources.

As a kind of model for this exercise, you might look again at the preceding example in which the student writer compares and contrasts two historical scholars on the nature of Renaissance humanism. This example demonstrates the difference between having an idea about someone else's idea and simply reacting to someone else's idea.

Keep in mind that your aim in this exercise is not to arrive at *your* opinion of the sources, but rather to construct the conversation that you think the author of one of your sources might have with the author of another. *How might they recast each other's ideas, as opposed to merely agreeing or disagreeing with those ideas?* It's useful to confine yourself to thinking as impartially as you can about the ideas found in your two sources.

## Strategy 4: Find Your Own Role in the Conversation

Even in cases in which you find a source's position entirely congenial, it is not enough simply to agree with it. In order to converse with a source, you need to find some way of having a distinct voice in that conversation. This does not mean that you should feel compelled to attack the source, but rather that you need to find something of your own to say about it.

In general, you have two options when you find yourself strongly in agreement with a source.

1. You can *work with* the source by expanding its implications, by applying it to new situations, and by pointing out areas in it that deserve more attention. In other words, you can maintain your general agreement with the source, but try to go somewhere else with it.
2. You can seek out other perspectives on the source in order to break the spell it has cast upon you. Breaking the spell means that you will necessarily become somewhat disillusioned, but not that you will then need to dismiss everything you previously believed.

How, in the first option, do you take a source somewhere else? Look again at the preceding example of Renaissance humanism. Rather than focusing solely on what the writer believes Kristeller finds most important, she might locate a point she finds especially interesting that Kristeller did not choose to emphasize and that she wished he had developed further. Then she could follow through on his lead and uncover new implications that depend upon Kristeller but that lie outside his own governing preoccupations. Or she might apply his principles to new geographic (rather than theoretical) areas, such as Germany instead of Italy.

The second option, researching new perspectives on the source, can also lead to uncovering new implications. Your aim need not be simply to find a source that disagrees with the one that has convinced you and then switch your allegiance, because this move would perpetuate the problem from which you are trying to escape. Instead, you would use additional perspectives to gain some critical distance on your source. An ideal way of sampling possible critical approaches to a source is to consult book reviews on it found in scholarly journals. Once the original source is taken down from the pedestal through additional reading, there is a greater likelihood that you will see how to distinguish your views from those it offers.

You may think, for example, that another source's critique of your original source is partly valid and that both sources miss things that you could point out, in effect refereeing the conversation between them. The writer on Kristeller might play this role by asking herself: "So what that subsequent historians have viewed his objective—a disinterested historical pluralism—as not necessarily desirable and in any case impossible? How might Kristeller respond to this charge, and how has he responded already in ways that his critics have failed to notice?" Using additional research in this way can lead you to *situate* your source more fully and fairly, acknowledging its limits as well as its strengths.

In other words, this writer, in using Kristeller to critique Tillyard, has arrived less at a conclusion than at her next point of departure. A good rule to follow, especially when you find a source entirely persuasive, is that *if you can't find a perspective on your source, you haven't done enough research.*

---

### ◢ APPLICATION:

### USING FREEWRITING TO CONVERSE WITH SOURCES

1. As we discussed in the "Application" that follows the "Focused Freewriting" section of Chapter 6, a twenty-minute focused freewrite on a single short passage taken from a text that you are studying is one of the best analytical exercises you can do.

   Try a twenty-minute freewrite on a selected passage from a secondary source. Choose the passage in answer to the following question: "What is the one passage in the source that I need to discuss, that poses a question or a problem or that seems, in some way perhaps difficult to pin down, anomalous or even just unclear?"

   *(continued)*

*(continued)*

Write the passage at the top of the page, and go. Force yourself to stay on task for the complete time, and if, at the end, you find you have more to say, keep going until you don't.

Here are a few general guidelines for focused freewriting, adapted from Chapter 6:

- Paraphrase key terms in the passage, laying out their possible meanings.
- Address how the passage is representative of broader issues in the source; you may wish to refer to a similar passage.
- Attend, at least briefly, to the context surrounding the passage, identifying the larger section from which it is taken.

2. As a variation on the preceding exercise, *apply a brief passage from a secondary source to a brief passage from a primary source.* Choose the secondary source passage first—one that you find particularly interesting, revealing, or problematic. Then locate a corresponding passage from the primary source to which the sentence from the first passage can be connected in some way. Write both passages at the top of the page, and then start writing. You should probably include paraphrases of key phrases in both; but your primary goal is to think about the two together, to allow them to interact. Try this for twenty minutes, and if you are getting somewhere, don't stop.

## Strategy 5: Supply Ongoing Analysis of Sources (Don't Wait Until the End)

Unless disciplinary conventions dictate otherwise, analyze *as* you quote or paraphrase sources, rather than summarizing everything first and leaving your analysis for the end. A good conversation does not consist of long monologues alternating among the speakers. Participants exchange views, query, and modify what other speakers have said. Similarly, when you orchestrate conversations with and among your sources, you need to *integrate your analysis into your presentation* of them.

---

**VOICES FROM ACROSS THE CURRICULUM**

**BRINGING SOURCES TOGETHER**

Avoid serial citation summaries; that is, rather than discussing what Author A found, then what Author B found, then what Author C found, and so

*(continued)*

*Bringing Sources Together (continued)*

forth, *integrate* material from all of your sources. For instance, if writing about the cause and treatment of a disorder, discuss what all authors say about cause, then what all authors say about treatment, and so forth, addressing any contradictions or tensions among authors.

—**ALAN TJELTVEIT,** *Professor of Psychology*

If you integrate your analysis as you go along, you will be more likely to explain how the information in the source fits into your unfolding presentation, and your readers will be more likely to follow your train of thought and grasp the logic of your organization. See the discussion of integrating analysis with the research paper later in this chapter.

## Strategy 6: Attend Carefully to the Language of Your Sources by Quoting or Paraphrasing It

Rather than generalizing broadly about ideas in your sources, you should spell out what you think is significant about their key words. In those disciplines in which it is permissible, *quote* sources—as opposed to paraphrasing them—*if the actual language that they use is important to your point.* This practice will help you to represent the view of your source fairly and accurately. In circumstances where quoting is not allowed—such as the report format in psychology—you still need to attend carefully to the meaning of key words in order to arrive at a paraphrase that is not overly general.

In most cases, paying close attention to the language will lead you to uncover attitudes implicit in the source. When you paraphrase, for example—as is not the case when summarizing—you necessarily come to terms with the language of the source. Paraphrasing doesn't just talk about the language; it takes that language and recasts it into synonymous terms. The process of arriving at suitable synonyms is unto itself an analytical task, one that inevitably moves you toward interpretation. In the act of creating a parallel phrase—which is what the term *paraphrase* means—you force yourself to specify what the language of the source means. It is almost impossible to not have ideas and not see the questions when you start paraphrasing.

Another reason that quoting and paraphrasing are important is that your analysis of a source will probably have to dwell as much on the *way* the source represents its position as on the information it contains. The information is not separable from how it is expressed. If you are quoting *Newsweek* on Bosnia, for example, you will be encountering not "the truth" about American involvement in this eastern European nation, but rather one particular representation of the situation—in this case, one crafted to meet the expectations of mainstream popular culture. Similarly, if you quote President Clinton on Bosnia, what probably matters most is that the president is choosing particular words to represent—and promote—the government's position. *It is not neutral information.* In short, the person speaking and the kind of source in which his or her words appear will acquire added significance when you make note of these words rather than just summarize them.

## APPLICATION:

### IDENTIFYING THE SIX STRATEGIES IN A PIECE OF CRITICAL ANALYSIS

A useful way of moving toward using the six strategies in your own writing is to make a point of seeing how other writers make these critical moves. The following paper by a student writer is a quite well-written critical summary that analyzes a piece of historical scholarship. Notice, for example, the concise, single-sentence summary of her author's thesis that the writer provides at the end of Paragraph 1. See how this sentence captures both the position that the article argues for and the position that the article argues against.

The piece also makes good use of all six of the strategies:

The review makes the source speak (Strategy 1).

The writer uses her source to ask questions, not just to provide answers (Strategy 2).

In two locations she puts the source into conversation with other sources with the aim of helping readers to see what is particularly valuable and problematic about the article (Strategy 3).

The writer finds her own role in the conversation (Strategy 4).

The review analyzes as it goes along, and as it proceeds, the amount of analysis increases (Strategy 5).

The writer quotes very selectively, usually follows quotes with helpful paraphrase, and attends to the significance of the source's language (Strategy 6).

Study the paper with an eye to locating each of these strategies. Find an example of each, and briefly try to explain how she has executed the particular strategy.

### A SUMMARY AND ANALYSIS OF AMANDA PORTERFIELD'S "WOMEN'S ATTRACTION TO PURITANISM"

[1] Amanda Porterfield, professor of religion at Syracuse University, attempts to explain the allure of sixteenth- and seventeenth-century women

*(continued)*

to Puritanism in her article "Women's Attraction to Puritanism."[1] She begins her article by analyzing the involvement of women in their daily church life through statistical data (196). She then proceeds to draw conclusions concerning the social implications of these statistics (198–208). Past research on Puritanism, Porterfield observes, analyzes only the male attitude toward women in Puritan society, mainly focusing on the subservience of women and discrimination toward them by the men (197). She proposes, however, that the benefits offered to women within Puritan theology and society outweighed their inferiority and that it was through the actual nature of their alleged subservience that they were able to gain these benefits.

[2] Her argument is based on the statistical evidence that Puritan women by 1660 made up the majority of communicants in every New England church (196). Their devotion stems from six benefits, or outlets, as determined by Porterfield. First, Puritanism attracted women because it provided them with symbols of "sexual satisfaction and emotional security" (199). Preachers encouraged them to visualize Christ as their bridegroom and God as their father figure. Women applied these relationships to their own lives in order to take away the guilt felt when searching for love and gratification. If a woman could think of her relationship with God and Christ as similar to her relationship with her father and husband, then she could accept their love and authority. Peace of mind would come through the "imaginary experiences of erotic satisfaction and emotional security" (197) provided by preachers in their sermons and their individual spiritual guidance.

[3] Women were further attracted to Puritanism because it gave them indirect and deliberate authority over the male figures in their lives. Preachers depended on the women's support and approval, because women made up the majority of the congregation. If preachers were going to encourage the women to view God in a personal way, and the preachers were representatives of Christ, then they were at the whim of the women's authority, since the women determined whether the images benefited them spiritually. Porterfield reports that John Cotton regretted his dependency on his women parishioners (200). Women's influence was equally established in the home. Puritans believed that ". . . male authority was actually contingent on female acceptance of that authority" (201). Thus, by giving up their authority to their husbands, they gained authority indirectly.

[4] Women were able to establish their own foundation of self-expression within this subservient position as wives and congregants. In giving up authority, they could express themselves by embracing Puritan values of self-control, humility, and soft-spokenness. Porterfield suggests that women overwhelmingly chose writing as the medium through which to achieve this self-expression. They wrote their husbands' memoirs when they died, wrote journals about their own lives, and wrote poetry with Puritan symbolism and values (201–03). She does not mention, however, that the actual acts of writing and reading themselves—not just what they wrote but the fact that they

*(continued)*

*(continued)*

had the ability to write—were a result of Puritan values and a direct, not indirect, way of establishing a voice of authority. In addition, Porterfield cites only the writings of Anne Bradstreet and Lucy Hutchinson, two very prominent women in Puritan New England (211–12). She does not mention that these women were atypical in their influence on the population through their writings and in the admiration and authority they gained. Instead, she uses their exceptional achievements to exemplify the generalities of the times.

[5] This outlet of writing fostered a radical movement among Puritan women. Porterfield uses Hutchinson as her one example in this discussion, except to note that in England more separatist women than men were sent to Bridewell prison for disrespecting the Church of England in 1568, implying that women took this radical Puritanism to the extreme to gain authority. Again, Porterfield does not support her arguments with conclusive evidence as she cites only the obvious, exceptional examples and claims that they support her generalizations. Radical Puritanism, she claims, allowed women the freedom to be outspoken because it utilized "public prophesy and spontaneous prayer" (204). Although these radical outlets attracted some women to Puritanism, others looked down upon the radicals because they did not exemplify the valued qualities of self-control, soft-spokenness, and humility (205).

[6] These other women were attracted to moderate Puritanism, which focused on social programs where the "well ordered" family was the foundation and example for the church and state (205). Marriage was the nucleus of this developing community. It was in this environment that women were aiding directly in the growth of a virtuous community by accepting their roles as mothers and wives. Women were essential to this social project. It is in this part of her discussion that Porterfield diverges from supporting her thesis and begins to discuss how the Puritans' commitment to the family influenced the development of modern-day society (206–07). She does not give examples of what women did that was important to the family, the actual acts of parenting that would support her argument that they were attracted to Puritanism because of this emphasis on family. She explains the Puritan view of families through quotes by preachers of significance—John Hooker, for example—but does not validate through examples from a broad sample base, the way that historians such as Jack Greene or John Horn would, as to why this viewpoint attracted women.

[7] The final benefit of Puritanism for women was its need to make women "the agents of the kind of domestic sociability that contributed to social stability" (208). In a time when England and New England were in states of upheaval, domestic comfort was of great concern. Porterfield argues that with the rise of Puritanism came a greater interest in amenities in the home, such as forks, plates, and chairs, in order to maintain a level of civility. Rooms became more specialized and private as Puritanism placed greater emphasis on intimate relationships in marriage (208). This need for social stability was central in defining women's responsibility and station in Puritan society.

*(continued)*

Porterfield implies that women were attracted to Puritanism because, by placing great emphasis on the home, it elevated the role of women in domestic life.

[8] Her conclusion restates these outlets that attracted women to Puritanism. Because Puritanism provided women with seductive imagery to give them comfort and security, placed them in subservient positions in a way that gave them indirect influence over their ministers and husbands, allowed personal expression through writing, and developed "domestic roles with great social influence," Puritan women benefited, religiously and socially, from the established society they existed in (209). It is here that I feel Porterfield should have included that her thesis is argued from the viewpoint of a Puritan woman. She expresses the women's plight in terms of Puritanism itself and does not draw from modern women's ideals. Although Porterfield's argument follows standard historical practice in not allowing for modern influence in her analysis of previous centuries, it would be interesting to consider how her arguments look from the perspective of the twentieth-century mind-set.

[9] When one looks at her arguments from a twentieth-century mind-set, they appear as rationalizations for women's subservient nature as opposed to positive attractions to Puritanism. Her idea that women gained authority by giving authority and gained benefits by submitting to Puritan values of humility, self-control, and inferiority does not adequately counter the fact that women were nevertheless consistently relegated to subordinate positions in the culture. Although a modern reader may have difficulty subscribing to the agenda that Puritan women accepted, it is revealing to see how a contemporary social phenomenon like the Feminist Movement may have been in some respects nourished by the Puritan past.

[10] Although not very persuasive due to the sweeping generalizations and lack of a broad sample base, this article is very intriguing and does give insight into the mind frame of Puritan women from a new perspective. Comparing Puritan women with those in the Chesapeake, one can see from her article the definite advantages for a woman living in a community that treasured the home and family (such as that provided by a Puritan congregation with its supportive preacher), as opposed to a predominantly male society that was chaotic, unstructured, and lacking a stabilizing spiritual force. With more research, as copious as James Horn's in his analysis of the Chesapeake, or a statement prefacing her article, declaring that not much evidence is actually in existence, her arguments could be made more valid. Winthrop D. Jordan in his essay "Enslavement of Negroes in America to 1700" explains that there is a definite lack of evidence available on the topic of slavery, and he uses what is available to him. If the case is the same for Porterfield, she should approach her article in the same respect.

ENDNOTE

[1]Amanda Porterfield, "Women's Attraction to Puritanism," *Church History* 60 (1991): 196–209.

# Finding Sources

Generally speaking, the best way to begin your research is to seek out an overview of materials available on your particular topic. What you don't want to do is to interface with your library's electronic card catalogue and check out the first book or books that attract your interest before you've taken the time to find out the range of views that are out there, the kinds of conversations that are going on about your topic. The strategies we will recommend aim to help you not only to find sources efficiently but also to evaluate their relative merits and locate them in the context of existing research.

The problem with doing research in the Information Age is that there is so much information available. How do you know which information is considered respectable in a particular discipline and which isn't? How can you avoid wasting time with source materials that have been effectively refuted and replaced by subsequent thinking? A short answer to these questions is that you should start not in the stacks but in the reference room of your library or its electronic equivalent.

## VOICES FROM ACROSS THE CURRICULUM

### BEGINNING RESEARCH WITH INDEXES

A useful research technique is to begin with indexes that will take you to specialized periodicals rather than beginning with books. Most scholarly journals have an index in the last issue for each year. Listed alphabetically by author, subject, or title are articles for a given year. Also, you may want to use any number of indexes. Here you look up a key word or phrase (of your choosing), and the index tells you when, what, where, and so forth for the word/phrase. Some of the key indexes are: *Social Science Index*, *Wall Street Journal Index* (for *WSJ* stories), *New York Times Index* (for *NYT* stories), and the *Public Affairs Information Service*.

—**FREDERICK NORLING,** *Professor of Business*

If you start with specialized dictionaries, abstracts, and bibliographies, you can rapidly gain both a broad perspective on your subject and a summary of what particular sources contain. This is the purpose of the reference room: it offers sources that review and summarize material for you in shorthand forms. In any case, you should take care not to get bogged down in one author's book-length argument until you've achieved a wider view of how other sources treat your subject.

You should be aware that reference sources use agreed-upon keywords for different subjects. Thus, don't be surprised if the subject headings you type in initially yield nothing. Always check first at the reference desk for the *Library of*

*Congress Subject Headings* to see what headings might be appropriate for your subject. It will tell you, for example, that fraternities and sororities are listed not under "fraternities and sororities," but rather under "Greek letter organizations."

Ask your reference librarian to direct you to the printed and online *indexes, bibliographies, specialized dictionaries,* and compilations of *abstracts* that are pertinent to your subject or discipline. These tools vary in their scope and in the information they contain.

**Indexes** offer a list of titles directing you to scholarly journals; often this list is sufficient to give you a clearer idea of the kinds of topics about which writers in the field are conversing. Here are a few titles, indicating the range of what's available: *Applied Science and Technology Index, Art Index, Biography Index, Business Periodicals Index, Education Index, General Science Index, Humanities Index, Literary Criticism Index, New York Times Index, Philosopher's Index, Religion Index, Reader's Guide to Periodical Literature, Social Sciences Index.* A number of these index both book reviews and scholarly articles. They are generally compiled annually.

**Compilations of abstracts and annotated bibliographies** provide more information—anywhere from a few sentences to a few pages that summarize each source. (See the section on abstracts and how to write them at the end of this chapter.) Here are a few commonly used titles: *Abstracts of English Studies, Chemical Abstracts, Communication Abstracts, Dissertation Abstracts, Historical Abstracts, MLA (Modern Language Association) International Bibliography, Psychological Abstracts, Monthly Catalog of United States Government Publications, Sociological Abstracts.*

**Specialized dictionaries and encyclopedias** are sometimes extraordinarily useful in sketching the general terrain for a subject, and they often include bibliographical leads as well. Here are some titles, ranging from the expected to the eccentric: *Dictionary of the History of Ideas, Dictionary of Literary Biography, Encyclopedia of American History, Encyclopedia of Bioethics, Encyclopedia of Crime and Justice, Encyclopedia of Economics, Encyclopedia of Native American Religions, Encyclopedia of Philosophy, Encyclopedia of Psychology, Encyclopedia of Unbelief, Encyclopedia of World Art, Encyclopedic Dictionary of Mathematics, Macmillan Encyclopedia of Computers, Encyclopedia of Medical History, McGraw Hill Encyclopedia of Science and Technology, New Grove Dictionary of Music and Musicians, Oxford English Dictionary.*

**Book review indexes** can direct you to how others in a particular field have evaluated a given book. If, for example, a given book seems to have said everything there is to say, a few book reviews can be invaluable in helping you to develop a different point of view toward the book in question. Most of the indexes just listed include book reviews. When looking for book reviews, you need to consider *audience:* whether you will be best served by newspapers and magazines or by specialized journals. The *Reader's Guide to Periodical Literature* will locate reviews as well as articles in popular—general audience—publications such as *Time* and *Newsweek.* For a broader range of titles, you might also consult *Book Review Index, Book Review Digest,* and *Subject Guide to Books in Print.* Indexes organized by discipline are more likely to take you to sources reviewed in academic journals; consult with your reference librarian for the ones most pertinent to your subject.

**Periodicals and journals** offer an effective next step in finding sources once you've surveyed your topic in digest form. These are generally more up to date than either reference materials or books. Most library reference rooms have either a booklet that lists all of the periodicals and journals they hold or a means of accessing a list of such holdings through the electronic catalogue. There are thousands of specialized journals available. If an index or bibliography refers you to a journal that your library does not hold, the library can usually get it for you (sometimes for a small fee) through a service known as Interlibrary Loan. Now many articles and reviews can be downloaded electronically; see the section entitled "Electronic Research" that follows.

---

## VOICES FROM ACROSS THE CURRICULUM

### TIPS FOR STARTING YOUR RESEARCH

A critical part of the bibliographic effort is to find a topic on which there are materials. Most topics can be researched. The key is to choose a flexible keyword/phrase and then try out different versions of it. For example, a bibliography on "women in management" might lead you to look up *women, females, business* (women in), *business* (females in), *gender in the workplace, sexism and the workplace, careers* (of men, of women, in business), *women and CEOs, women in management, affirmative action and women, women in corporations, female accountants,* and so forth. Be imaginative and flexible. A little bit of time with some of the indexes, listed earlier, will provide you with a wealth of sources.

    —**FREDERICK NORLING**, *Professor of Business*

❖ ❖ ❖

Use quality psychological references. That is, use references that professional psychologists use and regard highly. *Psychology Today* is not a good reference; *Newsweek* and *Reader's Digest* are worse. And don't even think about the *National Enquirer*. APA journals, such as the *Journal of Abnormal Psychology,* on the other hand, are excellent.

In looking for reference material, be sure to search under several headings. For example, look under *depression, affective disorders,* and *mood disorders.*

Books (e.g., *The Handbook of Affective Disorders*) are often very helpful, especially for giving a general overview of a topic. Books addressing a professional audience are generally preferable to those addressing a general, popular audience.

Finally, references should be reasonably current. In general, the newer, the better. For example, with rare exceptions (classic articles), articles from before 1970 are outdated and so should not be used.

    —**ALAN TJELTVEIT**, *Professor of Psychology*

We might generalize a rule from this professor's final comment: *start in the present and work backward.* Usually the most current materials will include bibliographical citations that can help you identify the most important sources in the past. We would also note that *Newsweek* can be a useful source if you want evidence about popular understanding of a subject or issue, but in this case, the fact that the material comes from *Newsweek* provides the central reason for citing it. As we discussed in Chapter 2, the evidence is always qualified by the frame. This matter of deciding what kind of source is best suited to your topic is the subject of the following extended "Voices" box, written by a reference librarian, on using and evaluating sources via the computer.

---

## VOICES FROM ACROSS THE CURRICULUM

### "ELECTRONIC RESEARCH: HOW DO I KNOW IF IT'S SCHOLARLY?," BY KELLY CANNON, REFERENCE LIBRARIAN

THE WORLD OF WEB

The Internet and its popular offspring, the World Wide Web, have dramatically improved public access to information. But the quality of information has also changed; traditional filters of peer editing and review are often sidestepped in the creation of Web documents, making it almost as easy to publish on the Web as to surf it. A general caveat might well be "reader beware." Users of the Web not only must learn how to find information, but also must acquire means of evaluating that information for reliability.

UNDERSTANDING DOMAIN NAMES

But how is the scholar to begin evaluating a Web document? Fortunately, there are several clues to assist you through the Internet labyrinth. One clue is in the Web site address itself. For example, the Internet Movie Database has http://us.imdb.com as its *Web address* (also known as *URL,* or *uniform resource locator*). The clue lies at the very end of the URL, in what is known as the *domain name,* in this case the abbreviation ".com." Web sites ending in ".com" are commercial, often with the purpose of marketing a product. Here are some other Web sites, each with a different domain name:

*National Right to Life Coalition*
http://www.nrlc.org/news/NRL2.98/green.html

*Valley of the Shadow*
http://jefferson.village.virginia.edu/vshadow2/

*Chronicle of Higher Education (subscription only)*
http://chronicle.com

*(continued)*

*(continued)*

*Mutual Funds Interactive*
http://www.brill.com

*Bureau of the Census*
http://www.census.gov/

*DCA Net Home Page*
http://www.dca.net

Note that ".net" stands for "network," ".edu" for "educational," ".gov" for "government," and ".org" for "organizations."

Much like sites ending in ".com," sites ending in ".org" may have a veiled agenda, whether marketing or politics. Also, ".net" sites are providers of Internet network services and are often in the marketing business themselves. On the other hand, ".edu" and ".gov" sites may indicate less bias, because they are ostensibly nonprofit and are often the producers of bonafide research.

In particular, ".gov" sites represent some of the best that is on the Internet. This is largely because the U.S. government is required by an act of Congress to disseminate to the general public a large portion of its data. The Web has in recent years been beset by a commercial motive, if only to pay the cost of Web site maintenance. The U.S. government, floated as it is by tax dollars, has largely escaped this consuming interest in moneymaking and provides the high quality, free Web sites reminiscent of the precommercial Internet era. This means that government sites offer high quality data, particularly of a statistical nature.

Scholars in the areas of business, law, and the social sciences may benefit tremendously, without subscription fees, from a variety of government databases. Prime examples are the legislative site known as Thomas (http://thomas.loc.gov) and data gathered at the Web site of the Census Bureau (http://www.census.gov). The Thomas site, named after—you guessed it—Thomas Jefferson, is maintained by the Library of Congress and is updated daily. Perhaps even more valuable to researchers than today's legislation is the archive of legislation going back to the Ninety-Third Congress (1973)—bills, resolutions, the U.S. Code, and so forth—allowing extensive research of the laws governing the United States. Archives, it should be noted, have come to be another hallmark of good Web sites, as the majority of the Web seems to offer only today's news.

## PRINT COROLLARIES

But a domain name can be misleading; it is simply one clue in the process of evaluation. Another clue, perhaps more significant, is the correlation between a Web site and the print world. Many Web sites offer print corollaries, and some have print equivalents. For example, Johns Hopkins University Press now publishes all its journals, known and respected for years by scholars, in both print and electronic formats. Many college and university libraries subscribe to these

*(continued)*

Johns Hopkins journals, collectively known on the Web as Project Muse (http://muse.jhu.edu/muse.html), in both the print and electronic formats. In this case, the scholar can assume that the electronic form of the journal undergoes the same editorial rigor as the print publication, because they are identical in content.

**FOR SUBSCRIBERS ONLY**

A collection of discrete pieces of information, or records, that is organized and indexed is called a *database*. Familiar examples of databases are a library card catalogue and a library online catalogue. The World Wide Web is full of databases, though these collections are often restricted to use by paying subscribers. The fees for these databases can be prohibitive, but fortunately for the average researcher, most college and university libraries foot the bill. The names of these databases are now well known and arguably contain the most thoroughly reviewed (scholarly) information available on the Web:

*Lexis-Nexis*
http://web.lexis-nexis.com/universe

*Ebsco*
http://www.epnet.com

*IAC*
http://www.informationaccess.com

*Dialog*
http://www.dialog.com

Inquire at your library to see if you are eligible to access any of these databases.

Each database contains its own proprietary search engine, allowing refinement of searches to a degree unmatched by search engines on the Web at large. Why? *One feature of databases is that they allow searching by subject heading, in addition to keyword searching.* This means that a human has defined the main subject areas of each entry, consequently allowing the user much greater control over the relevance of search retrievals. For example, if I type in the keywords "New York City" in a simple keyword search, I will retrieve everything that has the words *new* and *york* and *city* plus all of the records that simply mention "New York City" even once; in this case, the relevance can be very low in a search set. On the other hand, if subject headings have been assigned, I can do a subject search on "New York City" and find only records that are genuinely about New York City. This may sound trivial, but in the age of information overload, precision searching is a precious commodity.

**SEARCH ENGINE OR DIRECTORY?**

This is not to say that well-known search engines like AltaVista (http://www.altavista.digital.com) and HotBot (http://www.hotbot.com)

*(continued)*

*(continued)*

aren't wonderful, but they open a Pandora's box of unreviewed, "raw" information posted by anyone from expert to novice, and everything in between. Typically, such sites lack any sort of peer review.

One such site that is posted in jest is the Mankato Web site at http://www.lme.mankato.msus.edu/mankato/mankato.html. This site depicts the town of Mankato, Minnesota, as a tropical paradise, complete with wide, sandy beaches and palm trees. On a more sinister note, one arguably unscholarly Web site that frequently appears on searches dealing with sexuality, race, and religion is the Occidental Pan Aryan Crusader (http://www.crusader.net), a site that makes powerful claims, most lacking any substantiation or documentation.

Fortunately, there are Web search tools that offer evaluations of Web sites. Such evaluative search engines, called *directories,* include:

*Argus Clearinghouse*
http://www.clearinghouse.net

*Looksmart*
http://www.looksmart.com

*Magellan*
http://www.mckinley.com/magellan

*Yahoo!*
http://www.yahoo.com

The explicitness of the criteria and the rigor of the evaluation vary widely. Perhaps the most rigorous is the Argus site, which tends to point to subject-specific "clearinghouse" Web pages that provide links to, among other things, electronic magazines and journals on a subject. On the subject of *breweries,* for instance, Argus directs the searcher to the Beer Info. Source, which in turn points to the best in beer periodicals, including a trade publication called *Brewing Techniques: The Art and Science of Small Scale Brewing* (http://www.realbeer.com/brewingtechniques). Although directories like Argus are not adequate evaluators of information by themselves, they are excellent starting points, because they filter out sites they judge as less relevant to your search.

### ASKING THE RIGHT QUESTIONS

After all is said and done, it will be up to the individual scholar to assess each Web site independently. Here are some critical questions to consider:

Question:  who is the author?

Response:  check the Web page, probably near the bottom of the page.

Question:  is the author affiliated with any institution?

Response:  check the URL to see who sponsors the page.

Question:  what are the author's credentials?

*(continued)*

*"Electronic Research . . ."* (continued)

Response: check an online database (like Ebsco Academic Search 1,000 or Lexis-Nexis Academic Universe or Dialog) to see if this person is published in journals or books.

Question: has the information been reviewed or peer-edited before posting?

Response: probably not, unless the posting is part of a larger publication; if so, the submission process for publication can be verified at the publication's home page.

Question: is the page part of a larger publication?

Response: try the various links on the page to see if there is an access point to the home page of the publication. Or try the "backspacing" technique mentioned in the special tips that follow.

Question: is the information documented properly?

Response: check for footnotes or methodology.

Question: is the information current?

Response: check the "last update," usually printed at the bottom of the page.

Question: what is the purpose of the page?

Response: examine content and marginalia.

Question: does the Web site suit your purposes?

Response: review what the purpose of your project is. Review your information needs: primary versus secondary, academic versus popular. And always consult with your instructor.

### BIBLIOGRAPHIC RESEARCH

Up until now, we've addressed only electronic information that is full text. There may come a time when most all of the secondary information needed for research is available online and full text, but due to copyright and other restrictions, much of the most scholarly information is still available only in print. This almost always implies a slight delay in the amount of time it takes to retrieve the information: where full text databases and the World Wide Web promise instant gratification, more traditional modes of research necessitate either document delivery (fax or mail) or a visit to the library or other holding institution where a copy of the item can be retrieved. As individual journals begin to publish online (bypassing print altogether), the access to scholarly material may improve, but for now print copies remain the norm.

What has improved tremendously—with few exceptions—is the *indexing* of scholarly journals. Even if the journals themselves are not readily available in an electronic format, the indexing is available electronically. These

*(continued)*

*(continued)*

electronic indexes provide basic bibliographic information and sometimes an abstract (summary) of the article or book chapter. When professors refer to "bibliographic research," they probably mean research done with indexes. These indexes are available in any of three formats—print, CD-ROM, or on-line—depending on the academic institution. Inquire at your library about index availability.

Many academic institutions now subscribe to the following indexes electronically, whether CD-ROM or online:

*MLA* (literary criticism)

ERIC (education)

*PsycLit* (psychology)

*Historical Abstracts* (non-U.S. history)

*American History & Life* (U.S. history)

*Sociofile* (sociology)

*Biological Abstracts* (biology)

*Chemical Abstracts* (chemistry)

*ABI-Inform* (business)

*Anthropological Literature* (anthropology)

*Philosopher's Index* (philosophy)

*EconLit* (economics)

*Religion Index* (religion)

There are many others. Note that these indexes are specific to a particular subject area. Their coverage is not broad, but deep and very scholarly. These are the indexes to watch for when seeking the most scholarly information in your area of study. If a professor asks students to support their papers with scholarly secondary research, these indexes provide that kind of information. Although the full text is often not included, the indexing will provide information sufficient to track down the complete article, whether it is in the library or available through Interlibrary Loan or another document delivery service.

These indexes are a great aid in evaluating the scholarly merit of a publication, because they usually eliminate any reference that isn't considered scholarly by the academy. For example, the MLA only indexes literary criticism that appears in peer-reviewed journals and academically affiliated books. So consider the publications that appear in these indexes to have the academic "good housekeeping" seal of approval.

## POPULAR PRESS

Although the indexes just listed are scholarly, there are others that cover only the popular press. If information is needed, for example, from an issue of the *Los Angeles Times* in 1990, or a book review from *Time* magazine in

*(continued)*

1986, or a play review from the *Baltimore Sun* in 1996, popular indexes will cite these materials. *Book Review Digest,* available in print and online, indexes book reviews published in the popular press. *The National Newspaper Index* and the well-known *Reader's Guide to Periodical Literature,* available in CD-ROM and online, index newspapers, magazines, and reviews. Indeed, because the popular press profits tremendously from electronic access, indexing for popular titles appears all over the place; Lexis-Nexis and Ebsco Academic Search 1,000, to name two, index hundreds of newspapers, magazines, and reviews.

### TUNING IN TO YOUR ENVIRONMENT

Every university and college is different, each with its own points of access to information. Following are some exercises to help you familiarize yourself with your own scholarly environment.

### EXERCISE 1

Go to your library's reference desk and get a list of all scholarly journal indexes that are available electronically at your school. Then get a list of all online full text databases that are available to you.

### EXERCISE 2

Go to your library's reference desk and get a list of all the journals that the library subscribes to electronically. Then get a list of all journals that are available at your library either in print or electronically in your major area of study.

### EXERCISE 3

Ask the reference librarian about Web access in general for your major area of study. What tips can the library give you about doing electronic research at your academic institution? Are there any special databases, Web search engines/directories, or indexes that you should include in your research?

### EXERCISE 4

Try out some or all of the full text databases available on your campus. Then try the same searches on a scholarly index (CD-ROM or online). What differences do you see in the quality/scope of the information?

### TIP 1: BACKSPACING

"Backspacing" a URL can be an effective way to evaluate a Web site. It may reveal authorship or institutional affiliation. To do this, place the cursor at the end of the URL in the brower's URL dialogue box and then backspace to the last slash, and press "Enter." Continue backspacing to each preceding slash, examining each level as you go.

*(continued)*

*(continued)*

**TIP 2: WHAT A ~ MEANS**

Beware of the ~ in a Web address. Many educational institutions support personal home pages for students and faculty. Although the domain name remains ".edu" in these cases, the fact that they are personal means that pretty much anything can be posted.

**TIP 3: TITLE SEARCHING**

Not finding relevant information? Limit your search to the titles of Web documents. Title searches are available in several search engines, among them AltaVista (advanced mode) and HotBot.

**TIP 4: WHERE'S THE FULL TEXT?**

The best full text is available in subscription databases via the Web. Inquire at your library to see if you have access to Lexis-Nexis, FirstSearch, Ebsco Academic Search, UMI, Infotrac, or other full text databases.

**TIP 5: WHAT ABOUT OLDER INFORMATION?**

Full text for material published prior to 1990 is difficult to find. Use Interlibrary Loan or another document delivery service like CARL UnCover to have the print version of older titles sent to you. Electronic indexing (no full text) for older materials is readily available, back as early as 1900, sometimes earlier. Inquire at your library.

# Citing Sources

There are three ways of incorporating material from sources into your own text—summary, paraphrase, and quotation—and all three require citation. *Summarizing* condenses the information (often radically); *paraphrasing* restates the material in your own words, and *quoting* preserves it exactly as you found it in the source. In all three cases, because the information or ideas did not originate with you, it is *plagiarism* if you do not openly acknowledge the source. To do otherwise is misleading and dishonest.

From the early years of their schooling, most students have been lectured on the unethical nature of plagiarism, so we won't belabor the issue. You need to include a source citation unless the information or ideas are common knowledge (for example, the American Revolution was fought to free the colonies from England's economic and political domination; the technique of electrophoresis can separate various proteins from a given bacterium). If you're unsure whether a given fact or viewpoint is common knowledge, you're better off including a citation.

Another important reason for giving credit where it's due is that these references provide a courtesy to your readers. Citations enable them to find out more about a given position and to pursue other conversations on the subject. Along these lines, it is important to identify your source (make an attribution) *within* the text of your paper as well as in the parenthetical citation that follows your quotation or summary. *See the Appendix at the end of this book for the details of the various documentation styles for citing sources (MLA, APA, etc.).*

---

### VOICES FROM ACROSS THE CURRICULUM

#### ATTRIBUTING SOURCES CLEARLY

Provide sources (reference citations) for the factual claims you make, especially for specific information you obtain from a particular source and include in your paper. Make it clear which idea or information comes from which source. Where possible, integrate references into the structure of the paragraph (rather than listing sources at the end of the paragraph).

Also, as a general rule, you should not use as a reference any sources (1) for which you have read only the abstract or (2) that you have not read but that are cited in a source you have read.

—**ALAN TJELTVEIT,** *Professor of Psychology*

---

In other words, when you introduce a source, word that introduction so that readers can easily distinguish between what the source is saying and what you are saying. When you are including information from several sources, it is especially important that you attribute this information when you introduce it; otherwise, readers will encounter a series of citations at the end of a paragraph and will be bewildered about which information comes from which source.

## Six Techniques for Integrating Quotations into Your Paper

Integrating quotations into a paper is a technical matter that obeys a few basic rules, each of which is discussed briefly and exemplified here. An enormous number of writers don't know how to do this, and it makes them lose authority.

### Technique 1: Acknowledge Sources in Your Text, Not Just in Citations

*When you incorporate material from a source, attribute it to the source explicitly in your text—not just in a citation.* In other words, when you introduce the material, frame it with a phrase such as "according to Marsh" or "as Cartelli argues."

Such attributions are not required if you have cited the source within parentheses or with a footnote at the end of the last sentence you have quoted, paraphrased, or summarized. You are, however, usually much better off making the attribution overtly as well. If a passage does not contain an attribution, your readers will not know that it comes from a source until they reach the citation at the end. Attributing up front clearly distinguishes what one source says from what another says, and perhaps more importantly, what your sources say from what you say. Useful verbs for introducing attributions include the following: *notes, observes, argues, comments, writes, says, reports, suggests,* and *claims.* Note: generally speaking, you should cite the author by last name only—as *Cartelli,* not *Thomas Cartelli* and not *Mr. Cartelli.*

### Technique 2: Splice Quotations onto Your Own Words

*Always attach quotations to some of your own language; don't let them sit in your text as independent sentences with quotation marks around them.* You can normally satisfy this rule with an attributive phrase introducing the quotation—"As Bloom suggests, . . ." Alternatively, you can splice quotations into your text with a colon. For example:

> Patrick Henry's famous phrase is one of the first that American school-children memorize: "Give me liberty, or give me death."

(Note that in this usage the material that precedes the colon is normally an independent clause.) The rationale for this rule is essentially the same as for the previous one. If you are going to move to quotation, you first need to identify its author so that your readers will be able to put it in context quickly.

### Technique 3: Avoid Grammar and Punctuation Errors in Spliced Quotations

*Make sure that the quotation obeys the grammar of the sentence to which it is spliced.* You obviously don't want to commit a grammar error, and in many cases, such an error will render the sentence incoherent. Suppose, for example, you want to use at least a part of the following quotation:

> Where contemporaries like Wordsworth and Coleridge found their subject matter in a direct contemplation of the natural world, Keats was never more interested in nature than when it was mediated through art, through the words or pictures or statuary of other artists (Scott xi).

You would not want to preface this quotation with an opening such as "In Keats's 'Ode on a Grecian Urn,' the urn illustrates." Try to read such a sentence:

> In Keats's "Ode on a Grecian Urn," the urn illustrates, says Scott, "where contemporaries like Wordsworth and Coleridge found their subject matter in a direct contemplation of the natural world, Keats was never more

interested in nature than when it was mediated through art, through the words or pictures or statuary of other artists (Scott xi).

The splicing here is awkward and misleading. Scott is not referring explicitly to the ode, but the sentence suggests that the urn is an example of where the other poets find their subject matter.

There are various ways to insert quoted material smoothly and correctly into your sentences. We illustrate a few of these next, using revised versions of the prefatory statement about the urn.

### EXAMPLE 1

As is evident in his treatment of the urn in "Ode on a Grecian Urn," Keats was, as Scott observes, "never more interested. . . ."

Here the lead-in moves effortlessly into the second half of the original quotation.

### EXAMPLE 2

Keats's "Ode on a Grecian Urn" illustrates the poet's tendency, as Scott notes, "never [to be] more interested. . . ."

To maintain the grammatical fluency in the splicing just shown, it is necessary to add words inside *square brackets*. The brackets indicate that you are altering the original quotation. Brackets are also used when you insert explanatory information, such as a definition or example, within a quotation.

### EXAMPLE 3

As Scott has suggested, poems by Wordsworth and Coleridge find "their subject matter in a direct contemplation of the natural world," unlike those of Keats, who, in poems such as "Ode on a Grecian Urn," "was never more interested. . . ."

This version inserts pieces of the original quotation in two places in the sentence. Note that only the second insertion ("was never more interested") is preceded by a comma, because grammar requires it. *It is a common misconception that a comma always precedes a quotation,* whereas either a colon or no punctuation at all is also frequently correct.

### Technique 4: Use Ellipses to Shorten Quotations

*Use ellipsis points to shorten quotations.* These punctuation marks—typed as three dots with spaces around them—indicate that you have omitted words from within the quotation. Four dots indicates that the deletion continues to the end of the sentence (the fourth dot being a period). The following example illustrates both uses of ellipsis points, adding a sentence from later in Scott's paragraph.

Keats's "Ode on a Grecian Urn" illustrates Scott's argument that "Keats was . . . more interested in nature . . . when it was mediated . . . through the words or pictures or statuary of other artists. . . . His best poetry is composed largely of representations of representations" (Scott xi).

In most cases, the gap between quoted passages should be short, and in any case, you should be careful to preserve the sense of the original. The standard joke about ellipses is apposite here: a reviewer writes that a film "will delight no one and appeal to the intelligence of invertebrates only, but not average viewers." An unethical advertiser cobbles together pieces of the review to say that the film "will delight . . . and appeal to the intelligence of . . . average viewers."

### Technique 5: Cite Sources after Quotations

*Locate citations in parentheses after the quotation and before the final period.* As shown in the preceding citation of Scott, the information about the source appears at the end of the sentence, with the final period following the closing parenthesis. *There is normally no punctuation at the end of the quotation itself, either before or after the closing quotation mark.* A quotation that ends in a question mark or exclamation mark is an exception to this rule, because these signs are an integral part of the quotation's meaning. For example: "As Hamlet says to Rosencrantz and Guildenstern, 'And yet to me what is this quintessence of dust?'" (2.2.304-05).

### Technique 6: Use a Citation Form Appropriate to the Discipline

*Use the form of citation appropriate to the discipline in which you are writing.* In most academic writing, the division (humanities, social sciences, natural sciences) or the discipline (psychology) usually stipulates a particular citation form. Your best source on this matter is your professor and the specialized reference manual of the discipline in question. As the appendix on documentation styles at the end of this book demonstrates, the differences among the various formats are not limited to bibliographical citations. In APA form, for example, quotations of more than forty words should be indented to set them off from the text; in MLA form, quotations of more than three lines receive this treatment.

# Making the Research Paper
# More Analytical: A Sample Essay

The following is an example of "the research paper" as it often appears in college courses. We'll offer our analysis of what goes on in each paragraph of it, with an eye to (1) what typically goes wrong in research paper writing and (2) how a version of the "Six Strategies for Critical Analysis of Sources" could be used to revise it. At the end of the student paper you will find writing and revision strategies for the research paper that are adapted from the six strategies.

## EXTENDED
### ■✹ ANALYSIS

### THE FLIGHT FROM TEACHING

1 The "flight from teaching" (Smith 6) in higher education is a controversial issue of the aca-demic world. The amount of importance placed on research and publishing is the major cause of this flight. I will show different views and aspects concerning the problem plaguing our colleges and universities, through the authors whom I have consulted.

*[Introductory paragraph needs to be revised to eliminate prejudgment. Calling the issue "controversial" implies that there are different points of view on the subject. But the writer offers only one, and it is worded in a way that suggests she has prejudged the complex problem, leaping to a premature and oversimplified conclusion. Instead she needs to better frame the issue and then replace the procedural opening (see Chapter 6) with a more hypothetical working thesis that will enable her to explore the subject.]*

2 Page Smith takes an in-depth look at the "flight from teaching" in Killing the Spirit. Smith's views on this subject are interesting, because he is a professor with tenure at UCLA. Throughout the book, Smith stresses the sentiment of the student being the enemy, as expressed by many of his colleagues. Some professors resent the fact that the students take up their precious time—time that could be better used for research. Smith goes on about how much some of his colleagues go out of their way to avoid their students. They go as far as making strange office hours to avoid contact. Smith disagrees with the hands-off approach being taken by the professors: "There is no decent, adequate, respectable education, in the proper sense of that much-abused word, without personal involvement by a teacher with the needs and concerns, academic and personal, of his/her students. All the rest is 'instruction' or 'information transferral,' 'communication technique,' or some other impersonal and antiseptic phrase, but it is not teaching and the student is not truly learning" (7).

*[Writer summarizes one of her sources but does not analyze or offer any perspective on it.]*

3 Page Smith devotes a chapter to the ideal of "publish or perish," "since teaching is shunned in the name of research." Smith refutes the idea that "research enhances teaching" and that there is a "direct relationship between research and teaching" (178). In actuality, research inhibits teaching. The research that is being done, in most cases, is too specialized for the student. As with teaching and research, Smith believes there is not necessarily a relationship between research and publication. Unfortunately those professors who are devoted to teaching find themselves without a job and/or tenure unless they conform to the requirements of publishing. Smith asks, "Is not the atmosphere hopelessly polluted when professors are forced to do research in order to validate themselves, in order to make a living, in order to avoid being humiliated (and termi-

*(continued)*

---

nated)?" (197). Not only are the students and the professors suffering, but also as a whole, "Under the publish-or-perish standard, the university is perishing" (180).

*[Writer continues summary of source, using language that implies but does not make explicit her apparent agreement with it. She in effect appears to use the source to speak for her and does not distinguish her voice from that of her source. See, for example, the third sentence and the last sentence of the paragraph. Is the writer only reporting what Smith says or appropriating his view as her own?]*

4 Charles J. Sykes looks at the "flight from teaching" in Profscam: Professors and the Demise of Higher Education. Sykes cites statistics to show the results of the reduction of professors' teaching loads enabling them time for more research. The call to research is the cause of many problems. The reduced number of professors actually teaching increases both the size of classes and the likelihood that students will find at registration that their courses are closed. Students will also find they do not have to write papers, and often exams are multiple choice, because of the large classes. Consequently, the effects of the "flight from teaching" have "had dramatic ramifications for the way undergraduates are taught" (40).

*[Writer summarizes another of her sources without analysis of its reasoning and again blurs the distinction between the source's position and her own.]*

*[Here the writer includes two more paragraphs, each containing a summary of a different source.]*

5 E. Peter Volpe, in his chapter "Teaching, Research, and Service: Union or Coexistence?" in the book Whose Goals for American Higher Education?, disagrees strongly that there is an overemphasis on research. Volpe believes that only the research scholar can provide the best form of teaching because "Teaching and research are as inseparable as the two faces of the same coin" (80). The whole idea of education is to increase the student's curiosity. When the enthusiasm of the professor, because of his or her research, is brought into the classroom, it intensifies that curiosity and therefore provides "the deepest kind of intellectual enjoyment" (80). Volpe provides suggestions for solving the rift between students and professors, such as "replacing formal discourse by informal seminars and independent study programs" (81). He feels that this will get students to think for themselves and professors to learn to communicate with students again. Another suggestion is that the government provide funding for "research programs that are related to the education function" (82). This would allow students the opportunity to share in the research. In conclusion, Volpe states his thesis to be, "A professor in any discipline stays alive when he carries his enthusiasm for discovery into the classroom. The professor is academically dead when the spark of inquiry is extinguished within him. It

(continued)

✷

is then that he betrays his student. The student becomes merely an ac-quirer of knowledge rather than an inquirer into knowledge" (80).

*[Here the writer summarizes a source that offers an opposing point of view. It is good that she has begun to represent multiple perspectives, but as with the preceding summaries, there is not yet enough analysis. If she could put Volpe's argument into active conversation with those of Sykes and Smith, she might be able to articulate more clearly the assumptions her sources share and to distinguish their key differences. How, for example, do the three sources differ in their definitions of research and of teaching?]*

6 The "flight from teaching" is certainly a problem in colleges and univer-sities. When beginning to research this topic, I had some very definite opinions. I believed that research and publication should not play any role in teaching. Through the authors utilized in this paper and other sources, I have determined that there is a need for some "research" but not to the extent that teaching is pushed aside. College and universities exist to provide an education; therefore, their first responsibility is to the student.

*[Here the writer begins to offer her opinion of the material, which she does, in effect, by choosing sides. She appears to be compromising—"there is a need for some 'research' but not to the extent that teaching is pushed aside"—but as her last sentence shows, she has in fact dismissed the way that Volpe complicates the relationship between teaching and research.]*

7 I agree with Smith that research, such as reading in the professor's field, is beneficial to his or her teaching. But requiring research to the extent of publication in order to secure a tenured position is actually denying education to both the professors and their students. I understand that some of the pressure stems from the fact that it is easier to decide tenure by the "tang-ible" evidence of research and publication. The emphasis on "publish or perish" should revert to "teach or perish" (Smith 6). If more of an effort is required to base tenure upon teaching, then that ef-fort should be made. After all, it is the education of the people of our na-tion that is at risk.

*[The writer continues to align herself with one side of the issue, which she continues to summarize but does not raise questions about.]*

8 In conclusion, I believe that the problem of the "flight from teaching" can and must be addressed. The continuation of the problem will lead to greater damage in the academic community. The leaders of our colleges and universities will need to take the first steps toward a solution.

*[The writer concludes with a more strongly worded version of her endorsement of the position of Smith and Sykes on the threat of research to teaching. Notice that the paper has not really progressed from the unanalyzed position it articulated in Paragraph 2.]*

## Strategies for Writing and Revising Research Papers

The strategies here applied to "The Flight from Teaching" are versions of the strategies we have been providing throughout the chapter for making your uses of secondary sources more analytical.

### Be Sure to Make Clear Who Is Talking

Clarify for readers when you are speaking for your source and when you are speaking for yourself. Although the writer of the preceding research paper declares in the third sentence of the paper that she intends to "show different views and aspects concerning the problem," some of her remarks seem to be not just those of her sources, but interjections of her own opinions as well.

For example, when she refers to the professors' concern for their "precious time" in Paragraph 2, or when she writes that "In actuality, research inhibits teaching" in Paragraph 3, is she simply summarizing Smith or endorsing his position? The problem is not that she—or any writer—should stay out of the summary, but rather that she has not carefully differentiated her own remarks from those of her sources. You can, as noted earlier, easily achieve this clarity by inserting attributive tag phrases that distinguish who's saying what: "In Smith's view" or "In response to Smith, one might argue that."

Remember that your role is to provide explanation of and perspective on the ideas in your source. Your role is not, especially early on, to cheerlead for it or attack it. To fulfill this role, you will need to maintain some critical detachment, seeking to articulate your understanding of the position in the source before stating an opinion about it or "choosing sides."

On this note, it is worth remarking that most of the time you are not being asked for your point of view on the general subject that your sources are addressing. Rather, you are being asked for your point of view on your sources' points of view on the subject.

### Disciplinary Conventions Permitting, Analyze as You Go Along, Rather Than Saving Analysis for the End

It is no coincidence that a research paper that summarizes its sources and delays discussing them should have difficulty constructing a logically coherent and analytically revealing point of view. The *organization* of "The Flight from Teaching" obstructs the writer's ability to have ideas about her material. The alternative, where disciplinary conventions allow, is to analyze your sources as you go along.

The gap between presentation and discussion in the sample research paper leaves the analysis too loose: especially at first reading, we are left unsure how to interpret the various points of view that the writer is summarizing for us. Although it is beneficial to summarize sources, you need to do so in a way that locates the issues and breaks them down into their components.

On the following page, by contrast, is the opening paragraph of an essay that offers continual analysis of its sources:

Alan Friedman's *Spider's Web* argues in elaborate detail that the United States illegally armed Iraq prior to the Gulf War. Although the book relies on exhaustive description to focus on individual strands of the "web" in order to better understand the whole, it by no means offers the complete story. If anything, Friedman's accusations call for a comprehensive investigation. He has no pretensions about the book—that is, Friedman recognizes that his argument is only the first step. He writes in the closing paragraphs, "The issue far transcends Iraqgate or even the particular circumstances described in these pages. It is therefore up to Congress, the Clinton Administration, the Scott inquiry, and the British Parliament to pursue allegations wherever they lead" (287). It would almost be ridiculous to argue that Friedman's thesis is not based on some truth. There are far too many documents, testimonies, and coincidences for this entire situation to be a hoax. What is at issue is the extent of culpability.

At the very outset of his paper, the writer has synthesized his summary of the central source with a first stab at analyzing it. He tells us that Friedman's book does not offer "the complete story," quotes the author's closing admission to this effect, and suggests that at the least the book's argument contains (only) "some truth." It is worth noting that his summary could be made more analytical if the writer were to rank the information in some way, such as distinguishing cases in which evidence *strongly supports* a claim from cases in which evidence is *suggestive* or *speculative*.

### Quote and Paraphrase in Order to Analyze: Make Your Sources Speak

As with other uses of evidence, in analyzing secondary sources you will usually do better to say more about less, rather than less about more. If you include lots of quotation or paraphrase without explaining what it means or why it is important, you are leaving the source's language to speak for itself, as if it were self-evident. Even if this language is fairly clear in what it means to you, the aim of your analysis is to put what you have quoted or paraphrased into some kind of frame or perspective. *As a general rule, you should not end a discussion with a quotation, but rather with some point you want to make about the quotation.*

Your quoting can be *very* selective—a sentence or even a phrase will often suffice. After you quote, then you will usually need to paraphrase in order to help you realize and articulate the implications of the quotation's key terms.

Look at the opportunities for analysis that a writer can miss when allowing quotation to speak for itself. Consider the following single sentence from the second paragraph of "The Flight from Teaching" as a case in point:

> Page Smith disagrees with the hands-off approach being taken by the professors: "There is no decent, adequate, respectable education, in the proper sense of that much-abused word, without personal involvement by a teacher with the needs and concerns, academic and personal, of his/her students" (7).

The writer uses this passage as part of an apparently neutral summary of Smith's position, and she does not comment upon it further. But notice how

Smith's word choices provide additional information about the central idea being articulated. The repetition of "personal" and the quarrelsome tone of "much-abused" suggest that the writer's characterization of Smith as one who "disagrees with the hands-off approach" is extremely understated. Smith is writing a polemic, and he is preoccupied with the personal to the extent that he wishes to restrict the definition of education to it. The writer may agree or disagree with Smith's outlook, but the point is that if she attends to his actual language, she will be able to characterize that outlook much more accurately.

By contrast, the writer analyzing the *Spider's Web* quotes *in order to* analyze the implications of the source's language:

> If allegations that top levels of U.S. and British governments acted covertly to shape foreign policy are truthful, then this scandal, according to Friedman, poses serious questions concerning American democracy. Friedman explains, "The government's lack of accountability, either to Congress or to the public, was so egregious as to pose a silent threat to the principles of American democracy" (286). The word "principles" is especially important. In Friedman's view, without fundamental ideals such as a democracy based on rule by elected representatives *and* the people, where does the average citizen stand? What will happen to faith in the government, Friedman seems to be asking, if elected representatives such as the president sully that respected office?

This student writer's use of quotation serves not only to convey information but also to frame it. By emphasizing Friedman's diction ("principles"), he makes a point about that author's point of view.

### Try Converting Key Assertions in the Source into Questions

Often the style of a source will make its claims sound more final and unquestionably true than they actually are. So a useful habit of mind is to experiment with rewording selected assertions into questions. Consider, for example, what the writer of "The Flight from Teaching" might have discovered had she tried converting the following conclusions (in Paragraph 4) drawn from one of her sources into questions:

> The call to research is the cause of many problems. The reduced number of professors actually teaching increases both the size of classes and the likelihood that students will find at registration that their courses are closed. Students will also find they do not have to write papers, and often exams are multiple choice, because of the large classes.

Is it only professors' desire to be off doing their own research that explains closed courses, large class size, and multiple-choice tests? What about other causes for these problems, such as the cost of hiring additional professors or the pressure a university puts on professors to publish in order to increase the status of the institution? We do not intend to suggest that the writer should have recognized these particular problems with her sources but rather that she needs, somewhere in the paper, to raise questions about the reasoning implicit in them.

One good way to gain perspective on your secondary sources is to *query how they are defining, implicitly and explicitly, their key terms.* Notice all of the unstated assumptions about the meaning of key terms contained in the writer's fullest statement of her thesis: "Through the authors utilized in this paper and other sources, I have determined that there is a need for some 'research' but not to the extent that teaching is pushed aside. Colleges and universities exist to provide an education; therefore, their first responsibility is to the student" (Paragraph 6). What do she and her sources mean by "research" and what by "teaching"? To what extent can the writer fairly assume that the purpose of universities is "to provide an education"? Can't an education include being mentored in the skills that university teachers practice in their own research?

### Get Your Sources to Speak to One Another, and Actively Referee the Conflicts among Them

This means making clear to the reader how each source might respond to the other if they were in fact having a conversation. In "The Flight from Teaching," for example, Smith and Sykes assume that teaching is largely separable from scholarship, whereas Volpe sees teaching and scholarship as mutually re-inforcing. What, for example, does Volpe "say" to Smith, and how might Smith respond? Does Sykes "reply" in exactly the same way as Smith, or does the writer need to distinguish Sykes from Smith more accurately?

Her sources have repeatedly offered opposing answers that she should have put into debate. For example, Smith asserts that "research inhibits teaching" (Paragraph 3), whereas Volpe contends that "only the research scholar can provide the best form of teaching because 'teaching and research are as insepa-rable as the two faces of the same coin'" (Paragraph 5). Both sides *agree* that educating students is the "first responsibility" of colleges and universities, but they disagree radically on how this responsibility is best fulfilled. Smith believes that professors' research gets in the way of excellent teaching, whereas Volpe believes that research is essential to it. If the writer had brought these sources into dialogue, she could have discovered that the assertion she offers as her conclusion is, in fact, an evasion.

Once you've started thinking about the sources in terms of how you can get them to converse with one another on particular topics or questions, you've found the means to reorganize your paper around issues, rather than leaving readers to locate these issues for themselves as you move from source to source.

---

### APPLICATION:

### A RESEARCH SEQUENCE

This "Application" will show you how to write a prospectus, a "what's going on" survey of sources, an abstract, and a comparative summary.

The traditional sequence of steps for building a research paper—or for any writing that relies on secondary materials—is summary, comparative

*(continued)*

*(continued)*

analysis, and synthesis. The following sequence of four exercises addresses the first two steps as discrete activities. (You might, of course, choose to do only some of these exercises.)

1. **Compose a relatively informal prospectus,** in which you formulate your initial thinking on the subject before you do more research. This exercise will help to deter you from being overwhelmed by and absorbed into the sources you encounter.

2. **Conduct a "what's going on in the field" search.** This exercise is ideal for helping you to find a topic or, if you already have one, to narrow it. The kinds of bibliographic materials you consult for this portion of the research project will depend on the discipline within which you are writing. Whatever the discipline, start in the reference room of your library with specialized indexes (such as the *Social Sciences Index* or the *New York Times* Index), book review indexes, specialized encyclopedias and dictionaries, and bibliographies (print version or CD-ROM) that will give you an overview of your subject or topic. If you have access to databases through your computer network, you should also search them (see the "Electronic Research" section of this chapter).

The "what's going on in the field" search has two aims:

- To survey such materials in order to identify trends—the kinds of issues and questions that others in the field are talking about (and, thus, find important)

- To compile a bibliography that includes a range of titles that interest you, that could be relevant to your prospective topic, and that seem to you representative of research trends associated with your subject (or topic)

You will not be committed at this point to pursuing all of these sources, but rather to reporting what is being talked about. You might also compose a list of keywords (such as Library of Congress headings) that you have used in conducting your search. If you try (or are directed to try) this exercise, you will be surprised how much value there is in exploring indexes *just for titles,* to see the kinds of topics people are currently conversing about. And of particular aid in formulating and focusing your own topic, you will almost surely discover how *narrowly* focused most research is (which will get you off global questions).

Append to your bibliography a few paragraphs of informal discussion of how the information you have encountered (the titles, summaries, abstracts, etc.) has affected your thinking and plans for the paper. These paragraphs might respond to the following questions:

- In what ways has your "what's going on in the field" search led you to narrow or shift direction in or focus your thinking about your subject?

- How might you use one or more of these sources in your paper?

*(continued)*

*A Research Sequence (continued)*

- What has this phase of your research suggested you might need to look for next?

3. **Write an abstract** of an article (or book chapter) from your "what's going on" exercise that you think you might use in your final paper. Composing an academic abstract according to the conventions of the discipline in which you're writing is a necessary skill. Abstracts differ in format and length among disciplines, but by and large they follow a generalizable format like the one we offer next. You should look at some abstracts in the reference room and/or via your computer network to provide you with some models to imitate. Some abstracts, such as those in *Dissertation Abstracts,* are very brief—less than 250 words. You will probably need a little more space than this: aim for two pages. If other members of your class are working on the same or similar subjects, it is often extremely useful for everyone to share copies of their abstracts.

## HOW TO PREPARE A SCHOLARLY ABSTRACT

A scholarly abstract is a nonevaluative summary: that is, it presents rather than critiques the source's arguments. So, regardless of your opinions of the source, your first responsibility is to represent it as fairly and precisely as possible.

The abstract should begin with a clear and specific explanation of the work's thesis, its governing argument. In this opening paragraph, you should also define the work's purpose, possibly including established positions that it tries to refine, qualify, or argue against. What kind of critical approach does it adopt? What are its aims? On what assumptions does it rest? Why did the author feel it necessary to write the work—that is, what does he or she believe the work offers that other sources don't? What shortcomings or misrepresentations in other criticism does the work seek to correct?

You won't be able to produce detailed answers to all of these questions in your opening paragraph, but in trying to answer some of them in your note-taking and drafting, you should find it easier to arrive at the kind of concise, substantive, and focused overview that the first paragraph of your abstract should provide. Also be careful not to settle for bland, all-purpose generalities in this opening paragraph. And if you quote there, keep the selections short, and recognize that you will need to explain the quotations: don't expect them to speak for themselves.

In sum, your aim in Paragraph 1 is to define the source's particular angle of vision and articulate its main point or points, including the definition of key terms used in its title or elsewhere in its argument.

Once you've set up this overview of the source's central position(s), you should devote a paragraph or so to the source's *organization* (how it divides its subject into parts) and its *method* (how it goes about substantiating its argument). What kind of secondary material does the source use? How, that is, do its own bibliographic citations cue you to its school of thought, its point of view, its research traditions?

*(continued)*

*(continued)*

Your concluding paragraph should briefly recount some of the source's conclusions (related to but not necessarily the same as its thesis). In what way does it go about culminating its argument? What kind of significance does it claim for its position? What final qualifications does it raise?

As the preceding guidelines make clear, your primary concern should lie with representing the argument or point of view of the source as fairly and accurately as possible, rather than leading with evaluation (agree/disagree, like/dislike). Append to the end of the abstract a paragraph or two that addresses the question, "How has this exercise affected your thinking about your topic?" Objectifying your own research process in this way will help to move you away from the cut-and-paste, provide-only-the-transitions mode of writing research papers.

Here, as a model, is a good example of an abstract:

Abstract of "William Carlos Williams," an essay by Christopher Mac-Gowan in *The Columbia History of American Poetry,* pp. 395–418, Columbia University Press, 1993.

MacGowan's is a chronologically organized account of Williams's poetic career and of his relation to both modernism, as an international movement, and modernism as it affected the development of poetry in America. Mac-Gowan is at some pains both to differentiate Williams from some features of modernism (such as the tendency of American writers to write as well as live away from their own cultural roots) and to link Williams to modernism. Mac-Gowan argues, for example, that an essential feature of Williams's commitment as a poet was to "the local—to the clear presentation of what was under his nose and in front of his eyes" (385). But he also takes care to remind us that Williams was in no way narrowly provincial, having studied in Europe as a young man (at Leipzig), having had a Spanish mother and an English father, having become friendly with the poets Ezra Pound and H. D. while getting his medical degree at the University of Pennsylvania, and having continued to meet important figures in the literary and art worlds by making frequent visits to New York and by traveling on more than one occasion to Europe (where Pound introduced him to W. B. Yeats, among others). Williams corresponded with Marianne Moore, he continued to write to Pound and to show Pound some of his work, and he wrote critical essays on the works of other modernists. MacGowan reminds us that Williams also translated Spanish works (ballads) and so was not out of contact with European influences.

Williams had a long publishing career—beginning in 1909 with a self-published volume (paid for by himself) called *Poems* and ending more than fifty years later with *Pictures from Brueghel* in 1962. What MacGowan emphasizes about this career is not only the consistently high quality of work, but also its great influence on other artists (he names those who actually corresponded with Williams and visited with him, including Charles Olson, Robert Creeley, Robert Lowell, Allen Ginsberg, and Denise Levertov). MacGowan observes

*(continued)*

that Williams defined himself "against" T. S. Eliot—the more rewarded and internationally recognized of the two poets, especially during their lifetimes—searching for "alternatives to the prevailing mode of a complex, highly allusive poetics," which Williams saw as Eliot's legacy (395). MacGowan depicts Williams as setting "himself against the international school of Eliot and Pound—Americans he felt wrote about rootlessness and searched an alien past because of their failure to write about and live within their own culture" (397).

4. **Write a comparative summary of two reviews of a single source.** Most writers, before they invest the significant time and energy required to study a book-length source, take the much smaller amount of time and energy required to find out more about the book. Although you should always include in your final paper your own analytical summary of books you consult on your topic, it's extremely useful also to find out what experts in the field have to say about the source.

Select from your "what's going on" list one book-length source that you've discovered is vital to your subject or topic. As a general rule, if a number of your indexes, bibliographies, and so forth refer you to the same book, it's a good bet that this source merits consulting.

Locate two book reviews on the book, and write a summary that compares the two reviews. Ideally, you should locate two reviews that diverge in their point of view or in what they choose to emphasize. Depending on the length and complexity of the reviews, your comparative summary should require two or three pages.

In most cases, you will find that reviews are less neutral in their point of view than are abstracts, but they always do more than simply judge. A good review, like a good abstract, should communicate the essential ideas contained in the source. It is the reviewer's aim also to locate the source in some larger context, for example, comparing it to other works on the same subject and to the research tradition the book seeks to extend, modify, and so forth. Thus, your summary should try to encompass how the book contributes to the ongoing conversation on a given topic in the field.

Append to your comparative summary a paragraph or two answering the question, "How has this exercise affected your thinking about your topic?"

Obviously, you could choose to do a comparative summary of two articles, two book chapters, and so forth rather than of two book reviews. But in any event, if you use books in your research, you should always find a means of determining how these books are received in the relevant critical community.

Note: the next step, if you were writing a research paper, would involve the task known as *synthesis,* in which you essentially write a comparative discussion that includes more than two sources. Many research papers

*(continued)*

*(continued)*

start with an opening paragraph that synthesizes prevailing, perhaps competing, interpretations of the topic you are addressing. Few good research papers consist only of such synthesis, however. Instead, writers use synthesis to frame their ideas and to provide perspective on their own arguments; the synthesis provides a platform or foundation for their own subsequent analysis.

It is probably worth adding that bad research papers fail to use synthesis as a point of departure. Instead, they line up their sources and agree or disagree with them. To inoculate you against this unfortunate reflex, review "Six Strategies for Critical Analysis of Sources" (especially Strategy 4, "Find Your Own Voice in the Conversation") and "Strategies for Writing and Revising Research Papers."

We would like to emphasize, by way of conclusion, that these applications, and for that matter, the strategies this chapter recommends, share a common aim: to get you off the hotseat of judging the experts when you are not an expert. Most of us are more comfortable in situations in which we can converse amicably rather than judge and be judged. Think of that as you embark on research projects, and you will be far more likely to learn and to have a good time doing it.

## Key Words (in order of appearance)

| | |
|---|---|
| conversing with sources | .com |
| secondary source | .net |
| primary source | .edu |
| "source anxiety" | .gov |
| framing the discussion | .org |
| the straw man strategy | domain name |
| paraphrasing | print corollaries |
| online indexes | search engines |
| annotated bibliographies | online databases |
| specialized dictionaries | spliced quotations |
| book review indexes | ellipsis points |
| Library of Congress subject headings | scholarly abstract |
| Web address (URL) | synthesis |

## Guidelines for Using Secondary Sources

1. Avoid the temptation to plug in sources as "answers." Aim for a *conversation* with them. Think of sources as voices inviting you into a community of interpretation, discussion, and debate.

2. Quote, paraphrase, or summarize *in order to* analyze. Explain what you take the source to mean, showing the reasoning that has led to the conclusion you draw from it.

3. Quote sparingly. You are usually better off centering your analysis on a few quotations, analyzing their key terms, and branching out to aspects of your subject that the quotations illuminate.

4. Don't underestimate the value of close paraphrasing. You will almost invariably begin to interpret a source once you start paraphrasing its key language.

5. Locate and highlight what is at stake in your source. Which of its points does the source find most important? What positions does it want to modify or refute, and why?

6. Attribute sources ("According to Einstein, . . .") in the text of your paper, not just in parenthetical citations. This practice will distinguish source material from your remarks about it and allow readers to evaluate its credibility up front.

7. Look for ways to develop, modify, or apply what a source has said, rather than simply agreeing or disagreeing with it.

8. If you challenge a position found in a source, be sure to represent it fairly. First give the source some credit by identifying assumptions you share with it. Then isolate the part that you intend to complicate or dispute.

9. Look for sources that address your subject from different perspectives. Avoid relying too heavily on any one source.

10. When your sources disagree, consider playing mediator. Instead of immediately agreeing with one or the other, clarify areas of agreement and disagreement among them.

## CHAPTER 8

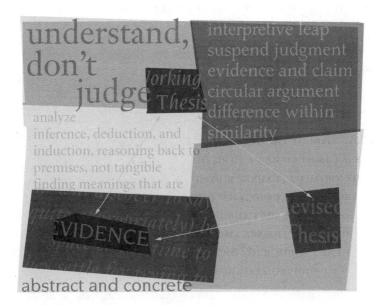

# EDITING FOR CORRECTNESS

**R**evising is the very heart of writing. The best ideas develop over time, through your repeated attempts to find the language that best articulates your thinking. Revision is a very broad term, however, and so it is useful to distinguish two kinds of revision: conceptual revision and technical editing.

## Conceptual Revision vs. Technical Editing

As we have been using the term thus far, *revision* refers to the process by which writers continually evaluate and rethink what they have written to improve the clarity and accuracy of their ideas. Revision, in this sense of "re-vision"—to see again—might involve choosing the best point you've made in an early draft and building the next draft around it, cutting the majority of what you had written. Or it might involve discovering an entirely different way of analyzing your topic and working to reconcile this viewpoint with your formulation from a previous draft. Such revisions are *conceptual:* they involve wide-scale changes in content and organization. In the first seven chapters, we have demonstrated how to do this kind of revision.

We now turn to the more *technical* kinds of revision associated with editing and correcting a draft. Chapter 8 addresses the issue of grammatical correctness and offers ways of recognizing and fixing (or avoiding) the most important errors. Chapter 9 concentrates on the stylistic choices that are available to you as you write and revise your draft for greater clarity and effect. Together the two chapters offer a minihandbook that, although not all-inclusive, nonetheless covers most of the important issues in editing a draft for correctness and style.

## Wait to Focus on Editing for Correctness

The first guideline in technical revision is to *wait* to do it until you have arrived at a reasonably complete conceptual draft. We have delayed until the end of the book our consideration of technical revisions precisely because most veteran writers avoid worrying about them in the early stages of the writing process. As we have suggested, writers need a stage in which they are allowed to make mistakes and use writing to help them discover what they want to say. If you get too focused on producing polished copy right up front, you may never explore the subject enough to learn how to have ideas about it. In other words, it doesn't make sense for you to let your worries about proper form or persuasive phrasing prematurely distract you from the more important matter of having something substantial to polish in the first place. But at the appropriate time—the later stages of the writing process—technical editing becomes very important.

## What Is Correctness, and Why Does It Matter?

When a paper obeys the rules of grammar, punctuation, and spelling, it has achieved *correctness*. Unlike editing for style, which involves you in making choices between more and less effective ways of phrasing (see Chapter 9), editing for correctness locates you in the domain of right or wrong. As you will see, there are usually a number of ways to correct an error, so you are still concerned with making choices, but leaving the error uncorrected is not really a viable option.

Correctness matters deeply because your prose may be unreadable without it. If your prose is ungrammatical, not only will you risk incoherence (in which case your readers will not be able to follow what you are saying), but also you will inadvertently invite readers to dismiss you as illiterate. Is it fair of readers to reject your ideas because of the way you've phrased them? Perhaps not, but the fact is they often will. A great many readers regard technical errors as an inattention to detail that also signals sloppiness at more important levels of thinking. In producing writing that contains such errors, you risk not only distracting readers from your message but also *undermining your authority* to deliver the message in the first place.

# The Concept of Basic Writing Errors (BWEs)

You get a paper back, and it's a sea of red ink. But if you look more closely, you'll often find that you haven't made a million mistakes—you've made only a few, but over and over in various forms. This phenomenon is what the rhetorician Mina Shaughnessy addressed in creating the category of "basic writing errors," or BWEs. Shaughnessy argues that in order to improve your writing for style and correctness, you need to do two things:

- Look for a pattern of error, which will require you to understand your own logic in the mistakes you typically make.
- Recognize that not all errors are created equal, which means that you need to address errors in some order of importance—beginning with those most likely to interfere with your readers' understanding.

The following BWE guide that we have composed reflects Shaughnessy's view. First, it aims to teach you how to recognize and correct the basic kinds of errors that are potentially the most damaging to the clarity of your writing and to your credibility with readers. Second, the discussions in the guide seek to help you become aware of the patterns of error in your writing and discover the logic that has misled you into making them. If you can learn to see the pattern and then look for it in your editing and proofreading—expecting to find it—you will quickly get in the habit of avoiding the error. In short, you will learn that your problem is not that you can't write correctly, but simply that you have to remember, for example, to check for possessive apostrophes.

Our BWE guide does not, as we've mentioned, cover *all* of the rules of grammar, punctuation, diction, and usage, such as where to place the comma or period when you close a quotation or whether or not to write out numerals. For comprehensive coverage of the conventions of standard written English, you can consult one of the many handbooks available for this purpose. Our purpose is to provide a short guide to grammar—identifying the most common errors, providing remedies, and offering the logic that underlies them. This chapter's coverage of nine basic writing errors and how to fix them will help you eliminate most of the problems that routinely occur. We have arranged the error types in a hierarchy, moving in descending order of severity (from most to least problematic).

Most of the relevant terminology for talking about grammar appears within the discussion of the basic writing errors. For definitions of terms that for reasons of space are not included there, we have compiled a "Glossary of Grammatical Terms." It appears near the end of the chapter, in place of the "Key Words" sections of earlier chapters. The key explanatory terms used in the BWE list have been boldfaced to indicate that they can also be found, alphabetically organized, in this glossary. Some of the nine BWEs also recur briefly in the glossary, but we have tried to avoid unnecessary repetition.

Throughout the chapter, at the ends of each BWE discussion, you will find brief self-tests entitled "Test Yourself" (these function in place of the "Applications" of previous chapters). Even if you believe that you already know how to find and fix a given BWE, it is probably a good idea to take each test—to write out corrections to the examples of each BWE. It is easy to conclude that you understand a problem when you are shown an example, told how to correct it, and then shown the correction. But understanding is not the same thing as practicing: taking the tests will help you learn to see and rectify the BWE yourself. Then, at the very end of the chapter, you will find a discussion of each example in "Answers to the 'Test Yourself' Sections," so that you can check your work.

# Nine Basic Writing Errors and How to Fix Them

## BWE 1: Sentence Fragments

The most basic of writing errors, a *sentence fragment,* is a group of words punctuated like a complete sentence but lacking the necessary structure: it is only part of a sentence. Typically, a sentence fragment occurs when the group of words in question (1) lacks a subject, (2) lacks a predicate, or (3) is a subordinate (or dependent) clause.

To fix a sentence fragment, either turn it into an independent clause by providing whatever is missing—a subject or a predicate—or attach it to an independent clause upon which it can depend.

### NOUN CLAUSE (NO PREDICATE) AS A FRAGMENT

A world where imagination takes over and sorrow is left behind.

This fragment is not a sentence but rather a noun clause—a sentence subject with no predicate. The fragment lacks a verb that would assert something about the subject. (The verbs *takes over* and *is left* are in a dependent clause created by the subordinating conjunction *where.*)

### CORRECTIONS

A world *arose* where imagination takes over and sorrow is left behind.
[new verb matched to *A world*]
*She entered* a world where imagination takes over and sorrow is left behind.
[new subject and verb added]

The first correction adds a new verb (*arose*). The second introduces a new subject and verb, converting the fragment into the direct object of *She entered.*

### VERBAL AS A FRAGMENT

Falling into debt for the fourth consecutive year.

*Falling* in the preceding fragment is not a verb. Depending on the correction, *Falling* is either a **verbal** or part of a verb phrase.

### CORRECTIONS

*The company was* falling into debt for the fourth consecutive year.
[subject and helping verb added]
Falling into debt for the fourth consecutive year *led the company to consider relocating.*
[new predicate added]
Falling into debt for the fourth consecutive year, *the company considered relocating.*
[new subject and verb added]

In the first correction, the addition of a subject and the helping verb *was* converts the fragment into a sentence. The second correction turns the fragment into a **gerund** phrase functioning as the subject of a new sentence. The third correction converts the fragment into a **participial phrase** attached to a new independent clause. (See the glossary under **verbal** for definitions of *gerund* and *participle.*)

### SUBORDINATE CLAUSE AS A FRAGMENT

I had an appointment for 11:00 and was still waiting at 11:30. Although I did get to see the dean before lunch.

*Although* is a **subordinating conjunction** that calls for some kind of completion. Like *if, when, because, whereas,* and other subordinating conjunctions (see the glossary), *although* always makes the clause that it introduces dependent.

### CORRECTIONS

I had an appointment for 11:00 and was still waiting at *11:30, although* I did get to see the dean before lunch.
[fragment attached to preceding sentence]

As the correction demonstrates, the remedy lies in attaching the fragment to an independent clause on which it can depend (or alternatively, making the fragment into a sentence by dropping the conjunction).

Sometimes writers use sentence fragments deliberately, usually for rhythm and emphasis or to create a conversational tone. In less formal contexts, they are generally permissible, but you run the risk that the fragment will not be perceived as intentional. In formal writing assignments, it is safer to avoid intentional fragments.

### TEST YOURSELF

## Fragments

There are fragments in each of the following three examples, probably the result of their proximity to legitimate sentences. What's the problem in each case, and how would you fix it? Write out your revisions, and then remember to check them against the answer key at the end of the chapter.

Margaret Mead studied non-Western cultures in such works as *Coming of Age in Samoa.* And influenced theories of childhood development in America.

The catastrophe resulted from an engineering flaw. Because the bridge lacked sufficient support.

In the 1840s the potato famine decimated Ireland. It being a country with poor soil and antiquated methods of agriculture.

> **? HINT BOX:**
>
> ## DASHES AND COLONS
>
> One way to correct a fragment is to replace the period with a dash: "The campaign required commitment. Not just money." becomes "The campaign required commitment—not just money." The dash offers you one way of attaching a phrase or clause to a sentence without having to construct another independent clause. In short, it's succinct. (Compare the correction that uses the dash with another possible correction: "The campaign required commitment. It also required money.") Moreover, with the air of sudden interruption that the dash conveys, it can capture the informality and immediacy that the intentional fragment offers a writer.
>
> You should be wary of overusing the dash in this way, as the slightly more presentable cousin of the intentional fragment. The energy it carries can clash with the decorum of formal writing contexts; for some readers, its staccato effect quickly becomes too much of a good thing.
>
> One alternative to this usage of the dash, in some cases, is the colon. It can substitute because it also can be followed by a phrase, a list, or a clause. As with the dash, it must be preceded by an independent clause. And it, too, carries dramatic force because it abruptly halts the flow of the sentence.
>
> The colon, however, does not convey informality. In place of a slapdash effect, it offers a spotlight on what is to follow it. Hence, as in this sentence you are reading, it is especially appropriate for setting up certain kinds of information: explanations, lists, or results. In the case of results, the cause or action precedes the colon; the effect or reaction follows it.
>
> Before leaving this "Hint Box," let us quickly offer the other legitimate use of the dash: to enclose information within a sentence. In this use, dashes precede and follow the information, taking the role usually assigned to commas. Consider the following example:
>
> Shortly before the election—timing its disclosures for maximal destructive effect—the candidate's campaign staff levied a series of charges against the incumbent.
>
> Note that if the information within the dashes is omitted, the sentence must still read grammatically. That is the rule for using dashes to sandwich information in this way.

## BWE 2: Comma Splices and Fused (or Run-On) Sentences

A **comma splice** consists of two independent clauses connected ("spliced") with a comma; a **fused** (or **run-on**) **sentence** combines two such clauses with no conjunction or punctuation. The solutions for both comma splices and fused sentences are the same:

1. Place a conjunction (such as *and* or *because*) between the clauses.
2. Place a semicolon between the clauses.
3. Make the clauses into separate sentences.

All of these solutions solve the same logical problem: they clarify the boundaries of the independent clauses for your readers.

**COMMA SPLICE**

He disliked discipline, he avoided anything demanding.

**CORRECTION**

*Because* he disliked discipline, he avoided anything demanding.
[subordinating conjunction added]

**COMMA SPLICE**

Today most TV programs are violent, almost every program is about cops and detectives.

**CORRECTION**

Today most TV programs are violent; almost every program is about cops and detectives.
[semicolon replaces comma]

Because the two independent clauses in the first example contain ideas that are closely connected logically, the most effective of the three comma-splice solutions is to add a subordinating conjunction (*Because*) to the first of the two clauses, making it depend on the second. For the same reason—close conceptual connection—the best solution for the next comma splice is to substitute a semicolon for the comma. The semicolon signals that the two independent clauses are closely linked in meaning. In general, you can use a semicolon where you could also use a period. (We will risk distracting you for a moment here to say that a semicolon does *not* signal a long pause; it virtually always separates two independent clauses not joined by a conjunction.)

The best cures for the perpetual comma splicer are to learn to recognize the difference between independent and dependent clauses and to get rid of "the pause theory" of punctuation. All of the clauses in our two examples are independent. As written, each of these should be punctuated not with a comma but rather with a period or a semicolon. Instead, the perpetual comma splicer usually acts on the pause theory: because the ideas in the independent clauses are closely connected, the writer hesitates to separate them with a period. And so the writer inserts what he or she takes to be a shorter pause—the comma. But a comma is not a breath mark; it provides readers with specific grammatical information, in this case (erroneously) that there is only one independent clause separated by the comma from modifying information. In the corrections, by contrast, the semicolon sends the appropriate signal to the reader: the message that it is joining two associated but independent statements. (A coordinating conjunction such as *and* would also be grammatically correct, though possibly awkward.)

### FUSED SENTENCE

The Indo-European language family includes many groups most languages in Europe belong to it.

### CORRECTION

The Indo-European language family includes many groups. Most languages in Europe belong to it.

[period inserted after first independent clause]

You could also fix this fused sentence with the coordinating conjunction *and*. Alternatively, you might condense the whole into a single independent clause:

Most languages in Europe belong to the Indo-European language family.

### COMMA SPLICES WITH CONJUNCTIVE ADVERBS

Quantitative methods of data collection show broad trends, however, they ignore specific cases.

Sociobiology poses a threat to traditional ethics, for example, it asserts that human behavior is genetically motivated by the "selfish gene" to perpetuate itself.

### CORRECTIONS

Quantitative methods of data collection show broad trends; however, they ignore specific cases.

[semicolon replaces comma before *however*]

Sociobiology poses a threat to traditional ethics; for example, it asserts that human behavior is genetically motivated by the "selfish gene" to perpetuate itself.

[semicolon replaces comma before *for example*]

Both of these examples contain one of the most common forms of comma splices. Both of them are **compound sentences**—that is, they contain two independent clauses. (See Chapter 9, "The Compound Sentence.") Normally, connecting the clauses with a comma and a conjunction would be correct: for example, "Most hawks hunt alone, but osprey hunt in pairs." In the preceding two comma splices, however, the independent clauses are joined by transitional expressions known as **conjunctive adverbs** (see the glossary). When conjunctive adverbs are used to link two independent clauses, they always require a semicolon. By contrast, when a coordinating conjunction links the two clauses of a compound sentence, it is always preceded by a comma.

In most cases, depending on the sense of the sentence, the semicolon precedes the conjunctive adverb and has the effect of clarifying the division between the two clauses. There are exceptions to this general rule, though, as in the following sentence:

The lazy boy did finally read a *book, however;* it was the least he could do.

Here *however* is a part of the first independent clause, qualifying its claim. The sentence thus suggests that the boy was not totally lazy, because he did get around to reading a book. Note how the meaning changes when *however* becomes the introductory word for the second independent clause:

The lazy boy did finally read a *book; however,* it was the least he could do.

Here the restricting force of *however* suggests that reading the book was not much of an accomplishment.

## TEST YOURSELF
### Comma Splices

What makes each of the following sentences a comma splice? Determine the best way to fix each one, and why, and then make the correction.

"Virtual reality" is a new buzzword, so is "hyperspace."
Many popular cures for cancer have been discredited, nevertheless, many people continue to buy them.
Elvis Presley's home, Graceland, attracts many musicians as a kind of shrine, even Paul Simon has been there.
She didn't play well with others, she sat on the bench and watched.

## BWE 3: Errors in Subject-Verb Agreement

The subject and the verb must agree in number, singular subjects taking singular verbs and plural subjects taking plural verbs. Errors in subject-verb agreement usually occur when a writer misidentifies the subject or verb of a clause.

**AGREEMENT PROBLEM**
Various kinds of vandalism has been rapidly increasing.

**CORRECTION**
Various kinds of vandalism *have* been rapidly increasing.
[verb made plural to match *kinds*]

When you isolate the grammatical subject (*kinds*) and the verb (*has*) of the original sentence, you can tell that they do not agree. Although *vandalism* might seem to be the subject because it is closest to the verb, it is actually the **object of the preposition** *of*. The majority of agreement problems arise from mistaking the object of a preposition for the actual subject of a sentence. If you habitually make this mistake, you can begin to remedy it by familiarizing yourself with the most common **prepositions.** (See the glossary, which contains a list of these.)

**AGREEMENT PROBLEM**

Another aspect of territoriality that differentiates humans from animals are their possession of ideas and objects.

**CORRECTION**

Another aspect of territoriality that differentiates humans from animals *is* their possession of ideas and objects.
[verb made singular to match subject *aspect*]

The subject of the sentence is *aspect*. The two plural nouns (*humans* and *animals*) probably encourage the mistake of using a plural verb (*are*), but *humans* is part of the *that* clause modifying *aspect,* and *animals* is the object of the preposition *from*.

**AGREEMENT PROBLEM**

The Republican and the Democrat both believe in doing what's best for America, but each believe that the other doesn't understand what's best.

**CORRECTION**

The Republican and the Democrat both believe in doing what's best for America, but each *believes* that the other doesn't understand what's best.
[verb made singular to agree with subject *each*]

The word *each* is always singular, so the verb must be singular as well (*believes*). The presence of a plural subject and verb in the sentence's first independent clause (*The Republican and the Democrat both believe*) has probably encouraged the error.

**TEST YOURSELF**

### *Subject-Verb Agreement*

Test yourself by diagnosing and correcting the error in the following example:

The controversies surrounding the placement of Arthur Ashe's statue in Richmond was difficult for the various factions to resolve.

**?**  **HINT BOX:**

## NONSTANDARD ENGLISH

The term *standard written English* refers to language that conforms to the rules and conventions adhered to by the majority of English-speaking writers. The fact is, however, that not all speakers of English grow up hearing, reading, and writing standard written English. Some linguistic cultures in America, for example, follow a different set of conventions for subject-verb agreement. Their speakers do not differentiate singular from plural verb forms with a terminal -*s*, as in standard English:

She walks home after work.

They walk home after work.

Some speakers of English do not observe this distinction, so that the first sentence becomes:

She walk home after work.

These two ways of handling subject-verb agreement are recognized by linguists not in terms of right versus wrong, but rather in terms of dialect difference. A *dialect* is a variety of a language that is characteristic of a region or culture and is sometimes unintelligible to outsiders. The problem for speakers of a dialect that differs from the norm is that they can't always rely on their ear—on what sounds right—when they are editing according to the rules of standard written English. If you consistently fail to detect a particular kind of error because it looks and sounds right to you, the best solution is to add a proofreading stage on your final draft in which you check every sentence only for that error.

## BWE 4: Shifts in Sentence Structure (Faulty Predication)

This error involves an illogical mismatch between subject and predicate. If you continually run afoul of faulty predication, you might use the exercises in a handbook to drill you on isolating the grammatical subjects and verbs of sentences, because that is the first move you need to make in fixing the problem.

**SHIFT**
    In 1987, the release of more information became available.

**CORRECTION**
    In 1987, more *information* became available *for release.*
    [new subject]

It was the *information,* not the *release,* that *become available.* The correction relocates *information* from its position as object of the preposition *of* to the subject position in the sentence; it also moves *release* into a prepositional phrase.

**SHIFT**

The busing controversy was intended to rectify the inequality of educational opportunities.

**CORRECTION**

*Busing* was intended to rectify the inequality of educational opportunities.
[new subject formulated to match verb]

The *controversy* wasn't *intended to rectify,* but *busing* was.

---

**TEST YOURSELF**

*Faulty Predication*

Identify and correct the faulty predication in this example:

The subject of learning disabilities is difficult to identify accurately.

---

## BWE 5: Errors in Pronoun Reference

There are at least three forms of this problem. All of them involve a lack of clarity about who or what a **pronoun** (a word that substitutes for a noun) refers to. The surest way to avoid difficulties is to make certain that the pronoun relates back unambiguously to a specific word, known as the **antecedent.** In the sentence "Nowadays appliances don't last as long as they once did," the noun *appliances* is the antecedent of the pronoun *they.*

**PRONOUN-ANTECEDENT AGREEMENT**

A pronoun must agree in number (and gender) with the noun or noun phrase that it refers to.

**PRONOUN ERROR**

It can be dangerous if a child, after watching TV, decides to practice what they saw.

**CORRECTIONS**

It can be dangerous if *children,* after watching TV, *decide* to practice what *they* saw.
[antecedent (and verb) made plural to agree with pronouns]
It can be dangerous if a child, after watching TV, decides to practice what *he or she* saw.
[singular pronouns substituted to match singular antecedent *child*]

The error occurs because *child* is singular, but its antecedent pronoun, *they,* is plural. The first correction makes both singular; the second makes both plural. You might also observe in the first word of the example—the impersonal *it*—an exception to the rule that pronouns must have antecedents.

---

**TEST YOURSELF**

*Pronoun-Antecedent Agreement*

What is wrong with the following sentence, and how would you fix it?

Every dog has its day, but all too often when that day happens, they can be found barking up the wrong tree.

---

**?** **HINT BOX:**

**SEXISM AND PRONOUN USAGE**

Errors in pronoun reference sometimes occur because of a writer's praiseworthy desire to avoid sexism. In most circles, the following correction of the preceding example would be considered sexist:

It can be dangerous if a child, after watching TV, decides to practice what *he* saw.

Though the writer of such a sentence may intend *he* to function as a gender-neutral impersonal pronoun, it in fact excludes girls on the basis of gender. Implicitly, it also conveys sexual stereotypes (for example, that only boys are violent, or perhaps stupid, enough to confuse TV with reality).

The easiest way to avoid the problem of sexism in pronoun usage usually lies in putting things into the plural, because plural pronouns (*we, you, they*) have no gender. (See the use of *children* in the first correction of the "Pronoun-Antecedent Agreement" example.) Alternatively, you can use the phrase *he or she*, as in the second preceding correction. Many readers, however, find *he or she* and its variant, *s/he,* to be awkward constructions. Another remedy lies in rewriting the sentence to avoid pronouns altogether, as in the following revision:

It can be dangerous if a child, after watching TV, decides to practice *some violent activity portrayed on the screen.*

---

### Ambiguous Reference

A pronoun should have only one possible antecedent.

**PRONOUN ERROR**

Children like comedians because they have a sense of humor.

**CORRECTIONS**

*Because children* have a sense of humor, *they* like comedians.
[subordinate *because* clause placed first, and relationship between noun *children* and pronoun *they* tightened]
Children like comedians because *comedians* have a sense of humor.
[pronoun eliminated and replaced by repetition of noun]

Does *they* in the original example refer to *children* or *comedians?* The rule in such cases of ambiguity is that the pronoun refers to the nearest possible antecedent, so here *comedians* possess the sense of humor, regardless of what the writer may intend. As the corrections demonstrate, either reordering the sentence or repeating the noun can remove the ambiguity.

---

**TEST YOURSELF**
### Ambiguous Reference

As you proofread, it's a good idea to target your pronouns to make sure that they cannot conceivably refer to more than one noun. What's wrong with the following sentences? Rewrite them correctly.

Alexander the Great's father, Philip of Macedon, died when he was twenty-six.
The committee could not look into the problem because it was too involved.

---

### Broad Reference

**Broad reference** occurs when a pronoun refers loosely to a number of ideas expressed in preceding clauses or sentences. It causes confusion because the reader cannot be sure which of the ideas the pronoun refers to.

**PRONOUN ERROR**

As a number of scholars have noted, Sigmund Freud and Karl Marx offered competing but also at times complementary critiques of the dehumanizing tendencies of Western capitalist society. We see this in Christopher Lasch's analysis of conspicuous consumption in *The Culture of Narcissism.*

**CORRECTION**

As a number of scholars have noted, Sigmund Freud and Karl Marx offered competing but also at times complementary critiques of the dehumanizing tendencies of Western capitalist society. We see *this complementary view*

in Christopher Lasch's analysis of conspicuous consumption in *The Culture of Narcissism.*
[broad *this* clarified by addition of noun phrase]

The word *this* in the second sentence of the uncorrected example could refer to the fact that *a number of scholars have noted* the relationship between Freud and Marx, or to the competition between Freud's and Marx's critiques of capitalism, or to the complementary nature of the two men's critiques.

Broad reference most commonly occurs when *this* is used as a pronoun; the remedy is generally to avoid using the word as a pronoun. Instead, convert *this* into an adjective, and let it modify some noun that more clearly specifies the referent: *this complementary view,* as in the correction, or alternatively, *this competition* or *this scholarly perspective.*

**TEST YOURSELF**

## Broad Reference

Locate the errors in the following examples, and provide a remedy for each:

Regardless of whether the film is foreign or domestic, they can be found in your neighborhood video store.

Many experts now claim that dogs and other higher mammals dream; for those who don't own such pets, this is often difficult to believe.

## BWE 6: Misplaced Modifiers and Dangling Participles

Before you can detect misplaced modifiers, you first need to understand what modifiers are. **Modifiers** are words or groups of words used to qualify, limit, intensify, or explain some other element in a sentence. A **misplaced modifier** is a word or phrase that appears to modify the wrong word or words.

**MISPLACED MODIFIER**
At the age of three he caught a fish with a broken arm.

**CORRECTION**
At the age of three *the boy with a broken arm* caught a fish.
[noun replaces pronoun; prepositional phrase revised and relocated]

The original sentence mistakenly implies that the fish had a broken arm.

**MISPLACED MODIFIER**
According to legend, General George Washington crossed the Delaware and celebrated Christmas in a small boat.

**CORRECTION**

According to legend, General George Washington crossed the Delaware *in a small boat* and *then* celebrated Christmas *on shore*.

[prepositional phrase relocated; modifiers added to second verb]

As a general rule, you can avoid misplacing a modifier by keeping it as close as possible to what it modifies. Thus, the second correction removes the implication that Washington celebrated Christmas in a small boat. When you cannot relocate the modifier, separate it from the rest of the sentence with a comma to prevent readers from connecting it to the nearest noun.

A **dangling participle** creates a particular kind of problem in modification: the noun or pronoun that the writer intends the participial phrase to modify is not actually present in the sentence.

**DANGLING PARTICIPLE**

After debating the issue of tax credits for the elderly, the bill passed in a close vote.

**CORRECTION**

After debating the issue of tax credits for the elderly, *the Senate passed the bill* in a close vote.

[appropriate noun added for participle to modify]

The bill did not debate the issue, as the original example implies. As the correction demonstrates, fixing a dangling participle involves tightening the link between the activity implied by the participle (*debating*) and the entity performing that activity (*the Senate*).

**TEST YOURSELF**

*Modification Errors*

Find the modification errors in the following examples, and correct them.

After eating their sandwiches, the steamboat left the dock.
The social workers saw an elderly woman on a bus with a cane standing up.
Crossing the street, a car hit the pedestrian.

## BWE 7: Errors in Using Possessive Apostrophes

Adding *'s* to most singular nouns will make them show possession: the plant*'s* roots, the accountant*'s* ledger. You can add the apostrophe alone, without the *s*, to make plural nouns that already end with *s* show possession: the flowers*'* fragrances, the ships*'* berths (although you may also add an additional *s*).

**APOSTROPHE ERROR**

    The loyal opposition scorned the committees decisions.

**CORRECTIONS**

    The loyal opposition scorned the *committee's* decisions.
    The loyal opposition scorned the *committees'* decisions.
       [possessive apostrophe added]

    The first correction assumes there was one committee; the second assumes there were two or more.

**APOSTROPHE ERROR**

    The advisory board swiftly transacted it's business.

**CORRECTION**

    The advisory board swiftly transacted *its* business.
       [apostrophe dropped]

    Unlike possessive nouns, possessive pronouns *(my, your, yours, her, hers, his, its, our, ours, their, theirs)* do not take an apostrophe.

**TEST YOURSELF**

## *Possessive Apostrophes*

Find and correct any errors in the following sentence.

    The womens movement has been misunderstood by many of its detractors.

## BWE 8: Comma Errors

As with other rules of punctuation and grammar, the many that pertain to comma usage share an underlying aim: to clarify the relationships among the parts of a sentence. Commas separate the parts of a sentence. They are particularly useful in separating the main clause from dependent elements, such as subordinate clauses and long prepositional phrases. One of their primary uses, then, is to help your readers distinguish the main clause from the rest of the sentence.

**COMMA ERROR**

    After eating the couple went home.

**CORRECTION**

    After *eating,* the couple went home.
       [comma added before independent clause]

The comma after *eating* is needed to keep the main clause "visible" or separate; it marks the point at which the prepositional phrase ends and the independent clause begins. Without this separation, readers would be invited to contemplate cannibalism as they move across the sentence.

**COMMA ERROR**

In the absence of rhetoric study teachers and students lack a vocabulary for talking about their prose.

**CORRECTION**

In the absence of rhetoric *study,* teachers and students lack a vocabulary for talking about their prose.
[comma added to separate prepositional phrase from main clause]

Readers have to read the sentence twice to find out where the prepositional phrase ends—with *study*—in order to figure out where the main clause begins.

**COMMA ERROR**

Dog owners, despite their many objections will have to obey the new law.

**CORRECTION**

Dog owners, despite their many *objections,* will have to obey the new law.
[single comma converted to a pair of commas]

A comma is needed after *objections* in order to isolate the phrase in the middle of the sentence (*despite their many objections*) from the main clause. This phrase is *nonrestrictive;* that is, the information it contains provides additional information that is not essential to the meaning of what it modifies. (Dog owners must obey the law whether they object or not.)

The test of nonrestrictive phrases and clauses is to see if they can be omitted without substantially changing the message that a sentence conveys ("Dog owners will have to obey the new law."). Nonrestrictive elements always take two commas—a comma "sandwich"—to set them off. Using only one comma illogically separates the sentence's subject (*dog owners*) from its predicate (*will have to obey*). This problem is easier to see in a shorter sentence. You wouldn't, for example, write "I, fell down." As a rule, commas virtually never separate the subject from the verb of a sentence. (Here's an exception: "Ms. Taloora, a high fashion model, watches her diet scrupulously.")

**COMMA ERROR**

Most people regardless of age like to spend money.

**CORRECTION**

Most *people,* regardless of age, like to spend money.
[comma sandwich added]

Commas enclose the nonrestrictive elements in the preceding corrected example. You could omit this information without significantly affecting the sense. Such is not the case in the following two examples.

**COMMA ERROR**

    People, who live in glass houses, should not throw stones.

**CORRECTION**

    People *who live in glass houses* should not throw stones.
      [commas omitted]

**COMMA ERROR**

    Please return the library book, that I left on the table.

**CORRECTION**

    Please return the library *book that* I left on the table.
      [comma omitted]

It is incorrect to place commas around *who live in glass houses* or a comma before *that I left on the table.* Each of these is a *restrictive clause*—that is, it contains information that is an essential part of what it modifies. In the first sentence, for example, if *who live in glass houses* is left out, the meaning of the sentence is lost: *People should not throw stones.* The word *who* is defined by restricting it to *people* in the category of glass house dwellers. Similarly, in the second example the *that* clause contributes an essential meaning to *book*—the sentence is referring to not just any book but to a particular one, the one *on the table.*

As a general rule, if the information in a phrase or clause can be omitted—if it is nonessential and therefore nonrestrictive—it needs to be separated by commas from the rest of the sentence. Moreover, you should note that nonrestrictive clauses are introduced by the word *which:* a *which* clause interpolated into a sentence takes a comma sandwich. By contrast, a restrictive clause, which takes no commas, is introduced by the word *that.*

**TEST YOURSELF**

        *Comma Errors*

Consider the following examples as a pair. Punctuate them as necessary, and then briefly articulate how the meanings of the two sentences differ:

The book which I had read a few years ago contained a lot of outdated data.

The book that I had read a few years ago contained a lot of outdated data.

## BWE 9: Spelling/Diction
## Errors That Interfere with Meaning

Misspellings are always a problem in a final draft, insofar as they under-mine your authority by inviting readers to perceive you as careless (at best). If you make a habit of using the spellchecker of a word processor, you will take care of most misspellings. But the problems that a spellchecker won't catch are the ones that can often hurt you most. These are actually **diction** errors—in-correct word choices in which you have confused one word with another that it closely resembles. In such cases, you have spelled the word correctly, but it's the wrong word. Because it means something other than what you've in-tended, you end up misleading your readers.

The best way to avoid this problem is to memorize the differences between pairs of words that are commonly confused with each other but that have dis-tinct meanings. The following examples illustrate a few of the most common and serious of these errors. Most handbooks contain a glossary of usage that *cites* more of these *sites* of confusion.

**SPELLING/DICTION ERROR: *IT'S* VS. *ITS***

Although you can't tell a book by its' cover, its fairly easy to get the gen-eral idea from the introduction.

**CORRECTION**

Although you can't tell a book by *its* cover, *it's* fairly easy to get the gen-eral idea from the introduction.

[apostrophe dropped from possessive and added to contraction]

*It's* is a contraction for *it is. Its* is a possessive pronoun meaning "belong-ing to it." If you confuse the two, *it's* likely that your sentence will, at least ini-tially, mislead *its* readers.

**SPELLING/DICTION ERROR: *THEIR* VS. *THERE* VS. *THEY'RE***

Their are ways of learning about the cuisine of northern India besides going their to watch the master chefs and learn there secrets—assuming their willing to share them.

**CORRECTION**

*There* are ways of learning about the cuisine of northern India besides going *there* to watch the master chefs and learn *their* secrets—assuming *they're* willing to share them.

[expletive *there*, adverb *there*, possessive pronoun *their*, and contraction *they're* inserted appropriately]

*There* as an adverb normally refers to a place; *there* can also be used as an **expletive** to introduce a clause, as in the first usage of the correction. (See the discussion of expletives in Chapter 9's "Cutting the Fat.") *Their* is a possessive pronoun meaning "belonging to them." *They're* is a contraction for *they are.*

**SPELLING/DICTION ERROR:** *THEN* **VS.** *THAN*

If a person would rather break a law then obey it, than he or she must be willing to face the consequences.

**CORRECTION**

If a person would rather break a law *than* obey it, *then* he or she must be willing to face the consequences.

[comparative *than* distinguished from temporal *then*]

*Than* is a conjunction used with comparisons: rather *x than y. Then* is an adverb used to indicate what comes next in relation to time: first *x, then y.*

**SPELLING/DICTION ERROR:** *EFFECT* **VS.** *AFFECT*

It is simply the case that BWEs adversely effect the way that readers judge what a writer has to say. It follows that writers who include lots of BWEs in their prose may not have calculated the disastrous affects of these mistakes.

**CORRECTION**

It is simply the case that BWEs adversely *affect* the way that readers judge what a writer has to say. It follows that writers who include lots of BWEs in their prose may not have calculated the disastrous *effects* of these mistakes.

[verb *affect* and noun *effects* inserted appropriately]

In their most common usages, *affect* is a verb meaning "to influence" and *effect* is a noun meaning "the result of an action or cause." The confusion of *affect* and *effect* is enlarged by the fact that both of these words have secondary meanings: the verb *to effect* means "to cause or bring about"; the noun *affect* is used in psychology to mean "emotion or feeling." Thus, if you confuse these two words, you will inadvertently make a meaning radically different from the one you intend.

**TEST YOURSELF**

*Spelling/Diction Errors*

Make corrections as necessary in the following paragraph.

Its not sufficiently acknowledged that the behavior of public officials is not just an ethical issue but one that effects the sale of newspapers and commercial bytes in television news. When public officials don't do what their supposed to do, than their sure to face the affects of public opinion— if they get caught—because there are dollars to be made. Its that simple: money more then morality is calling the tune in the way that the press treats it's superstars.

## Glossary of Grammatical Terms

**adjective**  An adjective is a part of speech that usually modifies a noun or pronoun: for example, *blue, boring, boisterous.*

**adverb**  An adverb is a part of speech that modifies an adjective, adverb, or verb: for example, *heavily, habitually, very.*

**clause (independent and dependent)**  A clause is any group of words that contains both a **subject** and a **predicate**. An **independent clause** (also known as a **main clause**) can stand alone as a sentence. For example:

> The most famous revolutionaries of this century have all, in one way or another, offered a vision of a classless society.

The subject of this independent clause is *revolutionaries,* the verb is *have offered,* and the direct object is *vision.* By contrast, a **dependent** (or **subordinate**) **clause** is any group of words containing a subject and verb that cannot stand alone as a separate sentence because it depends on an independent clause to complete its meaning. The following sentence adds two dependent clauses to our previous example:

> The most famous revolutionaries of this century have all, in one way or another, offered a vision of a classless society, *although* most historians would agree *that* this ideal has never been achieved.

The origin of the word *depend* is "to hang": a dependent clause literally hangs on the independent clause. In the preceding example, neither *although most historians would agree* nor *that this ideal has never been achieved* can stand independently. The *that* clause relies on the *although* clause, which in turn relies on the main clause. *That* and *although* function as **subordinating conjunctions;** by eliminating them, we could rewrite the sentence to contain three independent clauses:

> The most famous revolutionaries of this century have all, in one way or another, offered a vision of a classless society. Most historians would agree on one judgment about this vision: it has never been achieved.

**comma splice**  A comma splice consists of two independent clauses incorrectly connected ("spliced") with a comma. See BWE 2.

**conjunction (coordinating and subordinating)**  A conjunction is a part of speech that connects words, phrases, or clauses: for example, *and, but, although.* The conjunction in some way defines that connection: for example, *and* links; *but* separates. All conjunctions define connections in one of two basic ways. **Coordinating conjunctions** connect words or groups of words that have equal grammatical importance. The coordinating conjunctions are *and, but, or, nor, for, so,* and *yet.* **Subordinating conjunctions** introduce a dependent clause and connect it to a main clause. Here is a partial list of the most common subordinating conjunctions: *after, although, as, as if, as long as, because, before, if, rather than, since, than, that, though, unless, until, when, where, whether,* and *while.*

**conjunctive adverb**  A conjunctive adverb is a word that links two independent clauses (as a conjunction) but that also modifies the clause it introduces (as an adverb). Some of the most common conjunctive adverbs are *consequently, furthermore, however, moreover, nevertheless, similarly, therefore,* and *thus.* Phrases can also serve this function, such as *for example* and *on the other hand.* When conjunctive adverbs are used to link two independent clauses, they always require a semicolon:

> **Many pharmaceutical chains now offer their own generic versions of common drugs; however, many consumers continue to spend more for name brands that contain the same active ingredients as the generics.**

When conjunctive adverbs occur within an independent clause, however, they are enclosed in a pair of commas, as is the case with the use of *however* earlier in this sentence.

**coordination** *Coordination* refers to grammatically equal words, phrases, or clauses. Coordinate constructions are used to give elements in a sentence equal weight or importance. In the sentence "The tall, thin judge required the witness to answer the lawyer's question, but the witness refused," *The tall, thin judge required the witness to answer the lawyer's question* and *but the witness refused* are coordinate clauses; *tall* and *thin* are coordinate adjectives.

**dependent clause (see clause)**

**direct object** The direct object is a noun or pronoun that receives the action carried by the verb and performed by the subject. In the sentence "Certain mushrooms can kill you," *you* is the direct object.

**gerund (see verbals)**

**fused (or run-on) sentence** A fused sentence incorrectly combines two independent clauses with no conjunction or punctuation. See BWE 2.

**independent clause (see clause)**

**infinitive (see verbals)**

**main clause (see clause)**

**noun** A noun is a part of speech that names a person (*woman*), place (*town*), thing (*book*), idea (*justice*), quality (*irony*), or action (*betrayal*).

**object of the preposition (see preposition)**

**participle and participial phrase (see verbals)**

**phrase** A phrase is a group of words occurring in a meaningful sequence that lacks either a subject or a predicate. This absence distinguishes it from a clause, which contains both a subject and a predicate. Phrases function in sentences as adjectives, adverbs, nouns, or verbs. They are customarily classified according to the part of speech of their key word: *over the mountain* is a **prepositional phrase;** *running for office* is a **participial phrase;** *had been disciplined* is a **verb phrase;** *desktop graphics* is a **noun phrase;** and so forth.

**predicate** The predicate contains the verb of a sentence or clause, making some kind of statement about the subject. The predicate of the preceding sentence is *contains the verb, making some kind of statement about the subject.* The simple predicate—the verb to which the other words in the sentence are attached—is *contains.*

**preposition, prepositional phrase**   A preposition is a part of speech that links a noun or pronoun to some other word in the sentence. Prepositions usually express a relationship of time (*after*) or space (*above*) or direction (*toward*). The noun to which the preposition is attached is known as the **object of the preposition**. A preposition, its object, and any modifiers comprise a **prepositional phrase.** "*With* love *from* me *to* you" strings together three prepositional phrases. Here is a partial list of the most common prepositions: *about, above, across, after, among, at, before, behind, between, by, during, for, from, in, into, like, of, on, out, over, since, through, to, toward, under, until, up, upon, with, within,* and *without.*

**pronoun**   A pronoun is a part of speech that substitutes for a noun, such as *I, you, he, she, it, we,* and *they.*

**run-on (or fused) sentence**   A run-on sentence incorrectly combines two independent clauses with no conjunction or punctuation. See BWE 2.

**sentence**   A sentence is a unit of expression that can stand independently. It contains two parts, a **subject** and a **predicate.** The shortest sentence in the Bible, for example, is "Jesus wept." *Jesus* is the subject; *wept* is the predicate.

**sentence fragment**   A sentence fragment is a group of words incorrectly punctuated like a complete sentence but lacking the necessary structure; it is only a part of a sentence. "Walking down the road" and "The origin of the problem" are both fragments because neither contains a **predicate.** See BWE 1.

**subject**   The subject, in most cases a noun or pronoun, names the doer of the action in a sentence or identifies what the predicate is about. The subject of the previous sentence, for example, is *The subject, in most cases a noun or pronoun.* The simple subject of that sentence—the noun to which the other words in the sentence are attached—is *subject.*

**subordination, subordinating conjunctions**   *Subordination* refers to the placement of certain grammatical units, particularly phrases and clauses, at a lower, less important structural level than other elements. As with coordination, the grammatical ranking carries conceptual significance as well: whatever is grammatically subordinated appears less important than the information carried in the main clause. In the following example, the 486 personal computer is subordinated both grammatically and conceptually to the Pentium-based PC:

**Although 486-based personal computers continue to improve in speed, the new Pentium-based PC systems have thoroughly outclassed them.**

Here *Although* is a **subordinating conjunction** that introduces a subordinate clause, also known as a **dependent clause.**

**verb**   A verb is a part of speech that describes an action (*goes*), states how something was affected by an action (*became angered*), or expresses a state of being (*is*).

**verbals (participles, gerunds, and infinitives)**   Verbals are words derived from verbs. They are verb forms that look like verbs but instead function as nouns, adjectives, or adverbs. The three forms of verbals are identified next.

An **infinitive**—composed of the root form of a verb plus *to* (*to be, to vote*)—becomes a verbal when it is used as a noun (*To eat* is essential), an adjective (*These are the books **to read***), or an adverb (*He was too sick **to walk***).

Similarly, a **participle**—usually composed of the root form of a verb plus *-ing* (present participle) or *-ed* (past participle)—becomes a verbal when used as an adjective. It can occur as a single word, modifying a noun, as in *faltering negotiations* or *finished business*. But it also can occur in a **participial phrase**, consisting of the participle, its object, and any modifiers. Here are two examples:

> **Having been tried and convicted, the criminal was sentenced to life imprisonment.**
>
> **Following the path of most resistance, the masochist took deep pleasure in his frustration.**

*Having been tried and convicted* is a participial phrase that modifies *criminal; Following the path of most resistance* is a participial phrase that modifies *masochist.*

The third form of verbal, the **gerund**, resembles the participle. Like the participle, it adds *-ing* to the root form of the verb, but unlike the participle, it is used as a noun. In the sentence "Swimming is extraordinarily aerobic," the gerund *swimming* functions as the subject. Again like participles, gerunds can occur in phrases. The gerund phrases are italicized in the following example: "*Watching a film adaptation* takes less effort than *reading the book* from which it was made."

When using a verbal, remember that although it resembles a verb, it cannot function alone as the verb in a sentence: *Being a military genius* is a fragment, not a sentence.

## TEST YOURSELF
### *Grammar and Style Quiz*

Here is an error-laden paragraph to rewrite and correct. Unlike the other "Test Yourself" sections in this chapter, it does not categorize the errors it contains: you will need to diagnose and fix them yourself. It also includes a few stylistic problems to be discussed in Chapter 9, but we recommend that you take it now, as a quick check on your ability to recognize and fix BWEs. (At the end of the next chapter, you will have another opportunity to edit the paragraph for style.) A discussion of the errors and how to fix them occurs at the end of the final section of this chapter.

Rewrite the following paragraph, making changes in grammar and punctuation as necessary. You may need to add, drop, or rearrange words, but please do not add any periods. That way, you will be able to test yourself on your ability to use commas plus conjunctions, semicolons, colons, and dashes, rather than avoiding these options by separating each independent clause into a simple sentence.

1  It is a fact that fraternities and sororities are a major part of student life at

2  the university, students are preoccupied with pledging. This is not approved of by

3  most members of the faculty, however, they feel helpless about attacking them.

*(continued)*

| **TEST YOURSELF** *(continued* |

4    Perceiving that the greek societies are attractive to the students but at the same time

5    encouraging anti-intellectualism, it is not an issue that can be addressed

6    easily. The student, who wants to be popular and cool feels that he should not

7    talk in class, because interest in academics or having ideas outside class is

8    uncool. Its more important to pledge the right house then being smart. If the

9    administration would create alternatives to Greek life such as a honors program the

10   students lives would be more enriched. Although for now raising the cumulative

11   grade point necessary to pledge and remain active would be a good start.

12   Contrary to the Universitys stance against gender discrimination Greek life

13   perpetuates gender stereotypes; for example, the dances at each house for

14   freshman women but not men. Some of the best students agree with this but

15   mistakenly believes that most faculty endorse the system.

## Guidelines for Revising for Correctness

1. In correcting grammar, seek to discover the patterns of error in your writing, and unlearn the logic that has led you to make certain kinds of errors recurrently.

2. Check the draft for errors that obscure the boundaries of sentences: fragments, comma splices, and run-ons. Begin by isolating the simple subject and predicate in the main clause(s) of every sentence (to make sure they exist); this check will also help you to spot faulty predication and errors in subject-verb agreement. Then check to see that each independent clause is separated from others by a period, a comma plus coordinating conjunction, or a semicolon.

3. Check your sentences for ambiguity (capable of being read in more than one way) by deliberately trying to misread them. If your sentence can be read to mean something other than what you intended, the most common causes are misplaced and dangling modifiers and errors in pronoun reference.

4. Fix errors in pronoun reference and misplaced modifiers by making sure that every pronoun has only one clear antecedent and that every modifying word or phrase is placed as close as possible to the part of the sentence it modifies.

5. Avoid dangling modifiers by being sure that the noun or pronoun being modified is actually present in the sentence. Avoid broad refer-

ence by adding the appropriate noun or noun phrase after the pronoun *this*. (You can greatly improve the clarity of your prose just by avoiding use of the vague *this*, especially at the beginnings of sentences.)

6. Check that commas are separating dependent clauses, long prepositional phrases, or other modifying elements from the main clause. A comma is not a pause; its function is to help readers locate your sentence's main (independent) clause(s).

7. Enclose nonrestrictive modifiers placed between the subject and predicate of a sentence in a pair of commas or—for more emphasis—in a pair of dashes. A nonrestrictive modifier is a phrase, often beginning with *which*, that can be deleted from the sentence without changing the sentence's meaning.

## Answers to the "Test Yourself" Sections

### 1. **Test Yourself:** Fragments

**Original example:** Like many other anthropologists, Margaret Mead studied non-Western cultures in such works as *Coming of Age in Samoa*. And influenced theories of childhood development in America.

**Problem:** the second sentence is actually a fragment, a predicate in need of a subject.

**Possible correction:** Like many other anthropologists, Margaret Mead studied non-Western cultures (in such works as *Coming of Age in Samoa*) in ways that influenced theories of childhood development in America.

**Comment:** there are many ways to fix this example, but its original form leaves ambiguous whether the fragment refers only to Mead or to "many other anthropologists" as well. The correction offered includes the other anthropologists, diminishing the emphasis on Mead's book by placing it within parentheses. Although the correction uses a subordinating "that" to incorporate the fragment into the first sentence, it keeps this information in an emphatic position at the end of the sentence.

**Original example:** The catastrophe resulted from an engineering flaw. Because the bridge lacked sufficient support.

**Problem:** the second sentence is actually a dependent clause.

**Possible correction:** The catastrophe resulted from an engineering flaw: the bridge lacked sufficient support.

**Comment:** because the colon has causal force, this is an ideal spot to use one, identifying the "flaw."

**Original example:** In the 1840s the potato famine decimated Ireland. It being a country with poor soil and antiquated methods of agriculture.

**Problem:** the second sentence is actually a fragment, a subject plus a long participial phrase.

**Possible correction:** In the 1840s the potato famine decimated Ireland, a country with poor soil and antiquated methods of agriculture.

**Comment:** the cause of this kind of fragment is usually that the writer mistakenly believes that *being* is a verb rather than a participle that introduces a long modifying phrase ("Ireland" in this case). It would also be correct simply to change the period to a comma in the original sentence.

## 2. **Test Yourself:** Comma Splices

**Original example:** "Virtual reality" is a new buzzword, so is "hyperspace."

**Problem:** this is a comma splice—both clauses are independent, yet they are joined with a comma.

**Possible correction:** "Virtual reality" is a new buzzword; so is "hyperspace."

**Comment:** because the clauses are linked by association—both naming buzzwords—a semicolon would show that association. A writer could also condense the clauses into a simple sentence with a compound subject: "Both 'virtual reality' and 'hyperspace' are new buzzwords."

**Original example:** Many popular cures for cancer have been discredited, nevertheless, many people continue to buy them.

**Problem:** a comma splice results from the incorrectly punctuated conjunctive adverb "nevertheless."

**Possible correction:** Many popular cures for cancer have been discredited; nevertheless, many people continue to buy them.

**Comment:** without the semicolon to separate the independent clauses, the conjunctive adverb could conceivably modify either the preceding or the following clause. This problem is usually worse with *however.*

**Original example:** Elvis Presley's home, Graceland, attracts many musicians as a kind of shrine, even Paul Simon has been there.

**Problem:** this is a comma splice: the two independent clauses are linked by a comma without a conjunction. The problem is exacerbated by the number of commas in the sentence: the reader cannot easily tell which one is to separate the clauses.

**Possible correction:** Elvis Presley's home, Graceland, attracts many musicians as a kind of shrine—even Paul Simon has been there.

**Comment:** although one could justly use a semicolon here, the dash conveys the impromptu effect of an afterthought.

**Original example:** She didn't play well with others, she sat on the bench and watched.

**Problem:** because the second clause develops the first one, a writer might think that it is dependent on the first: conceptually, yes, but grammatically, no.

**Possible correction:** She didn't play well with others; she sat on the bench and watched.

**Comment:** if the writer wanted to link the two clauses more tightly, a colon would be appropriate instead of the semicolon.

### 3. **Test Yourself:** Subject-Verb Agreement

**Original example:** The controversies surrounding the placement of Arthur Ashe's statue in Richmond was difficult for the various factions to resolve.

**Problem:** the grammatical subject of the main clause is plural ("controversies"); the verb is singular ("was").

**Possible correction:** The controversies surrounding the placement of Arthur Ashe's statue in Richmond were difficult for the various factions to resolve (or "The controversy . . . was").

**Comment:** an error of this kind is encouraged by two factors: the distance of the verb from the subject and the presence of intervening prepositional phrases that use singular objects, which a writer might mistake for the grammatical subject of the main clause.

### 4. **Test Yourself:** Faulty Predication

**Original example:** The subject of learning disabilities is difficult to identify accurately.

**Problem:** the predicate matches the object of the preposition ("learning disabilities") rather than the subject of the main clause ("subject").

**Possible correction:** Learning disabilities are difficult to identify accurately.

**Comment:** omitting the abstract opening ("The subject of") enables the predicate to fit the new grammatical subject, "disabilities."

### 5. **Test Yourself:** Pronoun-Antecedent Agreement

**Original example:** Every dog has its day, but all too often when that day happens, they can be found barking up the wrong tree.

**Problem:** the plural pronoun "they" that is the grammatical subject of the second clause does not have a plural antecedent in the sentence.

**Possible correction:** Every dog has its day, but all too often when that day happens, the dog can be found barking up the wrong tree.

**Comment:** if a writer vigilantly checks all pronouns, he or she will identify the intended antecedent of the pronoun "they" to be the singular "dog" and revise accordingly. The sentence would still be incorrect if the pronoun "it" were used instead of the repeated "dog," because "it" would refer to the nearest preceding noun, "day."

### 6. **Test Yourself:** Ambiguous Reference

**Original example:** Alexander the Great's father, Philip of Macedon, died when he was twenty-six.

**Problem:** a reader can't be sure whether "he" refers to Alexander or to Philip.

**Possible correction:** Alexander the Great's father, Philip of Macedon, died at the age of twenty-six.

**Comment:** the correction rewords to remove the ambiguous pronoun. This solution is less awkward than repeating "Philip" in place of "he," though that would also be correct.

**Original example:** The committee could not look into the problem because it was too involved.

**Problem:** a reader can't be sure whether "it" refers to "the committee" or to "the problem."

**Possible correction:** The committee was too involved with other matters to look into the problem.

**Comment:** as with the previous example, rewording to eliminate the ambiguous pronoun is usually the best solution.

### 7. **Test Yourself:** Broad Reference

**Original example:** Regardless of whether the film is foreign or domestic, they can be found in your neighborhood video store.

**Problem:** the plural pronoun "they" does not have a plural antecedent in the sentence.

**Possible correction:** Regardless of whether the film is foreign or domestic, it can be found in your neighborhood video store.

**Comment:** although the sentence offers two options for films, the word "film" is singular and so, as antecedent, requires a singular pronoun ("it"). It is probably worth noting here that "it" would still be correct even if the original sentence began, "Regardless of whether the film is a foreign film or a domestic film." The rule for compound subjects that use an either/or construction is as follows: the number (singular or plural) of the noun or pronoun that follows "or" determines the number of the verb. Compare the following two examples:
"Either several of his aides *or* the *candidate is* going to speak."
"Either the candidate *or* several of his *aides are* going to speak."

**Original example:** Many experts now claim that dogs and other higher mammals dream; for those who don't own such pets, this is often difficult to believe.

**Problem:** the referent of the pronoun "this" is unclear. Precisely what is "difficult to believe"—that mammals dream or that experts would make such a claim?

**Possible correction:** Many experts now claim that dogs and other higher mammals dream; for those who don't own such pets, this claim is often difficult to believe.

**Comment:** often the best way to fix a problem with broad reference produced by "this" as a pronoun is to convert "this" to an adjective—a strategy that will require a writer to provide a specifying noun for "this" to modify. As a rule, when you find an isolated "this" in your draft, ask and answer the question "*this what?*"

### 8. **Test Yourself:** Modification Errors

**Original example:** After eating their sandwiches, the steamboat left the dock.

**Problem:** this is a dangling participle—the grammar of the sentence conveys that the steamboat ate their sandwiches.

**Corrections:** After the girls ate their sandwiches, the steamboat left the dock. Or: After eating their sandwiches, the girls boarded the steamboat, and it left the dock.

**Comment:** the two corrections model the two ways of remedying most dangling participles. Both provide an antecedent ("the girls") for the pronoun "their." The first correction eliminates the participial phrase, substituting a subordinate clause. The second correction adds to the existing main clause ("steamboat left") another one ("girls boarded") for the participial phrase to modify appropriately.

**Original example:** The social workers saw an elderly woman on a bus with a cane standing up.

**Problem:** misplaced modifiers create the problems in this sentence, which implies that the bus possessed a cane that was standing up. The problem exemplified here is produced from the series of prepositional phrases—"*on* a bus *with* a cane"—followed by the participial phrase "standing up," which is used as an adjective and intended to modify "woman."

**Possible correction:** The social workers saw an elderly woman on a bus. She was standing up with the help of a cane.

**Comment:** writers often try to cram too much into sentences, piling on the prepositions. The best remedy is sometimes to break up the sentence, a move that usually involves eliminating prepositions, which possess a sludgy kind of movement, and adding verbs, which possess more distinct movement.

**Original example:** Crossing the street, a car hit the pedestrian.

**Problem:** the dangling participle ("Crossing the street") does not have a word to modify in the sentence. The sentence conveys that the car crossed the street.

**Possible corrections:** Crossing the street, the pedestrian was hit by a car. Or: As the pedestrian crossed the street, a car hit him.

**Comment:** the first solution brings the participial phrase closest to the noun it modifies ("pedestrian"). The second converts the participial into the verb ("crossed") of a dependent clause ("As . . .") and moves "pedestrian" into the clause as the subject for that verb. As in the "steamboat" example, one correction provides an appropriate noun for the participial phrase to modify, and the other eliminates the participle.

### 9. **Test Yourself:** Possessive Apostrophes

**Original example:** The womens movement has been misunderstood by many of its detractors.

**Problem:** the possessive apostrophe for "womens" is missing. The trickiness here in inserting the apostrophe is that this word is already plural.

**Possible correction:** The women's movement has been misunderstood by many of its detractors.

**Comment:** because the word is already plural, it takes a simple *apostrophe s* to indicate a movement belonging to women—not "womens'."

### 10. **Test Yourself:** Comma Errors

**Original paired examples:** The book which I had read a few years ago contained a lot of outdated data.

The book that I had read a few years ago contained a lot of outdated data.

**Problem:** in the first example, the modifying clause "which I had read a few years ago" is nonrestrictive: it could be omitted without changing the essential meaning of the sentence. Therefore, it needs to be enclosed in commas—as the "which" signals.

**Possible correction:** The book, which I had read a few years ago, contained a lot of outdated data.

**Comment:** the second example in the pair—"The book that I had read a few years ago contained a lot of outdated data"—is correct as it stands. The restrictive clause, *that I had read a few years ago,* does not take commas around it, because the information it gives readers is an essential part of the meaning of *book.* That is, it refers to not just any book read a few years ago, as in the first example in the pair, but rather specifies the one containing outdated data. *The book that I had read a few years ago* thus functions as what is known as a *noun phrase.*

### 11. **Test Yourself:** Spelling/Diction Errors

**Original example:** Its not sufficiently acknowledged that the behavior of public officials is not just an ethical issue but one that effects the sale of newspapers and commercial bytes in television news. When public officials don't do what their supposed to do, than their sure to face the affects of public opinion—if they get caught—because there are dollars to be made. Its that simple: money more then morality is calling the tune in the way that the press treats it's superstars.

**Problems:** the paragraph confuses the paired terms discussed under BWE 9. It mistakes:

> "Its" for "It's" before "not sufficiently"
> "effects" for "affects" before "the sale"
> "their" for "they're" before "supposed"
> "than" for "then" before "their sure"
> "they're" for "their" before "sure"
> "affects" for "effects" before "of public opinion"

"Its" for "It's" before "that simple"

"then" for "than" before "morality"

"it's" for "its" before "superstars"

**Possible correction:** It's not sufficiently acknowledged that the behavior of public officials is not just an ethical issue but one that affects the sale of newspapers and commercial bytes in television news. When public officials don't do what they're supposed to do, then they're sure to face the effects of public opinion—if they get caught—because there are dollars to be made. It's that simple: money more than morality is calling the tune in the way that the press treats its superstars.

**Comment:** if you confuse similar words, the only solution is to memorize the differences and consciously check your drafts for any problems until habit takes hold.

### 12. **Test Yourself:** Grammar and Style Quiz

The answers offered here are not exclusive—the only ways to correct the problems. In some cases, we have offered various satisfactory remedies, and as previously noted, a few of the suggested revisions—marked by ▪▪—address editing for style (Chapter 9) rather than editing for correctness.

### LINE 1:

- ▪▪ There are no grammatical errors *per se,* but "It is a fact that" is a wordy expletive that should be cut.

### LINE 2:

- ▪ There is a comma splice between "university" and "students": insert semicolon as preferred option.
- ▪ "This," beginning the next sentence, is a broad reference and should be converted into an adjective, with a noun or noun phrase added, such as "This preoccupation" or "This dominance by Greek societies."
- ▪▪ In addition, a writer might recast the passive verb into the active: "Most faculty members do not approve of . . ."

### LINE 3:

- ▪ There is a comma splice after "faculty": insert semicolon.
- ▪ The antecedent of the pronoun "them" is ambiguous: substitute a noun such as "the Greeks."

### LINE 4:

- ▪ "Perceiving" is a dangling participle: either recast to include a subject in a dependent clause (such as "Because most faculty members perceive") or insert "most faculty members" as a referent for the participle before "it" in Line 5.

- Capitalize "Greek."

## LINE 5:

- Fix faulty parallelism: introduce the second item ("encouraging anti-intellectualism") with another "that" ("but at the same time that they encourage").
- The "it is" (an expletive) creates problems with broad reference. If Line 4 has been changed by eliminating the participle (using some version of the "Because most faculty members feel" option), recast the main clause. For example, following "anti-intellectualism" the sentence might read, "this issue cannot be addressed easily." If Line 4 has retained the participial phrase, then the revision would need to read something like "most faculty members believe that this issue cannot be addressed easily."

## LINE 6:

- The "who" clause is restrictive: the comma must be dropped.
- The "he" is sexist: use "he or she" or change the number—to "Students who want . . . feel that they."

## LINE 7:

- Fix faulty parallelism: change "interest in" to "be*ing* interested in" so as to match "hav*ing* ideas."

## LINE 8:

- Possessive "Its" should be the contraction "It's."
- Temporal "then" should be the comparative "than."
- Fix faulty parallelism: change "being" to "to be" to match "to pledge."

## LINE 9:

- Change "a honors" to "an honors."
- Insert commas around the nonrestrictive modifying phrase "such as an honors program": these will separate it from both the long introductory dependent ("if") clause that precedes it and the main clause that follows.

## LINE 10:

- Make "students" a plural possessive: "Students' lives."
- The "more enriched" is arguably wordy: "richer" is leaner.
- "Although" is a subordinating conjunction that creates a sentence fragment. The easiest solution is to cut it, though a writer could also attach the entire "although" clause to the previous sentence, using a comma or dash.

**LINE 11:**

- This is part of the fragment that began in Line 10.

**LINE 12:**

- Fix the possessive: "University's."
- Fix the case of the noun: "university's."
- Place a comma after "discrimination" to separate the long introductory modifying phrases from the main clause.

**LINE 13:**

- The semicolon is incorrect, because the sentence does not contain two independent clauses. A colon is better than a dash here, though both are technically correct.

**LINE 14:**

- Most rhetoricians consider "freshman" sexist: substitute "first-year."
- The use of "this" is another egregious case of broad reference ("agree with *this*" *what?*). The best solution is probably to rewrite this part of the sentence to clarify the meaning. For example, "Some of the best students object to Greek life in these terms and oppose the administration's handling of the Greeks . . ."

**LINE 15:**

- Fix subject-verb agreement: "some . . . believe."

Here is how one corrected version of the quiz might look:

Fraternities and sororities are a major part of student life at the university: students are preoccupied with pledging. Most faculty members do not approve of this dominance by Greek societies; however, they feel helpless about attacking the Greeks. Because faculty members perceive that the Greek societies are attractive to the students but at the same time that they encourage anti-intellectualism, this issue cannot be addressed easily. The student who wants to be popular and cool feels that he or she should not talk in class, because being interested in academics or having ideas outside class is uncool. It's more important to pledge the right house than to be smart. If the administration would create alternatives to Greek life, such as an honors program, the students' lives would be richer. For now, raising the cumulative grade point necessary to pledge and remain active would be a good start to solving the problem of Greek domination. Contrary to the university's stance against gender discrimination, Greek life perpetuates gender stereotypes: for example, the dances at each house for first-year women but not men. Some of the best students object to Greek life in these terms and oppose the administration's handling of the Greeks. But many of these same students mistakenly believe that most faculty members endorse the system.

## CHAPTER 9

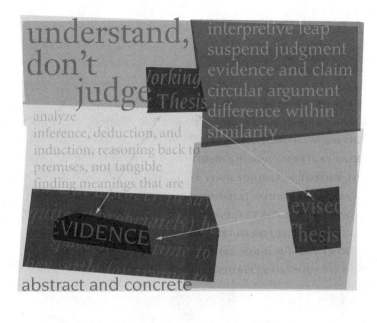

# EDITING FOR STYLE

Editing for style, unlike editing for correctness, does not occur in the comfortable land of simple right and wrong, but in the more exploratory terrain of making choices among more and less effective ways of formulating and communicating what you mean. At its most concrete, the domain of style can be divided into two broad categories:

- Diction—the words you choose
- Syntax—the sentence structure, the order in which you arrange your chosen words

In the previous chapter we advised that you delay editing for correctness until the end of the writing process, so that it would not interfere with your thinking. That advice remains only somewhat true in relation to editing for style. Although you should probably delay a full-fledged stylistic revision until a late stage of drafting, you probably should not totally ignore stylistic questions as you draft, because these decisions inevitably exert a powerful influence on the meaning you make. With regard to diction, the way you name key concepts and phrase significant distinctions is a crucial part of the analytical process of dividing a subject into parts. And with regard to syntax, the way you order your words will determine what you emphasize.

# What Is Style?

Broadly defined, *style* refers to all of a writer's decisions in selecting, arranging, and expressing what he or she has to say. Many factors affect your style: your aim and sense of audience, the ways you approach and develop a topic, the kinds of evidence you choose, and particularly, the kinds of syntax and diction you characteristically select. In this sense, style is personal.

The foundations of your style emerge in the dialogue you have with yourself about your topic. When you revise for style, you consciously reorient yourself toward communicating the results of that dialogue to your audience. Stylistic decisions, then, are a mix of the unconscious and conscious, of chance and choice. You don't simply impose style onto your prose; it's not a mask you don or your way of icing the cake. Revising for style is more like sculpting. As a sculptor uses a chisel to "bring out" a shape from a block of walnut or marble, a writer uses style to "bring out" the shape of the conceptual connections in a draft of an essay.

As the rest of this chapter will suggest in various ways, this "bringing out" demands a certain *detachment from your own language*. It requires that you *become aware of your words as words and of your sentences as sentences*.

## Editing for Style as a Form of Conceptual Revision: Two Brief Examples

Rethinking the way you have said something will often lead you to rethink the substance of what you have said. When you reorder the words in your sentences, you often will be able to recognize your ideas more clearly, and for that matter, discover new ideas that were shrouded in foggy constructions.

Suppose, for example, that in revising your sentence structure you decide to give more prominence to one of the two ideas that your original draft treated as equal. Your draft reads:

> The history of Indochina is marked by colonial exploitation as well as international cooperation.

Here, the claim that Indochina has experienced colonial exploitation is equal in weight to the claim that it has also experienced international cooperation. But consider what happens when your revision, by using an *although* clause, makes the claim of exploitation secondary to the claim of cooperation:

> The history of Indochina, *although* marked by colonial exploitation, testifies to the possibility of international cooperation.

The first version of the sentence would probably lead you to a broad survey of foreign intervention in Indochina. The result would likely be a static list in which you judged some interventions to be "beneficial" and others "not beneficial." The revised sentence redirects your thinking, tightens your paper's focus to prioritize evidence of cooperation, and presses you to make decisions, such as whether the positive consequences of cooperation outweigh the negative consequences of colonialism. In short, the revision leads you to examine the dynamic relations between your two initial claims.

Rethinking what you mean is just as likely to occur when you are revising at the level of word choice as at the level of syntax. Let's say that you've drafted an analysis of the president's approach to military spending, and, having encountered some apparently contradictory evidence, you've chosen to call his stance "ambiguous" (open to many interpretations). As you focus on the transitions among your examples, though, you realize that his approach actually tends to fall into one of two responses. You then understand that his approach should more accurately be termed "ambivalent" (possessing two opposite or conflicting views). This recognition, in turn, would lead you not only to reorganize your final version but also to refocus your argument, building to the significance of this ambivalence (that the president is trying to adopt two stances simultaneously) rather than to your previous conclusion (that presidential policy is simply incoherent).

As you read this chapter and apply its advice, keep in mind that revision is the essence of writing. Assume that your first draft will not—indeed, should not—be polished. But that's why you need to allocate time to rewrite: to dwell with your words and phrasings, so that you can begin to notice how to make your meaning cleaner, clearer, and more persuasive.

On the other hand, you should also recognize that the process of revision is, in theory, endless. Near the end of his career, Sigmund Freud considered the question of when a person should stop undergoing psychoanalysis, given that one is never totally "cured." His answer was that at a certain point, one has simply had enough and so stops arbitrarily. At some arbitrary point, you will have to decide to stop revising. The more of it you can find the time to do, however, the more successful your final product is likely to become.

## Levels of Style: Who's Writing to Whom, and Why Does It Matter?

*How* you say something is always a significant part of *what* you say. To look at words as words is to focus on the *how* as well as the *what*. Imagine that you call your friend on the phone, and a voice you don't recognize answers. You ask to speak with your friend, and the voice responds, "With whom have I the pleasure of speaking?" By contrast, what if the voice instead responds, "Who's this?" What information do these two versions of the question convey, beyond the obvious request for your name?

The first response—"With whom have I the pleasure of speaking?"—tells you that the speaker is formal and polite. He is also probably fastidiously well educated: he not only knows the difference between *who* and *whom,* but also obeys the etiquette that outlaws ending a sentence with a preposition ("Whom have I the pleasure of speaking *to?*"). The very formality of the utterance, however, might lead you to label the speaker pretentious. His assumption that conversing with you is a "pleasure" suggests empty flattery. On the other hand, the second version—"Who's this?"—while also grammatically correct, is less formal. It is more direct but also terse to a fault: the speaker does not seem particularly interested in treating you politely.

Is one response better than the other? The answer would seem to depend on your point of view and your understanding of the situation. Let's consider one more hypothetical example. You answer the phone, and a voice asks to speak with a member of your household but mispronounces the name. You might reasonably surmise that the caller is working from a list and trying to sell something. If you dislike telephone solicitation, you probably would be more likely to ask "Who's this?" than "With whom have I the pleasure of speaking?"

What generalizations about style do these examples suggest?

- There are many ways of conveying a message.
- The way you phrase a message constitutes a significant part of its meaning.
- Your phrasing gives your reader cues that suggest your attitude and your ways of thinking.
- All stylistic decisions depend on your sensitivity to context—who's talking to whom about what subject and with what aims.

The last of these generalizations concerns what is called the *rhetorical situation*. *Rhetoric* is the subject that deals with the use of language to inform or persuade or move an audience in some way. Obviously, as you make stylistic choices, you need to be aware of the possible consequences of making certain statements to a certain audience in a certain fashion. In reference to our telephone examples, for instance, you should recognize that in daily speech a proper *whom* and a polite *may* can lead others, however unfortunately, to view you with suspicion.

In an academic context, though, most of the analytical writing that you do occurs in a rhetorical situation that is quite formal. As Chapter 5 ("Matters of Form") discussed, academic discourse tends to be full of conventions—rules and protocols—and these are not simply a matter of etiquette. They can also provide guidelines designed to help writers organize and develop their thinking. Along similar lines, the diction you choose to use in academic situations will not only reflect your ability to "talk the talk" but, if you respect the terms, help you to think.

### Formal and Informal Styles

Formal English obeys the basic conventions of standard written prose, and most academic writing is fairly formal. An informal style—one that is conversational and full of slang—can have severe limitations in an academic setting. The syntax and vocabulary of written prose aren't the same as those of speech, and attempts to import the language of speech into academic writing can result in your communicating less meaning with less precision.

Let's take one brief example:

Internecine quarrels within the corporation destroyed morale and sent the value of the stock plummeting.

The phrase *internecine quarrels* may strike some readers as a pretentious display of formal language, but consider how difficult it is to communicate this concept economically. "Fights that go on between people related to each other" is awkward; "brother against brother" is sexist and a cliché; and "mutually destructive disputes" is acceptable but long-winded.

It is arguably a part of our national culture to value the simple and the direct as more genuine and democratic than the sophisticated, which is supposedly more aristocratic and pretentious. This "plain-speaking" style, however, can hinder your ability to develop and communicate your ideas. In the case of *internecine,* the more formal diction choice actually communicates more, and more effectively, than the less formal equivalents.

When in doubt about how your readers will respond to the formality or informality of your style, you are usually better off opting for some version of "With whom have I the pleasure of speaking?" rather than "Who's this?" The best solution will usually lie somewhere in between: "May I ask who's calling?" would protect you against the imputation of either priggishness or piggishness.

## Revising Word Choice (Diction)

The rest of this chapter examines the kinds of choices that you need to consider as you revise your drafts. The choices that arise in contemplating and reconsidering your words involve not only *precision* but also *appropriateness.* That is, you want the words with the most accurate meanings, but also those that are most acceptable in the given rhetorical situation within which you are writing.

### Getting the Right Word

The "right" word contributes accuracy and precision to your meaning. The "wrong" word, it follows, is inaccurate and vague. The most reliable guide to choosing the right word and avoiding the wrong word is the dictionary. A good one will give you not only concise definitions, but also the origin of the word (known as its *etymology*), and in some cases, synonyms and advice on the differences among related words. As an alternative to a dictionary, a thesaurus (a dictionary of synonyms) can provide a list of similar words from which to choose, but unless you are certain of the fine distinctions among related words (which a dictionary will generally provide), you run a fairly high risk of choosing an inappropriate word. In any case, you should not overlook one of the best ways to learn more about diction: pay attention in your reading to how unfamiliar words are used.

Some diction errors, as was discussed in "Spelling/Diction Errors That Interfere with Meaning" in Chapter 8, involve both correctness and style. If you confuse *then* and *than,* or *infer* and *imply,* you will not convey the meaning that you intend, and you will probably bewilder your readers. Getting the wrong word is, of course, not limited to pairs of words that are spelled similarly. A *notorious* figure is widely but unfavorably known, whereas a *famous* person is usually recognized for accomplishments that are praiseworthy.

### Shades of Meaning

A slightly less severe version of getting the wrong word occurs when a writer uses a word with a shade of meaning that is inappropriate or inaccurate in a particular context. Take, for example, the words *assertive* and *aggressive.* Often used interchangeably, they don't really mean the same thing—and the difference matters. Loosely defined, both terms mean "forceful." But *assertive* suggests being "bold and self-confident," whereas *aggressive* suggests being "eager to attack." In most cases, you compliment the person you call "assertive" but raise doubts about the person you call "aggressive" (depending on the situation: *aggressive* is a term of praise on the football field, but less so if used to describe an acquaintance's behavior during conversation at the dinner table).

One particularly charged context in which shades of meaning matter to many readers involves the potentially sexist implications of using one term for women and another for men. If, for example, in describing a woman and a man up for the same job, we referred to the woman as *aggressive* but the man as *assertive,* our diction would deservedly be considered sexist, because it would imply that her behavior was inappropriately belligerent and therefore "unwomanly," whereas his behavior was poised and therefore full of "manly" leadership potential. The sexism enters when word choice suggests that what is assertive in a man is aggressive in a woman.

In choosing the right shade of meaning, you can often get a sharper sense for the word by knowing its etymological history—the word or words from which it evolved. In the preceding example, *aggressive* derives from the Latin *aggressus,* meaning "to go to or approach"; and *aggressus* is itself a combination of *ad,* a prefix expressing motion, and *gradus,* "a step." An aggressive person, then, is "coming at you." *Assertive,* on the other hand, comes from the Latin *asserere,* combining *ad* and *serere,* meaning "to join or bind together." An assertive person is "coming to build or put things together"—certainly not to threaten.

The point is that words embody rich and complex histories that distinguish them from other words and that allow you to discriminate fine shades of meaning. The nineteenth-century English statesman Benjamin Disraeli once differentiated between *misfortune* and *calamity* by commenting on his political rival William Gladstone: "If Mr. Gladstone fell into the Thames, it would be a misfortune; but if someone dragged him out, it would be a calamity."

**APPLICATION:**

## WORKING WITH ETYMOLOGY

One of the best ways to get yourself to pay attention to words as words is to practice making fine distinctions among related words, as we did with "aggressive" and "assertive." The following exercise will not only increase your vocabulary but also acquaint you with the indispensable reference work for etymology, the *Oxford English Dictionary* (*OED*) and possibly specialized dictionaries as well.

Look up one of the following pairs of words in the *OED*. Write down the etymology of each word, and then, in a paragraph for each, summarize its linguistic history—how its meaning has evolved across time. (The dated examples of how the word has been used will be helpful here.)

| | |
|---|---|
| *ordinal* and *ordinary* | *explicate* and *implicate* |
| *tenacious* and *stubborn* | *induce* and *conducive* |
| *enthusiasm* and *ecstasy* | *adhere* and *inherent* |
| *monarchy* and *oligarchy* | *overt* and *covert* |

Alternatively, select a pair of similar words, or for that matter, any key words, from your reading for a course, and submit them to this exercise. There's no better way to learn about—and remember—a word.

### What's Bad about Good and Bad (and Other Broad Terms)

Vague terms such as *good* and *bad* can seduce you into stopping your thinking while it is still too general and ill-defined. If you train yourself to select a more precise word whenever you encounter these words in your drafts, not only will your prose become clearer, but the search for a new word will probably start you thinking again, sharpening your ideas. If, for example, you find a sentence such as "The subcommittee made a *bad* decision," ask yourself *why* you called it a bad decision. A revision to "The subcommittee made a shortsighted decision" indicates what in fact is "bad" about the decision and sets you up to discuss why the decision was myopic, further developing the idea. Nor are evaluative terms the only ones whose broadness can create problems. In a sentence such as "Society disapproves of interracial marriage," the broad term *society* can blind you to a host of important distinctions about social class, about a particular culture, and so on.

### Concrete and Abstract Diction

At its best, effective analytical prose uses both concrete and abstract words. Simply defined, *concrete diction* evokes: it brings things to life by offering your readers words that they can use their senses upon. *Telephone, eggshell, crystalline, azure, striped, kneel, flare,* and *burp* are examples of concrete diction. In academic writing, there is no substitute for concrete language whenever you are describing what happens or what something looks like—in a laboratory experiment, in a military action, in a painting or film sequence. In short, the language of evidence usually consists of concrete diction.

By contrast, *abstract diction* refers to words that lie beyond the senses, to concepts. *Virility, ideology, love, definitive, desultory, conscientious, classify,* and *ameliorate* are examples of abstract diction. In academic writing, by and large, this is the language of ideas.

Just as evidence needs to be organized by a thesis, and a thesis needs to be developed by evidence, so *concrete and abstract diction need each other.* Use concrete diction to illustrate and anchor the generalizations that abstract diction expresses. Note the concrete language used to define the abstraction *provinciality* in this example:

> There is no cure for *provinciality* like traveling abroad. In America the waiter who fails to bring the check promptly at the end of the meal we rightly convict for not being watchful. But in England, after waiting interminably for the check and becoming increasingly irate, we learn that only an ill-mannered waiter would bring it without being asked. We have been rude, not he.

In the following example, the abstract terms *causality, fiction,* and *conjunction* are integrated with concrete diction in the second sentence.

> According to the philosopher David Hume, *causality* is a kind of *fiction* that we ascribe to what he called "the constant *conjunction* of observed events." If a person gets hit in the eye and a black semicircle develops underneath it, that does not necessarily mean the blow caused the black eye.

The best academic writing integrates concrete and abstract diction. A style that omits concrete language can leave readers lost in a fog of abstraction that only tangible details can illuminate. The concrete language helps readers see what you mean, much in the way that examples help them understand your ideas. Without the shaping power of abstract diction, however, concrete evocation can leave you with a list of lively but, finally, pointless facts.

---

**?** **HINT BOX:**

**LATINATE DICTION**

Much abstract diction comes from Latin roots, words with such endings as *-tion, -ive, -ity, -ate,* and *-ent.* (Such words will be designated by an *L* in the etymological section of dictionary definitions.) Taken to an extreme, Latinate diction can leave your meaning vague and your readers confused. Note how impenetrable the Latinate terms make the following example:

*(continued)*

**?** *(continued)*

The examination of different perspectives on the representations of sociopolitical anarchy in media coverage of revolutions can be revelatory of the invisible biases that afflict television news.

This sentence actually makes sense, but the demands it makes upon readers will surely drive off most of them before they have gotten through it. Reducing the amount of Latinate diction can make it more readable:

Because we tend to believe what we see, the political biases that afflict television news coverage of revolutions are largely invisible. We can begin to see these biases when we focus on how the medium reports events, studying the kinds of footage used, for example, or finding facts from other sources that the news has left out.

Although the preceding revision retains a lot of Latinate words, it provides a ballast of concrete, sensory details that allows readers to follow the idea. Although many textbooks on writing argue against using Latinate terms where shorter, concrete terms (usually of Anglo-Saxon origin) might be used instead, such an argument seems needlessly limiting in comparison with the advantages offered by a thorough mixture of the two levels of diction. It's fine to use Latinate diction; just don't make it the sole staple of your verbal diet.

---

**APPLICATION:**

## RECASTING THE DICTION

Most people simply don't pay attention to words; that is, they use words as if their sounds and shapes were invisible and their meanings were unitary and self-evident. One goal of this chapter is to interest you in words themselves—as things with particularized qualities, complex histories, and varied shades of meaning. Such interest is enormously beneficial in improving your ability to write. There are various ways of nourishing this interest, all of which share the characteristic of focusing on the words as words. Here are three exercises designed to give practice with that focus:

1. Compose a paragraph using only concrete diction, and then one using only abstract diction. To what extent do your paragraphs share the strengths and weaknesses of concrete and abstract words previously discussed?
2. Select a paragraph or two from one of your papers and identify the Latin and Anglo-Saxon diction. Actually mark the draft—with an *L* or

*(continued)*

*Recasting the Diction (continued)*

an *A,* with a circle around one kind of word and a square around the other. Then find as many Anglo-Saxon substitutes for Latinate terms, and as many Latinate substitutes for Anglo-Saxon terms as you can (with the help of a dictionary and perhaps a thesaurus). Ideally, you might then do a final revision in which you synthesize the best from both paragraphs to arrive at a consummate revision of your original paragraph.

3. Rewrite the "To be or not to be" soliloquy from *Hamlet* (Act III, i) in Latinate terms ("to exist or not to exist"). This exercise, like the previous one, will probably lead you to discover how difficult it is to find substitutes for certain words. It is a lesson worth learning: how relatively rarely one word precisely "means the same thing" as another.

4. The following list of sentences offers somewhat exaggerated examples of vague diction. Rewrite them, substituting more concrete language, and supporting any abstractions you retain with appropriate detail. Just for the challenge, try rewrites that include no assertions, using only details to convey the point.

It was a great party; everybody had fun.

It was a lousy party; everybody disliked it.

The book was really boring.

The film was very interesting.

Marxism is stupid.

Asking that question to subjects is a waste of time.

The experiment has no point.

As a follow-up or an alternative, locate two examples of vague diction from one of your own papers, and give them this same treatment.

## Using and Avoiding Jargon

*Jargon*—the specialized vocabulary of a particular group—is one of those terms with unstable shades of meaning. Many people assume that all jargon is "bad": pretentious language designed to make most readers feel inferior. Many guidebooks on writing style attack jargon in similar terms, calling it either polysyllabic balderdash or a specialized, "gatekeeping" language designed by an in-group to keep others out.

Yet in many academic contexts, jargon is downright essential. It is a conceptual shorthand, a technical vocabulary that allows the members of a group (or a discipline) to converse with one another more clearly and efficiently. Certain words that may seem odd to outsiders in fact function as connective tissue for a way of thought shared by insiders. The following sentence, for example, although full of botanical jargon, is also admirably cogent:

In angiosperm reproduction, if the number of pollen grains deposited on the stigma exceeds the number of ovules in the ovary, then pollen tubes may compete for access to ovules, which results in fertilization by the fastest growing pollen tubes.

We would label this use of jargon acceptable, because it is written, clearly, *by* insiders *for* fellow insiders. It might not be acceptable language for an article intended for readers who are not botanists, or at least not scientists.

The problem with jargon comes when this insiders' language is ostensibly directed at outsiders as well. The language of contracts offers a prime example of such jargon at work:

The Author hereby indemnifies and agrees to hold the Publisher, its licensees, and any seller of the Work harmless from any liability, damage, cost, and expense, including reasonable attorney's fees and costs of settlement, for or in connection with any claim, action, or proceeding inconsistent with the Author's warranties or representations herein, or based upon or arising out of any contribution of the Author to the Work.

Run for the lawyer! What does it mean to "hold the Publisher . . . harmless"? To what do "the Author's warranties or representations" refer? What exactly is the author being asked to do here—release the publisher from all possible lawsuits that the author might bring? We might label this use of jargon *obfuscating:* although it may aim at precision, it leaves most readers bewildered. Although average readers are asked to sign them, such documents are really written by lawyers for other lawyers.

As the botanical and legal examples suggest, the line between *acceptable* and *obfuscating* has far more to do with the audience to whom the words are addressed than with the actual content of the language. Because most academic writing is addressed to insiders, you need to control the acceptable jargon in a given field. Your ability to use the technical language of the discipline is a necessary skill for conversing with others. Moreover, by demonstrating that you can "talk the talk," you will validate your authority to pronounce an opinion on matters in the discipline.

The following two guidelines can help you in your use of jargon:

1. When addressing *insiders,* use jargon accurately ("talk the talk").
2. When addressing *outsiders*—the general public or members of another discipline—either define the jargon carefully or avoid it altogether.

## Using Pronouns: The Person Question

The person of a pronoun takes one of three forms:

"I read Nietzsche" is in the first person. The pronoun (*I*) identifies the speaker.

"You read Nietzsche" is in the second person. The pronoun (*you*) identifies the person spoken to.

"He reads Nietzsche" is in the third person. The pronoun (*he*) identifies
the person or thing spoken about.

Table 9.1 distinguishes among first-, second-, and third-person pronouns,
indicating the various forms for each of the three persons.

"The person question" concerns which of these forms you should use
when you write. As a general rule, in academic writing you should discuss your
subject matter in the third person and avoid the first and second person.

**Third person:**    Heraclitus is an underrated philosopher.

**First person:**    I believe Heraclitus is an underrated philosopher.

**Second person:**    You should recognize that Heraclitus is an underrated
philosopher.

There is logic to this rule: most academic analysis focuses on the subject
matter rather than on you as you respond to it. If you use the third person,
you will keep the attention where it belongs. (This does *not* mean that you
should write about *yourself* in the third person—"This writer believes"—as we
discuss in the following section.)

## The First-Person *I*: Pro and Con

Using the first-person *I* throws the emphasis on the wrong place. Repeated assertions of "in my opinion" actually distract your readers from what you have to
say. Omit them except in the most informal cases. You might, however, consider
using the first person as a strategy for loosening up and saying what you really
think about a subject rather than adopting conventional and faceless positions.
This is not a bad idea in the drafting stage, especially if you are having trouble
bringing your own point of view to the forefront. In the final analysis, though,
most analytical prose will be more precise and direct in the third person.

**TABLE 9.1** First-, Second-, and Third-Person Pronouns.

|  | SINGULAR | PLURAL |
|---|---|---|
| **FIRST PERSON** | I, me, mine | we, us, ours |
| **SECOND PERSON** | you, yours | you, yours |
| **THIRD PERSON** | he, him, his<br>she, her, hers<br>it, its | they, them, theirs |

Let's take an example. Say that you are considering the extent to which models of local, state, and national government effectively provide social services for the homeless in an economy in which dwindling funds are available. After considering the strengths and weaknesses of each model, you might conclude, "I am convinced that local governments are most effective at providing services for the homeless, because they avoid the bureaucratic red tape that afflicts efforts on the state and national levels." The first four words of this sentence—although they may serve a rhetorical purpose by announcing to your audience your willingness to take a stand—are arguably an unnecessary and distracting addition. In fact, they grammatically subordinate the stand you have taken. If you cut "I am convinced that," what you lose in personal conviction you gain in concision and directness, by keeping the focus on the main idea in the main clause.

Are there cases when you should use *I?* Some professors do prefer the first-person pronoun in particular cases, as noted in the following three observations.

---

**VOICES FROM ACROSS THE CURRICULUM**

## USING THE FIRST-PERSON *I* in Academic Writing

I prefer that personal opinion or voice (for example, "I this," or "I that") appear throughout. I like the first person. No "the author feels" or "this author found that," please! Who is the author? Hey, it's you!
—**FREDERICK NORLING,** *Professor of Business*

❖ ❖ ❖

Avoid phrases like *"The author* believes (or will discuss). . . ." Except in the paper's abstract, *"I* believe (or will discuss)" is okay, and often best.
—**ALAN TJELTVEIT,** *Professor of Psychology*

❖ ❖ ❖

The biggest stylistic problem is that students tend to be too personal or colloquial in their writing, using phrases such as the following: *"Scientists all agree . . .*"; *"I find it amazing that . . .*"; *"the thing that I find most interesting . . ."* Students are urged to present data and existing information in their own words, but in an objective way. My preference in writing is to use the active voice in the past tense. I feel this is the most direct and least wordy approach: *I asked this . . . ; I found out that . . . ; These data show. . . .*
—**RICHARD NIESENBAUM,** *Professor of Biology*

---

Most professors prefer the first-person "I think" to the more awkward "the writer (or "one") thinks." We would point out only that, in the service of reducing wordiness, you can often avoid both options. One case in which the first person is particularly appropriate occurs when you are citing an example from your own experience (taking into account the danger of *merely* anecdotal evidence—see Chapter 2 for the section entitled "Anecdotal Evidence").

In certain contexts and disciplines, moreover, the first-person plural *we* is acceptable usage. When, for example, you are doing rhetorical analysis, studying the relation of a piece of writing to its audience, you might well write that "The president's speech assumes that *we* are all dutiful but disgruntled taxpayers" or "When we examine the president's actual program for cutting taxes, we discover a version of his opponents' proposals." Ultimately, if you are in doubt about using "I" or "we," either check with your professor or avoid these first-person pronouns.

### The Second-Person You and the Imperative Mood

As for the second person, proceed with caution. Using *you* is a fairly assertive gesture. Many readers will be annoyed, for example, by a paper about advertising that states, "When you read about a sale at the mall, you know it's hard to resist." Most readers resent having a writer airily making assumptions about them or telling them what to do. Some rhetorical situations, however, call for the use of *you*. Textbooks, for example, use *you* frequently because it creates a more direct relationship between authors and readers. Yet even in appropriate situations, directly addressing readers as *you* may alienate them by ascribing to them attitudes and needs they may not have.

The readiest alternative to *you,* the imperative mood, requires careful handling for similar reasons. The *imperative mood* of a verb expresses a direct request or command, leaving *you* understood, as in the following example: "Don't [you] scorn Aaron Burr too quickly." Such a sentence, though, runs the same kind of risk as the sentences discussed earlier that use the *you* explicitly: readers might resent your assumption that they would scorn Aaron Burr, or at any rate, dislike being told so forcefully how to think about him.

On the other hand, in certain writing situations—when, for instance, you are giving a set of step-by-step instructions or politely soliciting your readers' attention—the imperative address is both appropriate and useful. Here are two examples:

IMPERATIVES

*Remove* the cables and then *take* a spark plug wrench and *loosen* the plugs.
*Consider* how England responded to the new treaty between its historical enemies.

In the first sentence, the insertion of *you should* or *one should* before each verb would be wordy and distracting. In the second example, the imperative invites the readers into the discussion fairly unobtrusively.

The conventional argument for using the first and second person is that *I* and *you* are personal and engage readers. It is not necessarily the case, however, that the third person is therefore impersonal. Just as film directors put their stamp on a film by the way they organize the images, move among camera viewpoints, and orchestrate the soundtrack, so writers have a wide variety of resources at their disposal for making the writing more personal and accessible for their audiences, even when writing in the third person. Some of these resources, bound under the heading of "style," occupy the next section.

# Revising Sentence Structure (Syntax)

The term *syntax*, as previously defined, refers to a sentence's structure, the way it arranges words, phrases, and clauses. As such, it is an essential aspect of *grammar*, the systematic explanation of the structure of a language. *Syntax is, first and foremost, a tool of logic.* It clarifies the relationships within a sentence and gives some parts of the sentence more emphasis than others. *The key to revising the syntax of your sentences is to make sure that the relationships are clear and the emphasis falls where you intend.*

## Active and Passive Voices: Doing and Being Done To

In the *active voice*, the grammatical subject acts; in the *passive voice*, the subject is acted upon. Here are two examples:

**ACTIVE VOICE**
>Adam Smith wrote *The Wealth of Nations* in 1776.

**PASSIVE VOICE**
>*The Wealth of Nations* was written by Adam Smith in 1776.

The two sentences convey identical information, but the emphasis differs—the first focuses on the author, the second on the book. As the examples illustrate, using the passive normally results in a longer sentence than using the active. If we consider how to convert the passive into the active, you can see why. In the passive, the verb requires a form of *to be* plus a past participle (for more on *participles,* see the "Glossary of Grammatical Terms" in Chapter 8). In this case, the active *wrote* becomes the passive *was written,* the subject (*Smith*) becomes the object of the preposition *by,* and the direct object (*The Wealth of Nations*) becomes the grammatical subject.

### Passive Voice: Pro and Con

Consider the activity being described in the two versions of the preceding example about Adam Smith: a man wrote a book. That was what happened in life. The grammar of the active version captures that action most clearly: the grammatical subject (*Smith*) performs the action, and the direct object (*The Wealth of Nations*) receives it, just as in life. By contrast, the passive version alters the close link between the syntax and the event: the object of the action in life (*The Wealth of Nations*) has become the grammatical subject, whereas the doer in life (*Smith*) has become the grammatical object of a prepositional phrase.

Note, too, that the passive would allow us to omit *Smith* altogether: "*The Wealth of Nations* was written in 1776." A reader who desired to know more and was not aware of the author would not appreciate this sentence. More troublingly, the passive can also be used to avoid naming the doer of an action—not "I made a mistake" (active) but rather "A mistake has been made" (passive).

In sum, there are three reasons for avoiding the passive voice when you can:

1. It's longer.
2. Its grammatical relationships often reverse what happened in life.
3. It can omit the performer responsible for the action.

On the other hand, there are also good reasons for using the passive. If you want to emphasize the object or recipient of the action rather than the performer, the passive will do that for you: "*The Wealth of Nations* was written in 1776 by Adam Smith" places the stress on the book. The passive is also preferable when the doer remains unknown: "The president has been shot!" is probably a better sentence than "Some unknown assailant has shot the president!"

### Passive Voice and Scientific Writing

Especially in the natural sciences, the use of the passive voice is a standard practice. There are sound reasons for this disciplinary convention: *science tends to focus on what happens to something in a given experiment, rather than on the actions of that something.* Consider the following passive sentence:

Separation of the protein was achieved by using an electrophoretic gel.

Although you could convert this sentence into the active voice ("The researcher used an electrophoretic gel to separate the protein"), the emphasis would then rest, *illogically,* on the agent of the action (the researcher) rather than on what happened and how (electrophoretic separation of the protein).

More generally, the passive voice can provide a way to avoid using the pronoun *I,* whether for reasons of convention, as indicated earlier, or for other reasons. For example, the following passive sentence begins a business memo from a supervisor to the staff in her office.

**PASSIVE**

The Inventory and Reprint departments have recently been restructured and merged.

Like many passive sentences, this one names no actor; we do not know for sure who did the restructuring and merging, though we might imagine that the author of the memo is the responsible party. The supervisor might, then, have written the sentence as an active one:

**ACTIVE**

> I have recently restructured and merged the Inventory and Reprint departments.

But the active version is less satisfactory than the passive one for two reasons: one of practical emphasis and one of sensitivity to the audience (tone). First, the fact of the changes is more important for the memo's readers than is announcing who made the changes. The passive sentence appropriately emphasizes the changes; the active sentence inappropriately emphasizes the person who made the changes. Second, the emphasis of the active sentence on *I* (the supervisor) risks alienating the readers by taking an autocratic tone and by seeming to exclude all others from possible credit for the presumably worthwhile reorganization.

On balance, *consider* is the operative term when you choose between passive and active as you revise the syntax of your draft. What matters is that you recognize there is a choice—in emphasis, in relative directness, and in economy. All things being equal, and disciplinary conventions permitting, the active is usually the better choice.

## Static (Intransitive) vs. Active (Transitive) Verbs: *To Be or Not to Be*

Verbs energize a sentence. They do the work, connecting the parts of the sentence with each other. In a sentence of the subject-verb-direct object pattern, the verb functions as a kind of engine, driving the subject into the predicate, as in the following examples.

**TRANSITIVE VERBS**

A transitive verb takes (or could take) a direct object. Here are two examples:

> John F. Kennedy effectively *manipulated* his image in the media.
> Thomas Jefferson *embraced* the idea of America as a country of yeoman farmers.

By contrast, *is* and other forms of the verb *to be* provide an equal sign between the subject and the predicate but otherwise tell us nothing about the relationship between them. *To be* is an intransitive verb; it cannot take a direct object. Compare the preceding two sentences, which use transitive verbs, with the following versions of the same sentences using forms of the verb *to be*.

**To Be Verbs**

> John F. Kennedy *was* effective at the manipulation of his image in the media.
> Thomas Jefferson's idea *was* an America of yeoman farmers.

Rather than making things happen through an active transitive verb, these sentences let everything just hang around in a state of being. In the first version,

Kennedy did something—*manipulated* his image—but in the second he just *is* (or *was*), and the energy of the original verb has been siphoned into an abstract noun, *manipulation*. The revised Jefferson example suffers from a similar lack of momentum compared with the original version: the syntax doesn't help the sentence get anywhere. Yet because the forms of *to be* are so easy to use, writers tend to place them everywhere, habitually, producing relatively static and wordy sentences.

Certain situations, however, dictate the use of forms of *to be*. For definitions in particular, in which a term does in fact equal some meaning, *is* works well. For instance, "Organic gardening *is* a method of growing crops without using synthetic fertilizers or pesticides." As with choosing between active and passive voices, the decision to use *to be* or not should be just that—a conscious decision on your part.

If you can train yourself to eliminate every unnecessary use of *to be* in a draft, you will make your prose more vital and direct. In most cases, you will find the verb that you need to substitute for *is* lurking somewhere in the sentence in some other grammatical form. In the preceding sentence about Kennedy, *manipulate* is implicit in *manipulation*. In Table 9.2, each of the examples in the left-hand column uses a form of *to be* for its verb (italicized) and contains a potentially strong active verb lurking in the sentence in some other form (underlined). These "lurkers" have been converted into active verbs (italicized) in the revisions in the right-hand column.

Clearly, the examples in the left-hand column have problems other than their reliance on *to be* verbs—notably wordiness. *To be* syntax tends to encourage this circumlocution and verbosity. In revising a draft, try the following experiment. First, circle the sentences that rely on forms of *to be*. Then examine

**TABLE 9.2**  Static and Active Verbs.

| ACTION HIDDEN IN NOUNS AND *TO BE* VERBS | ACTION EMPHASIZED IN VERBS |
| --- | --- |
| The <u>cost</u> of the book *is* ten dollars. | The book *costs* ten dollars. |
| The <u>acknowledgment</u> of the fact *is* increasingly widespread that television *is* a <u>replacement</u> for reading in American culture. | People increasingly *acknowledge* that television *has replaced* reading in American culture. |
| A computer *is* ostensibly a labor-<u>saving</u> device—until the hard disk *is* the victim of a <u>crash</u>. | A computer ostensibly *saves* labor—until the hard disk *crashes*. |
| In the <u>laying</u> of a flagstone patio, the important preliminary steps to remember *are* the excavating and the <u>leveling</u> of the area and then the filling of it with a fine grade of gravel. | To *lay* a flagstone patio, first *excavate* and *level* the area and then *fill* it with a fine grade of gravel. |

the other words in these sentences, looking for "lurkers." Rewrite the sentences, converting the lurkers into vigorous verbs. You will usually discover many lurkers, and your revision will acquire more energy and directness.

## Coordination, Subordination, and the Order of Clauses

A *clause* is a group of words containing a subject and a predicate. As the first example in this chapter, about Indochina, demonstrated, the syntax of a sentence can give your readers cues about whether the idea in one clause is equal to (coordinate) or subordinate to the idea in another clause. In this context, grammar operates as a form of implicit logic, defining relationships among the clauses in a sentence according to the choices that you make about coordination, subordination, and the order of clauses. In revising your sentences, think of coordination and subordination as tools of logic and emphasis, helping to rank your meanings.

### Coordination

*Coordination* uses grammatically equivalent constructions to link ideas. These ideas should carry roughly equal weight as well. Sentences that use coordination connect clauses with coordinating conjunctions (such as *and, but,* and *or*). Here are two examples.

**COORDINATE SENTENCES WITH *AND***
Historians organize the past, *and* they can never do so with absolute neutrality.
Homegrown corn is incredibly sweet, *and* it is very difficult to grow.

If you ponder these sentences, you may begin to detect the danger of the word *and*. It does not specify a precise logical relationship between the things it connects, but instead simply adds them.
Notice that the sentences get more precise if we substitute *but* for *and*.

**COORDINATE SENTENCES WITH *BUT***
Historians organize the past, *but* they can never do so with absolute neutrality.
Homegrown corn is incredibly sweet, *but* it is very difficult to grow.

These sentences are still coordinate, but they achieve more emphasis than the *and* versions. In both cases, the *but* clause carries more weight, because *but* always introduces information that qualifies or contradicts what precedes it.

### Reversing the Order of Coordinate Clauses

In both the *and* and *but* examples, the second clause tends to be stressed. The reason is simple: *the end is usually a position of emphasis.*
You can see the effect of *clause order* more starkly if we reverse the clauses in our examples:

Historians are never absolutely neutral, but they organize the past.
Homegrown corn is very difficult to grow, but it is incredibly sweet.

Note how the meanings have changed in these versions by our emphasizing what now comes last. Rather than having their objectivity undermined ("Historians are never absolutely neutral"), historians are now credited with at least providing organization ("they organize the past"). Similarly, whereas the previous version of the "corn" sentence was likely to dissuade a gardener from trying to grow it ("it is very difficult to grow"), the preceding one is more likely to lure him or her to nurture corn ("it is incredibly sweet").

Nonetheless, all of these sentences are examples of coordination because the clauses are grammatically equal. As you revise, notice when you use coordinate syntax, and think about whether you really intend to give the ideas equal weight. Consider as well whether reversing the order of clauses will more accurately convey your desired emphasis to your readers.

### Subordination

A *main* or *independent clause* can stand alone, but a *subordinate* or *dependent clause* relies on some other statement to complete it. In sentences that contain *subordination,* there are two "levels" of grammar—the main clause and the subordinate clause—that create two levels of meaning. When you put something in a main clause, you emphasize its significance. When you put something in a subordinate clause, you make it less important than the main clause. (For more information, see the "Glossary of Grammatical Terms" and discussion of sentence fragments in Chapter 8.)

A subordinate clause is linked to a main clause by words known as *subordinating conjunctions*. Here is a list of the most common ones: *after, although, as, as if, as long as, because, before, if, rather than, since, than, that, though, unless, until, when, where, whether,* and *while.* All of these words define something *in relation to* something else:

*If* you study hard, you will continue to do well.
You will continue to do well, *if* you study hard.

In both of these examples, *if* subordinates "you study hard" to "you will continue to do well," regardless of whether the *if* clause comes first or last in the sentence.

### Reversing Main and Subordinate Clauses

Unlike the situation with coordinate clauses, the emphasis in sentences that use subordination virtually always rests on the main clause, regardless of the clause order. Nevertheless, the principle of end emphasis still applies, though to a lesser extent than among coordinate clauses. Let's consider two versions of the same sentence.

#### SUBORDINATE CLAUSE FIRST
Although the art of the people was crude, it was original.

SUBORDINATE CLAUSE LAST

The art of the people was original, although it was crude.

Both sentences emphasize the idea in the main clause ("original"). Because the second version locates the *although* clause at the end, however, the subordinated idea ("crude") has more emphasis than it does in the first version.

---

**APPLICATION:**

## EXPERIMENTING WITH EMPHASIS IN THE ARRANGEMENT OF CLAUSES

As the previous sections have demonstrated, depending on the ordering of the sections of a sentence, its emphasis changes. The exercises offered here are designed to help you recognize and experiment with the moveable parts of your own sentences.

1. There are four sections, separated by commas, in the following coordinate sentence. Rearrange the parts, and then briefly jot down how the meaning changes in each version.

I asked her to marry me, two years ago, in a shop on Tremont Street, late in the fall.

Then subject two sentences from one of your own papers to the same treatment.

2. Here is a sentence that contains a subordinate construction, chosen virtually at random from earlier in the chapter:

When you put something in a subordinate clause, you make it less important than the main clause.

This sentence can generate a range of transformations. Here are two, both of which reverse main and subordinate clauses:

a. Put information in a subordinate clause if you want to make it less important than what is in the main clause.
b. If you want to make information less important than what is in the main clause, put it in a subordinate clause.

Briefly note how these two versions change the meaning and emphasis of the original sentence.

Now you try writing the transformations. Change the order of clauses, and subordinate or coordinate as you wish. Do two rewrites of the following sentence; we recommend that you make one of them end with the word "friendly."

Faculty members came to speak at the forum, and they were friendly, but they were met with hostility, and this hostility was almost paranoid.

*(continued)*

*Experimenting with Emphasis in the Arrangement of Clauses (continued)*

Identify how each of your revisions changes the meaning and emphasis. Remember, by the way, that the end of a sentence is normally a forceful position.

3. Take any passage, and break it into a series of very simple sentences. Then rewrite the passage, combining the sentences in various ways by using coordinating and subordinating conjunctions. Here is one example:

There is an encyclopedia. It is a CD-ROM. It is inexpensive. It uses hypertext. There are options. Certain terms are capitalized. You can click on the capitalized terms. Clicking will give you more information about that term. You can construct a knowledge pathway. The information seems limited to fairly obvious facts. The information is superficial. The encyclopedia does not appear to interpret the information.

Ideally, you should then compare and contrast your version with that of others, in order to see how the different choices you have made shape the meaning of what is essentially the same information.

## Cutting the Fat

If you can reduce verbiage, your prose will communicate more directly and effectively. In cutting the fat, you need to consider both the diction and the syntax. As regards diction, the way to eliminate superfluous words is deceptively simple: ask yourself if you need all of the words you've included in order to say what you want to say. Such revision requires an aggressive attitude. *Expect* to find unnecessary restatements or intensifiers such as *quite* and *very* that add words but not significance.

As regards syntax, there are a few technical operations that you can perform on your sentences to reduce the number of words. The chapter has already mentioned most of these in other contexts. Here, with a slightly different focus, is a recap:

- Convert sentences from the passive into the active voice. Writing "He read the book" reduces by a third "The book was read by him," and eliminating the prepositional phrase ("by him") clarifies the relationships within the sentence.
- Replace anemic forms of *to be* with vigorous verbs and direct subject-verb-object syntax. Often you will find such verbs lurking in the original sentence, and once you've recognized them, conversion is easy: "The Watergate *scandal* was an event whose effects were felt across the nation" becomes "Watergate *scandalized* people across the nation."
- Avoid unnecessary subordination. It is illogical to write, "*It is true that* more government services mean higher taxes." If "it is true that," then

just write "More government services mean higher taxes"—don't muffle your meaning in a subordinate (*that*) clause.

Beyond these technical operations, perhaps the most useful way to cut the fat is to have confidence in your position on a subject and state it clearly in your paper. A lot of fat in essays consists of throat-clearings, attempts to avoid stating your position. Move quickly to an example that raises the question or issue you wish to analyze.

**? HINT BOX:**

## EXPLETIVE CONSTRUCTIONS

The syntactic pattern for "It is true *that* more government services mean higher taxes" is known as an *expletive* construction. The term *expletive* comes from a Latin word that means "serving to fill out." The most common expletives are *it* and *there*. Consider how the expletives function in the following examples.

EXPLETIVES

*There* are several prototypes for the artificial heart.
*It* is obvious that the American West exerted a profound influence on the photography of Ansel Adams.

EXPLETIVES ELIMINATED

The artificial heart has several prototypes.
The American West obviously exerted a profound influence on the photography of Ansel Adams.

As the revisions demonstrate, most of the time you can streamline your prose by getting rid of expletive constructions. The "It is obvious" opening, for example, causes the sentence to subordinate its real emphasis. In some cases, however, an expletive can provide a useful way of emphasizing, as in the following example: "There are three primary reasons that you should avoid litigation." Although this sentence subordinates its real content (avoiding litigation), the expletive provides a useful frame for what is to follow.

**▶ APPLICATION:**

## WORKING WITH VERBS TO CUT THE FAT

The chapter's discussion of verbs has been careful to represent the advantages of both the passive voice and forms of *to be,* especially as these are endorsed

*(continued)*

*Working with Verbs to Cut the Fat (continued)*

by disciplinary practices. Nonetheless, a significant amount of flabbiness can be attributed to the unself-conscious use of these forms. Here are a few simple exercises designed to help you to recognize the voice and forms of verbs and, where appropriate, to convert sentences that contain passives and expletives into more direct and vigorous sentences that use the active voice.

1. Circle and identify every verb in a passage (use the abbreviations *VA* = active voice, *VP* = passive voice, *VB* = verb of being). The passage might come from a book you are reading or from one of your own drafts. This exercise will give necessary training in identifying the forms of verbs. It can be sequenced with the next one.
2. Identify all of the sentences that use the passive voice in one of your papers. Then rewrite these sentences, converting passive into active wherever possible. Then count the total number of words, the total number of prepositions, and the average sentence length (words per sentence) in each version. What do you discover?
3. Using Table 9.2 as a guide, (a) circle every sentence in a passage from a paper you have written that uses a verb of being as its main verb. Then (b) examine every other word in these sentences for "lurkers" (potential active or passive verbs lurking in the sentences in some other form—see p. 318). Then (c) mark these with an *L,* and (d) rewrite every sentence that you can, converting the lurker into a verb in the active or passive voice.
4. Compose a paragraph of at least half a page in which you use only the passive voice and verbs of being, followed by a paragraph in which you use only the active voice. Then rewrite the first paragraph, using only active voice if possible; and rewrite the second paragraph, using only passive voice and verbs of being as much as possible. How do the paragraphs differ in shape and coherence?

## The Shapes of Sentences

When you write, you build. Writing, after all, is also known as composition—from the Latin *compositio,* meaning "made up of parts." We speak of *constructing* sentences and paragraphs and essays. The fundamental unit of composition is the sentence. *Every sentence has a shape, and learning to see that shape is essential to editing for style.* Once you can recognize the shape of a sentence, you can recast it to make it more graceful or logical or emphatic.

When you revise your sentences for style, your goal is not to prettify your language but rather to reveal the organization of your thought, clarifying your meaning and delivering it more accessibly to your readers. Because meanings are rarely simple themselves, clarifying often does not involve simplifying. Meanings usually involve complex relationships, placing two or more items in balance or elevating one over the others. These relationships can be built into the structure of your sentences. A series of short sentences that breaks up items that belong together will make your prose less readable than a long sentence that overtly makes the connections for your readers. Note the choppiness of the following passage.

> Interactive computer games teach children skills. The games introduce kids to computers. The games enact power fantasies of destroying enemies. These power fantasies are potentially disturbing.

Compare that to the following revision:

> Although interactive computer games teach children certain skills, they also encourage certain potentially disturbing power fantasies.

Because this version connects the items with tighter logic, it generates more forward momentum and is easier to comprehend than the first version, even though the sentence structure is more complex.

If you can approach stylistic editing in this technical, syntactic way, determining how to revise your sentences will become less vague and undirected. If something sounds awkward, but you don't know why, or if you want to make a passage more forceful, but you don't know how, there are fairly standard ways of assessing and altering the shapes of your sentences to make them communicate more effectively.

### How to Recognize the Four Basic Sentence Shapes

*Style,* as defined earlier, has to do with choice—the choices a writer makes about how to express something. But these decisions can be realized only if you can recognize and use the basic building blocks of composition.

Every sentence is built upon the skeleton of its independent clause(s), the subject and verb combination that can stand alone. Consider the following four sentences:

> Consumers shop.
> Consumers shop; producers manufacture.
> Consumers shop in predictable ways, so producers manufacture with different target groups in mind.
> Consumers shop in ways that can be predicted by such determinants as income level, gender, and age; consequently, producers use market research to identify different target groups for their products.

Certainly these four sentences become progressively longer, and the information that they contain becomes increasingly detailed, but they also differ in their structure—specifically, in the number of independent and dependent clauses they contain. Given that the sentence is the fundamental unit of composition, you will benefit immensely, both in composing and in revising your sentences, if you can identify and construct the four basic sentence types.

## THE SIMPLE SENTENCE

The *simple sentence* consists of a single independent clause. At its simplest, it contains a single subject and verb.

> Consumers shop.

Other words and phrases can be added to this sentence, but it will remain simple so long as "Consumers shop" is the only clause.

> Most consumers shop unwisely.

Even if the sentence contains more than one grammatical subject or more than one verb, it remains simple in structure.

> Most consumers *shop* unwisely and *spend* more than they can afford. [two verbs]
> Both female *consumers* and their *husbands* shop unwisely. [two subjects]

The sentence structure in the example that uses two verbs is known as a *compound predicate* (*shop* and *spend*). The sentence structure in the example that uses two subjects is known as a *compound subject* (*consumers* and *husbands*). If, however, you were to add both another subject and another verb to the original simple sentence, then you would have the next sentence type, a compound sentence.

## THE COMPOUND SENTENCE

The *compound sentence* consists of at least two independent clauses and no subordinate clauses. The information conveyed in these clauses should be of roughly equal importance:

> Producers manufacture, and consumers shop.
> Producers manufacture, marketers sell, and consumers shop.

As with the simple sentence, you can also add qualifying phrases to the compound sentence, and it will remain compound, as long as no dependent clauses are added:

> Consumers shop in predictable ways, so producers manufacture with different target groups in mind.
> Consumers shop recklessly during holidays; marketers are keenly aware of this fact.

Note that a compound sentence can connect its independent clauses with either a coordinate conjunction or a semicolon. (The primary use of the semicolon is as a substitute for a coordinate conjunction, separating two independent clauses.) If you were to substitute a subordinating conjunction for either of these connectors, however, you would then have a sentence with one independent clause and one dependent clause. For example:

> *Because* consumers shop in predictable ways, producers manufacture with different target groups in mind.

This revision changes the compound sentence into the next sentence type, the complex sentence.

### THE COMPLEX SENTENCE

The *complex sentence* consists of a single independent clause and one or more dependent clauses. As previously discussed under "Subordination, Coordination, and the Order of Clauses," the information conveyed in the dependent clause is subordinated to the more important independent clause. In the following example, the subject and verb of the main clause are underlined, and the subordinating conjunctions are italicized:

> *Although* mail-order merchandising—*which* generally saves shoppers money—has increased, most <u>consumers</u> still <u>shop</u> unwisely, buying on impulse rather than deliberation.

This sentence contains one independent clause (*consumers shop*). Hanging upon it are two introductory dependent clauses (*Although merchandising has increased* and *which saves*) and a participial phrase (*buying on impulse*). If you converted either of these dependent clauses into an independent clause, you would have a sentence with two independent clauses (a compound sentence) and a dependent clause. In the following example, the subjects and verbs of the two main clauses are underlined, and the conjunctions are italicized:

> Mail-order <u>merchandising</u>—*which* generally saves shoppers money—<u>has increased,</u> *but* <u>consumers</u> still <u>shop</u> unwisely, buying on impulse rather than deliberation.

This revision changes the complex sentence into the next sentence type, the compound-complex sentence.

### THE COMPOUND-COMPLEX SENTENCE

The *compound-complex sentence* consists of two or more independent clauses and one or more dependent clauses.

> Consumers shop in ways that can be predicted by such determinants as income level, gender, and age; consequently, producers use market research that aims to identify different target groups for their products.

This sentence contains two independent clauses (*Consumers shop* and *producers use*) and two dependent ones (*that can be predicted* and *that aims*).

> ### APPLICATION:
>
> ## BUILDING SENTENCE TYPES
>
> As we have done with the "Consumers shop" example, compose a simple sentence, and then expand it into the five other sentence shapes discussed earlier: a compound subject, a compound predicate, a compound sentence, a complex sentence, and a compound-complex sentence.
>
> To prevent this exercise from becoming merely mechanical, keep in mind how different sentence shapes accomplish different ends. In other words, make sure that your compound sentence balances two items of information, that your complex sentence emphasizes one thing (in the main clause) over another (in the subordinate clause), and that your compound-complex sentence is required to handle and organize complexity.
>
> In order to construct these sentence types, you will need to be able to distinguish independent clauses (sentences) from dependent clauses (fragments), and grammatical subjects or objects in the main clause from objects of prepositions. If you have difficulty making these distinctions, you should find it helpful to review parts of Chapter 8, particularly the discussion of sentence fragments and the following entries in the "Glossary of Grammatical Terms": *clause, conjunction, conjunctive adverb, coordination, direct object, phrase, preposition, subject, subordination,* and *verbals.*

### Parallel Structure

Besides sentence type, probably the most important and useful device for shaping sentences is *parallel structure,* or as it is also known, *parallelism.* Parallelism is a form of symmetry: it involves placing sentence elements that correspond in some way into the same (that is, parallel) grammatical form. Consider the following examples, in which the parallel items are underlined or italicized:

> The three kinds of partners in a law firm who receive money from a case are popularly known as <u>finders,</u> <u>binders,</u> and <u>grinders.</u>
>
> The Beatles acknowledged their musical debts <u>to</u> American rhythm and blues, <u>to</u> English music hall ballads and ditties, and later <u>to</u> classical Indian ragas.
>
> There was <u>no</u> <u>way</u> <u>that</u> the president <u>could gain</u> the support of party regulars *without alienating* the Congress, and <u>no</u> <u>way</u> <u>that</u> he <u>could appeal</u> to the electorate at large *without alienating* both of these groups.
>
> In the entertainment industry, the money that <u>goes</u> <u>out</u> to hire *film stars* or *sports stars* <u>comes</u> <u>back</u> in increased ticket sales and video or television rights.
>
> Where *bravura* <u>failed</u> to settle the negotiations, *tact* <u>and</u> *patience* <u>succeeded.</u>

As all of these examples illustrate, at the core of parallelism lies repetition—of a word, a phrase, or a grammatical structure. *Parallelism uses repetition to organize and emphasize certain elements in a sentence, so that readers can perceive more clearly the shape of your thought.* In the Beatles example, each of the prepositional phrases beginning with *to* contains a musical debt; in the president example, the repetition of the phrase *no way that* emphasizes the president's entrapment.

Parallelism has the added advantage of *economy:* each of the musical debts or presidential problems might have had its own sentence, but in that case, the prose would have been wordier and the relationships among the parallel items more obscure. Along with this economy come *balance* and *emphasis.* The trio of rhyming words (*finders, binders,* and *grinders*) that concludes the law firm example gives each item equal weight; in the entertainment industry example, *comes back* "answers" *goes out* in a way that accentuates their symmetry.

#### ANTITHESIS

One particularly useful form of balance that parallel structure accommodates is known as *antithesis* (from the Greek word for *opposition*), a conjoining of contrasting ideas. Here the pattern sets this against that, as in the last of the preceding parallelism examples:

Where <u>bravura</u> *failed* to settle the negotiations, <u>tact</u> and <u>patience</u> *succeeded.*

*Failed* is balanced antithetically against *succeeded,* as *bravura* is against *tact and patience.* Antithesis commonly takes the form of "if not *x,* at least *y*" or "not *x,* but *y.*"

#### FAULTY PARALLELISM

When you employ parallelism in revising for style, there is one grammatical rule you should obey. It is important to avoid what is known as *faulty parallelism,* which occurs when the items that are parallel in content are not placed in the same grammatical form.

**Faulty:**   *To study* hard for four years and then *getting* ignored once they enter the job market is a hard thing for many recent college graduates to accept.

**Revised:**   *To study* hard for four years and then *to get* ignored once they enter the job market is a hard thing for many recent college graduates to accept.

As you revise your draft for style, search for opportunities to place sentence elements in parallel structure. Often the parallels will be hidden in your sentences, but they can be brought out with a minimum of labor. In emphasizing the parallels, you will make your prose more graceful, clear, and logically connected.

> **APPLICATION:**
>
> ## PRACTICING PARALLELISM
>
> **1.** Rewrite the following examples of faulty parallelism, using correct parallel structure.
>
> a. Our personalities are shaped by both heredity and what type of environment we have been exposed to.
> b. Venus likes to play tennis and also watching baseball games.
> c. In the 1960s the use of drugs and being a hippie was a way for some people to let society know their political views and that they were alienated from the mainstream.
>
> The last of these sentences has a lot of problems; you will need to contemplate (speculate about) its thinking as well as its form. Are the parallel terms (in content if not in grammatical form) really parallel—that is, equal—or is one term actually an aspect of the other? If it is an aspect, included within the other term, how else would you rewrite that part of the sentence besides using parallelism?
>
> **2.** List all of the parallelisms in the following famous passage from the beginning of the Declaration of Independence:
>
> "We hold these truths to be self-evident: that all men are created equal; that they are endowed by their Creator with certain inalienable rights; that, among these, are life, liberty, and the pursuit of happiness."
>
> What do you notice about the way that the parallel structures accumulate? And how would you describe the effect produced by substituting "peanut butter" for "happiness"?
>
> In order to identify and compose parallel structures, it is helpful to remember that they can occur with *clauses, phrases,* and *prepositional phrases.* If you have difficulty recognizing these or differentiating among them, you should review the entries for these terms in Chapter 8's "Glossary of Grammatical Terms."
> Once you can recognize parallelism easily, practice it in your own writing. Do this consciously: include and underline three uses of it in a draft of your next writing assignment. After you've acquired the habit of casting your thinking in parallel structures, they will rapidly become a staple of your stylistic repertoire.

### The Periodic Sentence: Snapping Shut

The shape of a sentence governs the way it delivers information. The order of clauses, especially the placement of the main clause, affects what and how the sentence means. There are two common sentence shapes defined by their location of the main clause; these are known as *periodic* and *cumulative* sentences.

The main clause in a periodic sentence builds to a climax that is not completed until the end. Often, a piece of the main clause (such as the subject) is located earlier in the sentence, as in the following example.

> The *way* that beverage companies market health—"No Preservatives," "No Artificial Color," "All Natural," "Real Brewed"—*is* often, because the product also contains a high percentage of sugar or fructose, *misleading.*

We have italicized the main clause to clarify how various modifiers interrupt it. The effect is suspenseful: not until the final word does the sentence consummate its fundamental idea. The main clause is spread out across the sentence. (The term *periodic* originates in classical rhetoric to refer to the length of such sentences.)

Another version of the periodic sentence locates the entire main clause at the end, after introductory modifiers:

> Using labels that market health—such as "No Preservatives," "No Artificial Color," "All Natural," and "Real Brewed"—while producing drinks that contain a high percentage of sugar or fructose, *beverage companies are misleading.*

As we discussed in "Coordination, Subordination, and the Order of Clauses," the end of a sentence normally receives emphasis. When you use a periodic construction, the pressure on the end intensifies because the sentence needs the end to complete its grammatical sense. In both of the preceding examples, the sentences snap shut. They string readers along, delaying *grammatical closure*—the point at which the sentence can stand alone independently—until they arrive at a climactic end. (Periodic sentences are also known as *climactic sentences.*)

You should be aware of one risk that accompanies periodic constructions. If the delay lasts too long because there are too many "interrupters" before the main clause gets completed, your readers may forget the subject that is being predicated. To illustrate, let's add more subordinated material to one of the preceding examples:

> The way that beverage companies market health—"No Preservatives," "No Artificial Color," "All Natural," "Real Brewed"—is often, because the product also contains a high percentage of sugar or fructose, not just what New Agers would probably term "immoral" and "misleading," but what a government agency such as the Food and Drug Administration should find illegal.

Arguably, the additions (the *not just/but* clauses after *fructose*) push the sentence into incoherence. The main clause has been stretched past the breaking point. If readers don't get lost in such a sentence, they are at least likely to get irritated, wishing the writer would finally get to the point.

Nonetheless, with a little care, periodic sentences can be extraordinarily useful in giving emphasis. *If you are revising and want to underscore some point, try letting the sentence snap shut upon it.* Often the periodic *potential* will already be present in the draft, and stylistic editing can bring it out more forcefully. Note how minor the revisions are in the following example:

> **Draft:** The novelist Virginia Woolf suffered from acute anxieties for most of her life. She had several breakdowns and finally committed suicide on the eve of World War II.

> **Revision:** Suffering from acute anxieties for most of her life, the novelist Virginia *Woolf not only had* several *breakdowns, but* finally, on the eve of World War II, *committed suicide.*

This revision has made two primary changes. It has combined two short sentences into a longer sentence, and it has made the sentence periodic by stringing out the main clause (italicized). What is the effect of this revision? Stylistically speaking, the revision radiates a greater sense of its writer's authority. The information has been arranged for us. Following the opening dependent clause (*Suffering . . .*), the subject of the main clause (*Woolf*) is introduced, and the predicate is protracted in a *not only/but* parallelism. The interrupters that follow *had breakdowns* (*finally, on the eve of World War II*) increase the suspense, before the sentence snaps shut with *committed suicide*. In general, when you construct a periodic sentence with care, you can give readers the sense that you are in control of your material. You do not seem to be writing off the top of your ahead but rather, from a position of greater detachment, rationally composing your meaning.

### The Cumulative Sentence: Starting Fast

The cumulative sentence is in many respects the opposite of the periodic. Rather than delaying the main clause or its final piece, the cumulative sentence begins by presenting the independent clause as a foundation and then *accumulates* a number of modifications and qualifications. As the following examples illustrate, the independent clause provides quick grammatical closure, freeing the rest of the sentence to amplify and develop the main idea.

> *Robert F. Kennedy was assassinated* by Sirhan B. Sirhan, a twenty-four-year-old Palestinian immigrant, prone to occultism and unsophisticated left-wing politics and sociopathically devoted to leaving his mark in history, even if as a notorious figure.
>
> *There are two piano concerti* composed solely for the left hand, one by Serge Prokofiev and one by Maurice Ravel, and both commissioned by Paul Wittgenstein, a concert pianist (and the brother of the famous philosopher Ludwig Wittgenstein) who had lost his right hand in combat during World War I.

Anchored by the main clause, a cumulative sentence moves serially through this and that and the next thing, close to the associative manner in which people think. To an extent, then, cumulative sentences can convey more immediacy and a more conversational tone than can other sentence shapes. Look at the following example:

> The film version of *Lady Chatterley's Lover* changed D. H. Lawrence's famous novel a lot, omitting the heroine's adolescent experience in Germany, making her husband much older than she, leaving out her father and sister, including a lot more love-making, and virtually eliminating all of the philosophizing about sex and marriage.

Here we get the impression of a mind in the act of thinking. Using the generalization of changes in the film as a base, the sentence then appends a series of parallel participial phrases (*omitting, making, leaving, including, eliminating*) that moves forward associatively, gathering a range of information and laying out possibilities. Cumulative sentences perform this outlining and prospecting function very effectively. On the other hand, if we were to add four or five more changes to the sentence, readers would likely find it tedious, or worse, directionless. As with periodic sentences, overloading the shape can short-circuit its desired effect.

---

### APPLICATION:

## CONSTRUCTING PERIODIC AND CUMULATIVE SENTENCES

1. Compose a simple sentence on any subject, preferably one with a direct object. Then construct two variations expanding it, one periodic and one cumulative.

Here is an example using "James Joyce was a gifted singer":

*Periodic:* Although known primarily as one of the greatest novelists of the twentieth century, James Joyce, the son of a local political functionary who loved to tip a few too many at the pub, was also a gifted—and prize-winning—singer.

*Cumulative:* James Joyce was a gifted singer, having listened at his father's knee to the ballads sung in the pubs, having won an all-Ireland prize in his early teens, and having possessed a miraculous ear for the inflections of common speech that was to serve him throughout the career for which he is justly famous, that of a novelist.

2. Practice using periodic and cumulative constructions to produce their respective effects (where appropriate) in your own writing. As you go over a draft, look for opportunities to bring out these shapes, for you can assume that they are already present in some unrefined way in the sentence shapes you normally compose. Try including at least one of each in the next paper you write.

## Consistency of Tone

The *tone* of a piece of writing is its implied attitude toward its subject and audience. Whenever you revise for style, your choices in syntax and diction will affect the tone. There are no hard and fast rules to govern matters of tone, and your control of it will depend upon your sensitivity to the particular context—your understanding of your own intentions and your readers' expectations.

Let's consider, for example, the tonal implications of the warning signs in the subways of London and New York.

> London:   Leaning out of the window may cause harm.

> New York:   Do not lean out of the window.

Initially, you may find the English injunction laughably indirect and verbose in comparison with the shoot-from-the-hip clarity of the American sign. But that is to ignore the very thing we are calling "style." The American version appeals to authority, commanding readers what not to do without telling them why. The English version, by contrast, appeals to logic; it is more collegial toward its readers and assumes they are rational beings.

In revising for tone, you need to ask yourself if the attitude suggested by your language is appropriate to the aim of your message and to your audience. Your goal is to keep the tone *consistent* with your rhetorical intentions. The following paragraph, from a college catalogue, offers a classic mismatch between the overtly stated aim and the tonal implications:

> The student affairs staff believes that the college years provide a growth and development process for students. Students need to learn about themselves and others and to learn how to relate to individuals and groups of individuals with vastly different backgrounds, interests, attitudes and values. Not only is the tolerance of differences expected, but also an appreciation and a celebration of these differences must be an outcome of the student's experience. In addition, the student must progress toward self-reliance and independence tempered by a concern for the social order.

The explicit content of this passage—*what* it says—concerns tolerance. The professed point of view is student-friendly, asserting that the college exists to allow students *to learn about themselves and others* and to support the individual in accord with the *appreciation . . . of . . . differences.*

But note that the implicit tone—*how* the passage goes about saying *what* it says—is condescending and intolerant. Look at the verbs. An imperious authority lectures students about what they *need* to learn; tolerance is *expected;* celebration . . . *must* be an outcome; and the student *must* progress along these lines. Presumably, the paragraph does not intend to adopt this high-handed manner, but its deafness to tone subverts its desired meaning.

## APPLICATION:

## REWRITING PASSAGES TO MAKE THE TONE APPROPRIATE

1. Using the example from the college catalogue as a model, locate and bring to class examples of tonal inconsistency or inappropriateness that you encounter in your daily life. If you have difficulty finding examples, try memos from those in authority at your school or workplace, which often contain excruciating examples of officialese.

   Type one of your passages, and underneath it include a paragraph of analysis in which you single out particular words and phrases and explain how the tone is inappropriate. Then rewrite the passage to remedy the problem.

2. Find an example of tone that you think is just about perfect for the message and audience. Type it, and underneath discuss why it succeeds, being as specific as you can about how the passage functions stylistically—talking about particular phrasings and the match between what they are saying and the way they are saying it.

   If circumstances allow, collect a number of examples of effective tone and execrable tone, make copies, and discuss them with others. Developing a vocabulary for talking about tone will be an additional aid to discerning and managing your own tone in your writing.

3. Write a paper that analyzes the style of a particular group or profession (e.g., sports, advertising, bureaucracy, show business, music reviewing, etc.). Or as an alternative, adopt the voice of a member of this group, and write a parody that critiques or analyzes the language practices of the group.

By way of a few final words on how to improve your diction and syntax, consider the following two comments from professors. The first articulates the crucial interrelationship between writing well and reading attentively.

## VOICES FROM ACROSS THE CURRICULUM

## READING ATTENTIVELY TO IMPROVE ONE'S STYLE

Aside from the usual basic writing errors, the stylistic problems I most frequently encounter in students' papers are odd word selection and awkward

*(continued)*

---

*Reading Attentively to Improve One's Style (continued)*

sentence structure. I think both problems find their genesis in the same broader problem. You learn how to make telling use of the vocabulary you've been forced to memorize only by reading. You fashion an appealing sentence based on what you've read others doing.

—**JAMES MARSHALL,** *Professor of Economics*

---

The following anecdote, by contrast, argues for resisting the "officious" jargon of the workplace, in order to say what you mean.

---

## VOICES FROM ACROSS THE CURRICULUM

### RESISTING THE JARGON OF THE WORKPLACE

I worked for the Feds for many years before seeking the doctorate. My job required immense amounts of writing: reports, directives, correspondence, and so forth. But, on a day-to-day basis for almost seven years I had to write short "write-ups" assessing the qualifications of young people for the Peace Corps and VISTA programs. I'd generate "list-like," "bullet-like" assessments: "Looks good with farm machinery, has wonderful volunteer experience, would be best in a rural setting, speaks French." But I had to conclude each of these assessments with a one-page narrative. Here I tended to reject officious governmentese for a more personal style. I'd write as I spoke. Rather than "Has an inclination for a direction in the facilitation of regulation," I'd write "Would be very good directing people on projects." I'd drop the "-tion" stuff and write in "speak form," not incomplete sentences, but in what I call "candid, personal" style. I carry this with me today.

—**FREDERICK NORLING,** *Professor of Business*

---

## APPLICATION:

### EDITING A DRAFT FOR STYLE

Do a full-fledged stylistic revision of a paper. The best choice might well be an essay you have already revised, resubmitted, and had returned, because in that case, you will be less likely to get distracted by conceptual revision

*(continued)*

*(continued)*

and so can concentrate on stylistic issues. As you revise, try to accomplish each of the following:

Sharpen the diction.

Blend concrete and abstract diction.

Experiment with the order of and relation among (subordinate/coordinate) clauses.

Choose more knowingly between active and passive voice.

Cut the fat, especially by eliminating unnecessary "to be" constructions.

Vary sentence length and shape.

Use parallelism.

Experiment with periodic and cumulative sentences.

Fine-tune the tone.

## APPLICATION:

## RETAKING THE GRAMMAR QUIZ AS A STYLE QUIZ

The paragraph used for the grammar quiz at the end of the previous chapter also contained a plethora of stylistic errors (not to mention infelicities). If you have already edited the paragraph for correctness, now rewrite it, editing for style. If you have not yet taken the quiz, do so now as an overall check on your ability to recognize and remedy technical problems.

## Key Words (in order of appearance)

| | |
|---|---|
| diction | transitive (active) verb |
| syntax | intransitive (static) verb |
| style | "lurkers" |
| rhetorical situation | coordination |
| academic discourse | subordination |
| conventions | coordinating conjunctions |
| thesaurus | independent clause |
| sexist implications | dependent clause |
| etymological history | subordinating conjunctions |
| *OED* | expletives |

concrete diction    simple sentence
abstract diction    compound sentence
Latinate diction    complex sentence
Anglo-Saxon diction  compound-complex sentence
grammar      parallelism
first-person pronoun  antithesis
second-person pronoun periodic sentence
third-person pronoun  cumulative sentence
imperative mood   tone
active voice     grammatical closure
passive voice

## Guidelines for Editing for Style

1. Strive for distance as you edit: place yourself in the position of the reader, not the writer.
2. Check the diction. Is it precise? Have you pondered your definitions of terms? Is there sufficient balance between abstractions and concrete details?
3. Cut the fat. Don't use five words ("due to the fact that") when one will do ("because"). Root out expletives that needlessly subordinate ("It is true that . . ."). Avoid redundancy.
4. Tighten the syntax of your sentences by energizing the verbs. The active voice generally achieves directness and economy; it will promote clarity and cut fat.
5. Look for potentially strong active verbs "lurking" in sentences that use a form of *to be*. Beware habitual use of *to be* and passives, because these forms tend to blur or submerge the action, omit its performers, and generally lack momentum.
6. Look at the order and arrangement of clauses. Are ideas of equal importance placed in coordinate constructions? Have you used subordination to rank ideas? Have your sentences exploited the end as a position of emphasis?
7. Look at the shapes of your sentences. Do they use parallelism to keep your ideas clear? Where do you find opportunities for composing periodic and cumulative sentences that revision can bring out?

# Documentation Styles

There are a number of formalized styles of documentation, the most common being the MLA (Modern Language Association) style, which uses the author-work format, and the APA (American Psychological Association) style, which uses the author-date format. The various styles differ in the specific ways that they organize the bibliographical information, but all of them share the following characteristics:

1. They place an extended citation for each source at the end of the paper, including the author, the title, the date, and the place of publication. These citations are organized in a list, usually alphabetically.
2. They insert an abbreviated citation within the text, located within parentheses directly following every use of the source. Usually this in-text citation consists of the author's name and either the page (in MLA) or date (in APA).
3. They distinguish among different kinds of sources—providing slightly differing formulas for citing books, articles, encyclopedias, government documents, interviews, and so forth.
4. They have particular formats for citing electronic sources of various kinds, such as CD-ROMs, the World Wide Web, and online journals and databases.

Any writing handbook (a compilation of the rules of grammar and punctuation, available at most bookstores) will contain a detailed account of the various documentation styles. In addition, these are accessible on the World Wide Web. Some current Internet addresses that provide detailed instructions for using the MLA and APA styles are:

MLA: *http://owl.english.purdue.edu/Files/33.html*

APA: *http://owl.english.purdue.edu/Files/34.html*

An all-purpose style directory for citing resources is available at:

*http://www.muhlenberg.edu/library/ref/acad/ref_sty.html*

You have probably already discovered that some professors are more concerned than others that students obey the particulars of a given documentation style. Virtually all faculty across the curriculum agree, however, that *the most important rule for writers to follow in documenting sources is formal consistency.* That is, all of your in-text citations should follow the same abbreviated format, and all of your end-of-text citations should follow the same extended format.

Once you begin doing most of your writing in a particular discipline, you may want to purchase the more detailed style guide adhered to by that discipline. Toward this end we have included, as Section C, a brief list of style manuals at the end of the appendix. Because documentation styles differ not only from discipline to discipline, but also even from journal to journal within a discipline, you should consult your professor about which documentation format he or she wishes you to use in a given course.

# A. MLA (Modern Language Association) Style

## I. IN-TEXT CITATIONS

In-text citations indicate in shorthand form in the body of your paper the source you are using. All in-text citations direct your readers to the complete citation located in a list of references at the end of the paper or report. To keep attention focused on the form, we have used one basic source for all examples.

### 1. Single author

For both books and articles, include the author's name and the page number (without the abbreviation "p."). Note that there is no intervening punctuation between name and page and that the parentheses precede the period or other punctuation. If the sentence ends with a direct quotation, the parentheses come after the quotation marks but still before the closing period. Also note that no punctuation occurs between the last word of the quotation and the closing quotation mark:

> The influence of Seamus Heaney on younger poets in Northern
> Ireland has been widely acknowledged, but Patrick Kavanagh's
> "plain-speaking, pastoral" influence on him is "less recog-
> nized" (Smith 74).

In this case, (Smith 74) indicates the author's last name and the page number on which the cited passage appears. If the author's name has been mentioned in the sentence, you should include only the page number:

> According to Smith, Kavanagh's "plain-speaking, pastoral"
> style influenced Heaney (74).

One exception to these rules occurs with quotations of more than four typed lines. These are set off from the text by indenting one inch from the left margin and typing them double-spaced without quotation marks. The citation in such cases should appear in parentheses two spaces *after* the final punctuation. For example:

> According to Smith, Kavanagh's "plain-speaking, pastoral"
> style influenced Heaney (74). In such poems as Heaney's "Dig-
> ging," we encounter the presence of a rural voice offering

mordant commentary on his father's literal and figurative
roots. It is the same mordant tone we encounter in Kavanagh's
"The Great Hunger." (74)

Note that the author's name is not included in the citation because it appears in the text.

### 2. Two or three authors of a single work

List them all:

(Smith, Jones, and Adams 74).

Note that MLA spells out the word "and"; by contrast APA specifies an ampersand (&) in place of the "and."

### 3. More than three authors of a single work

Use the first author's name and "et al." This phrase, which means "and others," is neither italicized nor placed in quotes: (Smith et al. 74).

### 4. Two or more works by the same author

Include a short version of the title to identify which work by the same author you are citing. If the original title was *Belfast Poets and the Anxiety of Influence,* you could use (Smith, *Belfast Poets* 74).

### 5. A multivolume work

Include the volume number, followed by a colon and the page: (Smith 2: 74).

### 6. Unknown author

In the case of unsigned articles (usually brief newspaper or magazine pieces), use a short version of the title: ("Belfast Poets" 74).

### 7. Quoting a source's quotation

When you quote a quotation (commonly known as an indirect source), add the abbreviation "qtd. in."

According to Harriet Smith, the "plain-speaking, pastoral"
style of Irish poet Patrick Kavanagh heavily influenced
Seamus Heaney (qtd. in Marsh 57).

## II. END-OF-TEXT CITATIONS

All citations made in the body of your paper or report (in-text citations) are keyed to a list of references located at the end. This list, entitled "Works Cited" in MLA style, begins on a separate page. It presents in alphabetical order (by authors' last names) all sources actually cited in the body of the text and includes full publishing information for each source.

In general, the MLA style divides entries in the "Works Cited" list into three parts: author, title, and publication data. Each part is separated by a period from the others. Titles of book-length works are italicized, unless your instructor prefers underlining. Underlining is a means of indicating italics.

## 1. Book by a single author

> Douglas, Ann. *Terrible Honesty: Mongrel Manhattan in the 1920s.* New York: Farrar, Straus, and Giroux, 1995.

***More than one work by a single author:***
Organize the works alphabetically by the first major word in the titles. Provide the author's name with the first title, and then, for subsequent entries, insert three hyphens followed by a period (——.) in place of the author's name.

## 2. Book by multiple authors

For two or three authors, the form is the same as that for books by a single author, except that the names of authors after the first are not inverted: Marsh, Alec, and Linda Miller.

For more than three authors, include only the name of the first author followed by "et al.": Marsh, Alec, et al.

## 3. Book by a corporate author

Use the name of the corporation as the author (for example, American Medical Association).

## 4. Book by an unknown author

Alphabetize by the first significant word of the title.

## 5. Book with an editor (Ed.) and/or a translator (Trans.) in addition to author

> Durkheim, Emile. *Suicide: A Study in Sociology.* Trans. John Spaulding. Ed. George Simpson. New York: The Free Press, 1951.

Note: When a book has both a translator and an editor, the translator's name precedes the editor's.

## 6. Selection in an anthology or edited collection

> Levi-Strauss, Claude. "The Structural Study of Myth." *Critical Theory since 1965.* Eds. Hazard Adams and Leroy Searle. Tallahassee: Florida State UP, 1986. 809-22.

When you know where the selection originally appeared, you can give that publication information first and then supply the information on the source you actually consulted, preceded by "Rpt. in" (meaning "Reprinted in").

Do *not* include only the original source when you have actually consulted only the reprinted version.

### 8. Book in a series

> Fast, Robin Riley, and Christine Mack Gordon, eds. *Approaches to Teaching Dickinson's Poetry.* Approaches to Teaching World Literature 26. New York: MLA, 1989.

### 9. Editions of books after the first edition and republished books

> Hodges, John C., et al. *Harbrace College Handbook.* 13th ed. Fort Worth: Harcourt Brace College Publishers, 1998.

> Kavanagh, Patrick. *Collected Poems.* 1964. New York: W. W. Norton & Co., 1973.

The first date in the preceding example indicates the date of original publication.

### 10. Government publication

If no author is listed, start with the name of the government and the name of the agency.

> United States. Dept. of Transportation. *National Transportation Statistics.* Washington: GPO, 1990.

### 11. Articles in periodicals

References for articles differ from those for books in a few small ways:

- Article names go inside quotation marks.
- No punctuation follows the title of the periodical.
- A colon precedes the page numbers.

#### *Article in a journal:*

Journals, issued monthly or quarterly, are either separately or continuously paginated. In the latter, the page numbers of each issue within a given year begin where the previous issue ended.

> Cressy, David. "Foucault, Stone, Shakespeare and Social History." *English Literary Renaissance* 21 (1991): 121-33.

The number *21* here is the volume number. Although the title page also includes an issue number and a season, this information is not necessary to include in continuously paginated journals.

When the journal is separately paginated, include the issue number immediately after the volume number (separated by a period), as in the following example.

> Lazere, Donald. "Back to Basics: A Force for Oppression or Liberation?" *College English* 54.1 (1992): 7-21.

### Article in an encyclopedia:

If the articles are arranged alphabetically, do not include volume numbers or page numbers.

> "Bats." *The New Book of Knowledge.* 1981 ed.

### Article in a monthly or weekly magazine:

Articles in magazines are cited like articles in journals, except that you do not include volume and issue numbers for magazines.

> McPhee, John. "The Gravel Page." *The New Yorker* 29 Jan. 1996: 44-52.

If you are citing a magazine (or newspaper) article printed on nonconsecutive pages—for example, pages 11–16 and then pages 52–58—give only the first page number followed by a plus sign (11+).

### Article in a newspaper:

The format is the same as for magazines, except that the page reference indicates the number or letter of the section containing the article. Anonymous articles are alphabetized by the first significant word in the titles.

> Foreman, Bill. "Sculpture Evokes Memories of Young Bombing Victims." *The Morning Call* [Allentown, PA] 11 Feb. 1996: A17.

### Newspaper editorial or letter to the editor:

> "Unforgotten Crimes in Nigeria." Editorial. *New York Times* 10 Feb. 1996: 22.

## 12. Reviews

> Rorty, Richard. "Color-Blind in the Marketplace." Rev. of *The End of Racism: Principles for a Multiracial Society,* by Dinesh D'Souza. *The New York Times Book Review* 24 Sept. 1995: 9.

As with other sources, if the review is unsigned, begin with and alphabetize by the title of the review. If the review is untitled, begin with "Rev. of," and alphabetize by the title of the work being reviewed.

## 13. Interviews

For published interviews, start with the name of the person being interviewed, followed by the title (or, if untitled, the word "Interview"). Then add the name of the interviewer, followed by the source, which is cited as with any periodical. For a broadcast interview, include the name of the program, the station, and the date. For unpublished interviews, follow the name of the person interviewed with the phrase "Personal Interview" followed by the date.

**Published Interview**
>Adams, Anna. Interview. *Community Outreach*. WVIA, Allentown.
>>12 Jan. 1996.

**Unpublished Interview**
>Adams, Anna. Personal Interview. 26 Feb. 1996.

## III. CITING ELECTRONIC SOURCES IN MLA STYLE

The citation formats for electronic sources differ from those used for print sources in a few primary ways:

The method of accessing the information is included in what is called an *availability statement.* This statement replaces the publication information typically provided for text references. You should provide the information sufficient to retrieve the source.

In MLA style the phrase "Online" comes directly after the title and before the availability statement.

When an electronic source is available in both print and nonprint formats, generally you list both.

Citing the exact date for an electronic source is more complicated than for printed texts. Generally, you list the most recent update of the information, because electronic data is frequently revised. When a date cannot be determined, supply the date of your search (also known as the *access date*).

**Standard format:**

1. Name of the author if given

2. For a nonprint source, the title of the material accessed, inside quotation marks, followed by the date of the material, if given

If there is also a printed version of the source, provide the publication information in this slot, including the title and date. The nonprint information follows. The date of the nonprint information generally comes after the title of the database or other service from which the information was obtained.

3. The title of the database, underlined. If the source is an electronic journal or newsletter or conference, include the title, underlined, followed by volume and issue numbers, year or date of publication (in parentheses), and number of pages or paragraphs (if given) or "n. pag." (which stands for "no pagination").

4. Publication medium (CD-ROM or diskette or online)

5. Name of the vendor or publisher (with city of publication) or computer service

6. Electronic publication date, or, in the case of publications on diskette, year of publication. If you are using a computer service, list the date of access in this slot.

7. Electronic citations end with the URL (Universal Resource Locator) in angle brackets.

**Basic form for a Web page:**

```
Author. "Title of Part." Title of Work (Date of last update)
     Medium. URL. Access date.
```

**Basic form for a journal article available through an online database:**

```
Author. "Article Title." Journal Title Volume.Issue (Year):
     paging or number of paragraphs. Medium. Information sup-
     plier. URL. Access date.

Kupisch, Susan J. "Stepping In." Paper presented as part of
     the symposium Disrupted and Reorganized Families at the
     annual meeting of the Southeast Psychological Associa-
     tion, Atlanta, GA. (23-26 Mar. 1983): n. pag. Online.
     Dialog. ERIC. ED 233276.
```

In this case, the citation informs readers that the article can be accessed from a database called ERIC. The word "Dialog" is the name of the vendor of the electronic document service. ERIC is the service itself. The letters and numbers following identify the particular document.

Here are a few more examples:

```
Shearson Lehman Brothers, Inc. "Reebok: Company Report." 29
     July 1993. General Business File. CD-ROM. Information
     Access. Nov. 1993.

"Middle Ages." Academic American Encyclopedia. Online.
     Prodigy. 30 Mar. 1992.
```

# B. APA (American Psychological Association) Style

## I. IN-TEXT CITATIONS

In-text citations indicate within the body of your paper the source you are using. They appear in reduced form but direct your readers to the complete citation located in a list of references at the end of the paper or report. To keep attention focused on the form, we have used one basic source for all examples.

### 1. Single author

For both books and articles, include the author's name, followed by a comma, and then the date of publication. If you are quoting or referring to a specific passage, include the page number as well, separated from the date by a comma and the abbreviation "p." followed by a space.

Studies of students' changing attitudes towards the small colleges that they attend suggest that their loyalty to the institution declines steadily over a four-year period, whereas
their loyalty to individual professors or departments
increases "markedly, by as much as twenty-five percent over
the last two years" (Brown, 1994, p. 41).

If the author's name has been mentioned in the sentence, include only the
date in the parentheses immediately following the author's name:

Brown (1992) documents the decline in students' institutional
loyalty.

Quotations of forty words or more are set off from the text by indenting
five spaces from the left margin and typing, without quotation marks or
double-space. The citation should appear in parentheses one space *after* the
final punctuation.

Brown documents the decline in students' institutional
loyalty. In a survey of entering and graduating college students, Brown found that graduating seniors, while reporting
their highest loyalty to individual faculty members within
their majors, indicated significant decreases in enthusiasm
for the institution at large from what they had reported as
first-year students. (1992)

### 2. Multiple authors

For a work with two authors, include both names every time, connected with
an ampersand (&): (Brown & Greene, 1995).

For a work with three, four, or five authors, include all names in the first
reference: (Brown, Greene, Blue, Orange, & Square, 1995). In subsequent references use only the first author followed by "et al." (followed by a comma) and
the year: (Brown et al., 1995).

For a work with six or more authors, use only the first author's name followed by "et al." for all citations.

### 3. Two or more works by the same author

The date within the parenthetical citation will distinguish which of the two
works by the same author you are referring to. In the case of two or more works
by the same author in the same year, the in-text citation should distinguish
them with an "a" and a "b", and so forth: (Brown, 1994a). In the case of two or
more works by the same author but published in different years, list the years
separately: (Brown, 1992, 1993).

### 4. A corporate author or government agency

If the name is long, write it out the first time; then abbreviate it in subsequent
citations: (United States Department of Agriculture, 1992, p. 117). Subsequently, use: (USDA, 1992, p. 231).

### 5. Unknown author

Use the first few words of the title for unsigned pieces (usually brief newspaper or magazine articles). If the original title was "What Went Wrong During Their Four Years in College?" you would simply use: ("What went wrong," 1992, p. 69). Note that APA lowercases book and article titles except for the first letter of the first word.

### 6. Citing a source's quotation

To document material that your source quotes from another source (commonly known as an indirect source), identify the original source in your text by author's name, and in your citation precede your source with the phrase "cited in."

```
Orange observes that data about students' institutional loy-
alty must be adjusted not only for school size but also for
"such elusive factors as campus ambience" (cited in Brown,
1994, p. 12).
```

### 7. More than one work in a single citation

Alphabetize authors' last names and separate them with semicolons: (Brown, 1994; Greene, 1992, 1993; Orange, 1991). The two dates after "Greene" indicate two articles by that author. If you are citing two articles by the same author written in the same year, use "a" and "b" after the dates: (Taupe 1996a, 1996b).

## II. END-OF-TEXT CITATIONS

All citations made in the body of your paper or report (in-text citations) are keyed to a list of references located at the end. This list, entitled "References" in APA style, begins on a separate page. It presents in alphabetical order (by authors' last names) all sources actually cited in the body of the text and includes full publishing information for each source.

*Manuscript form:* The first line of the reference is not indented; subsequent lines for the reference are indented three spaces.

### APA References

The APA style divides entries into the following parts: author (using initials only for first and middle names), year of publication (in parentheses), title, and publication data. Each part is separated by a period from the others. In alphabetizing the "References" list, place entries for a single author before entries that he or she has co-authored, and arrange multiple entries by a single author by beginning with the earliest work. If there are two or more works by the same author in the same year, designate them with an "a" and a "b" and so forth directly after the year. For all subsequent entries by an author after the first, substitute three hyphens followed by a period (—-.) for his or her name.

## 1. Book by a single author

> Tannen, D. (1991). *You just don't understand: Women and men in conversation.* New York: Ballantine Books.

Note that only the first letter of the title and subtitle are capitalized (although proper nouns would be capitalized as necessary).

## 2. Book by multiple authors

> Ginsburg, H., & Opper, S. (1969). *Piaget's theory of intellectual development: An introduction.* Englewood Cliffs, NJ: Prentice-Hall.

Include all authors' names (although "et al." is used for in-text citations with three or more authors), separate them with commas, and use an ampersand (&) before the last author cited.

## 3. Book by a corporate author

Use the name of the corporation as the author (for example, the World Health Organization).

## 4. Book by an unknown author

Alphabetize by the first significant word of the title.

## 5. Book with a translator or editor

> Gimpel, J. (1984). *The cathedral builders.* (T. Waugh, Trans.). New York: Harper Colophon Books.

Note that the name of the translator is located within parentheses and appears in normal rather than inverted order after the title and before the publication data.

## 6. Edited book

> Arac, J. (Ed.). (1988). *After Foucault: Humanistic knowledge, postmodern challenges.* New Brunswick, NJ: Rutgers University Press.

## 7. Article or chapter in an edited book

> Sawicki, J. (1988). Feminism and the power of Foucauldian discourse. In J. Arac (Ed.), *After Foucault: Humanistic knowledge, postmodern challenges* (pp. 161-178). New Brunswick, NJ: Rutgers University Press.

Notice that there are no quotation marks around the title of the article, and no punctuation between the article title and the inclusive page numbers listed inside parentheses, prefaced by "pp."

## 8. Multivolume work

Johnson, B. D. (1978.) *National party platforms* (Vol. 1).
    Urbana: University of Illinois Press.

## 9. Editions of books after the first edition

Binkley, W. E. (1962). *American political parties: Their nat-
    ural history* (4th ed.). New York: Knopf.

## 10. Government document

U.S. Congress, Joint Committee on Printing. (1950). *Biograph-
    ical directory of the American Congress, 1774-1949* (81st
    Cong., House Document No. 607). Washington, DC: U.S. Gov-
    ernment Printing Office.

## 11. Articles in periodicals

References for articles differ from those for books in a few small ways:

- Neither underline (italicize) nor enclose in quotation marks the titles of articles.
- Capitalize the first word and all significant words in the titles of periodicals. The article title itself is lowercase.
- Underline or italicize the volume number (which is separated by a comma from the title of the journal) to distinguish it from the page reference.
- For periodicals with volume numbers, include the page numbers of the entire article, separated by a comma from the preceding volume number. Do not use "pp."
- For periodicals without volume numbers, use "p." or "pp." before the page number(s).

*Article in a journal:*

Baumeister, R. (1987). How the self became a problem: A psy-
    chological review of historical research. *Journal of Per-
    sonality and Psychology, 52,* 163-176.

For articles by two or more authors, use commas to connect the authors, and precede the last one with a comma and an ampersand (&).

If the journal is paginated by issue (rather than annually), place the issue number in parentheses following the volume number.

Wallston, B. S. (1981). What are the questions in psychology
    of women? A feminist approach to research. *Psychology of
    Women Quarterly, 5*(4), 597-617.

*Article in a monthly or weekly magazine:*

Rupley, S. (1995, September 26). Net worth: On-line invest-
    ing. *PC Magazine, 14*(16), 29.

***Article in a newspaper:***

> Foreman, B. (1996, February 11). Sculpture evokes memories of young bombing victims. *The Morning Call,* p. A17.

***Newspaper editorial or letter to the editor:***

> Faltysek. R. B. (1995, December 19). The price of company loyalty. [Letter to the editor]. *Tulsa World,* p. 13.

***Article in an encyclopedia:***

If the entry has no author, begin with the entry title.

> Irrigation. (1981). *The new book of knowledge.* (Vol. 9, pp. 408-410). Danbury, CT: Grolier.

## 12. Reviews

> Gorra, M. (1995, November 5). Taking the Freud out of Mother Goose. [Review of the book *From the beast to the blonde: On fairy tales and their tellers*]. *The New York Times Book Review,* pp. 7, 9.

## 13. Interviews

> Cleph, G. (1996). Drumming in my sleep. [Interview with Douglas Ovens]. *Po-Mo Percussion, 10,* 26-33.

If the interview is unpublished, do not include it in "References." Instead, mention the nature and date of the interview within the text of the paper.

## 14. Abstracts

Rather than use only an abstract culled from a collection of abstracts, it is preferable to locate and use the entire original article as a source. If you have used only an abstract from a collection, cite it in parentheses at the end of the entry. You would cite the article just as you would any article and then add, for example:

> (From *PsychSCAN: Neuropsychology,* 1996, 5, Abstract No. 422.)

## III. CITING ELECTRONIC SOURCES IN APA STYLE

The citation formats for electronic sources differ from those used for print sources in a few primary ways:

The method of accessing the information is included in what is called an *availability statement.* This statement replaces the publication information typically provided for text references. You provide the information sufficient to retrieve the source.

In APA style the phrase "[Online]" (in square brackets) comes directly after the title and before the availability statement.

When an electronic source is available in both print and nonprint formats, generally you list both.

Citing the exact date for an electronic source is more complicated than for printed texts. Generally, you list the most recent update of the information, because electronic data are frequently revised. When a date cannot be determined, supply the date of your search (also known as the *access date*).

**Standard format:**
1. Name of author
2. Date, in parentheses, of the year of publication or, in cases of revision, the most recent update. If you cannot determine the date, use the date of your search.
3. Title of article. This slot may also be filled with the title of a chapter.
4. Name of periodical, underlined, followed by the phrase [On-line] (in square brackets and hyphenated), a comma, and the volume number, also underlined. If the source is a chapter from a book, the title of the full work, underlined, fills this slot. If the article is on CD-ROM, use [CD-ROM] in this slot in place of [On-line].
5. Availability statement. This statement replaces the place and name of the publisher used in text references. Supply the information necessary for someone else to retrieve the source, such as the protocol (for example, FTP), the directory, and the filename.

Other forms of electronic correspondence—from bulletin boards, e-mail messages, and discussion groups—are not included in the reference list. Instead, cite them as personal communication within the text.

**Basic form for a Web page:**
```
Author. (Year). Title of part. Title of Work [Medium]. Avail-
    able: URL [Access date].
```

**Basic form for a journal article available through an online database:**
```
Author. (Year). Title. Journal Title [Medium], volume
    (issue), paging or number of paragraphs. Information sup-
    plier. Available: URL [Access date].

Summit, S. (1996). C.L.C-FAQ [On-line]. Available: by anony-
    mous FTP from

rtfm.mit.edu/pub/usenet-by-group/comp.lang.c/C-FAQ-list
```

# D. Bibliography of Style Manuals

The following bibliography contains a sampling of the major disciplinary style guides. These are usually available in the reference room of the library. Following each entry, in brackets, are the disciplines most likely to use the particular guide. Some disciplines accept more than one documentation style, and disciplines often prescribe their own variations on a standard style, as is the case, for example, with music's use of Chicago style.

American Chemical Society. *American Chemical Society Style Guide and Handbook.* Washington, DC: American Chemical Society, 1985. [**chemistry**]

American Institute of Physics. *Style Manual for Guidance in the Preparation of Papers.* 4th ed. New York: American Institute of Physics, 1990. [**physics**]

American Mathematical Society. *A Manual for Authors of Mathematical Papers.* 8th ed. Providence: American Mathematical Society, 1984. [**mathematics**]

American Medical Association-Scientific Publications Division. *Stylebook: Editorial Manual.* Littleton, MA: Publishing Sciences Group, 1976. [**medicine**]

American Psychological Association. *Publication Manual of the American Psychological Association.* 4th ed. Washington, DC: American Psychological Assn., 1994. [**psychology, many of the other social sciences**]

Associated Press. *The Associated Press Stylebook.* Reading, MA: Addison-Wesley, 1982. [**journalism**]

*The Chicago Manual of Style.* 14th ed. Chicago: University of Chicago Press, 1993. [**history, art, music, philosophy**]

Columbia Law Review. *A Uniform System of Citation.* 15th ed. Cambridge: Harvard Law Review, 1991. [**law**]

*The University of Chicago Manual of Legal Citation.* Chicago: University of Chicago Law Review, 1989. [**law**]

*The Bluebook: A Uniform System of Citation.* 15th ed. Cambridge, MA, 1991. [**law**]

Council of Biology Editors. Style Manual Committee. *CBE Style Manual: A Guide for Authors, Editors, and Publishers in the Biological Sciences.* 5th ed. Bethesda: Council of Biology Editors, 1983. [**biology**]

Dodd, Janet S., ed. *The ACS Style Manual: A Manual for Authors and Editors.* 2nd ed. Washington, DC: American Chemical Society, 1986. [**chemistry**]

Gibaldi, Joseph. *MLA Handbook for Writers of Research Papers.* 4th ed. New York: The Modern Language Assn. of America, 1995. [**English, classics, foreign languages**]

International Steering Committee of Medical Editors. "Uniform Requirements for Manuscripts Submitted to Biomedical Journals." *Annals of Internal Medicine* 90 (1978): 95-99. [**medicine**]

Irvine, Demar B. *Writing about Music: A Stylebook for Reports and Theses.* Seattle: University of Washington Press, 1968. [**music**]

Turabian, Kate L. *A Manual for Writers of Term Papers, Theses, and Dissertations.* 5th ed. Chicago: University of Chicago Press, 1987.

# CREDITS

## Photo

Page 23. Figure 1.2. Copyright © Eric Lessing/Art Resource, NY.
Page 48. Figure 2.3. Copyright © 1989 Jeff Widener/AP/Wide World Photos.
Page 130. Figure 4.5. Diego Velázquez, *Las Meninas*, 1656. Approx. 10'5" x 9'.
Museo del Prado, Madrid.

## Literary

Page 100. Fassin, Eric. "Playing by the Antioch Rules." Copyright (c) 1993 by
the *New York Times*. Reprinted by permission.

# INDEX